ZAGATSURVEY®

MUSIC GUIDE

1,000 Top Albums of All Time

Coordinator: Pat Blashill

Music Editor: Holly George-Warren

Editors: Betsy Andrews
and Randi Gollin

Published and distributed by
ZAGAT SURVEY, LLC
4 Columbus Circle
New York, New York 10019
Tel: 212 977 6000
E-mail: music@zagat.com
Web site: www.zagat.com

Acknowledgments

In the creation of this book, we appreciate the help of Mary Ascheim, Steve DeLorenzo, Tom Fatsi, Chet Flippo, Bob George of the Archive of Contemporary Music, Jonathan Hafter, Robert Kimball, Beth Piantidosi, Jonathan Schwartz, Beverly Sills, Jack Warren and Robert Warren. We would like to thank the following music experts for their work in putting together our initial *Survey*: Charles Cermele, John Diliberto, Jeffrey S. Kaye, Kathy O'Connell, Steve Smith and Kurt Wolff. We are also grateful to the following music writers, each of whom edited sections of this guide: Charles Cermele, Donald Elfman, Daniel Felsenfeld, John Ryan, Andy Schwartz, Andrew Simon, Malcolm Venable, Erin Stacey Visslailli and Kurt Wolff.

This guide would not have been possible without the hard work of our staff, especially Reni Chin, Larry Cohn, Griff Foxley, Schuyler Frazier, Jeff Freier, Katherine Harris, Natalie Lebert, Mike Liao, Dave Makulec, Jennifer Napuli, Rob Poole, Robert Seixas, Sharon Yates and Kyle Zolner.

The reviews published in this guide are based on public opinion surveys, with numerical ratings reflecting the average scores given by all survey participants who voted on each album and text based on direct quotes from, or fair paraphrasings of, participants' comments.

Contents

About This Survey

For 24 years, Zagat Survey has reported on the shared experiences of people like you. Originally focused on dining and travel, in recent years we've expanded our scope to cover entertaining, nightlife, movies, shopping, golf and theater. Now we are proud to bring you the ultimate music guide, a compilation of 1,000 of the top albums of all time.

There were over 10,600 participants in this *Survey*, each listening to an average of 24.2 hours of music per week (or 13.4 million total hours annually), spending more than $340 a year on recorded music and attending one live concert about once a month. With each surveyor having separately rated the albums for Overall Quality, Songwriting, Musicianship and Production Value, we hope to have achieved a new and uniquely reliable guide.

Of our surveyors, 41% are women, 59% men; the breakdown by age is 27% in their 20s; 33%, 30s; 21%, 40s; 14%, 50s; and 5%, 60s or above. Though living in all parts of the country and coming from highly diverse backgrounds, these surveyors share one common trait – they are all music lovers. In producing the reviews contained in this guide, our editors have synopsized surveyors' opinions, with their exact comments shown in quotation marks. We thank each of these participants for their thoughtful comments and ratings. This guide is really "theirs."

Of course, we are especially grateful to our coordinator, Pat Blashill, who has written about music for *Rolling Stone* and numerous other publications, and to our editor, Holly George-Warren, who has contributed to more than 40 books about contemporary music, including *The Rolling Stone Encyclopedia of Rock & Roll*.

To help you find the best music for each occasion, we have prepared a number of lists – see Top Ratings (pages 10–30) – and 67 handy indexes.

To join any of our upcoming *Surveys,* just register at **zagat.com.** Each participant will receive a free copy of the resulting guide when published. We would appreciate your comments, suggestions and even criticisms so that we can revise our future editions. Please contact us at music@zagat.com or by mail at Music – Zagat Survey, 4 Columbus Circle, New York, NY 10019. We look forward to hearing from you.

New York, NY
September 23, 2003

Nina and Tim

Nina and Tim Zagat

Zagat Tunes In

Don your Discman and take to the music racks with Zagat's first *Music Guide,* rating and reviewing 1,000 of the top albums of all time. Unlike other guides with reviews voiced by professional critics, this book shouts it out via feedback from over 10,600 avid listeners who own, on average, 516 CDs and records.

Hail, hail, rock & roll!: Reviewers rock out. Almost 50% listen to R&R more frequently than other genres, and nearly 40% of the albums chosen for this *Survey* are rockers. Classic rock reigns: almost a quarter of the guide was pressed on '70s vinyl, the Most Popular disc comes from Bruce Springsteen, and The Beatles were voted the most influential artists. But surveyors also root for contemporary artists like alternative outfits Sigur Rós and Wilco, garage upstarts The Strokes and The White Stripes, trippy jammers Dave Matthews Band and Phish, political art-rockers Radiohead and metal thrashers A Perfect Circle and System of a Down.

Strumming Heart Strings: Along with Bob Dylan, who rates No. 1 for Songwriting, Carole King, Joni Mitchell, Van Morrison and James Taylor quicken surveyors' pulse. There's room on the stereo for new bards too. Patty Griffin, India.Arie, Sarah McLachlan and decades-in-the-making overnight sensation Lucinda Williams rule the singer-songwriter roost, but the boys are catching up – just ask Ryan Adams, John Mayer and Rufus Wainwright.

Classical Gas: With classical music, opinions differ not so much on which composers to listen to, but which versions are best. Given 60 sets of Beethoven symphonies, who can pick? From the operatic enormity of Georg Solti's 16-CD Wagner *Ring Cycle* to Philip Glass' minimalism, selections made by surveyors who know their chops will help neophytes get their feet wet. Popular crossover Yo-Yo Ma has lots of fans, but veteran pianist Vladimir Horowitz tops the list.

All That Jazz: Jazz might earn a relatively small slice of the retail pie, but the American-born music is still bebopping. Miles Davis' *Kind of Blue* was voted No. 1 in the *Survey* for Overall Excellence (as well as Musicianship), followed by John Coltrane's *A Love Supreme.* Stepping into Ella Fitzgerald and Frank Sinatra's spotlight, pop-influenced crooners Harry Connick Jr., Norah Jones and Diana Krall cast a rekindled torch-song spell over listeners.

Kings and Queens of Soul: R.E.S.P.E.C.T. goes to Aretha Franklin, whose influence reverberates in the sounds of new R&B royalty Mary J. Blige, Alicia Keys and Jill Scott. Get-your-groove-on godfathers Marvin Gaye, Al Green and Otis Redding have passed the scepter to neo-soul heirs D'Angelo and Maxwell, by way of Prince and Stevie Wonder, while Brian McKnight channels the late, great Barry White.

Rave Faves: In the techno labs of robotic trailblazer Kraftwerk, avant-guardist Brian Eno and synthmeisters Jean-Michel Jarre and Vangelis, a sonic monster called electronica was born, mutating from dance floors to day spas to TV ads (yo, Moby). Ambient artists Enya and Kitaro shed light upon the New Age, while New Order and OMD unearthed the darkness, followed by noirish Everything But the Girl. French House popsters Air and St. Germain help chill out trendy hotel lobbies, while Deep Forest and Enigma bring global grooves to living rooms. Fatboy Slim's big beats, Basement Jaxx's electro-funk and Paul Oakenfold's tranced-out remixes keep the party going from Ibiza to Iceland, where alt-techno chanteuse Björk was born.

Hip-Hop Won't Stop: From pioneers like Eric B. & Rakim, Run-DMC and Slick Rick hip-hop has exploded, spawning political rap (Public Enemy, Boogie Down Productions), West Coast gangsta (Dr. Dre, N.W.A), East Coast flows (Notorious B.I.G., Tupac Shakur), feel-good grooves (De La Soul, A Tribe Called Quest), spacey beats (Dr. Octagon, Missy Elliot), Southern-fried bump (Arrested Development, OutKast), dense production (Wu-Tang), and even live instrumentation (The Roots). The Midwest (Eminem) and LA (Snoop Dogg) have produced some of today's biggest artists, while trip-hop Brits like Massive Attack are one indication that the sound's gone international.

Return to the Roots: Fabled Delta bluesman Robert Johnson and honky-tonker Hank Williams show up here, as do legends who lent their talents to the Nitty Gritty Dirt Band's top-rated C&W album. Neo-traditionalists Iris DeMent, Emmylou Harris and the hillbilly/gospel revival of *O Brother, Where Art Thou* prove the staying power of old-timey country, bluegrass and blues.

What a Production: As technology advances, so do our expectations of sound quality. Surveyors judged Production more harshly and rated it lower than other values. Peter Gabriel earned the No. 1 spot for Production by teaming world musicians with master engineering on his sexy soundtrack to *The Last Temptation of Christ,* followed by Pink Floyd's *Dark Side of the Moon,* and The Beatles' *Sgt. Pepper.*

Don't Buy the Hype: This guide is almost as interesting for who didn't make it in as for who did. Sorry, Avril, Britney and Mariah. While some big-name pop albums didn't rate highly enough to be included, non-commercial inclusions like New Latinist Manu Chao and indie iconoclasts They Might Be Giants suggest there's more to music than marketing.

From the sounds of past centuries to future sonics, from local listens to global grooves, this *Survey* is designed to help you choose from the wealth of tunes out there. So grab the guide, and crank it up!

New York, NY
September 23, 2003

Holly George-Warren

Buying Tips

Never has it been easier to get the sounds you want to hear. Back in the day, if you lived in the boonies and lusted after new 45s from The Clash or The Sex Pistols, you had to call on city pals to parcel the punk platters home for you. No more. Nowadays you can live anywhere and get as many cool CDs as you'd ever find at hip New York record outlets.

Treasure Hunt: Chains are everywhere, and it's not just music stores that carry the goods nowadays. You can flip through the racks for your faves at stereo outlets, book superstores and bulk discounters. If some traditional retail outlets seem to be going the way of the 8-track, user-friendly used CD stores and über-cool shops specializing in underground and club music still draw droves of die-hards determined to discover that definitive disc.

Surfin' USA: There's nothing like shopping in a *High Fidelity*-esque indie record store where the audiophilic staff can turn you onto new sounds. But 48% of our surveyors now listen to music on their computer and buy 32% of their tunes off the Internet. Browsing online CD stores is fast, easy and you don't have to dig out that well-worn Buzzcocks t-shirt to be cool enough to shop. Most Web outlets give you a few seconds to listen to tracks, and cruising the net for MP3s provides sonic excitement 24/7. Underground trading sites like Napster may not survive their brushes with the law, but smart businesses are stepping in to take over the trend. More than half of our surveyors download songs and burn their own CDs. For Apple users, iTunes software turns an iPod into a portable juke-box. (We've listed surveyors' favorite tracks for each album so you can make your own mixes).

Platters that Matter: Still thirst for obscure nuggets unrecognized by the masses and unavailable in digital? There's plenty of vinyl-only pay dirt to be dug up on eBay, at record fairs, flea markets and yard sales. And the best thing is, used wax is cheap. Since technology provides us with so much music on such little discs, there's lots more shelf space at home for those clunky 78s, LPs and singles.

Keepers of the Flame: While it's fun to root around for the originals, it's also exciting to explore decades-later versions. Specialty labels like Rhino are repackaging musical landmarks (many of which are reviewed in this guide) on remastered CDs, even reissuing chestnuts with extra tracks rescued from the vaults.

Thus, whether music is your constant companion, your party soundtrack, or your workout pal, today there are as many ways to make it yours as there are artists to listen to.

Key to Ratings/Symbols

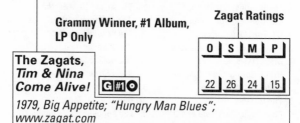

Artist, Album, Original Release Date, Original Label,
Favorite Track, Artist's Official Web Site

Grammy Winner, #1 Album, LP Only

Zagat Ratings

O	S	M	P
22	26	24	15

The Zagats, Tim & Nina Come Alive! 🄶 #1 ⊙

1979, Big Appetite; "Hungry Man Blues"; www.zagat.com

☑ The "dynamic duo of dining and whining (guitars)" "do it live" on this double album "bloated" with "monster rock hits"; Nina's "screaming, white-hot licks" on "catchy" cover tunes like *Do Fries Go With That Shake?* prove she's "still the greatest axe wielder around", but Tim's "gravelly" vocals often sound like "bouts of indigestion", and the production quality is so "lame" that "you'd think they were performing in the local diner restroom while the toilet was flushing."

Review, with surveyors' comments in quotes

Albums with highest overall ratings and greatest popularity are printed in CAPITAL LETTERS.

Symbols: Before each review the symbol ■ indicates responses were uniform, and ☑ means they were mixed. Other key symbols are:

🄶 Grammy Winner in an Album Category
#1 No. 1 album on Billboard Top 200 chart
⊙ LP only

Ratings: Given for Overall Quality, Songwriting, Musicianship and Production Value on a scale of **0** to **30**:

O Overall	S Songwriting	M Musicianship	P Production
25	19	25	12

0–9 poor to fair	**20–25** very good to excellent
10–15 fair to good	**26–30** extraordinary to perfection
16–19 good to very good	

Top Ratings*

Most Popular Albums

1. Bruce Springsteen, *Born to Run*
2. The Beatles, *Abbey Road*
3. The Beatles, *Sgt. Pepper*
4. U2, *The Joshua Tree*
5. The Beatles, *The White Album*
6. Miles Davis, *Kind of Blue*
7. Bruce Springsteen, *Darkness on the Edge of Town*
8. The Beatles, *Revolver*
9. Pink Floyd, *Dark Side of the Moon*
10. U2, *Achtung Baby*
11. The Clash, *London Calling*
12. Madonna, *Ray of Light*
13. Madonna, *Immaculate Collection*
14. Bob Marley and the Wailers, *Legend*
15. The Beach Boys, *Pet Sounds*
16. Bob Dylan, *Blood on the Tracks*
17. Dave Matthews Band, *Crash*
18. ABBA, *Gold/Greatest Hits*
19. Norah Jones, *Come Away with Me*
20. Bruce Springsteen, *The Rising*
21. Radiohead, *OK Computer*
22. Fleetwood Mac, *Rumours*
23. Nirvana, *Nevermind*
24. AC/DC, *Back in Black*
25. Pearl Jam, *Ten*
26. Bruce Springsteen, *Born in the USA*
27. Dave Brubeck, *Time Out*
28. Tori Amos, *Little Earthquakes*
29. *The Phantom of the Opera*
30. The Who, *Who's Next*
31. Bruce Springsteen, *Live/1975-85*
32. The Rolling Stones, *Exile on Main Street*
33. John Coltrane, *A Love Supreme*
34. Carole King, *Tapestry*
35. Led Zeppelin, *Led Zeppelin IV*
36. Pink Floyd, *The Wall*
37. Michael Jackson, *Thriller*
38. Counting Crows, *August and Everything After*
39. Grateful Dead, *American Beauty*
40. Paul Simon, *Graceland*
41. Guns n' Roses, *Appetite for Destruction*
42. Sarah McLachlan, *Fumbling Towards Ecstasy*
43. *Rent*
44. R.E.M., *Automatic for the People*
45. The Beatles, *Rubber Soul*
46. Bob Dylan, *Blonde on Blonde*
47. James Taylor, *Greatest Hits*
48. The Eagles, *Hotel California*
49. Van Morrison, *Moondance*
50. *West Side Story*

---

* An asterisk indicates a tie with the album above it.

Top 50 Overall Quality

30 Miles Davis, *Kind of Blue*
29 John Coltrane, *A Love Supreme*
Aretha Franklin, *Lady Soul*
Patty Griffin, *Living with Ghosts**
Bruce Springsteen, *Born to Run*
Howlin' Wolf, *Moanin' in the Moonlight*
Ella Fitzgerald, *Best of the Songbooks*
The Beatles, *Abbey Road*
The Who, *Who's Next*
Frank Sinatra, *In the Wee Small Hours*
Bill Evans, *Waltz for Debby*
Bob Marley and the Wailers, *Legend*
Bob Dylan, *Blood on the Tracks*
The Beatles, *Sgt. Pepper*
Nuggets: Original Artyfacts
Elvis Costello, *This Year's Model*
Stevie Wonder, *Innervisions*
Bruce Springsteen, *Darkness on the Edge of Town*
Hitsville USA
Nitty Gritty Dirt Band, *Will the Circle Be Unbroken*
Bob Dylan, *Blonde on Blonde*
Vladimir Horowitz, *Horowitz in Moscow*
Public Enemy, *It Takes a Nation*

J.S. Bach, *Mass in B minor*
Pink Floyd, *Dark Side of the Moon*
Charlie Parker, *Yardbird Suite*
J.S. Bach, *State of Wonder*
Dave Brubeck, *Time Out*
Mozart, *Piano Concertos 19-23*
The Clash, *London Calling*
Marvin Gaye, *What's Going On*
Mozart, *Don Giovanni**
The Beatles, *Revolver*
Carole King, *Tapestry*
My Fair Lady
*Sweeney Todd**
Aretha Franklin, *Queen of Soul*
Van Morrison, *Astral Weeks*
Joni Mitchell, *Blue*
28 Nat King Cole, *The Nat King Cole Story*
Joni Mitchell, *Court and Spark*
The Beach Boys, *Pet Sounds*
Barber, *Adagio for Strings*
Beethoven, *Symphony No. 9*
Frank Sinatra, *Only the Lonely*
Jascha Heifetz, *The Supreme*
The Replacements, *Let It Be*
Bartók, *Concerto for Orchestra*
Jimi Hendrix, *Electric Ladyland*
Beethoven, *Symphonies 5 & 7*

Top Overall Quality

By Genre

Blues

29 Howlin' Wolf, *Moanin' in the Moonlight*
The Red Rooster

28 Junior Wells, *Hoodoo Man Blues*
Snatch It Back and Hold It

Muddy Waters, *The Best*
Mannish Boy

Etta James, *The Essential*
At Last

Robert Johnson, *Complete Recordings*
Cross Road Blues

B.B. King, *Live at the Regal*
How Blue Can You Get?

Ray Charles, *Anthology*
Georgia on My Mind

Elmore James, *The Sky is Crying**
Dust My Broom

Albert King, *Ultimate Collection*
Born Under a Bad Sign

John Lee Hooker, *Ultimate Collection*
Boom Boom

27 Stevie Ray Vaughan, *Greatest Hits*
Pride and Joy

26 Paul Butterfield, *East-West*
East-West

Classical

29 Vladimir Horowitz, *Horowitz in Moscow*
Rachmaninoff Prelude in G Major

J.S. Bach, *Mass in B minor*
Agnus Dei

J.S. Bach, *State of Wonder*
Aria from the Goldberg Variations

Mozart, *Piano Concertos 19-23*
Piano Concerto No. 20

Mozart, *Don Giovanni*
Madamina, Il Catalogo E Questo

28 Barber, *Adagio for Strings*
Adagio for Strings

Beethoven, *Symphony No. 9*
Ode to Joy

Jascha Heifetz, *The Supreme*
Brahms Violin Concerto

Bartók, *Concerto for Orchestra*
Concerto for Orchestra

Beethoven, *Symphonies Nos. 5 & 7*
Symphony No. 7

Mstislav Rostropovich, *Dvořák; Tchaikovsky*
Dvořák Cello Concerto

Mozart, *Symphonies 35-41*
Jupiter Symphony

Country & Western

29 Nitty Gritty Dirt Band, *Will the Circle Be Unbroken*
Will the Circle Be Unbroken

28 Hank Williams, *40 Greatest Hits*
I'm So Lonesome I Could Cry

Gram Parsons, *Grievous Angel*
Return of the Grievous Angel

Willie Nelson, *Red Headed Stranger*
Blue Eyes Crying in the Rain

Patsy Cline, *Greatest Hits*
Crazy

Johnny Cash, *The Essential*
Ring of Fire

Emmylou Harris, *Pieces of the Sky*
Boulder to Birmingham

Alison Krauss, *Now That I've Found You*
When You Say Nothing at All

George Jones, *The Essential*
He Stopped Loving Her Today

27 Iris DeMent, *My Life*
My Life

Johnny Cash, *American Recordings*
Delia's Gone

Gillian Welch, *Revival*
Orphan Girl

Top Overall Quality

Dance

27 **Donna Summer,** *Dance Collection*
MacArthur Park Suite

Bee Gees, *Saturday Night Fever*
Stayin' Alive

26 **Madonna,** *Ray of Light*
Ray of Light

25 **Erasure,** *Erasure Pop!*
A Little Respect

Chemical Brothers, *Dig Your Own Hole*
Setting Sun

Paul Oakenfold, *Tranceport*
Someone

Pet Shop Boys, *Very*
Go West

Chic, *Dance Dance Dance*
Good Times

Björk, *Debut*
Big Time Sensuality

24 **Fatboy Slim,** *You've Come a Long Way, Baby*
The Rockafeller Skank

A Night at Studio 54
I Love the Night Life

Basement Jaxx, *Rooty*
Where's Your Head At

Electronica

28 **Massive Attack,** *Protection*
Protection

Joy Division, *Closer*
Isolation

27 **Kraftwerk,** *Trans-Europe Express*
Trans-Europe Express

Portishead, *Dummy*
Glory Box

New Order, *Substance*
Bizarre Love Triangle

Tricky, *Maxinquaye*
Overcome

Stereolab, *Emperor Tomato Ketchup*
Cybele's Reverie

New Order, *Power, Corruption and Lies*
Blue Monday

Massive Attack, *Blue Lines*
Unfinished Symphony

The Orb, *Adventures Beyond the Ultraworld*
Little Fluffy Clouds

Kruder & Dorfmeister, *The K & D Sessions*
Bug Powder Dust

26 **Depeche Mode,** *Music for the Masses*
Never Let Me Down Again

Folk

28 **John Prine,** *John Prine*
Hello in There

Nick Drake, *Bryter Later*
Northern Sky

Richard & Linda Thompson, *Shoot Out the Lights*
Wall of Death

The Weavers, *Weavers at Carnegie Hall*
Goodnight Irene

Leo Kottke, *6- and 12-String Guitar*
Vaseline Machine Gun

27 **Nick Drake,** *Pink Moon*
Pink Moon

Woody Guthrie, *The Greatest Songs*
This Land Is Your Land

Kate & Anna McGarrigle, *Kate & Anna McGarrigle*
Heart Like A Wheel

Ani DiFranco, *Living in Clip*
Both Hands

Joan Baez, *Joan Baez*
Silver Dagger

26 **Fairport Convention,** *Liege & Lief*
Matty Groves

Billy Bragg & Wilco, *Mermaid Avenue*
California Stars

Top Overall Quality

Funk

28 **The Meters,** *Funkify Your Life*
Cissy Strut

Funkadelic, *Maggot Brain*
Maggot Brain

27 **Isaac Hayes,** *Hot Buttered Soul*
Walk on By

Earth, Wind & Fire, *That's the Way of the World*
That's the Way of the World

Funkadelic, *One Nation Under a Groove*
One Nation Under a Groove

James Brown, *Live at the Apollo, Volume 1*
Lost Someone

James Brown, *Sex Machine*
Get Up (I Feel Like Being A) Sex Machine

26 **Parliament,** *Mothership Connection*
Mothership Connection (Star Child)

Isaac Hayes, *Shaft*
Theme from Shaft

Herbie Hancock, *Head Hunters*
Watermelon Man

24 **War,** *Greatest Hits*
Low Rider

AWB, *AWB*
Pick Up the Pieces

Hip-Hop

29 **Public Enemy,** *It Takes a Nation*
Bring the Noise

28 **Run-D.M.C.,** *Raising Hell*
Peter Piper

Dr. Dre, *The Chronic*
Nuthin' But a 'G' Thang

A Tribe Called Quest, *The Low End Theory*
Scenario

Wu-Tang Clan, *Enter the Wu-Tang*
C.R.E.A.M.

Boogie Down Productions, *Criminal Minded*
Criminal Minded

Nas, *Illmatic**
NY State of Mind

Tupac Shakur, *Greatest Hits*
I Get Around

27 **DJ Shadow,** *Endtroducing . . .*
Midnight in a Perfect World

A Tribe Called Quest, *People's Instinctive Travels*
Bonita Applebum

Notorious B.I.G., *Ready to Die*
Juicy

Notorious B.I.G., *Life After Death*
Hypnotize

Jazz

30 **Miles Davis,** *Kind of Blue*
So What

29 **John Coltrane,** *A Love Supreme*
Acknowledgement

Bill Evans, *Waltz for Debby*
Waltz for Debby

Charlie Parker, *Yardbird Suite: The Ultimate Collection*
Parker's Mood

Dave Brubeck, *Time Out*
Take Five

28 **John Coltrane,** *Blue Train*
Blue Train

Art Blakey & The Jazz Messengers, *Moanin'*
Moanin'

Sonny Rollins, *Saxophone Colossus*
St. Thomas

Charlie Parker, *Jazz at Massey Hall*
Salt Peanuts

Miles Davis w. Gil Evans, *Sketches of Spain*
Concierto de Aranjuez

Stan Getz, *Getz/Gilberto*
The Girl from Ipanema

Antonio Carlos Jobim, *Wave*
Wave

Top Overall Quality

Kids

28 Muppet Movie
The Rainbow Connection

27 They Might Be Giants, *NO!*
Bed Bed Bed

Sesame Street, *Platinum*
I Love Trash

The Lion King
Circle of Life

26 Mary Poppins
Feed the Birds

Jerry Garcia/David Grisman,
Not for Kids Only
There Ain't No Bugs on Me

Beauty and the Beast
Beauty and the Beast

25 Marlo Thomas, *Free to Be . . .*
You and Me
William's Doll

The Little Mermaid
Under the Sea

Carole King, *Really Rosie*
Chicken Soup with Rice

Best of Schoolhouse Rock
Conjunction Junction

24 Annie
Tomorrow

Musicals

29 My Fair Lady (Lerner and
Loewe)
I Could Have Danced All Night

***Sweeney Todd* (Sondheim)**
A Little Priest

28 Les Misérables (Kretzmer and
Schönberg)
On My Own

***West Side Story* (Bernstein and**
Sondheim)
Tonight

***Follies in Concert* (Sondheim)**
Losing My Mind

27 Fiddler on the Roof (Bock and
Harnick)
Sunrise, Sunset

***Company* (Sondheim)**
The Ladies Who Lunch

***Candide* (Bernstein and Wilbur)**
Glitter and Be Gay

***Gypsy* (Sondheim and Styne)**
Rose's Turn

***South Pacific* (Rodgers and**
Hammerstein)
Some Enchanted Evening

26 Ain't Misbehavin' (Waller)
Ain't Misbehavin'

The Phantom of the Opera
(Lloyd Webber)
The Music of the Night

New Age

27 Ottmar Liebert, *Nouveau*
Flamenco
Barcelona Nights

Enya, *Watermark*
Orinoco Flow

26 Enigma, *MCMXC A.D.*
Principles of Lust: Sadeness/
Find Love

George Winston, *Autumn*
Colors/Dance

Vangelis, *Chariots of Fire*
Titles

25 Koyaanisqatsi
Koyaanisqatsi

Jean-Michel Jarre, *Oxygene*
Oxygene, Part IV

Ray Lynch, *Deep Breakfast*
The Oh of Pleasure

Mannheim Steamroller, *Fresh*
Aire IV
The Dream

24 Kitaro, *Silk Road, Vol. 1*
Silk Road

Andreas Vollenweider, *Down to*
the Moon
Down to the Moon

Philip Glass, *Glassworks*
Facades

Top Overall Quality

Pop Vocal, Contemporary

28 **Michael Jackson,** *Thriller*
Billie Jean

27 **Madonna,** *Immaculate Collection*
Like a Prayer

Sade, *Diamond Life*
Smooth Operator

Dusty Springfield, *Dusty in Memphis*
Son of a Preacher Man

26 **Annie Lennox,** *Diva*
Why

Michael Jackson, *Off the Wall*
Don't Stop 'Til You Get Enough

Harry Nilsson, *Nilsson Schmilsson*
Without You

Tina Turner, *Private Dancer*
Private Dancer

Norah Jones, *Come Away with Me*
Come Away with Me

Roberta Flack, *Softly with These Songs*
Killing Me Softly with His Song

The Carpenters, *The Singles*
We've Only Just Begun

Linda Ronstadt, *Heart Like a Wheel*
You're No Good

Pop Vocal, Traditional

29 **Ella Fitzgerald,** *Best of the Songbooks*
Bewitched, Bothered and Bewildered

Frank Sinatra, *In the Wee Small Hours*
In the Wee Small Hours

28 **Nat King Cole,** *The Nat King Cole Story*
Unforgettable

Frank Sinatra, *Only the Lonely*
One for My Baby

Ella Fitzgerald, *The Complete Ella in Berlin*
Mack the Knife

Edith Piaf, *La Vie En Rose*
La Vie En Rose

Frank Sinatra, *Songs for Swingin' Lovers*
You Make Me Feel So Young

Frank Sinatra, *Sinatra Reprise*
Fly Me to the Moon

Barbra Streisand, *The Barbra Streisand Album*
Happy Days Are Here Again

Sarah Vaughan, *With Clifford Brown*
Lullaby of Birdland

Judy Garland, *Judy at Carnegie Hall*
Over the Rainbow

27 **Tony Bennett,** *I Left My Heart in San Francisco*
I Left My Heart in San Francisco

R&B

27 **Luther Vandross,** *The Best*
A House Is Not a Home

The Temptations, *Greatest Hits*
My Girl

Prince, *Sign 'O' the Times*
Adore

Barry White, *All-Time Greatest Hits*
Can't Get Enough of Your Love, Babe

Maxwell, *Urban Hang Suite*
Ascension (Don't Ever Wonder)

Jill Scott, *Who is Jill Scott?*
A Long Walk

Lauryn Hill, *The Miseducation*
Doo Wop (That Thing)

Prince, *1999*
Little Red Corvette

26 **Anita Baker,** *Rapture*
Sweet Love

Mary J. Blige, *No More Drama*
No More Drama

Mary J. Blige, *My Life*
My Life

D'Angelo, *Brown Sugar*
Brown Sugar

Rock, Overall

29 Bruce Springsteen, *Born to Run*
Thunder Road

The Beatles, *Abbey Road*
Here Comes the Sun

The Who, *Who's Next*
Won't Get Fooled Again

The Beatles, *Sgt. Pepper*
A Day In The Life

Nuggets: Original Artyfacts
Open My Eyes

Elvis Costello, *This Year's Model*
Radio, Radio

Bruce Springsteen, *Darkness on the Edge of Town*
Badlands

Pink Floyd, *Dark Side of the Moon*
Time

The Clash, *London Calling*
London Calling

The Beatles, *Revolver*
Tomorrow Never Knows

28 The Beach Boys, *Pet Sounds*
God Only Knows

The Replacements, *Let It Be*
Unsatisfied

Rock, Alternative

28 U2, *The Joshua Tree*
With or Without You

Nirvana, *Nevermind*
Smells Like Teen Spirit

Radiohead, *The Bends*
Fake Plastic Trees

Radiohead, *OK Computer*
Paranoid Android

R.E.M., *Murmur*
Radio Free Europe

Sigur Rós, *'Agaetis Byrjun*
Svefn G Englar

The Smiths, *The Queen is Dead*
There Is a Light that Never Goes Out

Wilco, *Yankee Hotel Foxtrot*
Jesus, Etc.

27 Pavement, *Slanted and Enchanted*
Summer Babe (Winter Version)

The Pretenders, *The Pretenders*
Brass in Pocket

Pearl Jam, *Ten*
Black

Big Star, *Sister Lovers/Third*
Jesus Christ

Rock, Art/Experimental

29 Pink Floyd, *Dark Side of the Moon*
Time

28 David Bowie, *The Rise and Fall of Ziggy Stardust*
Suffragette City

Pink Floyd, *Wish You Were Here*
Wish You Were Here

27 Pink Floyd, *The Wall*
Comfortably Numb

Brian Eno, *Before and After Science*
King's Lead Hat

Frank Zappa, *Apostrophe*
Apostrophe

David Bowie, *Changesbowie*
Changes

26 Peter Gabriel, *So*
In Your Eyes

Genesis, *Lamb Lies Down on Broadway*
Carpet Crawlers

David Bowie, *Station to Station*
Station to Station

25 David Bowie, *Heroes*
Heroes

Yes, *Fragile*
Roundabout

Top Overall Quality

Rock, Classic

29 **Bruce Springsteen**, *Born to Run*
Thunder Road

The Beatles, *Abbey Road*
Here Comes the Sun

The Who, *Who's Next*
Won't Get Fooled Again

The Beatles, *Sgt. Pepper*
A Day in the Life

Bruce Springsteen, *Darkness on the Edge of Town*
Badlands

The Beatles, *Revolver*
Tomorrow Never Knows

28 **The Beach Boys**, *Pet Sounds*
God Only Knows

Jimi Hendrix, *Electric Ladyland*
Voodoo Chile

The Rolling Stones, *Exile on Main Street*
Tumbling Dice

The Beatles, *The White Album*
While My Guitar Gently Weeps

The Beatles, *Rubber Soul*
In My Life

The Rolling Stones, *Beggar's Banquet*
Sympathy for the Devil

Rock, Garage/Underground

29 **Nuggets: Original Artyfacts**
Open My Eyes

28 **The Replacements**, *Let It Be*
Unsatisfied

Love, *Forever Changes*
Alone Again Or

The Replacements, *Tim*
Here Comes a Regular

Velvet Underground, *Velvet Underground and Nico*
Heroin

The Zombies, *Odessey and Oracle*
Time of the Season

27 **The Stooges**, *Funhouse*
TV Eye

Fugazi, *13 Songs*
Waiting Room

26 **Hüsker Dü**, *New Day Rising*
Celebrated Summer

25 **The Stooges**, *The Stooges*
I Wanna Be Your Dog

24 **Bob Mould**, *Workbook*
Wishing Well

The White Stripes, *White Blood Cells*
Fell in Love with a Girl

Rock, Hard/Heavy Metal

27 **Metallica**, *Master of Puppets*
Master of Puppets

Tool, *Aenima*
Aenima

Guns n' Roses, *Appetite for Destruction*
Welcome to the Jungle

Rush, *Moving Pictures*
Tom Sawyer

AC/DC, *Back in Black*
Back in Black

26 **Van Halen**, *Van Halen*
Ain't Talkin' 'Bout Love

Jethro Tull, *Aqualung*
Aqualung

25 **Metallica**, *Metallica*
Enter Sandman

Rush, *2112*
2112

Aerosmith, *Toys in the Attic*
Sweet Emotion

AC/DC, *Highway to Hell*
Highway to Hell

Slayer, *Reign in Blood*
Angel of Death

Rock, New Wave

29 **Elvis Costello**, *This Year's Model*
Radio, Radio

28 **Elvis Costello**, *My Aim Is True*
Alison

The Jam, *The Jam Collection*
To Be Someone (Didn't We Have a Nice Time)

27 **Talking Heads**, *Remain in Light*
Once in a Lifetime

Talking Heads, *Speaking in Tongues*
Burning Down the House

26 **Graham Parker**, *Squeezing Out Sparks*
Discovering Japan

XTC, *Drums and Wires*
Making Plans for Nigel

Nick Lowe, *Labour of Lust*
Cruel to Be Kind

Gang of Four, *Entertainment!*
I Found That Essence Rare

Squeeze, *Singles 45's and Under*
Tempted

25 **The English Beat**, *I Just Can't Stop It*
Mirror in the Bathroom

The Specials, *The Specials*
Message to you Rudy

Rock, Oldies

28 **Elvis Presley**, *Elvis (TV Special)*
If I Can Dream

Bo Diddley, *The Chess Box*
Bo Diddley

27 **Roy Orbison**, *All-Time Greatest Hits*
Crying

Chuck Berry, *Great Twenty-Eight*
Johnny B. Goode

Elvis Presley, *Elvis' Golden Records*
Jailhouse Rock

Buddy Holly, *The Best*
Peggy Sue

The Drifters, *All-Time Greatest Hits*
Under the Boardwalk

26 **Elvis Presley**, *From Elvis in Memphis*
In the Ghetto

Everly Brothers, *Cadence Classics*
Wake Up Little Susie

American Graffiti
Rock Around the Clock

The Four Seasons, *Anthology*
Sherry

The Righteous Brothers, *Anthology*
You've Lost That Lovin' Feeling

Rock, Punk

29 **The Clash**, *London Calling*
London Calling

28 **The Ramones**, *Ramones Mania*
I Wanna Be Sedated

The Ramones, *Ramones*
Blitzkrieg Bop

27 **Patti Smith**, *Horses*
Gloria

The Clash, *The Clash*
White Riot

Television, *Marquee Moon*
Marquee Moon

26 **Buzzcocks**, *Singles Going Steady*
What Do I Get

X, *Wild Gift*
White Girl

The Sex Pistols, *Never Mind the Bollocks*
God Save the Queen

MC 5, *Kick Out the Jams*
Kick Out the Jams

Bad Brains, *I Against I*
I Against I

25 **Patty Smith**, *Easter*
Because the Night

Top Overall Quality

Singer-Songwriter

29 **Patty Griffin,** *Living with Ghosts*
Every Little Bit

Bob Dylan, *Blood on the Tracks*
Tangled Up in Blue

Bob Dylan, *Blonde on Blonde*
Visions of Johanna

Carole King, *Tapestry*
So Far Away

Van Morrison, *Astral Weeks*
Madame George

Joni Mitchell, *Blue*
A Case of You

28 **Joni Mitchell,** *Court and Spark*
Help Me

Simon & Garfunkel, *Bridge over Troubled Water*
Bridge over Troubled Water

Simon & Garfunkel, *Parsley, Sage, Rosemary and Thyme*
Scarborough Fair/Canticle

Van Morrison, *Moondance*
Moondance

Tom Waits, *Rain Dogs*
Downtown Train

27 **James Taylor,** *Sweet Baby James*
Sweet Baby James

Soul

29 **Aretha Franklin,** *Lady Soul*
Chain of Fools

Stevie Wonder, *Innervisions*
Living for the City

Hitsville USA
Dancing in the Street

Marvin Gaye, *What's Going On*
What's Going On

Aretha Franklin, *Queen of Soul*
Respect

28 **Stevie Wonder,** *Talking Book*
Superstition

Sam Cooke, *The Man and his Music*
A Change Is Gonna Come

Curtis Mayfield, *Superfly*
Freddie's Dead

Solomon Burke, *Don't Give Up On Me*
Soul Searchin'

Otis Redding, *The Otis Redding Story*
Dock of the Bay

Stevie Wonder, *Songs in the Key of Life*
Sir Duke

Ray Charles, *Anthology*
Georgia on My Mind

Soundtracks

28 **Peter Gabriel,** *Passion*
It Is Accomplished

The Wizard of Oz
Over the Rainbow

Manhattan
He Loves and She Loves

Singin' in the Rain
Singin' in the Rain

The Sound of Music
Edelweiss

The Music from Peter Gunn
Peter Gunn Theme

27 *Star Wars*
Main Title

The Godfather
Love Theme from The Godfather

Funny Girl
Don't Rain on My Parade

Prince, *Purple Rain*
When Doves Cry

The King and I
Shall We Dance

Simon & Garfunkel, *The Graduate*
Mrs. Robinson

World

28 Paul Simon, *Graceland*
Diamonds on the Soles of her Shoes

Buena Vista Social Club
Chan Chan

27 *The Mambo Kings*
Beautiful Maria of My Soul

Cesaria Evora, Miss Perfumado
Sodade

26 The Chieftains, *Long Black Veil*
The Long Black Veil

Gipsy Kings, *Gipsy Kings*
Bamboleo

25 Loreena McKennitt, *Book of Secrets*
Highwayman

Amélie
La Valise d'Amélie

Manu Chao, *Clandestino*
Clandestino

24 Afro-Celt Sound System, *Sound Magic Vol. 1*
Saor/Free/News From Nowhere

Harry Belafonte, *Calypso*
The Banana Boat Song (Day-O)

Deep Forest, *Deep Forest*
Deep Forest

By Decade

Our editors' compilations of definitive discs, followed by our surveyors' favorite tracks.

1950s

28 Nat King Cole, *The Nat King Cole Story*
Unforgettable

Frank Sinatra, *Sinatra Reprise*
Fly Me to the Moon

Billie Holiday, *Lady Sings the Blues*
God Bless the Child

27 Cannonball Adderley, *Somethin' Else*
Autumn Leaves

Peggy Lee, *Spotlight on Peggy Lee*
Fever

An American in Paris
Love Is Here to Stay

Blossom Dearie, *Blossom Dearie*
I Won't Dance

26 Benny Goodman, *B. G. in Hi-Fi*
Stompin' at the Savoy

Dean Martin, *Capitol Collectors Series*
That's Amore

25 Louis Prima, *Zooma Zooma*
Just a Gigolo/I Ain't Got Nobody

A Star Is Born
The Man That Got Away

Chet Baker, *Chet Baker Sings*
My Funny Valentine

1960s

29 The Beatles, *Sgt. Pepper*
A Day In The Life

Aretha Franklin, *Queen of Soul*
Respect

28 Jimi Hendrix, *Are You Experienced?*
Purple Haze

27 Simon & Garfunkel, *The Graduate*
Mrs. Robinson

Cream, *Disraeli Gears*
Sunshine of Your Love

26 Phil Ochs, *I Ain't a'Marchin' Anymore*
Draft Dodger Rag

Jefferson Airplane, *Surrealistic Pillow*
White Rabbit

25 The Mamas and the Papas, *If You Can Believe Your Eyes . . .*
California Dreamin'

Big Brother and the Holding Co., *Cheap Thrills*
Piece of My Heart

24 Procol Harum, *Procol Harum*
Whiter Shade of Pale

Hair
Aquarius

22 Donovan, *Greatest Hits*
Mellow Yellow

Top Overall Quality

1970s

29 Marvin Gaye, *What's Going On*
What's Going On

28 Bob Marley and the Wailers, *Burnin'*
Get Up, Stand Up

David Bowie, *Ziggy Stardust*
Suffragette City

Led Zeppelin, *Led Zeppelin IV*
Stairway to Heaven

27 The Kinks, *Lola vs. The Powerman . . .*
Lola

John Lennon, *Imagine*
Imagine

Santana, *Abraxas*
Black Magic Woman

26 The Sex Pistols, *Never Mind the Bollocks*
God Save the Queen

Lou Reed, *Transformer*
Walk on the Wild Side

25 Lynyrd Skynrd, *Pronounced Leh-Nerd Skin-Nerd*
Free Bird

Yes, *Fragile*
Roundabout

Boston, *Boston*
More Than a Feeling

1980s

28 U2, *The Joshua Tree*
With or Without You

Michael Jackson, *Thriller*
Billie Jean

R.E.M., *Murmur*
Radio Free Europe

27 The Pretenders, *The Pretenders*
Brass in Pocket

Madonna, *Immaculate Collection*
Like a Prayer

Guns n' Roses, *Appetite for Destruction*
Welcome to the Jungle

Prince, *1999*
Little Red Corvette

26 Tina Turner, *Private Dancer*
Private Dancer

25 Tracy Chapman, *Tracy Chapman*
Fast Car

Van Halen, *1984*
Jump

23 *Flashdance*
What a Feeling

The Breakfast Club
Don't You (Forget About Me)

1990s

28 Nirvana, *Nevermind*
Smells Like Teen Spirit

27 Johnny Cash, *American Recordings*
Delia's Gone

Tupac Shakur, *All Eyez on Me*
California Love (Rmx)

26 Snoop Dogg, *Doggystyle*
Gin and Juice

Moby, *Play*
Porcelain

Red Hot Chili Peppers, *Blood Sugar Sex Magik*
Under the Bridge

25 Beck, *Odelay*
Devil's Haircut

The Fugees, *The Score*
Killing Me Softly with His Song

Björk, *Debut*
Big Time Sensuality

24 Fatboy Slim, *You've Come a Long Way, Baby*
The Rockafeller Skank

Dave Matthews Band, *Crash*
Crash

22 Sheryl Crow, *Tuesday Night Music Club*
Leaving Las Vegas

2000s

27 Bruce Springsteen, *The Rising*
The Rising

26 Coldplay, *A Rush of Blood to the Head*
Clocks

Mary J. Blige, *No More Drama*
No More Drama

Norah Jones, *Come Away with Me*
Come Away with Me

Thievery Corporation, *The Mirror Conspiracy*
Lebanese Blonde

The Roots, *Phrenology*
The Seed (2.0)

24 Daft Punk, *Discovery*
One More Time

The White Stripes, *White Blood Cells*
Fell in Love With a Girl

23 No Doubt, *Rock Steady*
Hella Good

22 The Strokes, *Is This It*
Last Night

P!nk, *M!ssundaztood*
Just Like a Pill

8 Mile
Lose Yourself

By Special Feature

Our editors' compilations of definitive discs, followed by our surveyors' favorite tracks.

Born in the USA

29 Marvin Gaye, *What's Going On*
What's Going On

28 Aaron Copland, *Appalachian Spring*
Appalachian Spring

27 Bruce Springsteen, *Born in the USA*
Born in the USA

Woody Guthrie, *Greatest Songs*
This Land Is Your Land

26 *Forrest Gump*
Fortunate Son

John Cougar Mellencamp, *Scarecrow*
Small Town

Woodstock
Star Spangled Banner

24 Arlo Guthrie, *Alice's Restaurant*
Alice's Restaurant Massacree

Dixie Chicks, *Home*
Travelin' Soldier

Neil Diamond, *The Jazz Singer*
America

23 Don McLean, *American Pie*
American Pie

Grateful Dead, *Steal Your Face*
U.S. Blues

Breakup

29 Bob Dylan, *Blood on the Tracks*
Tangled Up in Blue

Joni Mitchell, *Blue*
A Case of You

28 Patsy Cline, *Greatest Hits*
Crazy

George Jones, *Essential*
He Stopped Loving Her Today

27 Fleetwood Mac, *Rumours*
Go Your Own Way

26 The Rolling Stones, *Some Girls*
Miss You

Joy Division, *Substance*
Love Will Tear Us Apart

Rosanne Cash, *Interiors*
On the Surface

25 k.d. lang, *Ingenue*
Constant Craving

24 Alanis Morissette, *Jagged Little Pill*
You Oughta Know

Chris Isaak, *Heart Shaped World*
Wicked Game

Shawn Colvin, *A Few Small Repairs*
Sunny Came Home

Top Overall Quality

Chill-Out

27 A Tribe Called Quest, *People's Instinctive Travels . . .*
Bonita Applebum

Enya, *Watermark*
Orinoco Flow

26 Sarah McLachlan, *Surfacing*
Angel

Morcheeba, *Big Calm*
Part of the Process

Aimee Mann, *Magnolia*
Save Me

Bob Dylan, *Nashville Skyline*
Lay Lady Lay

Aphex Twin, *Selected Ambient Works 85-92*
Ageispolis

25 Air, *Moon Safari*
Sexy Boy

Leonard Cohen, *I'm Your Man*
Everybody knows

Twin Peaks
Falling

24 St. Germain, *Tourist*
Rose Rouge

Digable Planets, *Reachin' (A New Refutation of Time and Space)*
Rebirth of Slick (Cool Like Dat)

Cocktail Hour

28 Frank Sinatra, *Only the Lonely*
One for my Baby

Art Blakey & The Jazz Messengers, *Moanin'*
Moanin'

Stan Getz, *Getz/Gilberto*
Girl from Ipanema

Oscar Peterson, *On the Town*
Moonlight in Vermont

27 Stereolab, *Emperor Tomato Ketchup*
Cybele's Reverie

June Christy, *Something Cool*
Something Cool

Lee Morgan, *The Sidewinder*
The Sidewinder

26 *Pink Panther*
Pink Panther

25 Sergio Mendes, *Fool on the Hill*
Fool on the Hill

24 *Swingers*
You're Nobody Till Somebody Loves You

Tom Jones, *Greatest Hits*
It's Not Unusual

22 Herb Alpert and the Tijuana Brass, *Whipped Cream and Other Delights*
A Taste of Honey

Late Night

29 Frank Sinatra, *In the Wee Small Hours*
In the Wee Small Hours

Pink Floyd, *Dark Side of the Moon*
Time

28 Van Morrison, *Moondance*
Moondance

Tom Waits, *Rain Dogs*
Downtown Train

Nina Simone, *Wild Is the Wind*
Wild Is the Wind

27 Nick Drake, *Pink Moon*
Pink Moon

Jeff Buckley, *Grace*
Hallelujah

Tori Amos, *Little Earthquakes*
Winter

26 R.E.M., *Automatic for the People*
Nightswimming

Trainspotting
Born Slippy

25 Cassandra Wilson, *New Moon Daughter*
Last Train to Clarksville

The Chemical Brothers, *Dig Your Own Hole*
Setting Sun

Make-Out

27 Marvin Gaye, *Anthology*
Let's Get It On

Prince, *Purple Rain*
When Doves Cry

Massive Attack, *Blue Lines*
Unfinished Sympathy

Roxy Music, *Avalon*
Avalon

U2, *Achtung Baby*
One

Maxwell, *Urban Hang Suite*
Ascension (Don't Ever Wonder)

26 Diana Krall, *The Look of Love*
The Look of Love

D'Angelo, *Brown Sugar*
Brown Sugar

24 Erykah Badu, *Baduizm*
Next Lifetime

Olive, *Extra Virgin*
You're Not Alone

22 Terence Trent D'Arby, *Introducing . . .*
Wishing Well

Lenny Kravitz, *Are You Gonna Go My Way?*
Are You Gonna Go My Way?

Party

28 Run-D.M.C., *Raising Hell*
Peter Piper

The Ramones, *Ramones*
Blitzkrieg Bop

27 Funkadelic, *One Nation Under a Groove*
One Nation Under a Groove

26 Snoop Dogg, *Doggystyle*
Gin and Juice

25 Erasure, *Erasure Pop!*
A Little Respect

24 *A Night at Studio 54*
I Love the Night Life

The B-52's, *The B-52's*
Rock Lobster

Deee-Lite, *World Clique*
Groove is in the Heart

The Crystal Method, *Vegas*
Busy Child

23 Daft Punk, *Homework*
Around the World

INXS, *Kick*
Need You Tonight

21 KC & the Sunshine Band, *The Best*
Get Down Tonight

Rainy Day

28 Willie Nelson, *Red Headed Stranger*
Blue Eyes Crying in the Rain

Singin' in the Rain
Singin' in the Rain

27 Gillian Welch, *Revival*
Orphan Girl

26 Beth Orton, *Central Reservation*
Central Reservation

Everything But the Girl, *Walking Wounded*
Walking Wounded

25 Belle & Sebastian, *If You're Feeling Sinister*
The Stars of Track and Field

David Gray, *White Ladder*
Babylon

Seal, *Seal*
Kiss From a Rose

24 The Sundays, *Reading, Writing and Arithmetic*
Here's Where the Story Ends

The Crow
It Can't Rain All the Time

Dido, *No Angel*
Thank You

Missy Elliott, *Supa Dupa Fly*
The Rain (Supa Dupa Fly)

Top Overall Quality

Road Music

28 **Dr. Dre,** *The Chronic*
Nuthin' But a 'G' Thang

27 **Joni Mitchell,** *Hejira*
Coyote

The Allman Brothers, *Eat a Peach*
Melissa

26 **Dwight Yoakam,** *Guitars, Cadillacs*
Guitars, Cadillacs

The Eagles, *Their Greatest Hits*
Take It Easy

25 **Jackson Browne,** *Running on Empty*
Running on Empty

The Modern Lovers, *The Modern Lovers*
Roadrunner

AC/DC, *Highway to Hell*
Highway to Hell

Meat Loaf, *Bat out of Hell*
Paradise by the Dashboard Light

24 *Easy Rider*
Born to Be Wild

23 **Bob Seger & The Silver Bullet Band,** *Against the Wind*
Against the Wind

21 **Go-Go's,** *Beauty and the Beat*
We Got the Beat

Romantic

29 **Aretha Franklin,** *Queen of Soul*
Respect

28 **Stevie Wonder,** *Talking Book*
Superstition

27 **Al Green,** *Greatest Hits*
Let's Stay Together

26 **Matthew Sweet,** *Girlfriend*
Girlfriend

25 **Kate Bush,** *Hounds of Love*
Running Up That Hill

24 **Toni Braxton,** *Secrets*
Un-Break My Heart

Sleepless in Seattle
As Time Goes By

Natalie Cole, *Unforgettable: With Love*
Unforgettable

23 **Melissa Etheridge,** *Yes I Am*
Come to My Window

Faith Hill, *Breathe*
Breathe

22 **Celine Dion,** *Let's Talk About Love*
Let's Talk About Love

21 **John Lennon and Yoko Ono,** *Double Fantasy*
Watching the Wheels

Summer

29 **Bob Marley and the Wailers,** *Legend*
No Woman No Cry

27 **Creedence Clearwater Revival,** *Chronicle*
Bad Moon Rising

Jimmy Cliff, *The Harder They Come*
The Harder They Come

The Drifters, *1959-1965 All-Time Greatest Hits and More*
Under the Boardwalk

26 **Rod Stewart,** *Every Picture Tells A Story*
Maggie May

Grease
Summer Nights

25 **Jimmy Buffett,** *Songs You Know By Heart*
Margaritaville

George Benson, *Breezin'*
Breezin'

Alabama, *Mountain Music*
Mountain Music

24 **Don Henley,** *Building the Perfect Beast*
Boys of Summer

23 **Alice Cooper,** *Greatest Hits*
School's Out

22 **Steve Miller Band,** *Greatest Hits 1974-78*
The Joker

Sunday Mornings

28 Joni Mitchell, *Court and Spark*
Help Me

The Beatles, *Rubber Soul*
In My Life

Otis Redding, *The Otis Redding Story*
Dock of the Bay

Stevie Wonder, *Songs in the Key of Life*
Sir Duke

Oliver Nelson, *Blues and the Abstract Truth*
Stolen Moments

27 George Harrison, *All Things Must Pass*
My Sweet Lord

Vince Guaraldi, *A Boy Named Charlie Brown*
Linus and Lucy

26 The Roches, *The Roches*
Hammond Song

Phoebe Snow, *Phoebe Snow*
Poetry Man

Rickie Lee Jones, *Rickie Lee Jones*
Chuck E's in Love

24 John Mayer, *Room for Squares*
Your Body Is a Wonderland

23 The 5th Dimension, *Greatest Hits on Earth*
Up, Up and Away

Work-Out

26 Hairspray
You Can't Stop the Beat

Vangelis, *Chariots of Fire*
Titles

25 ABBA, *Gold/Greatest Hits*
Dancing Queen

Rocky
Gonna Fly Now

24 Gloria Estefan, *Greatest Hits*
Conga

George Michael, *Faith*
Faith

Kylie Minogue, *Fever*
Can't Get You Out of My Head

En Vogue, *Funky Divas*
Free Your Mind

Matrix
Spybreak! (Short One)

23 Flashdance
What a Feeling

No Doubt, *Rock Steady*
Hella Good

22 Joan Jett & the Blackhearts, *I Love Rock 'n' Roll*
I Love Rock 'n' Roll

Top 50 Songwriting

30 Bob Dylan, *Blood on the Tracks*
29 Patty Griffin, *Living with Ghosts*
Mozart, *Don Giovanni**
Mozart, *Piano Concertos 19-23*
Bob Dylan, *Blonde on Blonde*
Miles Davis with Gil Evans,
   Porgy and Bess
Bruce Springsteen, *Darkness on
   the Edge of Town*
Lucinda Williams, *Lucinda
   Williams*
Bruce Springsteen, *Born to Run*
John Prine, *John Prine*
Tom Lehrer, *That Was the Year
   That Was*
Woody Guthrie, *Greatest Songs*
Leonard Cohen, *I'm Your Man*
Simon & Garfunkel, *Bridge over
   Troubled Water*
Beethoven, *Symphony No. 9*
Nas, *Illmatic*
Mozart, *Requiem*
Carole King, *Tapestry*
Richard & Linda Thompson,
   Shoot Out the Lights
Simon & Garfunkel, *Parsley,
   Sage, Rosemary and Thyme*
Stravinsky, *Petrushka*
Public Enemy, *It Takes a Nation*
Beethoven, *Symphonies 5 & 7*

Joni Mitchell, *Blue*
Wagner, *Der Ring*
Curtis Mayfield, *Superfly*
Bruce Springsteen, *Live/1975-85*
Tom Waits, *Small Change*
Elvis Costello, *This Year's Model*
Sweeney Todd
The Beatles, *Abbey Road*
Mozart, *Symphonies Nos. 35-41*
The Beatles, *Sgt. Pepper*
Gram Parsons, *Grievous Angel**
The Beatles, *Revolver
Company*
Elvis Costello, *My Aim Is True*
Mos Def, *Black on Both Sides**
My Fair Lady*
The Beatles, *Rubber Soul*
Marvin Gaye, *What's Going On*
Brahms, *Symphony No. 4*
Gershwin, *Rhapsody in Blue*
28 Van Morrison, *Astral Weeks*
Laura Nyro, *Eli and the
   Thirteenth Confession*
Joni Mitchell, *Court and Spark*
Stevie Wonder, *Innervisions*
Stevie Wonder, *Talking Book*
Harry Chapin, *Verities &
   Balderdash*
The Replacements, *Tim**

Top 50 Musicianship

30 Miles Davis, *Kind of Blue*
Jimi Hendrix, *Electric Ladyland*

29 Leo Kottke, *6- and 12-String Guitar*
John Coltrane, *A Love Supreme*
Miles Davis with Gil Evans, *Porgy and Bess*
Jimi Hendrix, *Are You Experienced?*
Sonny Rollins, *Saxophone Colossus*
Charlie Parker, *Yardbird Suite*
Bill Evans, *Waltz for Debby*
Miles Davis, *Miles Ahead*
John Coltrane, *Blue Train*
Art Tatum, *Tatum Group Masterpieces*
Miles Davis with Gil Evans, *Sketches of Spain*
Derek & the Dominos, *Layla and Other Assorted Love Songs*
Keith Jarrett, *The Köln Concert*
Joe Satriani, *Surfing with the Alien*
Wayne Shorter, *Speak No Evil*
Nitty Gritty Dirt Band, *Will the Circle Be Unbroken*
Stevie Ray Vaughan, *Greatest Hits*
Ella Fitzgerald, *Best of the Songbooks*
The Meters, *Funkify Your Life*
Dave Brubeck, *Time Out*
Charlie Parker, *Jazz at Massey Hall*
Rush, *Moving Pictures*

A. Collins, J. Copeland, R. Cray, *Showdown!*
Vladimir Horowitz, *Horowitz in Moscow**
Chopin, *Nocturnes*
Lee Morgan, *The Sidewinder*
Cannonball Adderley, *Somethin' Else*
Peter Gabriel, *Passion*
Rimsky-Korsakov, *Scheherazade*
Barbra Streisand, *The Barbra Streisand Album**
Stevie Wonder, *Innervisions*
Curtis Mayfield, *Superfly*
Wes Montgomery, *Incredible Jazz Guitar**
Bruce Springsteen, *Live/1975-85*
Stan Getz, *Getz/Gilberto*
Henry Mancini, *Music from Peter Gunn*
B.B. King, *Live at the Regal*
Martha Argerich, *Début Recital*
J.S. Bach, *Mass in B minor**
Stevie Wonder, *Songs in the Key of Life*
Stevie Wonder, *Talking Book*
Oscar Peterson, *On the Town*
Bruce Springsteen, *Born to Run*
Aretha Franklin, *Lady Soul*
Art Blakey, *Moanin'*
Mstislav Rostropovich, *Dvorák; Tchaikovsky*
Richard & Linda Thompson, *Shoot Out the Lights*
The Who, *Who's Next*

Top 50 Production Values

29 Peter Gabriel, *Passion*
Pink Floyd, *Dark Side of the Moon*
The Beatles, *Sgt. Pepper*

28 Frank Sinatra, *Only the Lonely*
Dr. Octagon, *Dr. Octagonecologyst*
The Beatles, *Abbey Road*
The Beach Boys, *Pet Sounds*
DJ Shadow, *Endtroducing . . .*
Dr. Dre, *The Chronic*
Brian Eno, *Before and After Science*
Michael Jackson, *Thriller*
Pink Floyd, *The Wall*
Radiohead, *OK Computer*
Stevie Wonder, *Innervisions*
The Beatles, *The White Album*
Stevie Wonder, *Talking Book*
Tricky, *Maxinquaye*
Mozart, *Piano Concertos 19-23*
Thievery Corporation, *Mirror Conspiracy*
Nine Inch Nails, *Downward Spiral*
Sigur Rós, *'Agaetis Byrjun*
Wilco, *Yankee Hotel Foxtrot*
The Beatles, *Revolver*
Pink Floyd, *Wish You Were Here*
Paul Simon, *Graceland*

Bruce Springsteen, *The Rising*
Gillian Welch, *Revival*
Stevie Wonder, *Songs in the Key of Life*
The Lion King
Sweeney Todd
Kruder & Dorfmeister, *K & D Sessions*
Les Misérables
Puccini, *La Bohème*
Portishead, *Dummy*
Hitsville USA
They Might Be Giants, *NO!**

27 Steely Dan, *Aja*
Chemical Brothers, *Dig Your Own Hole*
Miles Davis, *Kind of Blue*
Star Wars
Emmylou Harris, *Wrecking Ball*
Massive Attack, *Protection*
U2, *The Joshua Tree*
The Beatles, *Rubber Soul*
Madonna, *Ray of Light*
Maxwell, *Urban Hang Suite*
A Tribe Called Quest, *Low End Theory*
J.S. Bach, *Mass in B minor*
Bruce Springsteen, *Born to Run*
Barbra Streisand, *The Barbra Streisand Album*

Directory

A

Aaliyah, *Aaliyah*
23 | 22 | 23 | 23
2001, Blackground; "Rock the Boat"
■ "The last account of R&B's sweetheart" shows the "sultry soul sister" "grown up" and "at the top of her game"; "singing with more emotion", branching out in topic, with Timbaland providing "haunting yet damn funky" production, the budding "superstar" is "honest" and persuasive: "if she wants you to dance, you will, and if she wants to seduce you, you're putty in her hands"; it's "a fabulous testament to greatness" "lost too soon."

ABBA, *GOLD/GREATEST HITS*
25 | 22 | 23 | 24
1993, Polydor/Universal; "Dancing Queen"; www.abbasite.com
■ If you "snuck ABBA into the house between Deep Purple and Led Zeppelin", let go of the shame because this "guilty pleasure feels less guilty all the time"; "unadulterated sugary perfection" with "a strong disco vibe", the sound of "the only palindrome in pop" "goes down easy"; for "cleaning", "the gym", a commuter "pick-me-up" or "bopping around in your undies", "put the CD in your pocket carrier – just don't sing aloud."

AC/DC, *BACK IN BLACK*
27 | 22 | 25 | 25
1980, Atlantic; "Back in Black"; www.ac-dc.net
■ "Awesome at 80 mph", "this high-water mark in hard rock" is "a tremendous rebound after the tragic death of original lead singer Bon Scott"; "once you hear the toll of *Hells Bells* you're hooked", and "you can't seem to listen to just one song" – "sex, drugs and R&R never sounded better"; this "archetypal head-banging masterpiece" comes courtesy of producer Mutt Lange (who "made real music before he got 'Twain'd'") who "makes it snap when it should and pop when it must."

AC/DC, *Highway to Hell*
25 | 21 | 25 | 23
1979, Atlantic; "Highway to Hell"; www.ac-dc.net
■ This "smoking album" with the "most prophetic title ever" marked the last time the world would hear "devilishly excellent" "founding lead singer Bon Scott's terrorizing yowl" as "the Brothers Young knocked out fast blues riffs and made schoolboy rock" with "blasting simplicity"; "crank it up in traffic to beat road rage" 'cause this "foray into mayhem" "kicks ass in the classic sense."

Adams, *The Chairman Dances*
24 | 23 | 26 | 25
1990, Nonesuch; "The Chairman Dances"; www.sfsymphony.org
■ "If it weren't for classical music programmers wishing they were living 200 years ago", Adams' "minimalist" "modern" "masterwork", "a clever little distillation" of his opera, *Nixon in China*, "would be performed as often as *Rhapsody in Blue*"; "Mao never danced like this": full of "percussive music with a nonstop forward motion"

"wonderfully captured by the San Francisco Symphony"
under Edo de Waart, the "winner" proves that "less is more."

Ryan Adams, _Gold_   23 | 25 | 23 | 23
2001, Lost Highway; "New York, New York";
www.ryan-adams.com
 The former Whiskeytown frontman "opens up, shares
his sojourn from NYC to LA" and "becomes a star on this
album"; less alt-country and "way more pop" than previous
outings, it's a "wonderful amalgam of genres tossed together
in a big salad of rockers and ballads", "full of attitude,
heartbreak and love stories"; the less-impressed declare
it "could've been great with some judicious editing."

Cannonball Adderley,   27 | 26 | 29 | 23
Somethin' Else
1958, Blue Note; "Autumn Leaves"
■ Cannonball "makes the alto sax sing" on this jazz "spine-
tingler" of "late '50s" "cool" by a "killer ensemble" including
pianist Hank Jones, bassist Sam Jones, drummer Art Blakey
and "featuring" Miles Davis on trumpet; "Adderley's warm
flow" contrasts with "the pithiness and spare notes" of his
sideman for a "heartbreaking _Autumn Leaves_" and an
"incredible _Love for Sale_"; it's "very chill throughout",
even if some say it's really "a Miles album in disguise."

Aerosmith, _Pump_   23 | 22 | 25 | 24
1989, Geffen; "Water Song/Janie's Got a Gun";
www.aerosmith.com
■ Sure, _Permanent Vacation_ placed the "Boston bad boys"
"back in the public eye" but this "rockin' good-time"
platinum seller "solidified" their "triumphant return", "re-
jump-starting their incredible, now-sober careers" and
"propelling them" "to permanent MTV residency"; packed
with "expertly crafted" hits like _Janie's Got a Gun_ and _Love
in an Elevator,_ this "comeback" is "one for the time capsule."

Aerosmith, _Toys in the Attic_   25 | 23 | 25 | 23
1975, Columbia; "Sweet Emotion"; www.aerosmith.com
■ The "toxic twins" deliver "pure, unadulterated", "raunchy
rock" on this "ground- and speaker-breaking" platinum
platter, released back "when their artistry matched their
blood-alcohol levels"; "Steven Tyler and the guys shine
like never before", "setting the bar" with "quintessential
signatures like _Sweet Emotion_ and _Walk This Way_"; the
"ultimate" 1970s "party album", it "still holds up well"
according to diehards who deem it their "favorite toy."

Afro-Celt Sound System,   24 | 23 | 28 | 26
Sound Magic Volume 1
1996, Real World; "Saor/Free/News From Nowhere";
www.afrocelts.com
■ "You got your Celt in my Afro! You got your Afro in my
Celt!" – but "together they sound great" on this multi-culti

crew's "seamless, accessible blend" of "two rhythmic musical" "traditions"; "upbeat and bass- and percussion-heavy", it's "perfect for showing off that new sound system", but "put on your dance shoes before you listen because you'll want to whirl and leap" to this "sonic blast."

Ain't Misbehavin' (Soundtrack) **G** 26 | 26 | 28 | 26
1978, RCA; "Ain't Misbehavin'"
■ "You don't even have to like musicals to love" this "jivin', good-time", Grammy-winning "celebration of Harlem" in "the early 20th century", from the Tony-winning revue; the "fantastic Fats Waller song collection" is "brilliantly brought to life" through the "wit and sass" of a "multitalented cast" led by Charlene Woodard and the "late and much-missed Nell Carter" – "what a party!"

Air, *Moon Safari*　　　　　25 | 21 | 24 | 27
1998, Astralwerks; "Sexy Boy";
www.source.astralwerks.com/air
■ "Like a dreamy French pillow to float away on", this "lavishly produced" "lounger" provides the "soundtrack for a dawn that should know better than to intrude on the night"; "spellbinding" electronica + "Bacharach + Beach Boys + Bond themes + Gainsbourg" = "airy" "kitsch" "bliss" from the "Euro-psychedelic" holy rollers of "after-hours" for "club-goers" "finishing the party with a pack of Gauloises" and "a rainy drive" home for an "afternoon nap."

Alabama, *Mountain Music* **G** **#1**　25 | 23 | 26 | 24
1982, RCA; "Mountain Music"
■ "Listening to the title track" of country cousins Randy Owen, Jeff Cook and Teddy Gentry's 1982 "toe-tappin'" breakthrough "transports you to a front-porch jam session somewhere in the Smoky Mountains"; "it's hard to dislike these guys" ("no scandals") – in fact, the "great harmonies" and "down-home storytelling" on this "Southern pride classic" will turn you into a "born-again cowboy or cowgirl in no time."

Aladdin (Soundtrack) **G**　　24 | 24 | 25 | 25
1992, Disney; "A Whole New World"
■ "It was a whole new world with Disney" in the '90s, and this "bouncy" soundtrack was part of the renaissance; "come on, admit it, you know you love singing along" with the "hilarious Robin Williams as the Genie" and the "great" Regina Belle with Peabo Bryson on the theme track; it's "clever and endearing" "music for kids as well as the kid inside you", so "pop it in, have a listen during your daily routine and just see how much easier things become."

Alice in Chains, *Dirt*　　24 | 24 | 25 | 24
1992, Columbia; "Would?"; www.aliceinchains.net
■ "Once you appreciate the suffering explored" on this "grunge benchmark", "you cannot let it go"; "propulsive,

punishing" and "beautifully depressing", this grunge "gift from the art gods" "foreshadowed" the late "Layne Staley's descent into substance abuse" – "you can almost feel the needle" when you drop into "Alice's scary wonderland"; with its "haunting riffs" and "dark, lovely delivery", one of the "most successful syntheses of alt-rock" out of Seattle "still gives some the creeps."

A Little Night Music   26 | 28 | 27 | 26
(Original cast recording)
1973, Columbia; "Send in the Clowns"
■ "You'll be laughing on the floor" at "the best comedic material Stephen Sondheim has ever written"; "set entirely in 3/4 time" and "witty as hell", this "lusty and romantic" "musical for grown-ups" is "far more than just *Send in the Clowns*"; "one must appreciate the musical theater voice: impure, sometimes ugly", but capable of executing "a lovely skewering of the idle class" – "as its director Hal Prince called it, [it's] 'whipped cream with knives.'"

Mose Allison,   25 | 26 | 24 | 22
Your Mind Is on Vacation
2000, Koch; "Your Mind Is on Vacation";
www.moseallison.net
☑ Mose Allison sure ain't on vacation because, as the title track says, his mouth is workin' overtime on this "super" jazz reissue of a 1976 Atlantic LP; the Mississippi "delight" "sings better than ever", "mixing Delta blues and biting Greenwich Village humor" in "a perfect setting with just the right balance of horn and trio tracks"; critics' only complaint with the "sophisticated interpreter's" rollicking keyboards is that he "plays the same riffs again and again."

The Allman Brothers, *Eat a Peach*   27 | 24 | 28 | 24
1972, Capricorn; "Melissa"; www.allmanbrothersband.com
■ "Master axeman" "Dickey is at his sweetest, Gregg at his most gravelly, the brothers at their tightest" on this "peachy keen" '70s "Southern rock landmark" "two-fer"; it's "a fitting swan song" for Duane, an "extraordinary electric slide player", who contributed three cuts, plus "mythic live tracks" from Fillmore East and tragically died before its completion; this "boatload of talent" "laid out the rudiments of the current jam band phenomenon" with "epics" from *Blue Skies* to the "hold-onto-your-hat" 33-minute *Mountain Jam*.

Herb Alpert and the Tijuana Brass,   22 | 22 | 26 | 24
Whipped Cream and Other Delights #1
1965, A&M; "A Taste of Honey"; www.herbalpert.com
■ "Alt-rock hipsters" who "long for velvet paintings of sumptuous blondes and all-night cocktail parties" can get their "sure-fire happiness fix" "from the '60s" with "sexpot Herb Alpert" and his "killer Tijuana jams" on this "catchy", food-themed concoction; "delightfully creamy", "brassy

and bouncy" describes both the "jazzy", "*Dating Game*" sound and the "pretty girl" covered in the stuff of the title track on the "racy" jacket.

Amélie (Soundtrack) | 25 | 23 | 25 | 24 |
2001, Virgin; "La Valise d'Amélie"

■ Yann Tiersen's "enchanting" soundtrack to the "quirky" French film "makes you want to jump on a Vespa with a baguette in your left hand and an espresso in your right"; "gorgeous instrumentals", replete with accordion and "a sense of humor", encompass the "whimsy, sadness and freedom" that make up the cinematic story of "bohemian romance"; it will have you "smiling with a naughty twinkle in your eye", just like its eponymous heroine.

America, | 22 | 22 | 20 | 20 |
History: America's Greatest Hits
1975, Warner Bros.; "Horse With No Name";
www.venturahighway.com

■ Born in the UK to U.S. parents, this trio's "gift to the colonists is" "a time capsule of folk rock" bursting with "great arrangements, many provided by Beatles' top dog George Martin"; a "fun sing-along" ("'70s cheese never sounded so sweet"), it includes "*Sister Golden Hair,* maybe the best song George Harrison never wrote", and "favorite", *Horse With No Name*; with a "cover designed by the late Phil Hartman in his pre-comic days, it's a must-have."

American Graffiti (Soundtrack) | 26 | 23 | 24 | 23 |
1973, MCA; "Rock Around the Clock"

■ "Where were you in '62?" – "if this doesn't take you older baby boomers back to your teens, you're brain dead", but even if you were "still in the womb", "you can be there" in the "happy days" of "drag races" and "young love" with this "fabulous collection of songs from the golden age of rock & roll"; on the soundtrack to "George Lucas' classic", "they're all here: Chuck Berry, Buddy Holly, Bo Diddley" and Bill Haley rockin' 'round the clock, "with Wolfman Jack DJ intros", to "perfectly capture the time."

An American in Paris (Soundtrack) | 27 | 27 | 27 | 25 |
1951, MGM; "Love Is Here to Stay"

■ With the "vastly superior" 1996 Rhino reissue, it's clear this "timeless" Gershwin score is here to stay; the "great variety" of tunes by Ira and George offer "everything you ever wanted in a musical", and "s'wonderful" "background music" for your daydreams, so "close your eyes", "relive the film" and remember Gene Kelly "gliding through some of most beautiful songs ever written."

TORI AMOS, *LITTLE EARTHQUAKES* #1 | 27 | 28 | 27 | 25 |
1992, Atlantic; "Winter"; www.toriamos.com

■ "Heartbreakingly honest", this "astonishingly assured debut" launched "quirky singer-songwriter" Tori's career with a "series of surreal musical portraits"; "strong yet fragile", she mixed a "remarkable vocal range", "prodigious piano prowess" and "incisive lyrics" – and "made a generation of girls feel it was ok to feel the way they did"; it's "an emotional journey" that "scares the bejesus out of you", but "never has an exorcism sounded so beautiful."

Animal House (Soundtrack)   21 | 19 | 20 | 20
1978, MCA; "Shout"

■ "Throw your own toga party" with this "oldies" and "Motown" soundtrack from the "frat" house flick about "the American college experience as seen through the eyes of Bluto and the boys"; "real gems" like Lloyd Williams' version of the Isley Brothers' "cult classic" *Shout* and Sam Cooke's "*Wonderful World,* aka the George Bush Song ('don't know much about history . . . don't know much geography')", are "not terribly high-brow, but they do evoke fond memories" of "seven years of college down the drain!"

Paul Anka,   24 | 25 | 23 | 24
Paul Anka Sings His Big 15, Vol. 1 ◉
1960, ABC/Paramount; "Diana"; www.paulanka.com

■ "Take yourself back to the good old days" with this "great collection" by "the former teen idol"; the guy who created "some of the best pop songs from the '50s", including *Diana, Puppy Love* and *Lonely Boy,* "has the timeless style" to make this LP, which spent an unprecendented 140 weeks on the charts, "worth a ton of pimple cream" even today; if you can't score the wax, make do with Rhino's *30th Anniversary Collection.*

Annie (Original cast recording) ▣ 24 | 23 | 24 | 24
1977, Sony; "Tomorrow"

▨ "The sun still comes out" when "little girls, their aunts and moms listen to" that "plucky predecessor to Punky Brewster" in Broadway's "bright splash of color set against Depression-era drab", a show that spawned "a billion community productions"; the "young" star's "screechy" vocals can be a little "hard to take", but "generation after generation" of "Andrea McArdle wanna-bes" in "red wigs" "belting *Tomorrow*" – "albeit off-key" – can't be wrong about this "kid-pleaser."

Annie Get Your Gun   24 | 25 | 24 | 22
(Original cast recording)
1946, MCA; "Anything You Can Do"

■ "Even while wearing a girdle", "the Merm does her stuff", "hammering" those "lighthearted", "hilarious" Irving Berlin songs to "the back row" on this cast recording from "the olden days" "when singers didn't have to be miked to be heard"; even if you don't "listen closely to the lyrics" of the show about shoot-'em-up Annie Oakley, especially on the 2000 Decca remaster, the foghorn "power of Ethel's voice" will "keep you awake."

Anonymous 4, *An English Ladymass* 27 | 25 | 28 | 26 |
1992, Hamonia Mundi; "Edi Beo Thu Hevene Quene";
www.anonymous4.com
☑ "Geeky musicology meets impeccable performance" in
the "hauntingly" "lovely period album" that "put this
talented quartet on the map"; the medieval Fab Four
"selected some of the best sacred music" for a "simple,
elegant", "magical experience for the listener"; even if "the
ladies sound a little shrill at moments", "nothing should be
anonymous about the *English Ladymass* or these vocalists."

Marc Anthony, *Marc Anthony* 23 | 21 | 24 | 23 |
1999, Columbia; "I Need to Know";
www.marcanthonyonline.com
■ Salsa's "great artist" "goes mainstream in the USA" and
proves "lyrical, sensuous and irresistible" "in both English
and Spanish" on this "charismatic" "crossover"; with a
"voice like buttah", Marc Anthony "seems to sing from deep
within", "bringing out the pain he feels" in "beautiful" but
"broody" songs about "life, love" and "his disintegrating
relationship with his wife"; "move over Ricky Martin" –
"Latino has a new grand name."

Anything Goes (Revival) 25 | 27 | 25 | 25 |
1987, RCA; "Anything Goes"
☑ "Broadway diva" Patti LuPone "at her brassy best" as
Reno Sweeney "really delivers", her "spunk and style
shining through in every note" of this "witty", "high-energy"
Cole Porter revival; a score that "sizzles" with "some of
the finest lyrics in theater history" and "a beat that will
make you tap your feet" are "infectiously fun" "for singing
along" 'cause the composer really was "the tops."

Aphex Twin, 26 | 22 | 24 | 25 |
Selected Ambient Works 85-92
1992, R & S; "Ageispolis"; www.aphextwin.org
■ "You are one with the world" "absorbing burbling
melodies and ingenius rhythms" from the "experimental
sketch" pad of "ambient electronica's" "doodler", Richard
James; "picking up where Brian Eno left off", the "pioneer"
put out "eerie masterpieces" that "sound like they came
from another planet" and touched down in the middle of
a "5 AM party" amid the "twilight fog" for a disc that's
"bleep bleep beautiful."

Apocalypse Now (Soundtrack) 24 | 22 | 23 | 25 |
1979, Wea/Elektra; "The End"
■ Frances Ford Coppola's Vietnam redux of Conrad's
Heart of Darkness "could never be considered one of the
greatest movies were it not for the incredible juxtaposition
of soundtrack to images"; *The End* by "The Doors, plus
Wagner", "Carmine Coppola's chilling synth score", "great
dialogue", helicopters, "machine guns and bomb sounds"
are like "watching the film with your eyes closed"; "try

using this CD as your alarm clock wake-up tune" – it's "brilliant", but you're "pretty warped" if you love "the sound of napalm in the morning."

Martha Argerich, *Début Recital* ⎸27⎸24⎸29⎸23⎸
1960, Deutsche Grammophon; "Liszt Sonata"
☑ On "arguably the most perfect debut recital of any keyboardist", Martha Argerich "shows her remarkable talent in its first form", creating an "instant classic"; the "pianist's pianist's" "fiery interpretations" "spark" with "electricity", and if it "does not represent her at her full maturity", a disc that displays the "world-class" "tigress" when she was yet a cub is nevertheless "a must."

Louis Armstrong, *Hello, Dolly!* ⎸27⎸24⎸28⎸24⎸
1964, Prime Cuts/Kapp; "Hello Dolly!"; www.satchmo.net
☑ "Ahhhhh", what a wonderful world – "no one does jazz the way Satchmo does jazz" proclaim "apple-pie" patriots of "America's music man"; with that "scratchy voice" and the "sweetest trumpet", "you can't mistake him for someone else" on this late-career listen that might be "more pop" than purists prefer but still serves as an "excellent" "intro" to the "lovable" "master"; so say "hello, Louie", because "there is no such thing as a bad Armstrong recording."

Arrested Development, *3 Years,* ⎸21⎸23⎸21⎸21⎸
5 *Months & 2 Days in the Life of* . . .
1992, Chrysalis; "Tennessee"
☑ "Clap your hands"! – "revolutionary" in their "positive", "thought-provoking" messages, Atlanta's crew of poets and musicians led by "socially conscious" rapper Speech mixes "blues, jazz, funk, reggae" and "hippie ideals" into a "groovy" stew; still, some say the single *Tennessee* "is the only track worth keeping" amid "lotsa filler" from an outfit that "served a long sentence with no parole" after this disc.

The Association, *Greatest Hits* ⎸21⎸21⎸22⎸20⎸
1968, Warner Bros.; "Cherish"
■ "Bad puns" aside, despite their "association with bubble gum" music, this group was "musically far and above the average", with "tight, distinctive harmonies", "peppy melodies and great arrangements" concocted by "pop genius" Terry Kirkman; beat a "mellow path back in time" to the "Summer of Love" with the "lush" and "breezy" "California sound" of *Windy* and that staple couples have vowed for thirtysomething years "to love and be loved to", *Cherish.*

AWB (Average White Band), *AWB* 🔢1 ⎸24⎸20⎸26⎸24⎸
1974, Atlantic; "Pick Up the Pieces";
www.averagewhiteband.com
☑ "The funkiest Scottish band ever", these "soulful" "emulators of Sly and the Family Stone and James Brown"

prove they "can get into a solid groove" with "excellent arrangements" like *Pick Up the Pieces*; this "treasure" brims with "dominant saxophones", "jazzed-up rock production", "great harmony vocals" and "some of the best drumming" in the genre; the less-impressed quip the '70s outfit "really lives up to their name."

B

J.S. Bach, *Brandenburg Concertos*   27 | 27 | 27 | 25
1987, Virgin; "Concerto No. 3"; www.oae.co.uk
■ "The Brandenbergs don't get a whole lot better" than this "spiritually purifying" "historical reproduction" of Bach's "sublime compositions"; the Orchestra of the Age of Enlightenment "adds a lot of style", playing the pieces as the composer "would have liked them", "with charm and motion" on period instruments; it "will remain a classic until people no longer listen to music, and that's a very long time!"

J.S. BACH, *MASS IN B MINOR* G   29 | 28 | 29 | 27
1985, Arkiv; "Agnus Dei"
■ The "strongest mass" from "the guy who invented heavy metal" is "a high mountain to climb", but this "definitive performance" by "one of the masters of Bach interpretation" "makes the ascent"; conductor John Eliot Gardiner "renders the oft-played sound fresh", leading the English Baroque Soloists in a "crisp rendition" with "impeccable choral singing"; hyperbolic partisans proclaim, "if this doesn't receive 'best record of all time', we should all give up on democracy."

J.S. Bach,   27 | 27 | 27 | 26
Six Unaccompanied Cello Suites G
1990, CBS Masterworks; "Suite No. 1, Prelude";
www.yo-yoma.com
■ "The perfect album for a sunny Sunday morning when you want to feel alive" might be this "glorious" "work of genius played by a genius"; "smooth as silk and nearly as delicate", Bach's solo suites are "pure heaven", and this "expressive recording" by arguably "our greatest living cellist" "creates its own emotional gravity", "stirring the soul" and "provoking thought"; "only once every 100 years does a talent like Yo-Yo Ma surface who has all the tools and personality" to deliver an "iconic interpretation."

J.S. BACH, *STATE OF WONDER: THE*   29 | 28 | 28 | 25
COMPLETE GOLDBERG VARIATIONS G
1981, Sony Classical; "Aria from the Goldberg Variations"
■ "A genius unfettered by conformity", Glenn Gould "began and ended his search for ecstasy with the *Goldberg*", recording it in 1955 and 1981; "part of the enjoyment is in the differences between the young, energetic pianist and the mature, measured man" on this "milestone" including

"alpha and omega" versions, outtakes and an interview; it's a CD "unrivalled in introspective fireworks", illuminating the musician "at his best": "playful", "eclectic" and "sui generis", "humming" along with "obvious joy."

Burt Bacharach,
26 | 28 | 26 | 25
Burt Bacharach's Greatest Hits
1974, A&M; "I'll Never Fall In Love Again"

■ "Who has never heard the opening lilt of *Close to You* by the Carpenters or the sauntering piano of *Say a Little Prayer* by Dionne Warwick", both crafted by "class personified", Burt Bacharach?; still, "one of the greatest tunesmiths of the '60s and '70s" stayed largely behind the scenes, and "few can actually connect his songs to him"; this "terrific primer to the musical world of *Austin Powers*' favorite composer" "gives him his due" by spotlighting the music of the "timeless writer" without the big-name voices.

Bad Brains, *I Against I*
26 | 24 | 25 | 21
1986, SST; "I Against I"; www.home.dti.net/joly/brains/

■ It's a no-brainer that "the godfathers of the hardcore movement" "rocked harder than any longhair metal band, yet their reggae jams expressed a softer, no less poignant side"; "fresh" and "ferocious", revealing "raw power, musical dexterity" and a "rasta edge", this "classic" helped "pave the way" for today's "new pop-punk wave."

Bad Company, *Bad Company* 🔳1
22 | 21 | 22 | 21
1974, Swan Song; "Bad Company"; www.badcompany.com

■ "Makes me want to buy a pickup truck and cheap beer" jest fans of this "stripped, smokin'", "straight-ahead" "classic '70s" disc; featuring ex–Mott the Hoople Mick Ralphs' "no-frills guitar", "strong hard rock–bluesy vocals from ex-Free" singer Paul Rodgers and charged with "lots of soul and depth", this multiplatinum "smash debut" "burst onto the scene", "dominated the airwaves" and "blew people away."

Erykah Badu, *Baduizm* 🄶
24 | 24 | 25 | 24
1997, Kedar; "Next Lifetime"; www.erykahbadu.com

■ "Billie Holiday meets Mary J. Blige" meets "a '70s soul goddess" on this "cathartic trip" to "the roots, man", fusing "heavy hip-hop beats" to blues and "jazz influences" for a "breakthrough R&B" debut that "shines" with "the neosoul earth mother's" "smooth", "sultry" "emoting" and "erotic rhythms"; it's so "romantic, soft and sexy", an album that might as well be called "Booty-ism" will "give you shivers."

Joan Baez, *Diamonds & Rust*
26 | 26 | 25 | 24
1975, A&M; "Diamonds & Rust"; www.baez.woz.org

■ With "diamond-sharp stylings and no rust whatsoever", the "enduring queen of folk" "tackles everyone from the Allman Brothers to John Prine to Bob Dylan" (her self-penned "haunting title song recounts their relationship") on what's "perhaps her most commercial success"; it's "a fine return to form" by "the mature Baez" – her "achingly pure soprano", as "impassioned" as ever, leaves listeners "in a state between euphoria and bittersweet sadness."

Joan Baez, *Joan Baez* | 27 | 25 | 26 | 23 |
1960, Vanguard; "Silver Dagger"; www.baez.woz.org
■ "The promise of what was to follow" shines through on this icon's "beautiful" debut that helped jump-"start the folk revival"; in a "pure voice" "as clear as a morning in the Rockies" she tenders "thrilling renditions of traditional tunes" – "this is the way" songs are "meant to be sung", "straight"-up, "no electrification"; "listen to it with someone who was there in the '60s", a time "when you felt you could still make a difference", and the "experience will be richer."

Anita Baker, *Rapture* G | 26 | 24 | 25 | 26 |
1986, Elektra; "Sweet Love"
■ "Husky" alto Anita Baker "could sing a McDonald's menu and make you want to light a fire and uncork a bottle of wine"; with "classic soul" and "gospel inspiration" and "elastic phrasing that's closer to jazz", this "rapturous" voice serves up "instant babymaking" R&B; "backed by an excellent band" that "never overwhelms" her "brilliant stylings", she "makes you feel every tremble of emotion" on "masterpieces" like *Sweet Love.*

Chet Baker, *Chet Baker Sings* | 25 | 23 | 26 | 23 |
1953, Pacific Jazz; "My Funny Valentine"; www.chetbaker.net
■ "He couldn't really sing, but boy, could he sing" – in the "almost androgynous" "whisper" "of a fallen angel", California's "cool cat" "approaches that pinpoint of truth in which sincerity and satire are one" on a "heartbreaking" jazz disc "redolent with ambiguity"; with his own "soulful trumpet" as backup, Baker's "intoxicating" "renditions of chestnuts" like *My Funny Valentine* "get to your soul" say "lonely" "romantics."

Afrika Bambaataa, | 25 | 23 | 25 | 24 |
Looking for the Perfect Beat 1980-1985
2001, Tommy Boy; "Planet Rock"
■ You'll find the perfect beat in "old-school heaven" with this "essential" disc that's stocked with "groundbreaking", "heavily sampled" "dance records" from "a godfather of hip-hop" who "took breakbeats to a higher level" and "set the stage for rap and electronica"; with its "free-flowing verse" and futuristic instrumentation, the Kraftwerk-inspired track, *Planet Rock,* "started a revolution" – as the people say, "praise the mighty."

The Band, *The Band* | 28 | 27 | 28 | 24 |
1969, Capitol; "Up on Cripple Creek"
■ By "bucking the psychedelic trend", "four Canadians [Robbie Robertson, Rick Danko, Garth Hudson, Richard

Manuel] and one Arkansas native [Levon Helm]" defined the Americana genre, with lyrics harkening back to the Civil War; a "brilliant" "compendium of gospel, blues, R&B and hillbilly wrapped up" in "roots rock", it "moves like the river" with "stellar" "intuitive group playing" and "tales of such legendary stature" they helped "change Clapton's mind about his musical direction."

BARBER, *ADAGIO FOR STRINGS;* *VIOLIN CONCERTO*   28 | 27 | 27 | 25

1964, Sony Classical; "Adagio for Strings"
■ "Thanks to Oliver Stone, who brought the classic to the masses through *Platoon*", the "haunting" *Adagio* is "inextricably linked to the folly of Vietnam", but the "elegant, lugubrious lament" has been performed during other "sad times", most recently after September 11th; "restful and moving" at once, it "produces tears" when they're most needed, and this "deeply felt and intensely presented performance" – coupled with the "achingly beautiful" *Violin Concerto* and two Schuman pieces – is "definitive."

Barenaked Ladies, *Stunt*   21 | 22 | 21 | 21

1998, Reprise; "Call and Answer"; www.bnlmusic.com
■ "These clever boys of Canadian rock" are "fully covered when it comes to" cranking out "catchy tunes" full of "tongue-in-cheek" lyrics that reveal a "knack for the wry turn of phrase"; "it doesn't take one week to like" this "naked pleasure" – "put it in, listen all the way through" and "you'll finish with a smile"; the "perfect intersection of comedy and music", this "guaranteed sing-along" is "only bettered by their live show."

BARTÓK, *CONCERTO FOR ORCHESTRA* G   28 | 28 | 29 | 24

1955, RCA; "Concerto for Orchestra"; www.cso.org
■ "Every track is a revelation" in this "fierce, earthy", "canonized" recording infused with "polish", "dazzling virtuosity" and "the greatest brass playing" by the Chicago Symphony Orchestra "in its prime"; "electrifying" conductor Fritz Reiner "looked like Grandpa Munster", and he created a sound to match his appearance: "powerful, slightly disturbing and not for the timid"; "the warmth of RCA Living Stereo" makes this disc "fundamental."

Bartók, *6 String Quartets* G   26 | 26 | 27 | 24

1989, Deutsche Grammophon; www.emersonquartet.com
◪ An "intense, fiery" but "clear presentation" of "difficult but important music", this "superbly done" collection made Bartok "accessible" and "the Emerson Quartet famous"; one of the "finest string outfits extant" "completely absorbs" the composer's "dynamic markings", "carrying them out with spooky attention", and though the disc "hardly replaces" "other sets in the can", it "remains a compelling contender" for "one of the finest chamber music recordings of all time."

Basement Jaxx, *Rooty*　　　　24 | 20 | 24 | 26
2001, Astralwerks; "Where's Your Head At"

⬛ "If you don't have this dance album, where's your head at?"; jus 1 listen and you'll be "moving your entire body, working all parts of the melody, harmony" and "great beats" on an "electric barrage of house, funk, techno, electro, rock and the kitchen sink" "mixed into one sexy disc"; if a few tracks are "tiresome", "catchy" cuts like *Romeo* "keep your spirits up" and your butt out of the chair 'cause "resisting the groove is futile."

Count Basie,　　　　　　　　28 | 27 | 28 | 23
The Complete Atomic Basie
1994, Roulette; "Lil' Darlin'"

⬛ The good Count "would get looser and more commercial later, but he's never more swinging" than on this big-band "blast from the past", "the best of Basie of the '50s", remastered and reissued with five newly unearthed tracks from his "second major period"; his ensemble is "in perfect form", with trumpeter "Joe Newman carrying the day" on Neal Hefti arrangements for a sound that's "pure magic."

Bauhaus, *Mask*　　　　　　25 | 26 | 23 | 21
1981, Beggars Banquet; "Kick in the Eye"

⬛ "Brilliantly cold, glacially bleak" and "full of wonderful angst", this "masterpiece of atmospheric post-Bowie, postpunk art glam" "helped usher in a new musical genre" that was the very "definition of goth"; to get into the "mood" of this "eerie" album, light some "candles in a bathroom" and "zone out" to "Peter Murphy's rich, haunting voice" – just try not to grow fangs, you "vampirey" fans.

THE BEACH BOYS, *PET SOUNDS*　　28 | 28 | 27 | 28
1966, Capitol; "God Only Knows"

⬛ "Brian Wilson dropped acid, spoke with God and composed" a "blissful listening experience" (his "genius never less clouded") full of "endless creativity and pure sadness – the aching 'nooooo' at the end of *Caroline No* may be the most heartbreaking moment on a pop record"; an "awesome departure from their squeaky-clean beach music", this pet project "translates adolescent angst, lust and paranoia" into "sonically ambitious", "shimmering songs with glorious instrumentation and harmonies" that "gave The Beatles a run for their money."

Beastie Boys, *Licensed to Ill* 🔢1　26 | 24 | 21 | 24
1986, Def Jam/Columbia; "Paul Revere"; www.beastieboys.com

⬛ A "smart and silly" "celebration of the nothingness of growing up in the '80s", this "ridiculous, obnoxious frat-rock rap" record helped "bring hip-hop to the suburbs" with "teen anthems" that thrive on "tongue-in-cheek irony" and "postpunk", "skateboard culture"; "classic" cuts like *Paul Revere, Girls* and *Fight for Your Right* "crash the party" to "get the crowd jumping" and shouting "hell, yeah!!"

Beastie Boys, *Paul's Boutique*   27 | 26 | 25 | 27
1989, Capitol; "Hey Ladies"; www.beastieboys.com
■ "Being a boy is so much fun" – backed by the Dust Brothers' "dope" production, the "three white guys from NYC" complement a "labyrinth" of "dusted-off" "'70s funk" samples with "bumpin' organ", "clever musicianship" and "dense", "humorous" wordplay to craft songs that "don't sound borrowed and have their own life and charm"; listening to the rappers "skewer" the tracks with "wit and snottiness" is like "walking through an all-you-can-eat buffet of pop culture."

THE BEATLES, *ABBEY ROAD* ⑤🏆   29 | 29 | 28 | 28
1969, Capitol; "Here Comes the Sun"; www.thebeatles.com
■ "Coming apart as a group, but still evolving as ace songwriters" the Fabs get "brilliant" exiled producer George Martin back on board to craft this "fitting swan song" (actually it was issued second-to-last, before *Let it Be*); considered their "apex", the "gloriously inventive" album "displays a maturity of theme, musicianship and sonic quality", the "synthesis of four masters"; "you couldn't ask for a better good-bye": "Harrison emerges as the equal of Lennon-McCartney" while "the suite that closes side two (part two) is the Sistine Chapel of rock & roll."

The Beatles, *The Beatles 1962-1966*   28 | 28 | 27 | 26
1973, Apple; "Yesterday"; www.thebeatles.com
☑ With "nostalgia on every track", this "pre-psychedelia" compendium is "great for a quick immersion into the early-mid period" when "the band was still having fun creating the magic"; "only a few are profound" but yeah, yeah, yeah, "these are the melodies that linger" and the "songs that turned a generation around"; still, Beatle-maniacs stridently suggest "get the individual albums (remastered by George Martin) – it's worth it."

THE BEATLES, *REVOLVER* 🏆   29 | 29 | 28 | 28
1966, Capitol; "Tomorrow Never Knows"; www.thebeatles.com
■ "Following Dylan's lead", "the Fab Four" "shaped their music to be more personal, poignant and fierce" creating a "breakthrough" that's their "trippiest", "most Eastern-influenced" yet somehow "the greatest sing-along album ever!"; it's "a historic turning point" that marks "Harrison's coming-out as a songwriter" as well as their "transition from pop" "Moptops" "to determinants of music and culture"; with "magical, mystical" "experiments in George Martin's lab", it meets approval here, there and everywhere.

THE BEATLES, *RUBBER SOUL*   28 | 29 | 28 | 27
1965, Capitol; "In My Life"; www.thebeatles.com
■ Showing the "demarcation between teen idols and cultural visionaries", this "revolutionary" release, "possibly their most romantic", has a "quieter" "folk feel", allowing their "wonderful teamwork" to shine through and "proving

that reflective songwriting can exist in rock"; as The Beatles "grew up" and "brought Indian music into their circle" they "turned pop music into a serious form of expression."

THE BEATLES, *SGT. PEPPER'S LONELY HEARTS CLUB BAND* 🅖 #1
29 | 29 | 28 | 29

1967, Capitol; "A Day in the Life"; www.thebeatles.com

■ "This Rosetta stone of '60s rock" "turned the world upside down"; considered "the birth of the concept album" in popular music, it's "theatrical from the cover" ("love those uniforms") "to the last note of *A Day in the Life*", inspiring "awe" with "a dramatic structure that's subtle and powerful"; "can you say 'counterculture'?" – "fresh, cheeky" "high art", this "benchmark" "did for psychedelic drugs what Marilyn Monroe did for peroxide."

THE BEATLES, *THE WHITE ALBUM* #1
28 | 28 | 28 | 28

1968, Apple; "While My Guitar Gently Weeps"; www.thebeatles.com

◪ "A big sprawling mess greater than the sum of its parts", this "fascinating snapshot of the group's divergent styles" is a "full-tilt buffet"; in "white there's might", with a "song for every mood", and four sides that feel like "separate solo outings", ranging "from avant garde" to "silly pop"; though lovingly referred to as a "shambolic, disjointed" "helluva ride", there are shades of gray for some lad-lovers who lament it's "too experimental" and "shoulda been one disc."

Beauty and the Beast (Studio) 🅖
26 | 26 | 26 | 26

1991, Disney; "Beauty and the Beast"

■ "Nothing brightens your day like imagining a candelabra serving you an eight-course dinner" with this Disney "triumph by Alan Menken and the late Howard Ashman"; with "tracks so vivid you can see the action as you listen" to Celine Dion, Peabo Bryson and "incomparable" veterans Jerry Orbach and Angela Lansbury, the "beautiful music for kids, parents and grandparents" just might "make you cry."

Beck, *Odelay* 🅖
25 | 25 | 25 | 26

1996, DGC; "Devil's Haircut"; www.beck.com

■ "An entertaining genre-hopper" mixing "a thousand little snippets" of rock, pop, electronica, country, low-fi, hip-hop, funk and "chunky, fat grooves", capped with "amazing tour-de-force production from the Dust Brothers", this "loopy mix o' tunes from the Beckmeister" shows where his "iconoclastic kitchensinkmanship" is at; "smart" and "subversive", this is "vital" "music with a healthy flea-market 'tude – it salvages old junk into eclectic treasures."

Jeff Beck, *Blow by Blow*
24 | 21 | 28 | 24

1975, Atlantic; "Freeway Jam"; www.jeffbeckmusic.com

■ "El Becko defied every convention" with this "genre-shifting" instrumental "classic" that took "prog rock to its highest level"; the "electric guitar wizard" "worked his magic with the bonus" of "top production" from Beatles' producer George Martin and Stevie Wonder on keyboards, creating one of the most "influential fusion" albums around.

The Bee Gees, Children of the World   24 | 24 | 26 | 25
1976, RSO; "You Should Be Dancing"
■ "The Bee Gees were well on their way to earning the 'Disco Kings' crown that would haunt them for the rest of their career" when they recorded this disc, which found the "kings of pop harmony" "self-producing" and "Barry Gibb experimenting with the falsetto that would mark a change in their singing style"; "great vocal interplay" and "gritty soul" combine for "fun" "party" hits, so get up on your feet, boogie child, 'cause "you should be dancing."

The Bee Gees,   27 | 25 | 26 | 27
Saturday Night Fever G #1
1977, RSO; "Stayin' Alive"
■ Grab your "white leisure suit", "get out that disco ball and boogie down" to the disc that "launched the craze"; "'seminal' doesn't do justice" to the soundtrack that "epitomized the '70s" when "The Bee Gees were at their height", pumping out the hits for John Travolta to dance his way to "stardom" "in those tight polyester bell bottoms"; Barry, Robin, Maurice and a host of "smooth" "contributing artists" "transport you back" to "shake your booty, baby!"

Beethoven, *Piano Concertos 3 & 5*   28 | 28 | 27 | 24
1964, Sony Classical; "Concerto No. 5"
■ Though pianist Rudolph Serkin "seems to have been forgotten", his "sensitive playing" on this disc "should remind listeners why he was considered one of the greats of the 20th century"; "monumentally performed" with the NY Philharmonic and conducted with the "utmost integrity" by Leonard Bernstein, it's "so upbeat that it should be recommended to fight off seasonal affected disorders!"

Beethoven,   28 | 27 | 28 | 26
Piano Sonatas Nos. 8, 13 & 14
1983, Deutsche Grammophon; "Moonlight Sonata: 1. Adagio Sostenuto"
■ You "can't go wrong" with Emil Gilels, "truly a giant of the keyboard" whose "absolutely riveting, deeply considered and humane performances" of these "wonderfully painful" mainstays "rank up there with Kemph, Schnabel, Goode and Brendel"; "once they start, they sound inevitable", establishing his position as "one of the supreme [classical] pianists of the postwar period."

BEETHOVEN, *SYMPHONIES NOS. 5 & 7*   28 | 29 | 28 | 26
1974, Deutsche Grammophon; "Symphony No. 7"; www.wienerphilharmoniker.at
■ You can "learn from old warhorses" – "reaching for former excellence under [Carlos] Kleiber", the Vienna Philharmonic turns out this "flawless", "legendary" set; the

"overplayed but underappreciated" *No. 5* "electrifies" with "white-hot intensity", and the "awesomely lyrical" *No. 7* "sings, it weeps, it dances, oh, does it dance."

BEETHOVEN, *SYMPHONY NO. 9*   28 | 29 | 28 | 26
1962, Deutsche Grammophon; "Ode to Joy";
www.berliner-philharmoniker.de
■ "Yes, Virginia, classical music rocks with the best of them" in this "monumental" recording of "one of the great masterpieces of all time"; under conductor Herbert von Karajan, the Berlin Philharmonic delivers the "goosebump"-raising "sine qua non" of the "soaring epic", "the essence of existence distilled"; "if one piece could speak for all of humanity, this is it" – "like readin', 'ritin' and 'rithmetic, it's something everyone must know"; "well, duh."

Beethoven,   26 | 27 | 26 | 24
Violin Sonatas Nos. 9 "Kreutzer" & 5 "Spring"
1974, Decca; "Kreutzer Sonata"
■ Itzhak "Perlman is magic", and "what a duo" he makes with pianist Vladimir Ashkenazy playing "the two most popular sonatas from a deservedly famous set"; the "*Kreutzer* is one of the most emotionally evocative pieces ever composed", and the violinist who "inherited Heifetz's mantle" "showcases his fabulous sound" with "fire."

Harry Belafonte, *Calypso* #1   24 | 23 | 24 | 23
1956, RCA Victor; "The Banana Boat Song (Day-O)"
■ "Before there was Bob Marley, there was Belafonte", bringing the Caribbean's "brown-skinned music to suburban America" back when "everyone was just wild about Harry"; with a "voice smooth as butter" and a "soft, sexy" delivery, the "fine performer" became "a household favorite", "launching a genre" stateside with this disc that "tallied him bananas" enough to top the charts; the "groovy" calypso collection "is as much fun now as it was in 1956."

Harry Belafonte and Lena Horne,   25 | 27 | 25 | 23
Porgy and Bess
1959, RCA; "Bess, You Is My Woman"
☑ Horne and Belafonte are "pure magic" on this first of four albums pairing the smooth Caribbean crooner with leading songbirds; though they only sing together twice on the disc, the pair "hit all of the emotions" of the "great Gershwin musical contribution" to "folk opera", "a powerful story" about "life in the Black South"; the album is "so novel, it was studied in school in the '60s", even though aficionados opine "there have been better productions."

Belle & Sebastian,   25 | 26 | 25 | 24
If You're Feeling Sinister
1996, Matador; "The Stars of Track and Field"
☑ In its early days, "Scotland's finest" was the "brainchild of witty Stuart Murdoch, possessor of Ray Davies' keen

eye and Nick Drake voice, with touches of trumpet and Isobel Campbell's mournful cello"; "delightfully" "dreamy", this "rainy day heartbreak music" is reminiscent of "The Smiths with a girl and a French twist"; still, cynics snipe "these champions of twee" "lack chutzpah."

Pat Benatar,   22 | 21 | 22 | 22
Crimes of Passion ⑤
1980, Chrysalis; "Hit Me With Your Best Shot";
www.benatar.com
■ It's a "crime not to own this" "seminal chick rock" disc that "propelled" Brooklyn's opera-trained "leotard-clad pixie to arena status", "inspiring the wardrobes of a million girls and the dreams of a million guys"; what a "powerful sound from a wisp of a girl" – it "brings me back to my MTV-watching days" wax the nostalgic, concluding "all the grrrls owe one to her" for this "incredible piece of ['80s] history."

Ben Folds Five, *Ben Folds Five*   23 | 25 | 24 | 20
1995, Passenger; "Philosophy"
■ "Answering Frank Zappa's question: does humor belong in music?" with a "good-time" "freshman effort", this "rockin'" "romp" "mixes piano-driven pop" with "deft", "cynical" lyrics, "carving out a unique sound" that "rivals Billy Joel"; a "modern-day crooner with something to say", Folds' songwriting "talent is surpassed only by how well he tickles the ivories"; "a future star is born" fawn fans who feel this frontman's "smarter-than-you approach kicked the door in on alternative music."

Tony Bennett,   27 | 26 | 27 | 26
I Left My Heart in San Francisco
1962, Columbia; "I Left My Heart in San Francisco";
www.tonybennett.com
■ "Bennett takes you into a lounge and opens his pipes" on this "sweet", "smooth", "smoky and sexy" album from "one of his career peaks"; "back in the '60s, he was in search of hits", and he found them with the "wonderful" *The Best Is Yet to Come* and a Grammy-winning title track that "makes you dream of romance in the most beautiful city in the world"; "fans for life" are "so glad that the MTV crowd has rediscovered" this "singer's singer."

Tony Bennett,   25 | 26 | 27 | 25
Playin' With My Friends: Bennett Sings the Blues
2001, RPM; "Stormy Weather"; www.tonybennett.net
☑ "Ah, Tony – the man's voice only gets smoother with age"; after fiftysome years in the biz, he's truly "better than ever", and some of the artists who duet with him on this "blues-based collaboration" disc "even do it [as] well" as he; "the best tracks feature vocalists adept at this style", including Natalie Cole on *Stormy Weather,* or folks like Billy Joel "reinterpreting their own material"; otherwise, critics croak this collection is "a tad spotty."

George Benson, *Breezin'* G #1   25 | 23 | 28 | 25
1976, Rhino; "Breezin'"; www.georgebenson.com
■ "Start your day in the right mood" and "breeze on through the afternoon" with this "mellow master's" pop "crossover", a "pivotal album in mainstreaming jazz"; though "people knew the man could play, most didn't know he could sing", but this disc convinced them – "a showcase for Benson's singular guitar talent" and "flirtatious" vocals, it combines "quiet fire and smooth soul in one fabulous package" of "light" hits.

Berlioz, *Symphonie Fantastique* G   26 | 26 | 28 | 24
1974, Philips; "March to the Scaffold"
☑ "Yes, Sir Colin is the man for Berlioz" – "proving that so-called 'classical' music can be as profound and modern as anything one is likely to hear today", the conductor leads the Royal Concertgebouw Orchestra of Amsterdam in a "beautifully interpreted", "stunningly performed", "superbly produced" recording of a composition by the musical "master of courage for his time"; still, some slam it as a rendition of a "Symphonie Overwrought" written by "a madman with no attention span."

Chuck Berry, *The Great Twenty-Eight*   27 | 26 | 27 | 21
1982, Chess; "Johnny B. Goode"; www.chuckberry.com
■ "If Elvis was the King", then "Chuck was the founding father" – "the Thomas Jefferson" of R&R just about "wrote the rulebook through his monumental guitar playing, vocal style and stage presence, as well as the subject matter and wit of his songwriting"; his "reelin' and rockin'" "teen anthems", from *Johnny B. Goode* to the double-entendres of *Maybellene,* "laid down the groundwork for" the genre.

Best of Schoolhouse Rock   25 | 27 | 21 | 22
(Soundtrack)
1998, Rhino; "Conjunction Junction"
■ Kids "rock out and learn at the same time", while "middle-aged people" "walk down memory lane" listening to this "classic" "blast from Saturday morning [TV's] past" when "an entire generation was taught grammar, math, science and history" via the "groovy" tunes of "clever 'toons"; "30 years later", parents who buy this "fun educational tool" to give their little ones "a head start in school" ask "how else would we know what an adverb is?"

The B-52's, *The B-52's*   24 | 22 | 20 | 22
1979, Warner Bros.; "Rock Lobster"; www.theb52s.com
■ "With a four-string guitar, two chicks in beehives and a spooky keyboard", "this little dance band from Athens, GA", "celebrates low-tech fun that speaks to the camp in all of us"; a "happiness bomb" "made for aliens hosting a party", it "bang, bang, banged on the door, baby!"; with

"Fred Schneider's nasal vocals balanced" by the "birdcall" "harmony of Kate Pierson and Cindy Wilson", it "gave us an excuse to wiggle on the floor" to such "kitschfest anthems" as *Rock Lobster* and *Planet Claire.*

Big Brother and the Holding Company, *Cheap Thrills* ⧇**1**
25 ｜ 21 ｜ 23 ｜ 20

1968, Columbia; "Piece of My Heart"

■ "Capturing the era of the 1960s with a great live sound", this sophomore effort from San Francisco's "psychedelic" blues "powerhouse" proved the breakthrough for "a little Texas gal" named Janis Joplin, who "could belt it out and belt it down better than anyone", "giving us a little piece of her heart and then some"; "raw and emotional", her "big, lusty, howling voice went on to rock immortality", while her backup band, deemed a "bloated barroom" outfit by a vocal few, "faded from the map."

The Big Chill (Soundtrack)
25 ｜ 24 ｜ 24 ｜ 24

1983, Motown; "I Heard It Through the Grapevine"

◨ "Especially fun to pop on after dinner to imitate the cast as you and your guest do the dishes and dance", this soundtrack is "decade-defining", but "which decade?": it's "perfect memory music" "not just of the movie or the generation depicted, but of the generations who grew up watching it" and "getting funky" to *Whiter Shade of Pale* and Marvin Gaye's "fantabulous *I Heard It Through the Grapevine*"; it's a "kick-ass" "party" disc but "where are the Stones?" – well, you can't always get what you want.

Big Star, *Sister Lovers/Third*
27 ｜ 26 ｜ 24 ｜ 22

1978, Rykodisc; "Jesus Christ"

■ "Phenomenal in its vulnerability", this "vastly influential" record captures the band on the brink of their breakup, offering "one last gorgeous gasp" as frontman "Alex Chilton falls apart and creates a beautiful, shimmering mess"; "*Holocaust* and *Big Black Car,* aching downers that stand in stark contrast to the joyous outbursts of *Kizza Me* or *O, Dana*", give a glimpse "inside the mind of a genius" while "providing a healthy argument for canonization by rock snobs."

Bizet, *Carmen Suites; L'Arlesienne Suites*
26 ｜ 27 ｜ 26 ｜ 24

1967, Sony Classical; www.newyorkphilharmonic.org

■ "In it's premiere it was booed off stage", but by the time Leonard Bernstein got a hold of it, Bizet's *Carmen* was "recognized" as "one of the world's most beautiful, powerful operas"; these "sweet" suites from the score reveal "another avatar" of the conductor's "amazing" "years with the NY Philharmonic", with "great playing" marked by his "typical flair"; as one shamed buff confesses "to think I fell in love with this music because of [its use in] *The Bad News Bears*."

Björk, *Debut* #1   25 | 23 | 24 | 25

1993, Elektra; "Big Time Sensuality"; www.bjork.com

■ "The quintessential Icelandic princess" "leaves the Sugarcubes far behind" on her second solo disc, "a luscious testament" of Nellee Hooper–produced "pixie-electronica" on which "she explores her sexuality and childlike psyche amid a techno-fueled soundtrack"; "combining the artiness" of her former band with dance-oriented tracks, the "quirky" "indie icon" creates a "fresh", "mystically unreal" "soundscape that complements" "her dazzling, otherworldly voice", leaving listeners violently happy.

Björk,   24 | 25 | 26 | 25
Selmasongs: Dancer in the Dark

2000, Polydor; "I've Seen It All"; www.dancerinthedark.com

■ "Sounding like Gershwin would if his songs were written in the year 3000" and in an "atypically dark" mood, "the queen of electronica" "shows she can write for orchestra", delivering a "show-tuney departure" on this "shocking" soundtrack for her death row debut in Lars von Trier's celluloid commentary on capital punishment; "wild and weird", she "pushes the breathy envelope and gives birth to a sound experience" as "haunting as her film performance."

Clint Black, *Killin' Time*   25 | 24 | 24 | 22

1989, RCA; "Killin' Time"; www.clintblack.com

■ "Pure country", rave fans of this "traditional sounding" "blockbuster" debut from the "damn cute" Texan–turned–Nashville star; spawning numerous hits and multiplatinum sales, this "hell of an album" is "marked by distinctive songwriting", "thoughtful lyrics" that "cut to the heart" and "a whiskey-tinged voice that's reminiscent of [Merle] Haggard", not to mention "one of the sexiest" in the genre.

Black Flag, *Damaged*   25 | 23 | 19 | 16

1981, SST; "Rise Above"

■ Rarely has "rage been better captured" than on this "raw, real" "hardcore masterpiece", a "pure slice of DIY punk" straight outta the SoCal scene that "defines a moment in time", and "gave voice to countless disaffected, disillusioned youths"; frontman "Henry Rollins is just so angry, he's lovable" as he "tears through" "rough and tumbling", "unbelievably intense" "staples", "laying the groundwork for generations to come."

Black Sabbath, *Paranoid*   25 | 22 | 24 | 20

1971, Warner Bros.; "Iron Man"; www.blacksabbath.com

■ Spotlighting "Tony Iommi's monster riffs and blistering solos", Geezer "Butler, the king of bass lines", and "vintage" "Ozzman at his Ozziest", this "template for a thousand" bands revealed "heavy metal at its finest and its first hour"; "iconic in the genre", these "lads from Birmingham" "knew how to make noise" "before thrash, before grunge", creating a "dark vision that's never been bested."

Art Blakey & The Jazz Messengers, *Moanin'*

28 | 26 | 29 | 25

1958, Blue Note; "Moanin'"; www.artblakey.com
■ "You can hear the glasses tinkle in a smoky nightclub" when you savor this "healthy dose" of '50s "hard-bop excellence" by the Jazz Messengers and their "prolific" leader; "what drive, what playing!" – with "Blakey's propulsive drumming", "Lee Morgan's exceptional" blowing and Bobby Timmons' "can't-be-beat" keys, this "definitive" disc "cooks", it "swings", "t'aint nothing better."

Mary J. Blige, *My Life*

26 | 25 | 25 | 25

1994, Uptown; "My Life"; www.mjblige.com
■ MJB "brings drama to a whole 'nother level with this soundtrack to a young woman in crisis", "vocalizing the heartbreak, pain" and hope that "every female can relate to"; "helped" by "soothing" hip-hop beats and Sean 'Puffy' Combs' "solid production", R&B's "successor to Aretha Franklin" "mellows the mood" with "spiritual" singing and "emotion that reads like an open book" – "use this album as a cathartic tool to get over your lost love."

Mary J. Blige, *No More Drama*

26 | 25 | 26 | 26

2002, MCA; "No More Drama"; www.mjblige.com
■ "You'd be hard pressed to find someone who likes R&B and gospel who doesn't find these" "soulful, classy songs" to be "pure therapy"; the "impassioned" "voice of her generation" is "happier and more mature", but she "retains the gritty" edge of someone who's "been through so much and keeps persevering"; sisters "hooked" on the title track's "*Young and the Restless* thing" insist "every woman who's ever been in love should have this disc."

Mary J. Blige, *What's the 411?*

25 | 23 | 25 | 24

1992, Uptown; "Real Love"; www.mjblige.com
■ "The queen of hip-hop/soul is born with this brutally honest", "seminal" debut "from the streets"; "sassy, slick and defiantly femme", "the lady kills it on this one", "with emotion that makes covers like *Sweet Thing* her own" and "hardcore delivery" on tracks like *Real Love* "sure to get everyone on the dance floor"; Sean Combs "helped craft" the "R&B masterpiece that heralded" "Mary bustin' out on the scene."

Blondie, *Parallel Lines*

24 | 23 | 23 | 23

1978, Chrysalis; "Heart of Glass"; www.blondie.net
■ "American pop perfection", this "attitude-heavy" combo's "brilliant" "breakout album" featuring "*Hanging on the Telephone*, a classic of the highest order", and *Heart of Glass* "launched new wave" as a "commercially viable genre" while "cementing the visage" of Debbie Harry, "punk rock's Marilyn Monroe"; capturing "the sound of CBGB's", producer Mike Chapman turned this "rock-disco fusion" "into the best thing to hit radio since the Ronettes."

Blood, Sweat and Tears, Blood, Sweat and Tears 🄶 #1 24 | 23 | 26 | 24
1969, Columbia; "And When I Die"

■ "They make me so very happy" agreed admirers of this "ambitious-as-hell" sophomore effort, a "perfect" combo of "great jazz masquerading as rock", enhanced by "crisp, clean, clear", "sharp horns" and the "bluesy", "soulful wailing" of Al Kooper's replacement, David Clayton-Thomas; "packed with hits", this "seminal work" that helped define "big band rock" rocketed up to No. 1, and is still "timeless", perhaps proving "what goes up" (like a *Spinning Wheel*) "doesn't grow old."

Mike Bloomfield, *Super Session* 25 | 20 | 28 | 21
1968, Columbia; "Season of the Witch";
www.mikebloomfield.com

■ Chicago's pioneering white bluesman, "at his sweetest", and keyboardist Al Kooper, "at the top of his game, joined forces with Stephen Stills, "the most underrated guitarist of his time", to create a "super" studio effort equivalent to their "live adventures"; this "blueprint for jam albums" features "a long riff on Donovan's *Season of the Witch*" and Dylan's *It Takes a Lot to Laugh, It Takes a Train to Cry*, bringing "tears to the eyes" from the axeman who "left earth too soon."

The Blues Brothers (Soundtrack) 25 | 23 | 25 | 23
1980, Atlantic; "Sweet Home Chicago"

■ "If you've got dark glasses, half a pack of cigarettes and a full tank of gas, hit it" on the downbeat and take this soundtrack on "an enjoyable cruise"; John Belushi and Dan Aykroyd "were on a mission from God" to build a "bridge between classic blues and unenlightened" "white kids", with "kick-ass" tracks by "legends like Aretha Franklin, Ray Charles, James Brown" and Cab Calloway, plus "superb arrangements"; "for a party or to lift your mood on a rainy day", it's "powerful good."

Bon Jovi, *New Jersey* #1 23 | 22 | 24 | 24
1988, Mercury; "Bad Medicine"; www.bonjovi.com

■ When you're "from New Jersey it's state law" that you like these "bad boys" and their multiplatinum "tribute to the Garden State", a "more mature" effort than "the mega-huge *Slippery*"; "if you made out in the '80s, you listened to" these "catchy" "feel-good songs" that conjure up "memories of teenage innocence" from groupies who gush "even if I didn't know what Jon Bon Jovi looked like, I'd still love his music."

Bon Jovi, *Slippery When Wet* #1 24 | 22 | 24 | 24
1986, Mercury; "Livin' on a Prayer"; www.bonjovi.com

■ "File under guilty pleasure" this breakout "album no one admits to owning, yet everyone knows all the words to"; "hairspray – check! high-heeled boots – check! silk scarves – check!" – a "power-pop" "classic", it "brings you back to the hair-band days" and "damn, it's fun"; "raise your fists" to "Jersey's own" for delivering "more hooks than a meatpacking plant" plus the "summer anthem *Livin' on a Prayer*" "that speaks volumes for the working class."

Boogie Down Productions, *Criminal Minded*
28 | 28 | 24 | 23

1987, B-Boy; "Criminal Minded"

■ "Hard-hitting", "stripped-down beats" backdrop the "the sheer intensity" of rapper KRS-One's "lethal rhymes" that "explicitly depict the harsh reality of life in the inner city" on this "seminal album" that "laid the foundation for hardcore rap"; "you can't seem to escape the urgency of the messages being rubbed onto your eardrum" by "a true hip-hop scholar" and his "chalk", the late Scott La Rock – "class is now in session."

Boston, *Boston*
25 | 22 | 25 | 25

1976, Epic (Sony); "More Than a Feeling"; www.bandboston.com

■ "It was more than a feeling" – "the nova that was Boston" sold over 16 million copies of its "blockbuster debut" and "still reverberates through R&R's celestial sky"; "oh-so-'70s, but oh-so-listenable" Tom Scholtz's "basement creation" revealed his "home-studio wizardry", "unleashing" "super anthems" and "a whole new spectrum" of "incredible sounds", "containing all the elements that make classic rock classic": from "the first note, it brings out the air guitar."

David Bowie, *Changesbowie*
27 | 26 | 26 | 26

1990, Rykodisc; "Changes"; www.davidbowie.com

■ An "excellent collection" spanning "the Thin White Duke's career from his Ziggy days up until his plastic soul stuff in the '80s", this "wonderful retrospective" documents the ever-"evolving" "trendsetter" who's "always testing our boundaries, making us think"; it's a "great beginner record" for novices to "ease into the catalogue."

David Bowie, *Heroes*
25 | 25 | 26 | 26

1977, Victor; "Heroes"; www.davidbowie.com

■ "The best-known album of the [Chameleon's] Berlin trilogy", this "sonically unique" effort "harnesses the creative talents of Brian Eno and guitarist Robert Fripp" and almost "sounds like a postwar German city: cold, angular, mechanical, yet with a delicious passion underneath"; side A offers "magical songs" "wrapped in fantasy" like the "passionate" title track, and "side B contains moody instrumentals", the precursor to "ambient" "music as art."

David Bowie, *The Rise and Fall of Ziggy Stardust and the Spiders from Mars*
28 | 28 | 26 | 26

1972, RCA Victor; "Suffragette City"; www.davidbowie.com

■ "With writing that has never been more insightful and deadpan", this "landmark glitter" "concept album traces the trials and tribulations of an alien supergroup, painting a dismal picture of stardom and its ensuing vices, from the apocalyptic opener *Five Years* to the epitaphic *Rock & Roll Suicide*": "opening the doors to glam rock with a bang" and "ushering in a new androgynous era", it's held together with sex, space and "Mick Ronson's charging guitar work" ("the stuff of legend").

David Bowie, *Station to Station*
26 | 26 | 26 | 26

1976, RCA Victor; "Station to Station";
www.davidbowie.com
■ "A very early expedition into cold techno-rock territory", this "crushingly dramatic" album reveals "emotional confusion sublimely rendered"; "disquieting" and "intense", with "production quality that's beyond words", it "chronicles Bowie's transformation from R&R singer to cocaine-fueled robot" or, according to others, "smooth crooner" "during the peak of his cool, detached LA phase" – "wow, paranoia never sounded so good!"

Boyz II Men, *Cooleyhighharmony* G
24 | 21 | 23 | 23

1991, Motown; "It's So Hard to Say Goodbye to Yesterday"
■ A throwback to '50s R&B group "harmonies", the mega-selling debut by this "Motown-reborn" group of urban preps balances "heartbreak ballads" like a cappella *It's So Hard to Say Goodbye to Yesterday* with "up-tempo doo-wop" numbers like "the autobiographical hoot", *Motownphilly*, "assisted with technology for the hip-hop generation"; the "fun", "smooth" and "funky" disc "brings joy every time you put it on and repeat the words."

Boyz II Men, *II* ▦
23 | 22 | 23 | 23

1994, Motown; "Water Runs Dry"
■ "If you loved them with *Cooleyhighharmony,* you loved them even more with *II*!!"; the Boyz's "well-crafted", chart-topping second album "shows how the group matured", with "amazing vocals" on "nice ballads" like the hit *I'll Make Love to You* and *Water Runs Dry,* plus "poppy, upbeat New Jack hits" such as *All Around the World*; like everything the "sultry quartet" does, this Grammy winner "makes you want to grind the one you love."

Billy Bragg & Wilco, *Mermaid Avenue*
26 | 27 | 26 | 24

1998, Elektra; "California Stars"; www.billybragg.co.uk;
www.wilcoworld.net
■ "Who was expecting to see British protest singer Billy Bragg hook up with alt-country gods Wilco", put "unheralded Guthrie" lyrics to music and "bring them to life?"; "Woody woulda approved" because this "fun sweep through Americana" "respectfully" "captures the everyman ethic found in his best work" with songs like

the "inspiring, uplifting *California Stars*"; thanks go to the dustbowl folky's daughter, Nora, for initiating this "impressive experiment"–cum–"celebration of life."

Brahms, *Symphony No. 4*   28 | 29 | 29 | 26
1980, Deutsche Grammophon
■ "Not for those who like their Brahms warm and fuzzy", this "riveting" recording "nails you to the wall with its bright sound and thrusting momentum"; conductor "Carlos Kleiber can be rather elusive, but when he works, he's marvelous", and here his "amazing, engaging performance" with the Vienna Philharmonic "makes the music new to a listener even years" after the disc was pressed; no matter when you take it for a spin, "you can't possibly not love it."

Toni Braxton, *Secrets*   24 | 23 | 24 | 25
1996, LaFace; "Un-Break My Heart";
www.tonibraxton.com
■ The "sexy", "husky" voice of R&B's barely clad siren soars all over a "soulful", "sultry" album of "touching" ballads like *Un-Break My Heart* and get-your-groove-on gems like *You're Making Me High* and *I Love Me Some Him*; "living up to the original's promise", it's the follow-up step in "the making of a diva."

Breakfast at Tiffany's   26 | 26 | 27 | 26
(Soundtrack) G #1
1961, RCA Victor; "Moon River"
■ "No film owes more to its music" – our huckleberry friend Henry Mancini "deserves high marks" for this "sophisticated", "delightful" "mood jazz", which reminds us "of a simpler time" when you could actually enjoy a coffee and a croissant on Fifth Avenue in solitude; from Audrey Hepburn's "incomparable" rendition of "dreamy *Moon River* to the *Latin Golightly* and *Moon River Cha Cha*", "loungers" ask "can there be anything more romantic?"

The Breakfast Club (Soundtrack)   23 | 20 | 21 | 21
1985, A&M; "Don't You (Forget About Me)"
☑ Don't you forget about this new-wave "time capsule", the "seminal" soundtrack to yet another John Hughes flick celebrating "'80s spoiled rich kids"; "pull on your leg warmers" and "do the Ally Sheedy dance" to the "high school agony and ecstasy" of the Simple Minds' smash single or Wang Chung's "rockin'" *Fire in the Twilight* on this "must-have for any future archaeologist who wants to understand the culture" of the era.

Sarah Brightman,   25 | 23 | 25 | 24
Time to Say Goodbye #1
1998, Angel; "Time to Say Goodbye";
www.sarah-brightman.com
■ Brightman "glows on pop" tunes like *Who Wants to Live Forever,* and "she's as bright as the sun when stretching

out her classical muscles" on cuts like Mozart's *Alleluja*; the Broadway muse burns it up with voice of "warmth" and "light" on this "operatic" crossover "blend" that even "guys" admit "makes me cry, for Pete's sake"; "the highlight" might be the "goosebump"-inducing title-track duet with Andrea Bocelli, which proves that the "soaring" soprano is "more than just Andrew Lloyd Webber's ex."

David Bromberg, *David Bromberg* | 26 | 24 | 26 | 23 |
1971, Columbia; "The Hold Up"

■ "David Bromberg 101" for novices, this "debut album that still holds up well" captures the "profoundly underrated" talents of this storyteller–cum–"musician's musician" who previously earned credits assisting the likes of Bob Dylan and Jerry Jeff Walker; deftly combining folk, bluegrass, rock and blues, his "guitar work is exceptional", his performance "energetic" and his style, nothing "uncompromised."

Brooks & Dunn, *Brand New Man* | 25 | 23 | 24 | 24 |
1991, Arista; "Neon Moon"; www.brooks-dunn.com

■ Kix Brooks and Ronnie Dunn, Nashville's "most honored", "fantastic duo", "kicked it up a notch" on their "terrific first album", turning out a "consistent", "quintessential '90s country" collection; "packed with feeling", "every tune" "gets the toes tapping and the beer flowing", especially the "quick-paced" hit *Boot Scootin' Boogie* – footloose fans feel "there will likely never be a better line dance."

Garth Brooks, *No Fences* | 26 | 25 | 25 | 25 |
1990, Capitol; "Friends in Low Places"; www.garthbrooks.com

■ "The reign of Garth began" with this "stellar sophomore" crossover that not only "put country on the map" again but brought it "into the realm of pop music"; he's "at his zenith" on this "sing-along favorite" bursting with "timeless" tunes "with a definite twang" that "well up the emotions" and get your "boot (and butt) twitching"; it's "required" listening, even for "purebred Yankees."

Garth Brooks, *Ropin' the Wind* 🄶 ▦ | 25 | 25 | 26 | 26 |
1991, Capitol; "Shameless"; www.garthbrooks.com

■ Rock "sensibilities meet country" on this "awesome" effort that, "from *The River* to the powerful *Shameless*" cover that "does Billy Joel proud", is "full of fun, familiar songs" and "scorching steel guitars"; it's the first C&W album to debut at No. 1 on Billboard's pop charts, "further explaining Mr. Brooks' magnetic hold on" "the rest of the decade" ("forget grunge", the early '90s "were all Garth").

Clarence "Gatemouth" Brown, *Texas Swing* | 25 | 19 | 28 | 21 |
1988, Rounder; "Frosty"; www.gatemouth.com

■ "Gate swings!" – from guitar to fiddle, this man can flat-out play" and that's just what the "national treasure" does on this "must-have for any collection", a Texas-size chunk of blues, jazz, swing and Cajun "classics" that combines his Grammy-winning album *Alright Again!* and follow-up *One More Mile*; ranging from tunes like *Frosty* to *Ain't that Dandy,* it's "almost as good as a live performance."

Clifford Brown, *Memorial Album* 27 24 28 23
1953, Blue Note; "Cherokee"
■ Throughout his "brilliant but all too brief career" before his "tragic" death in an auto accident at age 25, the trumpeter "genius" "never played a bad note"; this "stupendous bebop" "chronicle" compiles "some of his best recordings" – "fluid, forceful, melodic" and "clean", it's "top-notch Brownie", delivered in "a beautiful ringing tone that blows out the cobwebs and sings."

James Brown, 27 23 27 22
Live at the Apollo, Volume 1
1963, Polygram; "Lost Someone";
www.godfatherofsoul.com
■ What an "electrifying experience" – "it's live and you are there, sweatin' and swayin'" with the "'Godfather of Soul'" who gives a "simply astonishing performance" on this "driving, powerful" "definitive" release, proving that "'The Hardest Working Man in Show Business' isn't just a marketing phrase"; "one of the few" occasions "where the magic of being there translates to a recording", this funk "classic" "gives new definition to 'the slow burn.'"

James Brown, *Sex Machine* 27 24 27 23
1970, King; "Get Up (I Feel Like Being a) Sex Machine";
www.godfatherofsoul.com
■ "Put on your dancing shoes and get down" to the "master" "at the peak of his powers" because "music doesn't get any more feel-good" than this; "the first seven tracks are priceless" and perhaps "without equal in the canon", most notably *Get Up (I Feel Like Being a) Sex Machine,* while *Give It Up or Turnit a Loose* "may be the funkiest six minutes ever recorded" thanks to the "famous rhythm section", featuring bassist Bootsy Collins, reeds player Fred Wesley and drummer Clyde Stubblefield.

Jackson Browne, 25 26 25 23
Running on Empty
1977, Asylum; "Running on Empty";
www.jacksonbrowne.com
■ "An awesome on-the-road diary", this "sensitive singer-songwriter's" "eclectic mix of quasi-live" original tracks "compiled in hotel rooms, on tour buses" and onstage was "a risky undertaking" worth taking – years later, "classic '70s anthems" like *The Load Out* and the title track assure "you'll never run out of listening fuel"; a "terrific adventure", it "captured the performer's life" "so well" that it made a "lasting contribution to the musical landscape."

Jackson Browne,   25 | 28 | 24 | 22
Saturate Before Using
1972, Asylum; "Doctor My Eyes";
www.jacksonbrowne.com
■ This "amazing" debut "shows the promise of what
was to come" for the "talented singer-songwriter" who
would soon be a dominant force in pop radio and a mainstay
of the California soft-rock scene; only *Doctor My Eyes*
charted, but the entire disc is an "outstanding" collection of
"sincere and personal songs."

DAVE BRUBECK,   29 | 28 | 29 | 26
TIME OUT FEATURING "TAKE FIVE"
1959, Columbia; "Take Five"; www.brubeckinstitute.org
■ "Anyone who can write in a 5/4 rhythm and make it
swing has massive composing talent", and this pianist
puts out on this "masterwork of syncopation" "in time
signatures most of us never imagined existed"; featuring
the "sexy" sounds of Paul Desmond, "the Voltaire of sax",
the "seminal" *Take Five* is arguably the "best five minutes"
in the genre, but "the whole album shimmers" – it "brought
the music to the masses", made Brubeck a "superstar" and
still proves that "being smart is cool."

Jeff Buckley, *Grace*   27 | 27 | 27 | 25
1995, Columbia; "Hallelujah"; www.jeffbuckley.com
■ A "truly spiritual experience", this "divine" debut
from the late singer-songwriter "haunts" listeners with
"eerie", "fragile but powerful" songs that emphasize his
"equally ardent", "angelic voice"; it's "sophisticated
and elegant" with "lush arrangements" and "standout
tracks aplenty, including *Last Good-bye* and a cover of
Leonard Cohen's *Hallelujah*"; his drowning remains forever
"tragic", but "he did grace us with his gift, if only for
a fleeting moment."

Tim Buckley, *Happy Sad*   26 | 28 | 27 | 23
1969, Elektra; "Buzzin' Fly"
◩ "Hypnotically beautiful ballads" mark perhaps the "most
accessible album" from this "magnificent lost genius" of
the folk-rock world who, like his son Jeff, tragically died at
a young age; he shows an "amazing" vocal range and
"adventurous style" here – it's "deep and mystical" on one
hand but also just plain "pretty" and offers a "bittersweet
memory" of the late '60s.

Buckwheat Zydeco,   24 | 20 | 25 | 22
On a Night Like This
1987, Island; "On a Night Like This";
www.buckwheatzydeco.com
■ "Get out the gumbo", listen to Stanley 'Buckwheat' Dural's
"toe-tappin' bayou sounds as he plays the accordion and
sings in Creole French and English" and "let the good
times roll!"; "tight and fun", this breakthrough "catches

the excitement of seeing the band live" and "makes you want to party"; "where it lacks in self-penned consistency, it rescues with outstanding covers" of tunes from the Blasters and Bob Dylan, bringing "zydeco into R&R."

Buena Vista Social Club
28 25 28 27
(Soundtrack) 🄖 #1
1997, Nonesuch; "Chan Chan"
■ "*Viva la musica!*" – bluesman Ry Cooder "takes you back to another world" "frozen in time" and "introduces the work of [veteran] Cuban musicians", "letting everyone know what beauty comes from" our Caribbean neighbor; "love and loss run throughout the songs", and "with great rhythms" and "character in the voices" of "such talented old-timers", it's a "mini-vacation"; compadres concur that, accompanied by "Wim Wenders' must-see documentary", it's "another reason to stop the embargo."

Buffalo Springfield,
27 27 27 23
Buffalo Springfield Again
1967, Atco; "Bluebird"
■ The second of three "eclectic albums that melded folk, country" and psychedelic rock from the volatile "dream team" comprised of Neil Young, Stephen Stills, Richie Furay, Dewey Martin and Bruce Palmer, this "gem" yielded the "powerful, poetic, puzzling *Broken Arrow*" and "guitar extravaganzas *Mr. Soul* and *Bluebird*" – "proof that three distinct songwriters can come together to create one brilliant body of work"; "so smooth, so simple, so perfect" and so "short-lived, but oh-so-influential."

Jimmy Buffett,
25 25 23 23
Songs You Know by Heart
1985, MCA; "Margaritaville"; www.margaritaville.com
■ "Get the margaritas ready", "put on the flip-flops" and "transport yourself to a hammock" via "the laid-back prince of the Conch Republic of Key West"; "a nonstop party for life's castaways", this "guilty pleasure" offers "just the right amount of sing-along camp" that "goes great with alcohol and beaches"; while "every true Parrothead already has this in his or her collection", it is a must-get "for neophytes entering the mystical" land of perennial "summertime."

Solomon Burke,
28 27 26 25
Don't Give Up On Me
2002, Fat Possum; "Soul Searchin'"
■ A "master artist" of '60s soul makes "a triumphant return" to recording with this "outstanding" collection of rock covers "penned by greats" "the likes of Dylan, Van Morrison", "Elvis Costello and Tom Waits"; his "thundering voice imbues each song with a truthful grandeur that can't be matched" – you "can hear the heartbreak dripping from the speakers."

Burning Spear, *Marcus Garvey* 28 27 27 24
1975, Mango; "Marcus Garvey"; www.burningspear.net
■ Inspired by the leader of the 1920s' back-to-Africa movement, this "must-buy for all true roots reggae fans" relays "the message that one must take control of one's destiny"; "the horns go to your heart, the rhythms to your soul" and Burning Spear's "gravelly and impressive voice" "goes to your head" "so that the meaning comes through for real" on a "powerful" "classic" that's "political" and "grooving" all at once – "jah rasta!"

Kate Bush, *Hounds of Love* 25 26 25 24
1985, EMI America; "Running Up That Hill"
■ "There are strange dreams we forget, but Kate Bush remembers" on this "intensely personal" "masterpiece" that "transports you to another reality"; "Ms. Amos, Ms. Apple, Ms. Morissette" . . . "no one should be late to her 'class' on old-school" "mythic", "neurotically intelligent" music – especially for this "punkishly charming" "'lesson' offering lyrics full of wit, grace" and "poetry", "idiosyncratic in the extreme" and underscored by a "beautiful voice" "that makes your heart beat faster."

The Paul Butterfield Blues Band, *East-West* 26 24 27 23
1966, Elektra; "East-West"
■ "Genre bending/blending" "jazz, world, rock and folk", this "pioneering masterpiece" also "stretched the blues into the Middle East, while honoring the classics with Butterfield's impeccable harp work"; "if the twin guitars of the Yardbirds' Jimmy Page and Jeff Beck had worked as well as those of Mike Bloomfield and Elvin Bishop do here, Led Zeppelin would never have happened."

Buzzcocks, *Singles Going Steady* 26 25 22 21
1979, I.R.S.; "What Do I Get?"
■ Led by "punk Beatle" Pete Shelley, this "UK powerpop combo" "understood the value of a hook" and "never sneered at a finely crafted song"; "this blitz through their early" years is "comprised of eight perfect A sides", "from the comical *Orgasm Addict* to a great song about having no one, *What Do I Get?*", as well as "their B sides – in a twist, they're as good as the flips."

Bye Bye Birdie (Soundtrack) 22 22 21 22
1963, RCA Victor; "Bye Bye Birdie"
■ The story, morning glory, is that this "catchy" soundtrack is "nostalgia all the way", "capturing the era" of the 1950s, America's "teenage years"; the word, hummingbird, is that "even with Ann Margret's strange singing" and the "reverb-obsessed '60s engineering", "it's a lot of fun", thanks to "screams" like Paul Lynde and Maureen Stapleton – baby boomers blubber "the sad part is people, like my mom, used to be like that."

The Byrds, *Fifth Dimension* 26 | 25 | 25 | 23
1966, Columbia; "Eight Miles High"
■ The "revolutionary" group that "stretched from folk rock to full-blown electric" is showcased here and includes founder Roger McGuinn ("the word 'jangly' was created to describe his 12-string guitar, which sets the tone"), David Crosby (whose "high harmonies gave the band a sound no other combo could duplicate"), Chris Hillman, Gene Clark and Michael Clarke; "any album that contains a musical interpretation of Einstein's theory" – the "majestic *Eight Miles High*" – "is alright by me" rave relativists.

C

Cabaret (Soundtrack) **G** 27 | 27 | 26 | 26
1972, MCA; "Cabaret"
■ *Willkommen* to the "divine decadence" of the Berlin cabaret set against the "chilling horror" of the Nazis on this "fabulous" soundtrack to "the Kander and Ebb classic brought to vivid life on screen by Bob Fosse" and starring "spellbinding" Joel Grey and "amazing" Liza Minnelli at her "knock-'em-dead" "peak"; "poignant and hedonistic with a gay subplot" and "serious undertones", the "catchy" album has "all the elements" to "draw you in."

Maria Callas, 28 | 26 | 28 | 24
The Very Best of Maria Callas
1953, EMI; "Casta Diva"
☑ When Callas "was on stage, there wasn't anybody else", and this disc is "a rare opportunity to hear the arias that made the diva" "a magnificent singing actress"; "there are times we should remember her", like when we want to hear *Casta Diva* or "her heartbreaking *Mamma Morte* from the *Philadelphia* soundtrack"; "she emotes" so much, she could "blow out your stereo", but sensitive ears say her "almost harsh voice" is "not the apparatus to support the music."

Camelot (Soundtrack) 24 | 26 | 23 | 22
1967, Warner Bros.; "Camelot"
☑ The "simple folk" say the "knights of the turntable score big" with Lerner and Loewe's "tuneful poetry" on this "schmaltzy" soundtrack; the cast "can't really sing, but who cares" when "Richard Harris is fabulous" and "Vanessa Redgrave turns *The Lusty Month of May* into a longing song instead of that trippy number in the original?"; still, show tune royalty decree "you have to be nuts" to prefer the film recording to Julie Andrews and Robert Goulet "in fine voice" on the Broadway album.

Glen Campbell, *Wichita Lineman* **#1** 24 | 25 | 26 | 23
1968, Capitol; "Wichita Lineman"; www.glencampbellshow.com
■ "Evocative of an era", this "essential-to-the-'60s" "great album of country-pop tunes" bottles "vintage Campbell" at

his "professional best"; while the "timeless interpretation of Jimmy Webb's" title track is "constantly sung in karaoke bars", die-hard C&W fans wonder how "anyone can hear the yearning" song and "not be moved"; this "solid" hitmaker may be "underrated" but he's still on the line and "will never be forgotten."

Candide (Original cast recording)   27 | 27 | 29 | 26
1956, Columbia; "Glitter and Be Gay"

■ "Thank God this was made so that future generations would know the masterpiece" "that brought opera to the middle class"; "avoiding the show's notorious book problems" (sorry, Lillian Hellman), "the record captures the genius of Leonard Bernstein's score", "reducing the most sophisticated ear to a giddy school girl" ready to "glitter and be gay" over Voltaire's "involved story"; "a young Barbara Cook", her "radiant soprano" "ranging beyond most singers", is "heavenly."

Captain Beefheart, *Safe as Milk*   24 | 24 | 23 | 20
1967, Buddah; "Electricity"

■ "Cut from the same cloth as Zappa", innovator "Van Vliet (aka Beefheart) is as eccentric as they come and therein lies his charm"; mixing "imaginative arrangements topped by post–Howlin' Wolf vocals" and "Ry Cooder's superb" guitar throughout, it's "scary, wired music", perhaps the "weirdest white-boy blues-rock"; while it's "his most accessible" effort, "there's nothing safe" about it – it's "so ahead of its time, we still haven't caught up to it."

Carousel (Soundtrack)   26 | 27 | 26 | 24
1956, Angel; "If I Loved You"

■ "Joyous" tunes "are bustin' out all over" this "riotous" Rodgers and Hammerstein score, which includes the "best overture in musical theater", the "tearjerker" *I Loved You* and the "outstanding" *You'll Never Walk Alone*; Gordon McCrae and "nightingale" Shirley "Partridge" Jones simply "break your heart" on the "oldie but goody" soundtrack to the groundbreaking musical psychodrama, setting "standards by which all performances are judged."

Mary Chapin Carpenter,   26 | 27 | 25 | 25
Shooting Straight in the Dark
1990, Columbia; "Down at the Twist and Shout";
www.marychapincarpenter.com

■ "From high-energy country hits (*Down at the Twist and Shout*) to gritty, embittered battle cries (*You Win Again*) on to mournful tearjerkers (*When She's Gone*)", this "wise, womanly, wonderful" "storyteller's" "distinguished lyrics" always "ring true" making this "one of the best single-girl albums ever"; "play it on dateless Saturday nights – or anytime, for that matter" – this "gifted" "triple threat" is "all one could ask for in a singer-songwriter."

The Carpenters, *The Singles 1969-1973* ☝#1

26 | 25 | 25 | 25 |

1973, A&M; "We've Only Just Begun"

■ "It's yesterday once more" with "the early best" of the sibling duo; "dismissed by critics" as "saccharine pop", "it isn't cutting edge", no – it's "bubblegum but delicious", with Richard's "outstanding production" backing his sister's "heavenly voice" on "fireplace" "love songs" like *We've Only Just Begun*; "optimistic" with a tad of "sadness", Karen's "vocals are even more moving in light of her death" due to anorexia; swallow the "lump in your throat", "sing along" and it'll put you "on the top of the world."

The Cars, *The Cars*

24 | 22 | 23 | 24 |

1978, Elektra; "Just What I Needed"

■ This "exceptional debut" from a "groundbreaking" Boston band "combines slick new wave with cheeky rock" via "beautifully stylized", "catchy nuggets" with "wheezing synths, super-sized vocals", "killer hooks" and "quirky lyrics that shake it up" crossed with a "truckload of personality"; "illustrating why Ric Ocasek is a great producer", this "superior effort" also features "Elliott Easton's tasty guitar work" – "if the bass lines don't get your ass out of the chair, you're dead."

Johnny Cash, *American Recordings* Ⓖ

27 | 25 | 26 | 26 |

1994, American/Sony; "Delia's Gone"; www.johnnycash.com

■ Producer "Rick Rubin created a gem of a crossover" with this "first sure-shot in the American Recordings canon", bringing one of C&W's "greatest singer-songwriters to grace this earth" to a "whole new" hipster following; "stripped down" and "stark", "Cash's spookiest" effort catapults his "unique voice front and center" – it's "just the Man in Black with his acoustic guitar" pouring his heart into "monumental" murder ballads (*Delia's Gone*) and "stand-out covers" while "pondering his dark past."

Johnny Cash, *At Folsom Prison* ☝#1

27 | 26 | 26 | 23 |

1968, Columbia; "Folsom Prison Blues"; www.johnnycash.com

■ "Can you get more country?" drawl denizens of this "true classic" in which the "baddest musician on the planet" "performs from inside one of America's infamous prisons", "delighting thieves, murderers and junkies with songs about authority, death and drugs"; this "gritty, real" and recently expanded set shows this "national treasure" "at the peak of his powers" (and includes a few "smoking June Carter duets"), making it a "must for any collection."

Johnny Cash, *The Essential Johnny Cash*

28 | 28 | 27 | 25 |

1992, Columbia/Legacy; "Ring of Fire"; www.johnnycash.com

■ Though "all Cash is essential", this "exhaustive" three-disc box, compiling the early Sun classics and select

Columbia recordings from the "original American badass", is the "best of the best" – it "should be required listening for fans of all genres"; with his "low gravelly voice that always sounds like he's seen and done it all" and "gut-level" songs that touch on "spirituality" and "carnality", "'Old Golden Throat'" "strikes an imposing pose over country music."

Rosanne Cash, *Interiors*   26 | 26 | 24 | 23 |
1990, Columbia; "On the Surface";
www.rosannecash.com
■ "Johnny's daughter does him proud" on a "tremendous album" of "literate, compassionate" songs that show "the introspective side of country"; "hauntingly beautiful", this "exorcism of demons" "set the bar for divorce albums" (Cash cut it after splitting with husband Rodney Crowell) while representing this onetime Nashville star's "most intimate, mature work"; it's "an injustice" "to call it" C&W – it's "really beyond genre", establishing a "new direction for a great artist."

Nick Cave and the Bad Seeds,   25 | 28 | 24 | 22 |
From Her to Eternity
1984, Mute/Elektra; "From Her to Eternity";
www.nickcaveandthebadseeds.com
■ After Australia's Birthday Party combusted along came its leader ("a reformed punk rocker with the soul of a poet") with this "feral", "spooky", "brilliant beginning" featuring the Bad Seeds (including guitarist Blixa Bargeld, bassist/keyboardist Barry Adamson and organist/bassist Mick Harvey) playing "provocative music delivered with" "dramatic presentation"; "in Nick's hands, love is serious business" say fans who anoint him "the Black Crow King" and "the Voice of the Grim Reaper Calling You Home."

Manu Chao, *Clandestino*   25 | 25 | 26 | 24 |
1998, Virgin; "Clandestino"; www.manuchao.net
■ "What if the mike were passed to a trilingual tequila worm?" – "only [French-born Spaniard] Manu Chao can show you", so drink in his "exuberance distilled into" this "super-cool, circuslike production" from the "new wave of Latin music"; recorded in Central and South America, it's "so bouncy, so multinational", "you can't stop singing" "and dancing along" to the "interesting mix of languages, lyrics, beats and instruments"; audophilic oracles opine it's the "jubilant sound" "of the future."

Harry Chapin, *Verities & Balderdash*   26 | 28 | 24 | 23 |
1974, Elektra; "Cat's in the Cradle";
www.harrychapinmusic.com
■ "The story song was Chapin's specialty, and this collection more than satisfies as it leaves a lush legacy of the singer-social activist" "taken from us way too young" after a 1981 auto accident; with the "perennial hit *Cat's in the Cradle,* this "thoughtful, insightful, entertaining and amusing

performer", who could "make us cry and laugh in the course of a few tracks", "etched his place in history" – it's the "most timeless" "tearjerker" ever.

Tracy Chapman, *New Beginning* 24 26 23 22
1995, Elektra; "Give Me One Reason";
www.tracychapman.com
■ "Truly a new beginning", this "inspiring" fourth effort is "something of a comeback" for a "superb" singer-songwriter "who might have been destined to one-hit-wonderdom" but instead reached out and "connected with people", especially with her "glorious, bluesy" hit *Give Me One Reason*"; she "holds nothing back, offering her emotions freely", making this "feel-good record with positive vibrations" a "transporting, calming" experience.

Tracy Chapman, 25 27 24 23
Tracy Chapman G #1
1988, Elektra; "Fast Car"; www.tracychapman.com
■ "A sensitive poet" whose "compelling" "lyrics are brought to life" with "raw emotion" in a "hauntingly beautiful voice" that "quivers and swoops with urgency", this "supreme talent's" "almost unbearably good" Grammy-winning debut "gave America a new view of urban life"; in the heat of the Reagan-Bush years, the "soulful" guitarist helped "bring the singer-songwriter genre back from the dead", with "earthy songs" "rife with political commentary and moving balladry."

Ray Charles, *Anthology* 28 27 28 25
1989, Rhino; "Georgia on My Mind";
www.raycharles.com
■ "Brother Ray is called a genius for good reason" – the "class and talent" of the "godfather" of soul "shines through" on this genre-defying "must-have" of R&B, "blues, jazz and country tunes"; packed with "heaps of real goodies", including *Georgia on My Mind,* his "fine version of *America the Beautiful* and his deeply moving *Lucky Old Sin*", it's "suitable for rainy nights, loneliness and bittersweet" nostalgia; "once you hear it, you'll realize how important Mr. Charles has been."

Cheap Trick, *Live at Budokan* 24 21 23 20
1979, Epic; "I Want You To Want Me";
www.cheaptrick.com
■ "So good it made me want to move to Japan", this "guilty pleasure" was "the perfect album for all the dumb rockers who secretly wanted to be sensitive types – or vice-versa"; "you can't overlook how influential" this "snapshot of Cheap Trick's career" was "to a generation" of fans: it had "incredible chops, a sense of humor and songs you couldn't help but sing along to"; sure, "screams blanket every track", but Budokan's shrieking girls "enhance the energy", making this "pop treat" "trashy but fun."

The Chemical Brothers, *Dig Your Own Hole*

1997, Astralwerks; "Setting Sun"

■ "A monster combining rock, hip-hop, techno" and "punk" into one "exhilarating, continuous kaleidoscope of sound", this "trendsetter" "explodes from every angle", "escalating the intensity of a club or party" and sending "sweaty" "dancers" scurrying onto the floor; winding down with "Beth Orton's wonderful vocals" on *Where Do I Begin,* the "fast-paced" "standard" for "surreal" supersonics ends in "some mellow tracks to finish off a night of excess pleasure."

Chic, *Dance Dance Dance: The Best of Chic*

1991, Atlantic; "Good Times"

■ "Producing not only for themselves, but for Sister Sledge, Diana Ross", Madonna and others, "two of the finest pop songwriters of the '70s and '80s – Chic's "pioneer" "kings" Nile Rodgers and the late Bernard Edwards – "reigned" over the club floors, creating "innovative" "masterpieces" that "funk so well", they "move your body all night"; it's good times working "your dancin' shoes" and your brain to this "thinking man's disco" – in other words, "yeah, baby!"

Chicago, *Chicago IX: Greatest Hits* 🔢

1975, Columbia; "25 or 6 to 4"; www.chicagotheband.com

■ "Bring on the horns!" hoot hordes hot for this "brassy, jazz-influenced rock group" and their "crisp, clean" '70s sound; bursting with hits that "make you smile", like *Color My World* and *25 or 6 to 4,* this "fine compilation" has "all the flavor you need for hours of listening"; sure, it's "mushy love music" ("cheesy schmaltz to make-out by") but you can "also listen to it when your heart is broken" ("their ballads are so dead on").

The Chieftains, *Long Black Veil* 🔢

1995, RCA Victor; "The Long Black Veil"

■ "You don't have to be" from the Emerald Isle to "love the Chieftains", who unveil an "absolutely brilliant" blend of "modern-day rock", folk and "Irish music for the everyman" on this "super album" "festooned with high-profile guests", among them Sinéad O'Connor, the Rolling Stones, Ry Cooder, Van Morrison, Sting – "even Tom Jones fits in"; it's "like listening to a pint of Guinness" – "after a few" sips you'll be "hooked and enamored forever."

Chopin, *Nocturnes*

1965, RCA; "Op. 27, No. 1"

■ "Nobody, repeat nobody, plays the *Nocturnes* like [Arthur] Rubenstein"; his name is "synonymous with Chopin piano works", and indeed, "the king" of these "finest of musical vignettes" "displays his masterful artistry", "executing, with sheer brilliance and introspection, the most colorful interpretations"; though "the sound quality isn't all there" on this "old recording", even a classical "novice" can clearly hear that "two of the greatest Polish musicians" "were made for each other."

A Chorus Line | 26 | 26 | 25 | 24 |
(Original cast recording)
1975, RCA; "One"
☑ "God, I'm glad I own it, I'm glad I own it" sing surveyors spoofing the opener to this "singular sensation", the "electrifying" album to one of "Broadways' longest-running shows"; with "brilliant writing" by Ed Kleban and Marvin Hamlisch and the "energy", "humor and sadness" of a cast that "does it for love", musical "vignettes about chorus line wanna-bes" "pop" with "excitement", even if the disc "sounds like it was recorded in a tin can."

June Christy, *Something Cool* | 27 | 26 | 28 | 25 |
1954, Capitol; "Something Cool"
■ "The lady has a way with a sultry song", say "blissed out Christy fans" "enjoying their favorite cocktail" to this disc of "ultracool jazz vocals" by Stan Kenton's former crooner, "perfectly complemented by Pete Rugolo's" "lovely West Coast arrangements"; "as good today as it was 50 years ago", it's has been reissued on Blue Note with bonus tracks for a lush listen that's "like sipping a top martini."

Eric Clapton, *Slowhand* | 26 | 25 | 28 | 24 |
1977, RSO; "Wonderful Tonight"; www.claptononline.com
■ On this platinum-selling disc, the "guitar god" delivers "an eclectic group of songs" that go "from blues to country to straight-up rock", including "the soft *Lay Down Sally*", "the anthem for the time", J.J. Cale's *Cocaine* and "that wedding mainstay *Wonderful Tonight*"; this "classic" is "the pinnacle of laid-back '70s", a handful advise: "ignore the words and enjoy the mastery" of his instrument – "his music says so much more than what he is singing."

Eric Clapton, *Unplugged* 🄶 #1 | 26 | 25 | 28 | 25 |
1992, Reprise; "Layla"; www.claptononline.com
☑ This "understated surprise" blends "mellow Clapton" "with the tingle of a live performance", "demonstrating that he could reimagine his style" with "smooth" acoustic interpretations; "stripped to its best", the "granddaddy of the MTV Unplugged CDs" finds "this amazing talent" "expressing his love for rollicking blues and his lost son" with a "new spin on *Layla*" and the "touching" *Tears in Heaven*; still a few fret he "plays it safe as milk with these 'no-I-never-really-rocked' versions of old classics."

Stanley Clarke, *School Days* | 24 | 20 | 28 | 23 |
1976, Nemperor; "School Days"; www.stanleyclarke.com
☑ The "fast-fingered" "funkmeister" of "bass pyrotechnics" schools students of sound with this "bible for die-hard fans

of soloing chops and improvisation"; "standard for hip", "high-energy" jazz-meets-rock, it "shows the incredible power and beauty" of the big axe, but "the production is a bit dated", and "anyone not interested in fusion" might bomb it as "bombastic."

The Clash, *The Clash* $\boxed{27}$ $\boxed{26}$ $\boxed{24}$ $\boxed{22}$
1977, Epic; "White Riot"
■ "Loud, angry, intelligent and witty", this "frighteningly good" debut represented "a new statement of music at the time of its release, taking what the Ramones and the Sex Pistols started, but adding better lyrics and tunes"; "though relegated to the punk ghetto", this "mighty powerhouse of conviction", "street smarts" and "real social justice" "delves into a wide variety of influences such as rockabilly and reggae" – it's "raw, unbuttoned, slightly sloppy but relentlessly brilliant."

THE CLASH, *LONDON CALLING* $\boxed{29}$ $\boxed{27}$ $\boxed{26}$ $\boxed{25}$
1979, Epic; "London Calling"
■ A "revolutionary" double album that "proved to be the voice of a generation", this "sonic potpourri of rock, rockabilly, reggae and dub" "defines an era, yet remains relevant today"; the UK "godfathers of punk" "cast their jaundiced eye on politics, pop, consumer culture and, surprisingly, love" on this "staggering achievement"–cum– "encyclopedia for questioning authority" and "laid down the law – which side are you on?", this "landmark" "screamed", "making people want to dance, shout and incite riots."

Jimmy Cliff, *The Harder They Come* $\boxed{27}$ $\boxed{25}$ $\boxed{26}$ $\boxed{22}$
1973, Island; "The Harder They Come";
www.jimmycliff.com
■ "It's hard to imagine a finer multi-artist reggae collection" than this "deep soundtrack" to the "outstanding movie" starring Cliff and featuring his music, including the "pure bliss" of the title track; the album "tells the great story" of Jamaican rude boy culture and the struggle to "escape from poverty" with an "uplifting spirit" that's "soulful" and "real"; "still fresh after thirty years" despite its "primitive production", it "hooked" the mainstream on the genre.

Patsy Cline, $\boxed{28}$ $\boxed{25}$ $\boxed{25}$ $\boxed{22}$
Patsy Cline's Greatest Hits
1967, MCA; "Crazy"; www.patsycline.com
■ Conveying "power, majesty" and "emotion in every note", the "12 legendary tracks" on the "'Queen of Country's'" "fantastic compilation" feel like "heartache personified" – you can't help but "sense a lingering sadness" from "a brilliant talent whose life was tragically cut short" by a plane crash in 1963; the "first lady" of the genre who could fall to pieces and have sweet dreams fully "lived life" – no wonder faithful fans "crazy about Patsy" ask, "can you imagine C&W without her?"

Rosemary Clooney,   26 | 27 | 27 | 25
Rosemary Clooney Sings the Music of Cole Porter
1980, Concord Jazz; "My Heart Belongs to Daddy"
■ If you're throwing a clambake, "how can you not have a Rosemary Clooney album?" – "one of the best stylists warbling" "wonderful songs" from crafty Cole Porter sets the mood for a "great dinner party"; her "superb" "version of *My Heart Belongs to Daddy* beats out Mary Martin's by a long shot", proving that she's not only George's aunt – she's an "excellent musician" with a "remarkable" voice.

Close Encounters of the Third Kind   24 | 26 | 26 | 25
(Soundtrack) ☒
1978, Arista; "Main Title"
■ "It is near-impossible to listen to this music in the middle of a field on a starry night, no light around, without feeling a little excited and uneasy", so pop it in the stereo of your "mothership", head for the hills and take a spin to the far side; "spectacular" composer John Williams "captures the mystery of a possible contact with alien life forms" on the "avant-garde" soundtrack to Steven Spielberg's film; it's "soaring, majestic" and might just "contain the most recognizable five notes" in the galaxy.

Joe Cocker,   24 | 22 | 23 | 23
With a Little Help from My Friends
1969, A&M; "With a Little Help from My Friends";
www.cocker.com
■ "A unique talent with style and soul to spare" who "makes the mike his audience", this "timeless rocker does timeless work" on a bluesy "bombshell of raw originality", backed by guests including Steve Winwood and Jimmy Page; "part gravel, part velvet", "like a male Janis Joplin", "his voice is so distinctively engaging it makes your throat raspy just listening" to him cover Dylan and Beatles tunes.

Cocteau Twins,   25 | 24 | 26 | 26
Heaven or Las Vegas
1990, 4AD/Capitol; "Heaven or Las Vegas";
www.cocteautwins.com
■ Swooping down like an "ethereal voice from the nether-regions, come to share with us" all that is "sublime", "Elizabeth Fraser's haunting", "wondrous", "unearthly" vocals bring "pure bliss and tranquility", "spanning the entire range of what is possible"; simply "enchanting", this "user-friendly alternative record" "moves gracefully straight through, from start to finish", making it a "captivating" choice when you want to "relax, reflect or make-out."

Leonard Cohen, *I'm Your Man*   25 | 29 | 23 | 23
1988, Columbia; "Everybody Knows"; www.leonardcohen.com
■ After a hiatus, this "lyrical genius" with the "husky voice" "picks up where he left off", offering a "tasty sandwich of

self-loathing and love gone wrong"; "sexy, dark and thoughtful", it's more keyboard-centric, but still "full of soul, truth and insight"; he's as "eerie, elegant and funny" as ever, "and more prescient-sounding" with each listen – he remains "the perfect companion on a lonely night."

Leonard Cohen, | 26 | 28 | 21 | 21 |
The Songs of Leonard Cohen
1968, Columbia; "Suzanne"; www.leonardcohen.com
■ "When you're in the mood, there's no one better" than Canada's "über-cool" "troubled troubadour", whose "melancholy" debut is the source of many "classics", from *Suzanne* to *Sisters of Mercy*; the "lyrics are provocative", "the sparse instrumentation fits perfectly" and "his deep voice captivates" on songs that "stick to your bones long after the album is over."

Coldplay, *Parachutes* G #1 | 24 | 25 | 25 | 25 |
2000, Nettwerk; "Yellow"; www.coldplay.com
■ "It's been a while since a debut showed such promise for the future of British Sad Bastard Music", quip supporters of this "polished pop" effort revealing "shades of U2"; offering "cerebral lyrics", these "heartfelt tunes for a rainy day" feel like *Dark Side of the Moon* for the introspective Gen-Y crowd"; thanks to "beautiful piano, clear guitar chords and Chris Martin's emotive falsetto", it "has the power to relax like a tranquilizer (but is in no way 'lite.'")

Coldplay, | 26 | 26 | 27 | 27 |
A Rush of Blood to the Head
2002, Capitol; "Clocks"; www.coldplay.com
■ An "emotional tour de force" that "far exceeds follow-up expectations", this "magnificent" sophomore effort is considered "a watershed", a "swirling mix of atmospheric sounds, gorgeous melodies and meaningful songs" with a "soulful vibe" – everything "just gels"; its message of "hope for the new millennium" feels "cathartically perfect for dealing with breakups, death or utter sadness."

Lloyd Cole and the Commotions, | 24 | 28 | 22 | 21 |
Rattlesnakes
1984, Chrysalis; "Perfect Skin"; www.lloydcole.com
■ A "crafty tunesmith", ex-philosophy student Cole and his rocking crew "create the template for earnest irony" on this "world-weary" debut; from "the opening of *Perfect Skin*, a life-affirming moment", to "*Are You Ready to Be Heartbroken*, perhaps no finer breakup song", Scotland's "melancholy wit" is "smarter than most out there."

Ornette Coleman, | 28 | 26 | 28 | 24 |
Shape of Jazz to Come
1959, Atlantic; "Lonely Woman"
◪ "Improvisational impresario" and alto sax "vanguardist" Coleman "bursts onto the scene with an avant-garde

masterpiece filled with wild harmonics"; "engrossing and challenging", it's "difficult but worth listening to enough to get it", so "open your mind" to a "groundbreaking" free-jazz set that remains "stunning", even if it is "still frustrating [almost] 50 years after" it first "raised hackles."

Natalie Cole,   24 23 25 26
Unforgettable: With Love G #1
1991, Elektra; "Unforgettable"; www.nataliecole.com
■ Natalie drops her "typical R&B career" and "comes out from her father's shadow", "doing an excellent job singing dad's classics"; this "tribute" "brings the legacy of Nat King Cole to a new generation", but it's also the statement of "a daughter claiming her own" and "returning to romance with a voice" that "puts you in the mood for wine, roses and love"; though some find the "dead dad duet creepy", everyone agrees she was "born" for this music.

NAT KING COLE,   28 25 28 25
THE NAT KING COLE STORY
1961, Capitol; "Unforgettable"; www.nat-king-cole.org
■ With his "voice, phrasing and style" all "as smooth as velvet", "Mr. Mellow" "could cause a meltdown" on this "must-have" "overview" showcasing new versions of "many of his best-known songs"; on both his cuts performed "with the trio, as in *Route 66*", and "his more lush pop songs" like *Darling, Je Vous Aime Beaucoup,* "the real King" Cole is "one word: unforgettable."

Nat King Cole and George Shearing,   25 25 28 25
Nat King Cole Sings/George Shearing Plays
1961, Capitol; "Pick Yourself Up"; www.nat-king-cole.org
■ This "fantastic combination of the cool style of Shearing and the mellow tones of Nat King Cole" serves up "smooth jazz to fall in love with"; with a choir of strings as backup, the pianist caresses the keys as the singer waxes "lyrical" on hits like *Let There Be Love*; could it be anything other than "sweet listening" with this "delightful" duo?

Albert Collins, *Ice Pickin'*   25 21 28 22
1978, Alligator; "Cold, Cold Feeling"
■ "The Iceman shines, unleashing his piercing, shivering" "open-D tuning" on "classics like *Honey Hush* and *Cold, Cold Feeling*"; "with his Telecaster slung side shoulder", Collins played "funky, exuberant, caressing blues"; this cat "prowled even in the studio", "kicking ass" with a "razor-sharp guitar attack" on an "album that helped him move past the roadhouses and develop a widespread following."

Albert Collins, Johnny Copeland   26 23 29 24
and Robert Cray, *Showdown!* G
1985, Alligator; "T-Bone Shuffle"
■ "All legends in their own time", "these three great blues guitarists have one thing in mind – the music"; "they sound

loose and relaxed" with "an interesting blend of styles", and "everyone chips in the right amount, no one hogging the spotlight, a sign of mutual respect"; with the former two "now gone, Cray must carry on for future axe slingers."

Judy Collins, *Wildflowers*
26 | 25 | 26 | 23

1968, Elektra; "Both Sides Now"

■ A collection of "anthems for a new era", this "timeless masterpiece" of "soft, gentle" folk-pop, Collins' first to go gold, showcases her soprano "voice like liquid silver"; she's "one of music's treasures", with a knack for turning songs by then-unknowns Leonard Cohen and Joni Mitchell, including her version of *Both Sides Now,* into "unforgettable" "classics" that live in your "memory forever."

Phil Collins, *No Jacket Required* Ⓖ ▦
22 | 23 | 23 | 23

1985, Atlantic; "Sussudio"

■ No hair required for the man who "makes being bald cool"; from "atmospheric" ballads like *One More Night* to the "pleading" pop of *Take Me Home* to "dance" tunes like *Sussudio,* "there's a bit of everything" on this "versatile" Grammy winner; Collins climbed from behind Genesis' drum kit and "showed he had his own style", with "hooks" so "inescapable" and a voice so "recognizable" that this "standout" could double as "the soundtrack of the '80s."

John Coltrane, *Blue Train*
28 | 27 | 29 | 25

1957, Blue Note; "Blue Train"; www.johncoltrane.com

■ "Imagine great ensemble playing wedded to the passionate mastery" of one of "the best saxophonists to roam the planet", and you've got this "early Coltrane" from the "pre-quartet" period when he was "emerging from hard bop" but "not yet delving into free jazz"; "each solo is a compositional masterpiece", accompanied by a "beautiful mix of instruments", most notably Curtis Fuller's "emotionally compelling trombone"; hepcats "herald" "ya gotta have it."

JOHN COLTRANE, *A LOVE SUPREME*
29 | 28 | 29 | 26

1964, impulse!; "Acknowledgement"; www.johncoltrane.com

■ "Was this the work of a mere mortal?" – "renaissance artist" John Coltrane "reaches for the heavens and comes up with one of the most compelling works in music history"; one of the first "jazz theme albums" treats the subject of "spirituality" with "passion, quietude, celebration and resolution" on four "beautiful compositions" that take you on a "transcendental trip" that "will forever linger in your head" and "soul"; Trane's "genius" is so "close to divine", it's as if "God is speaking through his sax."

Shawn Colvin, *A Few Small Repairs*
24 | 25 | 24 | 23

1996, Columbia; "Sunny Came Home"; www.shawncolvin.com

▨ "The world finally caught on to Colvin" who "reached her creative and commercial peak" with this "breakthrough" that combined "her folk roots with pop appeal" and spawned the "smash hit" *Sunny Came Home*; she's a "storyteller with a voice to boot" and on this near-diary of divorce she "sounds more world-weary" than before; still, some fans feel a few small repairs may have been in order, moaning we "miss her more acoustic sound" of *Fat City* and *Cover Girl*.

The Commitments (Soundtrack) <u>24</u> <u>22</u> <u>24</u> <u>23</u>
1991, MCA; "Mustang Sally"

■ "Who knew a group of Irish men and women could do soul and R&B so well?"; "the energized climax of *Try a Little Tenderness,* the bellowing heartache of *Do Right Woman, Do Right Man* and everything in between tells the story" of these "entrancing and invigorating" "tribute" artists, "even if you haven't seen the movie"; a "fun romp", it's "responsible for the overuse of *Mustang Sally* by every bar band in America."

Common, Like Water for Chocolate <u>24</u> <u>26</u> <u>24</u> <u>24</u>
2000, MCA; "The Light"

■ A "progressive" rapper, this "new voice in hip-hop" "is not afraid to speak of the lovelier things in life but still makes heads nod"; with backup by D'Angelo, Roots drummer ?uestlove, trumpeter Roy Hargrove and an all-star cast of track performers, "Chi-town's one and only" spits about relationships and urban life over "jazzy, soulful" instrumentation on an album that's "crunchy and rootsy in tone" and "refreshing" in its subject matter.

Company <u>27</u> <u>29</u> <u>26</u> <u>26</u>
(Original cast recording) **G**
1998, Columbia; "The Ladies Who Lunch";
www.sondheim.com

■ Elaine "Stritch is at her foghorn best", "blasting herself into Broadway history with her searing *Ladies Who Lunch*" on this "groundbreaking" cast recording; the Tony-winning "concept musical about marriage" includes "dizzying electric locution" by Dean Jones and Charles Kimbrough on "some of Stephen Sondheim's most bitingly satirical songs"; a "pulsating score that captures the sound of 1970s New York City", this survivor remains "surprisingly undated" – "everybody, rise!"

Sam Cooke, The Man and his Music <u>28</u> <u>26</u> <u>26</u> <u>23</u>
1986, RCA; "A Change Is Gonna Come"

■ "From the gospel of *Touch the Hem of His Garment* to the swinging groove of *Twisting the Night Away* to the gut-busting *Bring It on Home to Me* and the transcendent *A Change Is Gonna Come*", this "essential" disc "captures everything" that made the "singer/writer/producer"/"soul pioneer" "so great: his charisma, his arrangements and, most of all, his voice", "sweet" and "smooth" as ever; "what a loss when he was killed."

Alice Cooper, *Greatest Hits* | 23 | 21 | 21 | 21 |
1974, Warner Bros.; "School's Out"; www.alicecoopershow.com
■ "Snakes alive", "you gotta love the trashiness" – "laugh now, but if you're old enough to remember, you used to" adore this "pop genius"; "here is a good helping from the king of macabre shock-rock, who, long before there was a Marilyn Manson" or Kiss, "went to the gallows" for his makeup and symbolism; these "angsty teenage anthems", including *School's Out* and *I'm Eighteen,* are delivered with "hooks, riffs and attitude."

Aaron Copland, *Appalachian Spring, Rodeo, Billy the Kid, Fanfare for the Common Man* 🄶 | 28 | 27 | 28 | 26 |
1966, Sony Classical; "Appalachian Spring"
■ "Nothing beats driving through the countryside with" Copland's *Appalachian Spring* "soaring" from your speakers, and once you park your buggy, it's "impossible not to get up and dance the hoedown to" Bernstein's "absolutely swaggering and dazzling" interpretation; as for *Billy the Kid,* "oh, to be out west" with "a spring in your step"; "thank you, Lenny" and Aaron, for this "watershed work" that made it conceivable "to sound American and to sound classical, and both superbly."

Chick Corea, *Return to Forever* | 26 | 25 | 27 | 25 |
1972, ECM; "Sometime Ago/La Fiesta"; chickcorea.com
■ Return to "brilliant pianist" Chick Corea as he "leads the fusion dream team of the '70s in an assault of electric and acoustic textures" on this disc of "excellent songs" that "inspired a generation of musicians"; with "great playing" by Chick and the band plus Flora Purim's "spooky" vocals, it's "smooth, enveloping, stimulating and relaxing", plus "it's obscure enough that you won't look like you're trying to fake the funk" when you "add it to your Case Logic."

Elvis Costello, *My Aim Is True* | 28 | 29 | 25 | 24 |
1977, Columbia; "Alison"; www.elviscostello.com
■ "Bespectacled and angry", the "original talent" "who made nerd glasses cool" "shook up the landscape of rock" by delivering "punk attitude in a radio-friendly package"; "paranoid, voyeuristic and loaded with insight beyond the young man's years", this "phenomenal debut leaps off the stereo and grabs your attention with sex-obsessed cynicism and Dylanesque poignancy" – "you'll marvel at *Alison*", "while grooving to the bouncy" *Watching the Detectives,* "a new wave anthem."

ELVIS COSTELLO, *THIS YEAR'S MODEL* | 29 | 29 | 27 | 26 |
1978, Columbia; "Radio, Radio"; www.elviscostello.com
■ "The new wave Cole Porter's" "amazing follow-up to an amazing debut" features the Attractions, with their "high-energy rhythm section" and "the incomparable Steve Nieve on keyboards"; "this blistering indictment of everything

and everyone that had ever gotten in his way" includes such "brilliant songs dripping with vile" as *Radio, Radio*, the "hard-edged" *Pump It Up* and the "kinetic" *Lipstick Vogue*; P.S. if "you pogoed your butt off back in the day", "check out the Ryko reissue with extra" tunes.

COUNTING CROWS, | 25 | 25 | 23 | 24 |
AUGUST AND EVERYTHING AFTER

1994, DGC; "Mr. Jones"; www.countingcrows.com

■ This "extraordinary debut" showcases "storytelling in the vein of Springsteen", conveyed through the "wounded agony" of singer Adam Duritz's "nasally, whiny but likable" "unique voice"; "with great production" by T Bone Burnett and "flawless arrangements with breathing room", this "anthem for lonely singles" "blends passion, poetry and musical punch", with a "hint of Van Morrison" – "youthful longing has seldom been so beautifully expressed."

The Cramps, | 24 | 21 | 20 | 20 |
Songs the Lord Taught Us

1980, I.R.S.; "TV Set"

■ "Who else can do psycho-rockabilly-horror-surf-country like this? Nobody!" – this act is "in a special-ed class of their own", and their first full album of "sleazy fun", produced by Alex Chilton, is "one easy lesson on how to be cool"; "vocalist Lux Interior is fantastic and, though you may question either his or your sanity, has to be heard to be believed" – sure, it's "sick, but that's why you need it."

Robert Cray, *Strong Persuader* | 25 | 24 | 27 | 24 |

1986, Mercury; "Smoking Gun"; www.robertcray.com

■ "A great performance by a young cat right out of the gate", this Seattle native's debut mixes "cool urban blues", soul and "booming bass lines" while the "tight" Memphis Horns "support his distinctive guitar work"; the "unusually insightful writing", "memorable tunes" and "sexy music" show a "wit" and "irony" that's "true to the bone."

Crazy for You | 23 | 26 | 25 | 24 |
(Original cast recording)

1992, Angel Records; "Someone to Watch Over Me"

■ "*The Little Mermaid* soars on land" as the voice of Disney's Ariel, Jodi Benson, "plays the temptress and the fellas fall for her" in this "sweet, light" "throwback to an earlier carefree time"; "while the story is as corny as it gets", "glorious" George Gershwin watches over this "perky", "uplifting" "celebration" of his "classics woven into a fine musical", which is bound to have "Fred and Ginger fans" "smiling from ear to ear."

Cream, *Disraeli Gears* | 27 | 24 | 28 | 23 |
1967, Polydor; "Sunshine of Your Love"; www.claptononline.com

■ "Rock's first big power trio", featuring "Eric Clapton, young, rash and fresh" on guitar, Jack Bruce on bass and

Ginger Baker on drums, "defined 'supergroup' before the phrase was coined"; "taking the mantle from the Jimi Hendrix Experience", they "created walls of sound that slammed your eardrums and tugged at your emotions", exuding "psychedelia in all its excessive glory"; hey, "let's get naked and smoke" and "crank up the stereo!"

Creedence Clearwater Revival, *Chronicle*   27 | 26 | 26 | 23
1976, Fantasy; "Bad Moon Rising";
www.creedence-revisited.com
■ "Certainly the best Bay Area group" with a "raised-in-the-swamps"-of-"Louisiana sound", CCR features the "awesome" vocals of John Fogerty, who "seemed to have an endless supply of three-minute songs that captured the ears and imagination of everyone who had a radio"; this "excellent" collection of hits represents "pure Americana, up there with baseball and apple pie" — "so go for it, relive the memories."

Jim Croce, *I Got a Name*   26 | 27 | 25 | 23
1973, ABC; "I Got a Name"; www.jimcroce.com
■ "A master of easy folk" "with a hook", this "stellar storyteller", whose "life was cut short" by a plane crash "at the height of his rising career", sure had a name — it was "a major part of the soundtrack to the '70s"; even today "his understanding of the fragility of the human heart" leaves a "tear in your beer" – this "superlative" posthumous release, featuring the "gorgeous ballad" *I'll Have to Say I Love You in a Song* "speaks volumes" about "how precious time can be."

Bing Crosby, *A Merry Christmas*   27 | 25 | 26 | 23
with Bing Crosby and The Andrews Sisters 🔢
1949, Decca; "White Christmas"
■ "Would there still be the holiday if Bing hadn't made records?" – this "bona fide classic" amid many such Crosby discs is so "smooth, it reminds you of home" as the crooner, accompanied by the "icing on the cake, The Andrews Sisters", leaves visions of sugar plums dancing in your head; the "eclectic mix" of seasonal tunes, including "Hawaiian music and church hymns", is really all about the title – "why anybody else bothers to record *White Christmas* is beyond" comprehension.

Crosby, Stills & Nash,   28 | 27 | 27 | 25
Crosby, Stills & Nash
1969, Atlantic; "Suite: Judy Blue Eyes";
www.crosbystillsnash.com
■ "A '60s signpost" offering "harmonies with a message" from former members of the Byrds, Buffalo Springfield and the Hollies, this "impeccable debut" featuring the "epic *Suite: Judy Blue Eyes*" and "classic *Wooden Ships*" "took rock to a new place"; it introduced a "sweet blend of

voices and instruments" to a "loud guitar"-oriented audience "and powerful musicianship to folk" listeners, bestowing "seminal peace in its purest form."

Crosby, Stills, Nash & Young, Déjà Vu ⚊1️⃣   27 | 27 | 27 | 25
1970, Atlantic; "Carry On"; www.csny.net

■ Stephen Stills' ex-Springfield bandmate Neil Young joined the "supergroup" in time for Woodstock and their second "superb" album, adding his unique tenor, songs of "depth and passion" and "fluid guitar work" to the mix; the result: a "soul snatcher" that "transformed their sound from folk to rock" and became "part of the collective unconscious"; unfortunately, "four guys this talented just can't fit their egos on one bus for very long" – "they perfected it here and then blew up."

Crosby, Stills, Nash & Young, Four Way Street ⚊1️⃣   26 | 27 | 27 | 23
1971, Atlantic; "Ohio"; www.csny.net

■ "I only wish this had been a six-album set" instead of a double declare admirers of this "landmark" "time capsule" that captures the "excellent" quartet in a live setting; "vital and unpredictable", it "sums up the late '60s/early '70s" with "political, anthemlike, multi-harmonized home-hitting songs" like *Ohio* (it's "eerie hearing it after Kent State") and *Southern Man*; the "legendary" supergroup's "synergy defies description."

The Crow (Soundtrack) ⚊1️⃣   24 | 21 | 23 | 24
1994, Atlantic; "It Can't Rain All the Time"

■ "Goths" "love the feeling this music gives you", i.e. "gloomy" and "intense"; "as heavy a soundtrack as ever", this "excellent alt-rock sampler" featuring Jane Siberry's sad and sultry *It Can't Rain All the Time,* plus "exclusive tracks by leading" "metal bands" and "hard rockers", including The Cure, Nine Inch Nails and Stone Temple Pilots, is "rough, loud" and "very fitting for such a dark movie"; with an industrial squeak, it "opened the door for later compilations such as *The Matrix.*"

Sheryl Crow, Tuesday Night Music Club   22 | 23 | 22 | 22
1993, A&M/Universal; "Leaving Las Vegas";
www.sherylcrow.com

■ "Down-to-earth", "easy folk rock" with "non-sugar-pop lyrics", this "insightful account of self doubt gone good" was "a surprising first effort that came out of nowhere" and "justifiably brought Crow into prominence", earning her an armful of Grammys; "assisted by David Baerwald's songwriting", this "great storyteller" delivers "danceable" tunes that are "soulful yet commercially rhythmic", prompting supporters to proclaim "all I wanna do is listen."

Crowded House, *Crowded House* 26 | 26 | 25 | 24
1986, Capitol; "Don't Dream It's Over"
■ "Exhibit A on how to do pop music" was "sprung on an unsuspecting public" by "frontman Neil Finn who proved to be a most sensitive songwriter", as well as a "gorgeous vocalist", on this "brilliantly assembled" "debut from the Split Enz splinter group"; "complex lyrics" "counterpoint" "melodic" keyboards with "clever" "twists and drops" to "capture something pure" on this "marvelous" disc – "Beatlesque is a valid description."

The Crystal Method, *Vegas* 24 | 19 | 22 | 25
1997, Outpost; "Busy Child"; www.thecrystalmethod.com
■ "If AC/DC were born 20 years later" ... "the Led Zeppelin riffs of the electronic age" ... "the '90s equivalent of The Monkees" – name-drop all ya want, the point is "America's answer to The Chemical Brothers" serves up the "butt-shakin' party tracks" to keep you a busy child; "techno that makes anti-techno folks take notice", the "bombastic" debut struck the jackpot and went gold for an "aural sensation" that "fits stylistically with Bruckheimer movies" and "car commercials" alike.

The Cure, *Boys Don't Cry* 25 | 25 | 23 | 22
1980, Elektra/Asylum; "Boys Don't Cry"; www.thecure.com
■ A "stellar" "compilation of singles and selected tracks from the band's UK debut, *Three Imaginary Boys*", this "witty and edgy" release, full of "clever" "lyrics that made you want to have your heart broken", introduced "seminal mope rock" stateside; Robert Smith's "poetic genius" yielded "an enlightening", "poignant goth pop" "album to listen to while pining away for misspent youth" – "who didn't go through this phase?"

Cypress Hill, *Cypress Hill* 23 | 22 | 21 | 23
1991, Ruffhouse; "How I Could Just Kill a Man";
www.cypressonline.com
■ "Stoners" "choked" with "shock" when this trio's "excellent debut" "burst on the scene seemingly out of nowhere"; "innovative production, lingo, flows and attitude" permeate a "hit parade of weed-smoking anthems" underscored by DJ Muggs' "vicious beats", rapper B-Real's nasal, "comic" "sing-song" and Sen-Dog's "well-placed", grimy rhymes; "hardcore gangsta", trunk-rattling tracks like *How I Could Just Kill a Man* "put Hispanic rap on the map."

D

Daft Punk, *Discovery* 24 | 21 | 23 | 26
2001, Virgin; "One More Time"
■ "Do ya hear a party comin' on?"; "harder, better, faster and stronger" with "disco attitude and pumped up chops",

the "magnifique" sophomore disc shows how D'Punk's "music has grown"; proving they're "more than jack-beat distributors", the "Europop techno" duo "deliver a heaping dose of quality dance-pop songs" with an "intricate Philip Glass–esque circular rhythm" to "make you shake your rump" and get "psyched up for a good night at the club."

Daft Punk, *Homework*   23 | 20 | 22 | 26
1997, Virgin; "Around the World"
■ "Play that funky music, French boys" – a "house party is at your disposal" with this "utterly original" debut from the "leaders of the Franco-house revolution"; "recorded entirely in their bedroom" and subsequently "used to pitch everything from bras to cell phones", the "instant classic is minimalist but robust", with "quirky beats colored by '70s pimp-disco" and "hammering hooks deep as vats of taffy" to get you to do your homework, which entails "bouncing on your own bed" moving that "booty."

Damn Yankees   24 | 24 | 24 | 24
(Original cast recording)
1955, RCA Victor; "Whatever Lola Wants";
www.damnyankees.com
◨ The "utterly perfect" Gwen Vernon hits 'em outa the park in this "damn good" "true-to-life" update of the *Faust* "story that is never dated"; whether you "despise the Yankees" or love 'em, "you've got to have heart" for this "'50s favorite" that brought "baseball to Broadway"; if you've got a turntable, try to score it on wax – "the new CD remaster has no bass", so it's "like listening to a radio."

D'Angelo, *Brown Sugar*   26 | 25 | 26 | 26
1995, EMI; "Brown Sugar";
www.okayplayer.com/dangelo/interface
■ This "wonderful singer and songwriter" "is probably responsible for a lot of the babies born the year" his "spectacular" debut descended; drawing comparisons to "Prince", "Marvin Gaye" and "Al Green", the "sensual" "neosoul"/R&B "superstar" lathers on "laid-back", "get-down" grooves like an update of Smokey Robinson's *Cruisin'* with his "high-pitched" croon and "funky", "excellent musicianship" – it's so "shmoooth-uh", it's "all about licking your lips and his."

D'Angelo, *Voodoo* ⓖ▮1▮   24 | 23 | 26 | 26
2000, Virgin; "Untitled (How Does It Feel)";
www.okayplayer.com/dangelo/interface.htm
■ "Light the candles and break out the massage oil" 'cause when R&B's "sexiest man" does his voodoo, "anyone gets in the mood"; but he's not just about "lovemaking": his long-awaited follow-up is a "hybrid of black music" "held together by a creamy falsetto" that "traces back the roots and boils them in a stew of hip-hop sensibilities" stirred by "talented musicians" ranging from jazzman Charlie Hunter

to Roots drummer ?uestlove; D'Angelo digs "a deep groove and pocket on this disc."

Charlie Daniels Band, *Fire on the Mountain*

24 | 24 | 27 | 23

1974, Kama Sutra; "Long Haired Country Boy";
www.charliedaniels.com
■ "Southern rock at its best" cheer longhaired country boys and girls of this "snappy old favorite", which crosses the Mason-Dixon line to R&R and features none other than The Allman Brothers' Dickey Betts on guitar; though his biggest hit *The Devil Went Down to Georgia* was still four years down the road, this was "the record that made" the bearded fiddler "a star."

Terence Trent D'Arby, *Introducing the Hardline According to Terence Trent D'Arby* 🄶 🎵

22 | 22 | 22 | 22

1987, Columbia; "Wishing Well";
www.sanandapromotion.com
☑ "Oh the promise" this "new R&B force held" when his "groundbreaking" debut came out – "an absolutely stunning album", it "skirted from pop (*Wishing Well*) to balladry (*Sign Your Name*) to classic soul" (Smokey Robinson's *Who's Loving You*); "smooth with an edge", this "high flier's" "soaring voice" "exudes a sexual energy that's irresistible", even if he "seemed to get derailed by ego"; "love him or hate him", there's no denying he "made his mark" with this "moment of genius."

Miles Davis, *Bitches Brew* 🄶

26 | 24 | 28 | 25

1970, Columbia; "Spanish Key"; www.milesdavis.com
☑ They don't call him Miles for nothing – "the iconoclast" takes "a gargantuan leap forward" on "a milestone in the transformation of jazz"; "everyone who was anyone in what was to become fusion is on this classic", including Chick Corea on keys and Wayne Shorter on sax; with "tasty snippets from great players thrown against a backdrop of noise", an album that "angered as many critics as it influenced musicians" is so "funky and hypnotic", it "casts a voodoo spell" that "gets you groovin' at every listen."

MILES DAVIS, *KIND OF BLUE*

30 | 28 | 30 | 27

1959, Columbia; "So What"; www.milesdavis.com
■ "If you could play one disc for visitors from outer space, this would be it" rave earthlings; this *Survey*'s Top album for Overall Excellence and Musicianship is the "Mount Olympus" of jazz, "featuring brilliant improvisation and tight musicianship" by Miles, "John Coltrane, Bill Evans and a host of other greats" with a "sultry" "melodic theme" that "sounds like wet streets and flashing neon"; "add some wine and a good book", "cigarettes and scotch", "a beautiful woman and an ice-cold martini" – add whatever – "and you've got the perfect evening."

Miles Davis, *Miles Ahead*   27 | 27 | 29 | 25
1957, Columbia/Legacy; "The Duke"; www.milesdavis.com
◪ "Every note of every tune" on "one of the best jazz
albums of the late '50s" is "so cool, it sounds like it could
have been recorded yesterday"; this "wonderful marriage
of Gil Evans' creative orchestrations" for big-band backup
of "Miles' soulful" solos revived the "collaboration" that
would birth *Porgy and Bess* and *Sketches of Spain*; still,
aficionados assert "if you're going to skip an Evans/Davis"
disc, this "lesser album" is "the one" to miss.

Miles Davis with Gil Evans,   28 | 29 | 29 | 27
Porgy and Bess
1958, Columbia/Legacy; "Summertime"; www.milesdavis.com
■ "Opera never sounded so good" say hipsters more
atuned to smoky clubs than Met box seats; "Gil Evans is
perhaps the master at orchestrated jazz arrangements
from the cool school", "Davis displays exceptional talent
by redefining" the score and there's "perfect synchronicity"
between them on this "essential" album that's so "brilliant",
"it gives you butterflies"; "what could be bad?" ask
"blissed"-out listeners – "Gershwin grooves!"

Miles Davis with Gil Evans,   28 | 28 | 29 | 27
Sketches of Spain ▣
1959, Columbia/Legacy; "Concierto de Aranjuez";
www.milesdavis.com
■ How can an album "provoke such an emotional response
every time you hear it?" – how can it not, when you combine
"Miles at his peak" with "Gil Evans' instrumentation and
vision"?; the "two brilliant innovators" lead "one of the
most beautiful large jazz ensembles ever" in "revolutionized
conceptions" of "melancholy Spanish blues" that "sustain
a mood and a sound" "evocative of a far-off and mystical
land" where the "unending trumpet sweetness" flows.

Dead Kennedys,   25 | 25 | 20 | 18
Fresh Fruit for Rotting Vegetables
1980, Alternative Tentacles; "Holiday in Cambodia";
www.deadkennedys.com
■ "The fun-sized bites" of Jello Biafra's "venomous"
"social-political rants that get you to think for yourself"
crossed with "East Bay Ray's raw guitar that sounds like
someone surfing over garbage cans" make this "powerful
statement" "one of the best" "classic old-school" "punk
albums, bar none"; "too perfect in feeling and too impactful
to mention", this "trailblazer" gave "kids their first taste of
hardcore", "actually scaring people" with its "brilliance."

Blossom Dearie, *Blossom Dearie*   27 | 26 | 25 | 24
1956, Verve; "I Won't Dance"; www.angelfire.com/ny/
blossomdearie
■ "The queen of jazz cabaret" is as "endearing and
eccentric as her name"; giving us that "ooh-la-la" in a

"wee", "little girl voice" full of "vulnerability", she's "subtle but packs a punch", "a true song stylist" who may "not be for everyone" but at seventysomething is "still going" and "still great"; fans find her "better in person", but if you can't catch her live, these "Verve sessions are [so] fresh and charming", you'll probably "fall in love."

Deee-Lite, *World Clique*
24 | 20 | 22 | 25

1991, Elektra; "Groove Is in the Heart"

■ Travel "back in time to your fag-hag years" and "get goosebumps" bumping to this deee-liteful dance disc that "holds up 12 years later" from a clique that was "way ahead of their time" in "their own groovalicious" ways; the "funky", "fresh" beats took you on a "campy romp through the lives of the denizens of St. Mark's Place" as "Lady Miss Kier, with killer voice and style, helped propel" DJ Dmitry and Towa Tei "into history", "giving us a good look behind the turntables"; "their disappearance is the world's loss."

Deep Forest, *Deep Forest*
24 | 22 | 24 | 25

1993, 550 Music; "Deep Forest"

■ What "originated as a chill-out album after a good, sweaty rave" is "now a favorite of the nesting Banana Republic couple", but it's still as "weird" and "wonderful" as ever, say "break-dancing techno pygmies"; "it's hard to imagine" how the voices of those diminutive "native Africans" "could be integrated seamlessly with Western-style ambient dubbing", but here it is, "done so well" to create an "incredible" "atmosphere of meditative adventure" for New Age armchair travelers.

Deep Purple, *Machine Head*
24 | 21 | 25 | 22

1972, Warner Bros.; "Smoke on the Water";
www.deep-purple.com

■ "How can you listen to *Smoke on the Water* and not play air guitar?" – that "menacing opening riff" is perhaps the "most recognized in rock history"; thanks to the "clash of five creative geniuses", this "high-water mark of heavy-osity" showed "sparkling musicianship" with Ian Gillian's "soaring vocals" and Ritchie Blackmore's "searing guitar work" evident on "concert staples *Lazy* and *Space Trucking*" and the "epic girl anthem *Highway Star* that's worth the price of admission alone."

Def Leppard, *Hysteria* ⊞1
24 | 21 | 24 | 25

1987, Mercury; "Pour Some Sugar on Me";
www.defleppard.com

■ When you "want to lose control" and "play loud" heavy metal "all night long", this "adrenaline-charged, full-on" "cock rock" is the way to go; boasting a string of "sexy", "unavoidably addictive" hits, it's the "perfect high school soft head-banger album" – "every inch" of this "polished *Pyromania* follow-up" ("what a comeback after drummer Rick Allen lost one arm") has "production value bleeding from its pores"; it's "dripping in clichés, but it works and don't say it doesn't."

Def Leppard, *Pyromania*   25 | 21 | 24 | 25
1983, Mercury; "Photograph"; www.defleppard.com
■ "The boys from Sheffield" "blew the door open" with this "classic" that "kicked the U.S. metal scene in the ass"; "harmonies! big rock choruses! Steve Clark's wailing guitar solos!" – this "decade-defining" disc "represented" what "Mutt Lange's excellent production" could do, helping to make DL "a household name"; "Gunter glieben glauten globen, indeed!" – any "child of the '80s" can tell you where these "four famous nonsensical words" come from.

De La Soul,   26 | 27 | 24 | 25
3 Feet High and Rising 🔢1
1989, Tommy Boy; "Me, Myself and I"
■ "The cleverest trio in hip-hop" "laid the groundwork for today's non-bling rappers" with a debut that combines "insightful", "happy-go-lucky" lyrics and "genius" producer Prince Paul's "eclectic sampling"; the "bright, flowery" cover art is a clue-in to "fun" tunes like *Me, Myself and I* that helped "change the whole dynamic of the genre" with their "mixture of funk, schoolhouse rock, folk and comedy" on a "revolutionary" disc that "made it cool to be a hippie."

Iris DeMent, *My Life*   27 | 28 | 25 | 25
1994, Warner Bros.; "My Life"; www.irisdement.com
■ Thanks to her "consummate writing", "unforgettable" sound and "remarkable" ability "to give voice to teardrops", "Iris is the real deal: "an artist with a capital A"; "unique and haunting", this "talented young lady's" "remarkable" second album, dedicated to her late father, communicates "country the way it was meant to sound"; "her music isn't easy", fawn fans, "and we thank her for that."

John Denver, *Greatest Hits* 🔢1   25 | 26 | 24 | 23
1974, RCA Victor; "Take Me Home, Country Roads"; www.johndenver.com
■ "The album everyone loves from the artist everyone mocked" – no matter "how cool you think you are", "who can resist belting out" the late singer-songwriter's hits like "*Take Me Home, Country Roads* along with the jukebox?"; "reassuringly familiar" ("weaned on Denver, what can I say?"), this "warm, fuzzy" collection of "corny, but uplifting" country-folk tunes leaves many "high on nostalgia" – "I don't love the mountains, but his tunes make me think I do!"

Depeche Mode,   26 | 25 | 25 | 26
Music for the Masses
1987, Sire/WB; "Never Let Me Down Again"; www.depechemode.com
■ "Aptly titled", this "peak" disc from "one of the most influential bands of the '80s" "set the bar" for "teen angst

everywhere", and the "masses liked it"; "one-half dark and tortured and one-half lively dance staple", its "beautiful lyrics, sublime melodies" and "electronic soundscapes become lush tracks that wrap the listener in seductive languor"; take it for a spin and remember the days of "Converses, cut-offs and [close]-shaved purple hair" when D'Mode was "walking on hallowed ground."

Depeche Mode, *Violator* 　　　26 | 25 | 25 | 27
1990, Sire/WB; "Enjoy the Silence"; www.depechemode.com
■ Practically "defining melodramatica", "like a corpse with a passionate pulse", like "philosophy with a beat and a heart", this "revolutionary, dark", "sensual" album "violates all the senses" with "lush, organic, beautiful" beats, David Gahan's "haunting", "deep croons" and Martin Gore's "angelic sighs"; "every song is an earworm" on a "synth-delicious" disc that "ruled both the dance floor and the bedroom"; worshipers swear, it's "the only place I ever found Jesus."

Derek & the Dominos, 　　　28 | 27 | 29 | 26
Layla and Other Assorted Love Songs
1970, RSO; "Layla"; www.claptononline.com
■ "Clapton leads a crackerjack group, with standout slide guitarist Duane Allman", creating "one of the greatest collaborations ever recorded", "the two musicians prodding each other to mystical heights"; "pain drips from the grooves of this seminal record" that has "something for everyone – hard-driving rockers, stormy blues, wailing solos", including "*Layla*, as it was meant to be sung", "with the most stunning opening riff" "written by Eric for his secret love Patti Boyd, then married to his best pal George Harrison."

Devo, *Q: Are We Not Men?* 　　　23 | 22 | 20 | 22
A: We Are Devo!
1978, Warner Bros.; "Mongoloid"; www.mutato.com
■ Q: "Who else could take *Satisfaction* and turn it into a new wave hit?" A: no one but these "progenitors of geek-rock who married synth and satire", "wrote scathing lyrics, delivered in earnest" and "spit" their Brian Eno–produced "sound in the face of an industry then defined by disco"; "if the Gang of Four infused their music with Marxism, then Devo doused theirs with the theory of de-evolution" – yeah, they were "rebels", so "don't let their plastic suits and flowerpot hats fool you."

Neil Diamond, *The Jazz Singer* 　　　24 | 23 | 24 | 23
(Soundtrack)
1980, Capitol; "America"; www.neildiamond.com
■ "That husky voice singing 'just pour me a drink, and I'll tell you some lies' gets me every time", "admit" "guilty pleasure" seekers; *Love on the Rocks* is just one of the "tremendous songs" off this "good soundtrack" of a "lame" remake starring the "hippie-turned-cheeseball"; Diamond

practices "the fine art of schmaltz at its best", writing and performing in "so many styles, you can slow dance, Charleston or folk dance without turning over the record."

Bo Diddley, *The Chess Box*   28 | 25 | 27 | 23
1990, Chess/MCA; "Bo Diddley"

■ "He will always be the greatest self-name dropper", but "it ain't bragging if you can do it, and all Bo did was practically invent R&R", as he reveals with "humor" on this double disc "must-have"; the "great" "progenitor" "created his own beat", which "became the bedrock" of the genre – no wonder "flamboyant" classics like *I'm a Man* and *Who Do You Love* are "fun for young and old."

Dido, *No Angel*   24 | 23 | 23 | 23
1999, Arista; "Thank You"; www.didotv.com

■ "Slap some electronic beats on a pretty girl with a guitar" and an "ethereal voice", and "you've got a great album"; still, "stores couldn't give it away" until "a sample of *Thank You* on Eminem's *Stan* sent sales through the roof", and even "metal fans" fell for Dido's "New Age"–meets–"soft rock", "heartfelt first effort"; let this "moody" "chick" music "float in the air" "for a romantic date at home" – just don't "fall asleep" on your sweetie 'cause the songs are so "very soothing."

Ani DiFranco, *Living in Clip*   27 | 28 | 26 | 24
1997, Righteous Babe; "Both Hands"; www.righteousbabe.com

■ "The original 'Righteous Babe'" ("one of the saviors of folk music") creates "poignant" "poetry with gutteral speak" on this "potent" double album that "shows the power of her live performances" ("hear me roar, strum and jam"); it isn't just about "the great mix of new and old songs", it's about the "visceral feelings" – Ani "offers slices of life", delivering "issues of importance" to "adolescents and 50-year-olds alike" with "more energy than a bullet train."

Digable Planets,   24 | 24 | 24 | 24
Reachin' (A New Refutation of Time and Space)
1993, Pendulum/EMI; "Rebirth of Slick (Cool Like Dat)"

■ On a disc that's "silkier than Frederick's of Hollywood panties", these "jazz-hop heads" mix live instrumentation, "ultrahip", "mellow" grooves and "bohemian rhymes" that "touch on issues such as racism and women's rights"; the bass line to *Rebirth of Slick (Cool Like Dat)* is "funky as anything", and "*Femme Fatale* is one of the strongest political hip-hop moments ever"; it's just "too bad" these "phat" Planets "flamed out early."

Sasha & John Digweed,   26 | 21 | 26 | 26
Northern Exposure 2: East Coast Edition
1997, Ministry of Sound/Ultra; "Symphony "

■ "Bring on the glowsticks", Mr. Toad, 'cause this album is a "wild ride from start to finish"; serving up some of the "funkiest shit you're ever gonna hear", the "masters of the art" of "trippy", "late-night", "Eurodance" remixes take you on a "hypnotic and energizing" journey that's "worth going" on "often", "if only for their 12-minute version of Hybrid's *Symphony*"; "long live Sasha and Digweed!" – "they get it", and then they give it back "so nicely."

Dinosaur Jr,   24 | 22 | 25 | 17
You're Living All Over Me
1987, SST; "Little Fury Things"
■ "An ear-blasting", "indie classic" from the "frontrunners of grunge", this "high point of Dinosaur Jr's output, released before the exit of Lou Barlow" and including background vocals from Sonic Youth's Lee Ranaldo, "blows the genre wide open"; it "sounds great at excessive volume" – "virtuoso" J. Mascis throws down "slabs of guitar" while "remaining true to building melodies" and the "fuzzy", "murky production suits the music perfectly."

Celine Dion, *Let's Talk About Love* #1   22 | 21 | 23 | 23
1997, 550 Music; "Let's Talk About Love";
www.celinedion.com
☑ "How do you out-sing Streisand?" – take a lesson from "a real diva", who busts the charts with her 10th disc, as "slick" and "dramatic as usual", with "so many big moments", from duets with Babs and The Bee Gees to the "in-the-mood" title track to the "famed *Titanic*" "love song" that "brings you back to the ship"; not everyone has a "taste" for "strong vocals and beautiful lyrics" as "schmaltz"- busters boo "do us a favor and shut up."

Dire Straits, *Brothers in Arms* G #1   25 | 24 | 27 | 25
1985, Warner Bros.; "Brothers in Arms"
■ "Sonically brilliant", this "must-have record for serious audiophiles" "perfectly evokes its period" ("great for flashbacks to *Miami Vice*") with a "terrific mix of commercial pop" (the song *Money for Nothing* "made us all want our MTV") and "musical exploration crafted" in an "atmosphere of power and mystery" by "supremely talented guitarist" and "literary songwriter" Mark Knopfler; Dire diehards declare that "some of the best tracks are those that got little to no exposure."

Dirty Dancing (Soundtrack) #1   24 | 22 | 23 | 23
1987, RCA Victor; "(I've Had) the Time of My Life"
■ We know, we know – you've "had the time of your life listening to this" CD featuring that Bill Medley/Jennifer Warnes hit; "Swayze sings" on the "new cuts", which "mix with the oldies without clashing, and the whole thing does what any great soundtrack should do": it "reminds you of why you loved the movie"; "great dance music and kitsch" bring back "sweet memories" "of your free spirit, hot summers, good friends" and Jennifer Grey before the nose job.

Dixie Chicks, *Home* **#1**   24 | 23 | 25 | 24
2002, Open Wide; "Travelin' Soldier"; www.dixiechicks.com
■ A "great bluegrass sound" dominates this "back-to-basics acoustic album by the reigning queens of country"; though "they've scaled the ladder of success", this "talented" trio still sings "from the heart", "taking chances that bar bands wouldn't be brave enough" to attempt; you "gotta love *White Trash Wedding*" and their "incredible cover of Stevie Nicks' *Landslide*", plus the "tearjerker" "*Travelin' Soldier* should quiet anyone who calls the Chicks un-American."

Dixie Chicks,   25 | 25 | 26 | 24
Wide Open Spaces **G #1**
1998, Monument; "Wide Open Spaces"; www.dixiechicks.com
■ Coming "out of nowhere", the Chicks "earned their rocket trip to the top" with this "fresh, edgy", "energetic" major label debut that helped "revolutionize country music"; "if you like a little bit of sweetness, spunk and tenderness in one package", you'll find it on this "instant classic", along with "traditional instruments"; "the girls sashay their way" through songs that "speak to the challenges of life", bolstered by "honest lyrics anyone can relate to."

DJ Shadow, *Endtroducing . . .*   27 | 22 | 27 | 28
1996, Mo' Wax; "Midnight in a Perfect World";
www.djshadow.com
■ "As clear a voice as there may ever be from the turntablist revolution", Shadow brings "trip-hop" and "sampling" "to new heights"; "like something a linguistics professor would dream up to hold a mirror to our naked souls", the "dark", at times "apocalyptic" disc displays the DJ "collaging" "Bach, Ted Nugent and the theme to *Crocodile Dundee*" into "mesmerizing" "metaphors"; "a production wet dream", this "definitive instrumentalist collection" "gives hip-hop a vital shot in the arm."

Eric Dolphy, *Out to Lunch!*   27 | 25 | 28 | 26
1963, Blue Note; "Hat and Beard"
◪ "One can only imagine the title" of this LP is cribbed from "commentary overheard in one of his audiences" say "novice jazz ears challenged" by the "atonal" "intensity and originality" of Dolphy's "conversational approach"; this disc might "not be the kind of lunch that is a crowd-pleaser", but with "Freddie Hubbard's buttery tone balancing Eric's flights of fancy", it does "manage to evoke aural landscapes" for a satisfying "start to enjoying" the sound dished out by this "brilliant avant-garde musician."

Fats Domino, *My Blue Heaven:*   26 | 23 | 25 | 23
The Best of Fats Domino
1990, EMI; "Blueberry Hill"
■ "One of those CDs you gotta have", this collection, crammed with Fats' '50s and '60s Imperial hits, including

the title track, *Blueberry Hill* and *Ain't That a Shame,* "truly the best from a great artist that spanned genres" and eras, "holds up pretty well"; a New Orleans R&B boogie-woogie piano player at the forefront of "rollicking American roots music", he "belongs in the pantheon with Chuck Berry and Little Richard."

Donovan, *Donovan's Greatest Hits* 22 24 21 21
1969, Epic; "Mellow Yellow"
■ "He may have been criticized at the time for being a Dylan clone, but this" "hippest of the high hippies" "was original in his own way", fashioning "pleasant folky headtrip diversions" "worth recalling, from *Atlantis* to *Jennifer Juniper*"; this "surreal pop" feels like a "moment frozen in time" – "flash your peace sign" and soak up the "sweet '60s" sensation of "sunshine and poetry" from the "too-cute tunesmith" who "made girls want to wear flowy, innocent dresses and smoke banana peels."

Doobie Brothers, 24 22 24 22
Best of the Doobies
1976, Warner Bros.; "Black Water"; www.doobiebros.com
■ "The Doobies are more than just alright with me" quip fans, and while they had "many lineup changes over the years", this "must-have" "captures the original essence of their '70s rock" with tunes like the "great sing-along *Black Water*" and "fabulous *Long Train Running*"; this "catchy, fun" "toe-tappin' stuff" "appealed to bikers, guitar junkies and Middle America" and came on "like a shot of adrenaline, reliable and dependable to jack you up."

The Doors, *The Doors* 27 26 25 24
1967, Elektra; "Light My Fire"; www.thedoors.com
■ "An astonishing debut" "by some UCLA students" and friends who "take a trip to the other side and show us mere mortals how horrifying and beautiful it can be"; "John Densmore is an underrated genius on skins, Ray Manzarek the backbone on keyboards and Robby Krieger a revelation on guitar", while "Jim's throaty growl makes you want to rip off your clothes and dance on a table!" ("whoosh, this lit my fire!"); "today's bad boys don't have a clue – Morrison "did it all before, when it was truly shocking."

The Doors, *L.A. Woman* 25 26 24 23
1971, Elektra; "L.A. Woman"; www.thedoors.com
■ "Summing up the City of Angels as well as Didion, Chandler or Nathaniel West ever did", the title track "screams out the pain of the times slathered with the excitement of LA" – "there's nothing better for zooming up the 405 freeway"; "bluesy and manic", "the arrangements and singing fit together like some puzzle never completed in previous" releases while revealing "the Lizard King as a lyrical god"; released after "Jimbo's flameout" in Paris, "the final chapter" "leaves us wanting more."

Nick Drake, *Bryter Later*　　28 | 28 | 25 | 23
1970, Hannibal; "Northern Sky"

■ "A sad guy's happiest album", this second "more up-tempo" effort from the late British singer-songwriter–cum–cult figure "gives lie to those who call Drake a miserablist"; a "lovely poetic work" of "pastoral, transcendent chamber-folk", this "influential disc" features members of Fairport Convention, including Richard Thompson, and brings together "a touch of jazz and a dash of pop" in "swirling, spellbinding", "lush settings" – it's "perfect to chill to."

Nick Drake, *Pink Moon*　　27 | 28 | 26 | 22
1972, Hannibal; "Pink Moon"

■ "Thanks to a VW commercial", "this lost classic" from a "lost soul" "was revived for later generations" – "long before quiet was the new loud, this bleak", "brooding" "record revealed just how achingly beautiful depression could be"; "a bold contrast" to previous efforts but "fitting for his final" album two years before his death in 1974, it captures "sparse arrangements" and his "peaceful" approach ("the sound of stars falling"), making it "the ultimate dark-night-of-the-soul" listen.

Dr. Dre, *The Chronic* ①　　28 | 27 | 26 | 28
1992, Death Row/Interscope; "Nuthin' But a 'G' Thang";
www.dre2001.com

■ "Bringing West Coast rap to the mainstream", this "milestone" "defines gangsta hip-hop"; fueled by George Clinton/Parliament-Funkadelic samples and the "rude, lewd, funky-as-hell" rhymes of a young Snoop Dogg, the album's "summer afternoon grooves" mark Dre's "preeminence" as producer while "making a strong case for the legalization of marijuana"; "an album to play at a house party or rollin' in your car", it's the "perfect fusion of life, fantasy and phenomenal beats" – "just don't let your kids listen."

Dreamgirls　　24 | 23 | 26 | 24
(Original cast recording) ⑥
1982, Geffen; "And I Am Telling You I'm Not Going"

☑ "The cast did not fake their way to the top of this" "sizzling Motown-Broadway fusion" loosely based on the Supremes: "Diana was never as good" as Sheryl Lee Ralph, and "Jennifer Holliday blows the roof off your speakers"; "sing it, my sisters" – too bad your "fabulous voices" are so "poorly preserved for history" on a "badly truncated recording"; try Nonesuch's 2000 "concert version" – the divas are different, but the CD "restores every sublime note" of "one of the finest shows ever written."

The Drifters, *1959-1965*　　27 | 26 | 25 | 24
All-Time Greatest Hits and More
1988, Atlantic; "Under the Boardwalk"

■ "R&B goes uptown but retains its soul" on a collection of "some of the best pop-soul ever made" by a gospel-influenced vocal group "backed by top studio musicians" on "tunes by some of the best songwriters of the day"; the "assemblage" went through "several iterations", helping to launch the solo careers of lead singers Clyde McPhatter and Ben E. King, but it's the sweet tenor voices of Johnny Moore and Rudy Lewis that anchor "vintage" hits like *Under the Boardwalk* and *Up on the Roof.*

Dr. Octagon,   25 | 24 | 24 | 28
Dr. Octagonecologyst
1996, Bulk; "Blue Flowers"
■ "Journey deep into Kool Keith's warped brain" where his "hysterical", "diabolical" alter ego, "a verbal surgeon and Beethoven enthusiast" "from Jupiter", lays down "beats so spooky, you feel like you're being wheeled on a gurney through a gruesome hospital"; "the Lon Chaney of hip-hop" gets a hand from producers Dan the Automator and Q-Bert on this "demented porno movie in musical form" – just "make sure you don't bob your head enough to warrant decapitation."

Dr. Zhivago (Soundtrack) **G** **#1**   27 | 25 | 26 | 25
1966, MGM; "Lara's Theme"
■ "Haunting and chilling to the bone", Maurice Jarre's "instrumental score captures the mood of this excellent film" adaptation of Boris Pasternak's novel so well that snow-bound czarist scholars say "every time I read the book, I hear the soundtrack in the background"; revel in "Russia by way of Hollywood" with "stirring melodies" of "epic romanticism" that "bring to life the beautiful scenery and Lara", as played by the lovely Julie Christie.

Duran Duran, *Duran Duran*   22 | 19 | 20 | 22
1981, Capitol; "Girls on Film"; www.duranduran.com
■ "Pure trendsetters, from their signature" "David Bowie–influenced" "synth-pop sound" to their "telegenic" image, these "pretty boy" "pioneers of the New Romantic movement" arrived at the "dawn of the video age" with "one of *the* must-have" albums of the '80s"; though often "more remembered for their racy *Girls on Film*" MTV staple than their "infectious tunes", this "blast from the past", boasting "poetic", "bawdy, lyrical themes", helped "define British new wave."

Duran Duran, *Rio*   22 | 20 | 20 | 23
1982, Capitol; "Rio"; www.duranduran.com
■ "Nothing says 1982 like this" "arty soundtrack to the sun-soaked" era packed with "stylish mood pieces" and "fun pop" tunes; "hip, fashionable and exciting", the "consummate MTV band" "made every girl want to skip puberty and go right to marriage with any of them"; it's a "guilty pleasure", but it's also "worth replacing the vinyl with a new CD" to conjure "wonderful memories for those of us who covered our walls with John Taylor posters."

BOB DYLAN, *BLONDE ON BLONDE*   29 | 29 | 25 | 25
1966, Columbia; "Visions of Johanna";
www.bobdylan.com
■ "The fog and amphetamine haze" of this double album
"masterpiece" feels like "a carnival ride through old, weird
America" with the "prophet's" "wild imagery" "floating
over a swirl of guitar and churning harmonica", backed by
Al Kooper and Band members Robbie Robertson, Garth
Hudson and Rick Danko; "by going electric, he changed
folk forever and set a new standard of poetry with a
backbeat" – "invective and tenderness have never come
together with such power."

BOB DYLAN,   29 | 30 | 26 | 26
BLOOD ON THE TRACKS 🔢1
1975, Columbia; "Tangled Up in Blue";
www.bobdylan.com
■ On "this phenomenal comeback of poetic beauty" after
"five years of nondescript releases", "America's greatest"
bard's "failing marriage inspired a flawless string of songs
that demonstrate his suffering in every line"; his "meditation
on lost love covers every feeling", going from his most
caustic (*Idiot Wind*), to lamentative (*Simple Twist of Fate*)
to romantic (*You're Gonna Make Me Lonesome*); voted this
Survey's No. 1 for Songwriting, it's "venom and heartbreak
perfected", and it's "quite amazing."

Bob Dylan, *Nashville Skyline*   26 | 27 | 25 | 25
1969, Columbia; "Lay Lady Lay"; www.bobdylan.com
■ "A complete change of pace" for the "crown prince of
protest songs", this "towering achievement" "put country
music in the broader limelight", "taking a sizable chunk of
the rock world along for the ride"; it was an "interesting
foray" – with a "chillingly great" "back-to-the-woods feel"
featuring "a laid-back Dylan, singing in a voice that's
barely recognizable" on "the sweet, gentle *Lay, Lady, Lay*"
and "a timeless duet with Johnny Cash on *Girl from
the North Country.*

E

The Eagles, *Their Greatest Hits*   26 | 26 | 25 | 25
1971-1975 🔢1
1976, Asylum; "Take It Easy"; www.eagles.yahoo.com
■ On "deservedly" one of the "best-selling discs of all
time", "every song is an ingrained part of popular culture";
"hey girls, have you ever cheated on your boyfriend? then
you know *Lyin' Eyes*", and "if you never made out in the
backseat while listening to *Take It to the Limit,* then you've
never made out" . . . and you know "it's hard not to press
the accelerator when *Already Gone* comes on" – yeah,
this "'70s flashback" "makes you long for adventure and a
time when you had no commitments."

THE EAGLES, *HOTEL CALIFORNIA* 🔢1 | 26 | 26 | 26 | 26 |
1976, Asylum; "Hotel California"; www.eagles.yahoo.com
■ The album that took the LA out of Shangri-La", this "snide aside on the California lifestyle" "rocks more than previous" efforts, "thanks to the triple-threat guitar attack from Don Felder, Glenn Frey and new member Joe Walsh, who play a game of one-upmanship", and "Don Henley's ability to paint a picture", especially on the "sultry title track"; "like the great line 'you can check out any time you like, but you can never leave'" ("who hasn't looked for that creepy hotel?"), this "masterpiece" "attaches itself forever."

The Eagles, *The Long Run* 🔢1 | 22 | 22 | 24 | 24 |
1979, Asylum; "The Long Run"; www.eagles.yahoo.com
◪ "The disjointed but catchy batch of tunes that presaged the breakup of LA's famous band" on "this cynical follow-up to *Hotel California*" is even "darker, but a great swan song"; fans feel it has "some wonderful moments" and newcomer "Timothy B. Schmit's high-range vocals on *I Can't Tell You Why* are excellent", yet critics carp that "Joe Walsh is this album's only saving grace – it's bloated '70s indulgence at its worse", so "let's make it a short run!"

Steve Earle, *Guitar Town* | 27 | 27 | 26 | 23 |
1986, MCA; "Guitar Town"
■ "A seminal", "stunning debut" from "one of America's most brutally honest songwriters", this collection of "gorgeously simple" tunes "hit like a meteor when it arrived" in the "post–*Urban Cowboy*" era, helping to nurture what "blossomed into the alt-country movement"; while later efforts underscore his "integrity and resilience", this "pre-prison disc" "packed with promise" establishes this "modern bad boy" as "a voice to reckon with."

Earth, Wind & Fire, *That's the Way of the World* 🔢1 | 27 | 25 | 27 | 27 |
1975, Columbia; "That's the Way of the World"; www.earthwindandfire.com
■ "A stew of all the best elements that make up the universe", this "amazing" group is the "real deal", delivering "seminal galactic funk" via a "rocking horn section", matched by "moving ballads" from "legendary" shining star Philip Bailey; the "deep sounds" "span the test of time" – decades later, "today's hip-hop" generation is "still sampling" this "fun stuff."

Easy Rider (Soundtrack) | 24 | 24 | 25 | 24 |
1969, Dunhill/ABC; "Born to Be Wild"
■ Get your motor running with this "blast from the past", the soundtrack to Dennis Hopper's "classic" '60s hippie biker flick; it may be "a period piece", but tunes by The Byrds, Steppenwolf and more "had a big impact on the mainstream", as kids just realizing they were born to be wild "couldn't believe they were hearing 'goddamn' on

the radio"; "on a cold night with time to kill", "listen and relive" the second "age of American independence."

Echo & the Bunnymen, *Crocodiles*   25 | 24 | 24 | 22 |
1980, Sire; "Do It Clean"; www.bunnymen.com
■ "Out of the ashes of punk" came this "completely different" Liverpool-based group led by vocalist Ian McCulloch and guitarist Will Sergeant on their "psychedelic, brooding" debut; "undeniably cool", it held the "promise of Echo, which appeared poised to become" big, but instead "settled for critical acclaim" and the adoration of a "small, discerning core of fans."

Linda Eder, *It's No Secret Anymore*   26 | 25 | 28 | 26 |
2000, Atlantic; "Vienna"; www.lindaeder.com
■ It's no secret that "Linda Eder could sing the phone book" and give you "chills, chills, chills"; in a "technically stunning" "Broadway voice" "backed by wonderful arrangements", the "powerful singer" "belts" "emotional ballads" "like no one else" – including, "yes, Streisand in her prime" – hitting the "high notes" with "amazing" "beauty"; the former *Jekyll and Hyde* star's laboratory of sound features tunes by "songwriter/husband Frank Wildhorn" for "a marriage made in musical heaven."

8 Mile (Soundtrack)   22 | 22 | 20 | 22 |
2002, Shady/Interscope; "Lose Yourself"
■ "The bad boy that you love to hate" "does seamless storytelling on *Lose Yourself*", the Oscar-winning "summary of the movie" that "showcased" "Eminem's genuine talent" as an actor/MC, "renewing faith" among his fans and making him "as popular as the chocolate candies" he's named for; the rest of the hip-hop soundtrack is "off the hook" too: "Nas is incredible followed by 50 Cent's equally hot *Wanksta*" and "Rakim's *R.A.K.I.M.* will totally flip you out"; it's "gritty", "profane" and "very catchy" – in other words, "damn."

Electric Light Orchestra, *ELO's Greatest Hits*   24 | 22 | 25 | 24 |
1979, Jet; "Can't Get It Out of My Head"; www.elomusic.com
■ You "can't live without a little ELO" or this "time capsule" that "captures their essence"; "endlessly entertaining", it includes "songs from the ether", ranging from orchestral tracks to "pithy pop tunes that soared them into the charts" and "fueled many a starlit idyll"; with Jeff Lynne at the helm, they "combined craftsmanship and innovative arrangements" and bestowed this "oeuvre of lasting songs."

Duke Ellington with John Coltrane, *Duke Ellington & John Coltrane*   26 | 26 | 28 | 24 |
1962, Impulse!; "In a Sentimental Mood"; www.johncoltrane.com, www.dukeellington.com
◩ You "can't go wrong" when "one of the great ones" meets another, and this "excellent" combo of "two masters" is a

"must-have", say pals of the "perfect pairing"; Ellington brought a "wonderful mix" of his own tunes to the sitdown with Coltrane's quartet for a "solid disc" that's "an enjoyable listen"; however, "large-band" boosters bluster "the album just doesn't live up to the immensity of its talents", preferring Duke with his orchestra rather than on this "sleepy" set.

Missy Elliott, *Supa Dupa Fly* | 24 | 23 | 22 | 26 |
1997, EastWest/Elektra; "The Rain (Supa Dupa Fly)";
www.missy-elliott.com
■ "A girl shows she can play with the boys" on this "futuristic", "funky hip-hop" disc from the "king and queen of new beats", "real talent" Missy 'Misdemeanor' Elliot and "great" avant-trackmaster Timbaland; "combining wry humor, wit and drum 'n' bass"–driven grooves on "catchy" tracks that help you "get yer freak on", it "started a whole trend for female rappers."

Emerson, Lake and Palmer, | 23 | 21 | 27 | 24 |
Brain Salad Surgery
1973, Atlantic; "Karn Evil 9: First Impression - Part 1";
www.emersonlakepalmer.com
☑ A "deliciously grandiose" "opus" that "solidified" this trio "as one of the premier practitioners of progressive rock", this "artistic piece" "of epic magnitude" is "just short of pretentious making it, well, brilliant"; "their supreme mastery of instruments" ("long live the Moog synthesizer") and "blending of classical" music was "way ahead of its time, perhaps too far" for a few who bristle at its "overblown", "bombastic UK" "excess."

Eminem, *The Eminem Show* ▣ | 25 | 26 | 23 | 25 |
2002, Aftermath/Interscope; "Without Me"; www.eminem.com
☑ "He's come a long way, baby" – "the rapper you love to hate and hate to love" lays down his "most personal album" with an "intensity" and "cohesiveness" that "reflects the maturity of a tortured young man" who "speaks to anyone who has ever felt a little different or marginalized"; despite the "addictive beats" on tracks like the "infectious" *Without Me,* harder ears say the "over-produced", "radio-friendly" stuff "lacks some of the gritty rawness that is Eminem."

Eminem, | 24 | 25 | 22 | 25 |
***The Marshall Mathers LP* ▣▣**
2000, Aftermath/Interscope; "Stan"; www.eminem.com
☑ "With a biting sense of humor", "in-your-face" "genius" "Eminem flexes storytelling muscle that even the finest folk writers would envy", "exercising the First Amendment", "channeling anger into art" and conveying "a well-masked understanding of human suffering" over "Dr. Dre's catchy-as-ever beats"; though the white rapper's "incisive writing" and razor-sharp flow may have "raised the bar for lyricism much higher", others yawn that the "bigoted jerk's" "stories of poor ol' me are getting tired."

Eminem, *The Slim Shady LP* 🅖   23 | 24 | 21 | 23

1999, Aftermath; "My Name Is"; www.eminem.com

☑ "Pushing the limits of censorship", the "audacious debut from the snot heard round the world" – "more shocking than Marilyn Manson, more offensive than Andrew Dice Clay" – "gives a glimpse into the life of a poor white kid from Detroit", "showing off lyrical potential and brutal honesty" on tracks like the "self-aggrandizing, self-immolating" *My Name Is*; smoother operators find the disc "rough around the edges", while feminists feel "his talent doesn't outweigh the misogynistic lyrics."

The English Beat,   25 | 23 | 24 | 23
I Just Can't Stop It

1980, Sire/WEA; "Mirror in the Bathroom"

■ Looking for "fun, fun and more fun" "party music enriched by social commentary"? "ska to the rescue": "just thinking about" this "vital" "piece of British pop circa 1980" "makes you want to dance" – "'I just can't stop it' is right!"; while you're at it, "catch the rhythm section" and give toaster-rapper Ranking Roger and vocalist Dave Wakeling a listen – this onetime 2-Tone outfit "ranks with The Specials."

Enigma, *MCMXC A.D.*   26 | 22 | 25 | 26

1991, Charisma/Virgin/EMI; "Principles of Lust: Sadeness/ Find Love"

■ "Strip your partner" to the "chanting monks, lush female vocals and heavy breathing" of this "techno-jazz–New Age" "fusion" "fairytale"; "perfectly melding electronica with medievalism", it sets a "magical" "mood for romance", but it's "wonderfully spiritual and inspirational at the same time", and "the funky *Sadeness*" was a dance hall hit; so, "let it be the soundtrack to your own porno" or party – the Catholic church might not have appreciated it, but you'll "love" the "journey."

Brian Eno, *Before and After Science*   27 | 25 | 26 | 28

1977, EG Records; "King's Lead Hat"

■ "Ever the consummate perfectionist, Eno has too many albums to consider", but this "glistening, mysterious", "sonically layered masterpiece" is the "seminal one to have"; "the father of ambient, perhaps now best known as producer" (U2, Bowie, Devo, Talking Heads, etc., etc.), concocts the most "gently, beautiful songs one can imagine, marrying perfect pop moments to experimentalism" while "validating the synthesizer as a musical instrument" – surely this is what Stanley Kubrick's "Hal listens to."

En Vogue, *Born to Sing*   24 | 22 | 24 | 23

1990, Atlantic; "Hold On"; www.en-vogue.net

■ "Giving girls growing up a song to test their pipes on" with their hit *Hold On*, R&B's fearsome foursome of "female a cappella" sirens "represent for the ladies", crafting "outrageous harmonies and heartfelt soul" on a "bold and

beautiful", hip-hop–tinged debut that is both "elegant"
and "danceable"; though "their voices blend together"
"like well-tuned instruments", "each artist gets to lead"
and all of them are "born to sing."

En Vogue, *Funky Divas*

24 | 23 | 24 | 24

1992, EastWest; "Free Your Mind"; www.en-vogue.net
■ Living up to the title, "the Supremes of the '90s" came
with "more attitude" and "sass" to this session, mixing
"sex appeal" with "messages of female empowerment"
for an "explosive" follow-up album; from the rock-driven
Free Your Mind to the straight-ahead hip-hop groove of
My Lovin', the disc displays the divas' "versatility" and
"amazing" "musical ability", helping to "set the stage" for
groups like TLC.

Enya, *Watermark*

27 | 24 | 26 | 26

1989, Geffen; "Orinoco Flow"; www.enya.com
■ "Take a bath, have a massage" and "wind down" with
this "watershed" "nightcap" of "beauty and eeriness" from
"the New Age icon"; "the other side of Celtic music", the
solo crossover from the former Clannad "songbird jumped
onto the charts" in a world in need of "spiritual and
intellectual" "rejuvenation"; "Enya's voice is an amazing
instrument", and the album's "lush vocals, pillowy synths
and unusual rhythms" are so "mellow", it's "sleep inducing."

Erasure,

25 | 24 | 24 | 25

Erasure Pop!: The First 20 Hits

1992, Sire; "A Little Respect"
■ Packed to the rim with "goodies" for gettin' down, this
"trendsetting" "gay man's paradise" of electropop is "a
mélange of the most popular and everlasting favorites of
the duo", ex-Depeche Moder Vince Clarke and the out-
and-about Andy Bell, who "could sing the ingredients of a
can of soup and make it sound catchy"; once you're on this
"heady trip back to the wild '80s", "it's harder to press stop
than it is to get chewing gum off your shoe."

Eric B. & Rakim, *Paid in Full*

27 | 27 | 24 | 24

1987, 4th & Broadway; "Paid in Full"
■ "Hip-hop at its purest", this "classic" by "possibly the
best DJ/MC combo from rap's old-school days" features
Eric B.'s "sophisticated" samples and "jazzy", "intoxicating"
beats as groundwork for lyrical "god" "Rakim's double
and triple entendres, which you'll only figure out after years
of listening"; "copied by so many others", "even today" the
album is so "influential" that "after one time through, you will
sink into the paper like ink" to lay down rhymes yourself.

Gloria Estefan, *Greatest Hits*

24 | 22 | 26 | 25

1992, Epic; "Conga"; www.gloriaestefan.com
■ Estefan's got "energy up the wazoo" on this "get-up-
and-boogie" pop platter that even hipsters report being "a

little bit embarrassed to enjoy"; "it's hard to listen to without dancing" to the "Latin beat" of her band, the Miami Sound Machine, so "join in the conga", but don't dismiss the "thoughtful" "tearjerkers" ripe for "post-breakup, mope-around-your-room" sessions; "how can you not love" a "hot", "proud", "rockin'" lady who's a "true survivor and true talent"?

Melissa Etheridge, *Yes I Am*   23 | 24 | 24 | 23
1993, Island; "Come to My Window";
www.melissaetheridge.com
■ "News alert: Women Can Rock" – just tune in to this "female Bruce Springsteen's" "raw", "emotional", "earthy voice belting out" "fist-pumping" songs "without peer" "that come from the deepest part of her being"; "how do you not love this little ball of fire" who, "by being true to who she is", scooped up a Grammy and inspired women fans to exclaim "even tho I'm not, I kinda wish I was."

E.T. The Extra-Terrestrial   26 | 25 | 28 | 26
(Soundtrack) **G**
1982, MCA; "Escape/Chase/Saying Goodbye"
■ "Out-of-this-world" composer "John Williams shocks us all, following the stratospheric success of *Star Wars* with yet another memorable theme"; "instantaneously recognizable" to just about "anyone who grew up in the early '80s", the "symphonic score" to "the alien's soul" "contains beautiful movements and exciting action cues", with "just a touch of saccharine"; go ahead, give in to the "goosebumps" for *Escape/Chase/Saying Goodbye,* "the song where E.T. goes home."

Eurythmics, *Greatest Hits*   24 | 23 | 24 | 24
1991, Arista; "Sweet Dreams"
■ "Like one big 'nah nah' to everyone who wasn't with them from the start", this triple-platinum compilation "rocks you, cradles you and then rocks you again"; Annie Lennox's "hauntingly beautiful" "voice for the ages" complemented by "Dave Stewart's musicianship and production proficiency, a wonderful part of the equation", make each tune a "perfect pop-synth masterpiece", indeed, "their brilliance is all over every track."

BILL EVANS, *WALTZ FOR DEBBY*   29 | 28 | 29 | 25
1961, Riverside; "Waltz for Debby"; www.billevans.org
■ "Bill Evans could play *Chopsticks* and it would be fabulous", fawn fans of this "legendary" "low lights–and-cabaret" live set recorded during the same date as his *Sunday at the Village Vanguard*; the man "could provide more expression with fewer notes than any other pianist" for "instant sincerity" on "bittersweet" takes of "mellow", "timeless melodies" like *My Foolish Heart* and the title track; but he "isn't just lyrical, he swings", and bassist Scott LaFaro and drummer Paul Motian "are just cool."

The Everly Brothers,   26 | 26 | 24 | 23
Cadence Classics (Their 20 Greatest Hits)
1985, Rhino; "Wake Up Little Susie"
■ While "Elvis gave rock its rhythm & blues and gospel strains", brothers Phil and Don, a rockabilly duo from Kentucky, "brought the aching harmonies of Appalachia" and "bridged country and pop in a new way"; "these oldies really are goodies" and "this compilation from their Cadence years features all their biggest hits except *Cathy's Clown*" – "hats off to Rhino for capturing the original sound!"

Everything But the Girl,   24 | 24 | 21 | 23
Amplified Heart
1994, Atlantic; "Missing"; www.ebtg.com
■ Previously known for jazz-pop "standouts" that "fit into several categories", British duo Tracey Thorn and Ben Watt broke through to a "new sound" with this "transitional" effort, boosted by a post-album Todd Terry remix of the "moody, heartwrenching" *Missing*; a few feel the dance single "overshadowed" the disc's "gentle perfection" – it's really an "outpouring of searing sentiments" that comes on "like soft lips brushing your neck and a walk on a beach at sunset, all at the same time."

Everything But the Girl,   26 | 25 | 25 | 26
Walking Wounded
1996, Atlantic; "Walking Wounded"; www.ebtg.com
■ "Seamless techno-pop" "meets emotions" on this "amazing rebirth by a once-acoustic duo"; "finally – intelligent, adult dance music, and oh ... that voice" – Tracey Thorn's "ice-cool vocals" bespeak a "postmodern ache of loneliness and passion" for today's walking wounded; with Ben Watt's "unparalleled musicianship" on "sexy", "soulful", "beat-driven tracks", they delivered a "masterpiece" of "come-down" tunes for a "late-night dinner party" and the "cab ride home after."

Evita (London cast recording)   25 | 24 | 26 | 25
1978, MCA; "Don't Cry for Me Argentina"
☑ "You can smell the cigars" burning when you listen to this "political tearjerker", a musical "way to learn the history of Argentina" and its dictator's sainted wife, Eva Peron; scored "before Andrew Lloyd Webber sold his soul to the devil", it's "still great after a quarter-century", and though "some may prefer the Broadway cast", "which launched the careers of Patti LuPone and Mandy Patinkin", don't cry for the "true superstar" Elaine Page in "the "best of all *Evita* recordings."

Cesaria Evora, *Miss Perfumado*   27 | 23 | 28 | 23
1992, Windham Hill; "Sodade"
■ "The Queen of Cape Verde" is known for performing sans shoes, and on this disc, she "makes you want to go barefoot with her", "singing velvety Portuguese" in a

"beautiful voice" with "soulful style and phrasings"; "a truly unique diva", the fiftysomething songstress brings *morna,* the multicultural musical stew of her native West African island, to an international audience that has come to "love" her sound; "like great jazz and gospel", "it's all pathos, logos and ethos, baby", and it "rocks."

F

Fairport Convention, *Liege & Lief*   26 25 28 22
1969, A&M; "Matty Groves"
■ "An undeniable classic" from the UK's "answer to the Byrds", this fourth Fairport phenom can be summed up in "one word: magnificent"; "it was a risk at the time" to "mix traditional songs" "telling stories of bygone days" of old England with "1960s folk-rock music", but this "creative group" made something "amazing to ponder"; "haunting and absorbing", it marks their last release with guitarist Richard Thompson and Sandy Denny, whose voice "illuminates the lyrics."

Marianne Faithfull, *Broken English*   25 24 23 24
1980, Island; "Broken English";
www.marianne-faithfull.net
■ "Take all the bitterness and anger of her storied life" as onetime rising pop star and Mick Jagger's girlfriend, "mix in guitar and tears", and you've got this "raw, scathing, infectious" "comeback" "triumph"; revealing a "weathered voice and weathered soul", "she's been down and out and understands what she's singing about", from her "gritty" rendition of Lennon's *Working Class Hero* to the "superb song *The Ballad of Lucy Jordan.*"

Faith No More, *The Real Thing*   21 20 22 21
1990, Slash; "Epic"; www.fnm.com
■ "Influential is not the word" to describe this "seminal recording" that "really came from out of nowhere", jump-starting a "whole new genre"; whether this "metal-rap fusion" was the "catalyst for this direction or one step ahead of their peers we'll never know" but there's no denying that frontman "Mike Patton's voice is extraordinary" and that *Epic,* "one of the neatest rock singles", "still makes you want to flop around like a fish out of water."

Fame (Soundtrack)   23 22 23 23
1980, RSO; "Fame"
■ "Danceable angst" meets "joie de vivre" on this "sincere and lovely soundtrack" "about NYC's High School of Performing Arts" that makes you "see kids singing and dancing in the city streets" "on people's cars"; "work out" with Irene Cara to "great" pop-rock tunes "written for the film, rather than compiled from previous top 40 hits" – "you will laugh, you will cry, it will become a part of you" 'cause "this album really does live forever."

Fatboy Slim, | 24 | 20 | 23 | 26 |
You've Come a Long Way, Baby
1998, Astralwerks; "The Rockafeller Skank";
www.gutterandstars.com
■ With a "flamboyance only surpassed by keep-you-moving-till-dawn" "big beats, hypnotic rhythm tracks and hooks that won't let go", Fatboy Slim, aka Norman Cook, serves up "a fun ride from beginning to end"; with hits like *Praise You* and *The Rockafeller Skank* to "bring a smile to the grumpiest person's face", "the professor of DJ electronica" "puts one more notch on the bedpost" for "commercialized techno"; "believe the hype for once – this *is* as good as" "f#@king in heaven."

Fiddler on the Roof | 27 | 28 | 26 | 26 |
(Original cast recording)
1964, RCA; "Sunrise, Sunset"
■ "No Jewish house should be without this recording", and neither should the *goyim*; "a true classic about life in turn-of-the-century Eastern Europe" based on Sholom Aleichem's stories, the album "beautifully captures the spirit" of both the *shtetl* and the "universal" "common man"; "bravo, Zero" Mostel, whose "huge personality booms through" his performance of *If I Were a Rich Man* and "family anthem" *Sunrise, Sunset*; it's "Jew-topia" because, "after all, it's tradition."

The 5th Dimension, | 23 | 23 | 25 | 24 |
Greatest Hits on Earth
1972, Bell; "Up, Up and Away"
■ At the dawning of the age of Aquarius, "this group helped pop usher in the '70s" with a "groovy" "cotton-candy" mix of "classic songs from the era's best writers, including Jimmy Webb and Laura Nyro", "stunningly arranged by Bones Howe", with "beautifully blended vocals" featuring Marilyn McCoo "singing her heart out"; "from the sultry *Stoned Soul Picnic* to the heartfelt *Last Night I Didn't Get to Sleep at All*", this CD "transports you" up, up and away on a "lush" "sing-along ride."

50 Cent, *Get Rich or Die Tryin'* 🔢 | 22 | 20 | 20 | 24 |
2003, Aftermath; "In Da Club"; www.50cent.com
◪ "Dr. Dre and Eminem's protégé" brings "hardcore" "gangsta" "street cred" to his "tight" debut reminiscent of the late "Tupac Shakur" with its "off-the-hook" lyricism featuring "amusing jabs at fellow artists"; while the production is "brilliant" on tracks like *In Da Club,* which "gets the crowd going", some won't pony up the "sucka" change for a rapper they consider "overhyped."

Fishbone, *Truth and Soul* | 24 | 22 | 26 | 22 |
1988, Columbia; "Ma and Pa"
■ Serving up "brassy, ballsy ska-soul-punk-funk at its finest", the "unsung heroes" of the '80s "can make your

head bob, make you rip an air guitar or shake your booty"; "the Bone's massive chops are funneled into great songs" that "ooze with conviction" – "you name it, it's here", including a cover of Curtis Mayfield's *Freddie's Dead*; dude, "this album smokes."

ELLA FITZGERALD, THE BEST OF THE SONGBOOKS

29 | 28 | 29 | 27

1993, Polgram; "Bewitched, Bothered and Bewildered"; www.ellafitzgerald.net
■ That "voice is one in a million", which is why it's ranked No. 1 in the *Survey* for Pop Vocals; Fitzgerald's "unparalleled" singing "coupled with couldn't-be-better tunes" culled from her composer tribute series "makes for an achingly good listen" – she "swings" with Johnny Mercer, "gets soulful" with Rogers & Hart and "brings the wit of Porter and Gershwin to life"; "if you're [too] cheap" for the "glorious box set" of all sixteen *Songbooks,* you "can't top" this compilation for, "oooooh", "Ella-gance!"

Ella Fitzgerald, The Complete Ella in Berlin: Mack the Knife

28 | 25 | 28 | 24

1960, Verve; "Mack the Knife"; www.ellafitzgerald.net
■ "What beauty! what grace!" – even when she is "butchering" a "standard", "Ella makes you happy you're alive"; "the queen of jazz" "can't remember the words to *Mack the Knife*", but she "wings it beautifully" on the "live album that all others are judged by"; though "honors need to be shared with the countless others who are responsible for the lovely writing, composing and instrumentals", Ms. Fitzgerald's "sugar and spice" is so nice, "you'll forget the real lyrics."

Roberta Flack, *Softly With These Songs: The Best of Roberta Flack*

26 | 25 | 26 | 23

1993, Atlantic; "Killing Me Softly With His Song"
■ "The woman has soul", alright – "Ms. Flack's career songbook" "shines" with "exceptional artistry and enough emotion to color the world in whatever hue she chooses", which is usually a shade of "pure romance"; "break out the candles" and get "mellow" with the "sensual" singer/pianist's "all-time mush" hits, including *The First Time Ever I Saw His Face* (which is actually about Don McLean in concert) and *Killing Me Softly With His Song*.

Flaming Lips, Transmissions from the Satellite Heart

24 | 23 | 23 | 24

1995, Warner Bros.; "She Don't Use Jelly"; www.flaminglips.com
■ "Another out-there album from the kings of weird", this "dorky, fun" effort marked "a great point" in the "imaginative band's" "career when they transitioned from indie-punk" to mainstream renown; the hit *She Don't Use Jelly* put Wayne Coyne and company "on the map", but in the transmission "a great album was overlooked", insist Lips-lovers.

Flashdance (Soundtrack) **G** **#1**   23 | 20 | 22 | 23
1983, Casablanca; "What a Feeling"
■ The soundtrack "that had girls dressed in leg warmers and cut-out sweatshirts" dreaming of "becoming welder/dancers when they grew up" still has a "nice beat to wiggle to"; "you know why aerobics was so popular in the '80s" as Irene Cara and a "sexy", "driving beat" "get you moving" as enthusiastically as Jennifer Beals' body double; the outfits may be "out of style, but this one's a classic", not in the least because it conjures that "wet dream" of a "water scene" – "what a feeling."

Fleetwood Mac, *Fleetwood Mac* #1   26 | 26 | 26 | 25
1975, Reprise; "Landslide"; www.fleetwoodmac.com
■ "Amazing how a band can reinvent itself and release an incredible 'debut' over seven years after it formed" – "enter Lindsey Buckingham and Stevie Nicks" "with her voice of gold", and "the rest is history"; their "infusion" "showed how brilliant Mick Fleetwood and John McVie were at putting together combos", "Christine McVie's vocals blend with the newcomers' gloriously" and "the good white witch knows how to write a song" – together they "make magic before your ears."

FLEETWOOD MAC, *RUMOURS* G #1   27 | 27 | 27 | 26
1977, Warner Bros.; "Go Your Own Way";
www.fleetwoodmac.com
■ "Seamless and timeless", this "blockbuster" combines "incredible writing" with "sweet music": "Buckingham's banjo-style guitar playing cut new ground", while Mick and John were "the best rhythm section in R&R"; with "Nicks at her smoky-voiced best", it documents "five people working as one" "in the face of" "two bitter breakups among band members"; "the emotion screams out", especially in "the palpable tension between Lindsey and Stevie", resulting in the "timeless treasures" *Dreams* and *Go Your On Way.*

Dan Fogelberg, *Phoenix*   24 | 24 | 24 | 23
1979, Full Moon; "Longer"; www.danfogelberg.com
◪ This is "the way a heart would sound if it could sing", confess fans who feel this "vastly underrated talent's" "wimpy, yet hefty" sixth album is the one where he "shed his 1970s roots and honed his songwriting"; sure, the pop hit "*Longer* has been mandatory listening at weddings since", but it's "the lesser-known tracks that stand out"; still, a few find it doesn't rise to the level of "his best work."

John Fogerty, *Centerfield* #1   22 | 23 | 24 | 22
1985, Warner Bros.; "Centerfield"; www.johnfogerty.com
■ "John's songwriting genius is given credence with this" "excellent comeback, a reminder of the good old days when CCR rocked" the bayou; a solo showcase from the "original DIYer", it includes the title track "winner" that "still reins as a sports bar anthem"; listening to this

"wonderful romp" from "one of the most recognizable voices in classic R&R" is "like inviting an old friend into your home" – or out to the ballgame.

Follies in Concert (Revival) **G**   28 | 28 | 28 | 27
1985, RCA; "Losing My Mind"

☑ "Sondheim's amazing score gets the star treatment" for the "all-time best statement of what it means to get older" on "one of the most exciting concert albums in any genre"; Broadway babies agree that the "restoration of music cut from the original", plus "thrillingly" "brilliant" performances by an "incredible" cast, including Barbara "Never Better" Cook, Elaine "A Hoot" Stritch and Mandy "Way Over the Top" Patinkin, add up to "pure theatrical" "heaven for show-tune queens" and neophytes alike.

Foo Fighters, *Foo Fighters*   24 | 22 | 25 | 22
1995, Roswell/Capitol; "I'll Stick Around"; www.foofighters.com

■ "After grunge burned out", Nirvana's Dave Grohl emerged "from the shadow of Kurt Cobain" and "let fans in on a little known secret": "he's more than an excellent drummer", he's an "all-around musician" and, hello, he "did the whole damn thing" himself, playing almost "all the instruments, singing all the vocals"; "not a sad rip-off" of his past "glory", this debut is "humorous and fun, with real rock cred" that reveals him to be a "great frontman."

Foo Fighters, *One By One*   24 | 23 | 25 | 25
2002, Roswell; "All My Life"; www.foofighters.com

■ "All hail Dave Grohl's" "introspective lyrics and confident singing" "anchored by musical explosions" on this "standout" effort that "solidifies" the band's status as the "premier un-angry rock group"; "gritty and smooth, gentle and rough", with "devastating drumming and sharp guitar hooks", it's "phenomenally well-rounded" – Foo freaks fawn "they seem to get better with each album."

Footloose (Soundtrack) **#1**   23 | 21 | 22 | 23
1984, Columbia; "Footloose"

■ The "feet-tapping, finger-snapping" soundtrack to the fellas' *Flashdance* forms "a time capsule of the early '80s" when "catchy rockers, unadulterated pop" and "rebellious dance tunes" were the rage, and women swore "Kevin Bacon was the only man they'd leave their husbands for"; "cut loose" with Kenny Loggins' "energetic" title track and Deniece Williams' "fun" *Let's Hear It for the Boy*, and get "nostalgic" wondering "were we ever really that young and horny?"

Forrest Gump (Soundtrack)   26 | 24 | 25 | 25
1994, Epic; "Fortunate Son"

☑ "They sure did a good job of covering that much music history in two discs" of soundtrack "representing the changing face of America"; this R&R "road trip" "touches on every decade" "from Elvis to peace ballads" to "classic singles" including CCR's *Fortunate Son,* songs from Wilson Pickett, Willie Nelson, Bob Dylan, Fleetwood Mac and more; it's "like a box of chocolates" you can listen to: the truncated tunes "don't [always] fit well together", but you can gorge yourself on "moldie oldies."

The Four Seasons, *Anthology*   26 | 23 | 24 | 23
1988, Rhino; "Sherry"
■ He might have sang in "falsetto", but Frankie Valli "walked like a man", leading one of the "greatest American quartets of the '60s" to doo-wop pop stardom; this "excellent compilation" includes familiar hits like *Dawn* and *Sherry*, which "make you smile", mixed in with obscurities like "a weird cover of a Dylan song"; it's "solid proof" that the Rock and Roll Hall of Famer's "unusual voice" remains "somehow amazingly appealing" from season to season.

The Four Tops, *Anthology*   26 | 24 | 27 | 26
1974, Motown; "I Can't Help Myself"
■ Almost "nobody from Motown does it better" than "one of the great boy groups of all time", the hit-friendly vocal quartet of Lawrence Payton, Renaldo Benson, Levi Stubbs and Abdul Fakir, whose radio classics *I Can't Help Myself (Sugar Pie, Honey Bunch), Reach Out (I'll Be There), It's the Same Old Song* and *Baby I Need Your Loving* are collected on this genre-defining set; "still tops after all these years", "these dudes have ultra-soul."

Peter Frampton,   22 | 19 | 23 | 22
Frampton Comes Alive! 🔢1
1976, A&M; "Do You Feel Like We Do";
www.frampton.com
☑ "Light yer Bics!" cheer crowds who consider this the "granddaddy of live albums" ("whaa, whaa" – "remember when guitars could talk?"); "do you feel like we do? then show me the way" to "the bong", quip the nostalgists convinced it "captured a moment"; bashers boo it's "dated", "self-indulgent tripe", adding "it's one of the great mysteries" how this double "wonder" could have sold over six-million copies in the U.S. alone.

Frankie Goes to Hollywood,   23 | 20 | 21 | 24
Welcome to the Pleasuredome
1984, Island; "Relax"
■ "Back in the day", before we "realized some musicians were silly, silly people", this "wildly popular" debut "had us dancing on the bar"; "politically incorrect" and "so cheesy", it "manages to pull off grandeur" with a "sense of humor ("c'mon, *Do You Know the Way to San Jose?* and *Born to Run* in one?), "helping straight people see that they could groove to gay music"; "with insistent keyboards and giddily flirtatious lyrics" produced by "genius Trevor Horn", "*Relax* still kicks today's collective ass."

ARETHA FRANKLIN, *LADY SOUL*　29 | 27 | 29 | 26
1968, Atlantic; "Chain of Fools"
■ Though the song isn't on this *Survey*'s top-rated soul record, R-E-S-P-E-C-T "cannot be denied" to a "searing", gospel-trained voice that "melts the ice in anyone's veins"; "putting others to shame", Aretha "reinvigorates" *People Get Ready,* turns out a "model" *(You Make Me Feel Like) A Natural Woman* and "swings" with "power" on *Chain of Fools,* "fastening to your brain's pleasure sensors and not letting go" for a "stellar work" that suggests this "legend" is "the greatest female performer of all time."

ARETHA FRANKLIN, *QUEEN OF SOUL:*　29 | 27 | 28 | 27
THE VERY BEST OF ARETHA FRANKLIN
1994, Rhino; "Respect"
■ "The title says it all", as "the queen proves why she took her throne" on this "flawless" set collecting "her incredible performances", including *Respect, I Never Loved a Man (the Way I Love You)* and "all the essentials", plus "early recordings" featuring the "diva" on piano; with "soul oozing from her pores" and "blistering vocal prowess", the "goddess" "with roots in gospel" makes "your hairs stand on end" because, "honey, if she's singing it, it's the best."

Fugazi, *13 Songs*　27 | 25 | 24 | 21
1990, Dischord; "Waiting Room"
■ The "quintessential DIY indie band" put together two EPs – *Fugazi* and *Margin Walker* – "to create one great", "trademark album" of "fast, furious and borderline frenzied" yet "intelligent punk" rock; "representing" DC's "burgeoning hardcore scene" in the late '80s, these "antiheroes" didn't "sugarcoat" their subjects, instead they threw "political and poetic" anthems "right in your face", spawning "the blueprint for countless emo rip-offs" and a sound that's "energy personified."

The Fugees, *The Score* G #1　25 | 24 | 25 | 25
1996, Ruffhouse; "Killing Me Softly With His Song"
■ "Lyrical gymnast" "Lauryn Hill shines" on this record that "everybody and their brother wore out", mostly thanks to "one of the best remakes ever", Roberta Flack's *Killing Me Softly,* and a gumbo of "jazz, rap, reggae" and "dancehall elements" driving the "excellent production"; "revolutionary in the world of hip-hop", the trio's "streetwise, smart, political" rhymes and "infectious beats" still have surveyors wondering, "will they ever get back together?"

Funkadelic, *Maggot Brain*　28 | 26 | 28 | 23
1971, Westbound; "Maggot Brain"
■ "Funkier than Sly, harder than Sabbath", George Clinton's "mind-blowing" clan of space-aged musicians – namely "underrated" phenom guitarist Eddie Hazel – stuffed a "veritable medley" of soul, "gospel, acid rock and pretty much everything else" into "steady, psychedelic grooves",

as in the "high-water mark", album-opening title cut; a few feel the "band would never sound this hot again."

Funkadelic,　　　　　　　　27 | 25 | 28 | 26
One Nation Under a Groove
1978, Warner Bros.; "One Nation Under a Groove"
■ "The crazed genius of George Clinton – part Sun Ra, part stadium rock", part "playful" "free-for-all" – is in full effect here, with horn-driven, "freaky-yet-accessible", "truly danceable" "layers of sound" bound to make any listener believe "there ain't much else funkier than takin' a ride on the mothership"; "fun"-seekers with a groove allegiance swear "nobody else has that" much "mojo goin'."

Funny Girl (Soundtrack) **G**　　27 | 26 | 26 | 27
1968, Columbia; "Don't Rain on My Parade"
■ "Life's candy" with this soundtrack for fans of Ms. Streisand; "boisterous baby Babs" belts out an Oscar-winning, "stunning interpretation" of Jule Styne and Bob Merrill's "sweet and up-tempo" "smash" score that "still sends chills up your spine" thirtysome years after it was recorded; "laugh, cry", "sing these songs in the shower trying to sound" an iota as "thrilling" as the precocious "powerhouse" and "remember why we loved her."

G

PETER GABRIEL, *PASSION* G　　28 | 26 | 29 | 29
1989, Geffen; "It Is Accomplished"; www.petergabriel.com
■ "It is rare that one finds an album that so eloquently expresses the gamut of human emotion", but this *Survey*'s No. 1 for Soundtrack and Overall Production bears the cross; Gabriel's "powerfully moving" score to Martin Scorcese's controversial *The Last Temptation of Christ* is "recommended for active listening" to contemplate its "mystical" "beauty" in full; "one of the most varied musicians of our time" teams with artists like Nusrat Fateh Ali Khan for world-infused "trance before trance was mainstream."

Peter Gabriel, *So*　　　　　26 | 27 | 26 | 27
1986, Geffen; "In Your Eyes"; www.petergabriel.com
■ "A brilliant fusion of British prog and world beat", "Gabriel's rock and soul background is infused with African and Middle Eastern elements", plus "irresistible hooks, layered textures, intelligent lyrics" and "innovative production"; from the "funky" *Sledgehammer* and *Don't Give Up,* "the tear-jerking duet with Kate Bush", to *In Your Eyes* (remember when "John Cusack made it a teen anthem in *Say Anything*"?), there's "not a lame track in the litter."

Gang of Four, *Entertainment!*　　26 | 25 | 23 | 22
1979, Warner Bros.; "I Found That Essence Rare"
■ "The raw truth shines through" on this Leeds UK quartet's "staccato, danceable" disc, a "vital", "seminal" set of

"neo-Marxist rock" that remains one of "the greatest political albums", making the Gang "what Rage Against the Machine always wanted to be"; with its "shockingly" "sharp songs and ironic, striking", "socially conscious lyrics" "wrapped in dissonance", it's a "model for all to follow" and "highly recommended for anyone who missed the punk revolution" of the late 1970s.

Garbage, *Garbage* 24 | 22 | 24 | 25 |
1995, Almo Sounds; "Stupid Girl"; www.garbage.com
■ Three "phenomenal" producer-musicians (including "genius Butch Vig" of Nirvana *Nevermind* fame) plus one Scottish "super-vixen equals" this "delicious" debut that "mixes techno beats" with "alternative pop"; "edgy and melodic", it's a "crown gem of the post-grunge scene" thanks to "modern rock goddess" "Shirley Manson's pout" and "masterful vocals" that come on "like a sexy swagger"; "trashy in the right ways", this "awesome effort" "kicks ass."

Jerry Garcia and David Grisman, 26 | 24 | 28 | 24 |
Not for Kids Only
1993, Acoustic Disc; "There Ain't No Bugs on Me"
■ The "Grateful Dead meets Mister Rogers" and, man, is it "cool" on this "gem" for children "of all ages" by "two talented musicians", legendary frontman Jerry Garcia and mandolin player David Grisman; the "fab arrangements" on originals like *There Ain't No Bugs on Me* and traditional folk tunes such as *Arkansas Traveller* make for a "sittin' 'round the fire" sound that's so "enchanting", overgrown hippies sigh, "I think I like it more than my kid."

Judy Garland, 28 | 27 | 27 | 25 |
Judy at Carnegie Hall 🄖
2001, Capitol; "Over the Rainbow"
■ "Just when they thought Garland was washed up, she blazed forth with a newfound determination" in a 1961 "historic" comeback at Carnegie Hall; re-released with "better sound", this 40th anniversary disc "captures the magic of two incredible performances: Judy's and the audience's", sending "chills down your spine" as her "fans" "feed" at a "fever pitch" on the "tragic legend's" "full range of emotion" on signatures like *Over the Rainbow*.

Erroll Garner, *Concert by the Sea* 27 | 26 | 28 | 24 |
1956, Columbia; "It's All Right By Me"
■ Back in the early '60s "when you should have been listening to Elvis", if you "were a jazz buff", you probably thought this "powerful" disc "was so cool as you entered high school" and fumbled through your "collegiate make-out" years; Garner was "a one-of-a-kind performer who enriched the repertoire" with "amazing left-hand" "piano prowess", "true showmanship" and that crazy humming along, and he's "in top form for this live performance" that is "incomparable" for "a romantic evening."

Marvin Gaye, *Anthology*

27 | 26 | 27 | 25

1995, Motown; "Let's Get It On"

■ "There is nothing sweeter" than the "pure-honey" voice of soul music's "gone but hardly forgotten" "icon", whose well-rounded best-of collection is expanded here on CD; Marvin can "make your heart ache" on *You're All I Need to Get By*, featuring Tammi Terrell, make you want to holler with *Inner City Blues* or "put you in the mood" for some lovin' with *Let's Get It On*; so, "slip this into your player, light a candle, pour a glass of wine" and do as the sexy song says.

MARVIN GAYE, *WHAT'S GOING ON* 🔟

29 | 29 | 28 | 27

1971, Motown; "What's Going On"

■ "Social statement and pure soul peacefully co-exist" on a "gorgeous" yet "gritty" "concept album", "a visionary" "apogee" that "provides a snapshot of a different time and culture in our country", with "landmark" cuts that are "poignant" in message, yet "smooth" in sound; Motown "almost rejected it for not being outwardly commercial", but in the end, it "changed the face" of popular music, with "spacey" grooves driving "stream of consciousness" delivered by the "voice of an angel."

Genesis, *The Lamb Lies Down on Broadway*

26 | 27 | 27 | 25

1974, Atlantic; "Carpet Crawlers"; www.genesis-music.com

■ "In its prime", this English prog band set "the standard for concept albums" with this "weird", "wild" but "incredibly coherent" "tour de force"; an "art-rock" "classic among theatrical, story-driven" efforts, if a trifle "bloated and pretentious", this "intense" double record was an "epic swan song" for "charismatic" singer Peter Gabriel before, some disgruntled fans say, "Phil Collins turned the group into a shallow hit machine."

Gershwin, *Rhapsody in Blue; American in Paris; Grand Canyon Suite* 🄶

28 | 29 | 28 | 26

1959, Sony Classical; "Rhapsody in Blue"

■ "If you love jazz but are not sure about classical, here is your portal to the other side"; from its "opening notes", *Rhapsody in Blue* "runs chills down your arms", "reminding you of how much you love New York City"; "show-biz Lenny" Bernstein, on piano and with baton, delivers an "astonishingly idiomatic, fun and zippy" performance of "one of the cheeriest pieces of all time", plus other "glittering", "God-bless-America" Gershwins; "come on over – you'll love what you find."

Stan Getz, *Getz/Gilberto* 🄶

28 | 27 | 29 | 26

1963, Verve; "The Girl from Ipanema"

■ "Feel the warm breezes of the Copacabana in your living room" as "Stan Getz's sax, João Gilberto's guitar with Astrud Gilberto's vocals and Antonio Carlos Jobim's

piano" "whisk you down to Rio" on this "bossa nova
masterpiece" "embodying" the "cocktail music of the JFK
era"; "light some candles, get in a bubble bath" and go
"mellow" in your "lower latitudes with its hip-swaying
harmonies", until you burst forth with the realization that,
"hey, this album beat out the Beatles for a Grammy!"

Gigi (Soundtrack) G #1   24 | 25 | 23 | 24
1958, EMI; "Thank Heaven for Little Girls"
■ "Ah Gigi, ah Maurice", "ah . . . Paris!"; this "charming"
chart-topper is "a perfect synergy of topic, songwriters
and performers" with "surprising" Louis Jourdan, "brilliant"
Hermione Gingold and "spry, roué" Chevalier delivering the
"lovely" Lerner and Loewe score; with so many "brilliant"
songs to enjoy, "thank heaven" for Rhino for a reissue that
is "superior to the original" vinyl.

Dizzy Gillespie, *At Newport*   27 | 26 | 28 | 24
1957, Verve; "Manteca"
■ "No tops list would be complete without Dizzy" say
hepcats whose heads spin over the "legend's" "awesome"
live "classic"; "this recording not only shows Gillespie's
fantastic playing and skills as a bandleader" on songs like
the "vibrant" *Manteca,* but also "how an entertainer brings
the audience into the performance" with "comic" turns
and "great interplay."

Vince Gill, *When I Call Your Name*   26 | 25 | 27 | 25
1989, MCA; "When I Call Your Name"; www.vincegill.com
■ You just may "cry" as this "down-home boy" with the
"voice of an angel" "croons fantastic love ballads" like the
title track, which, "when it comes to hurtin' country", is
"right up there with George Jones' *He Stopped Loving Her
Today*"; "one of the classiest men in the business", this
"hunk" with the "sweetest smile" possesses pipes that
are "as pure and real as they come", prompting the con-
Vinced to coo "he can call my name anytime."

Gipsy Kings, *Gipsy Kings*   26 | 23 | 27 | 25
1988, Elektra; "Bamboleo"; www.gipsykings.com
■ "Just try not to dance while listening" to the "French-
Spanish gypsy" guitar band that "brought flamenco to the
pop mainstream", "setting a world music standard" for
"cool" with their "infectious and uplifting" "mélange of
Mediterranean and Continental sounds"; "accessible" to
everyone from "the average college kid" to "advertising
teams" to legions of "tapas restaurant" owners, it may
have "been played to death", but the disc remains a "down
'n' dirty good time."

Philip Glass, *Glassworks*   24 | 21 | 24 | 23
1982, CBS Masterworks; "Facades"; www.philipglass.com
◪ "Anything from this innovative man is brilliance",
including "minimalism, minimalism, minimalism, oh, and

some repetition" in this "hypnotic" work of "unparalleled rhythm"; "the next step in American music" for its time, the album retains a "transporting ambiance that never reveals its age"; that's because Glass keeps "imitating himself", diss detractors who "grab the aspirin" and call this "dreck" "the aural equivalent of the Chinese water torture."

The Godfather (Soundtrack) G   27 | 26 | 26 | 26
1972, Paramount; "Love Theme from The Godfather"
■ "Gangster-chic music to whack someone by", the "perfect complement to the greatest movie of all time" "teaches" goodfellas "respect for the family"; composer "Nino Rota rocks", scoring "haunting horns" for a "universally recognized theme" that "helps set the tone" for Frances Ford Coppola's "dark look into organized crime"; "it's rare that an instrumental soundtrack is worth getting in total", but this is "an offer you can't refuse."

Godspell (Original cast recording)   22 | 22 | 21 | 20
1971, Arista; "Day By Day"
◪ "We beseech thee": "dance, dance, dance, mismatch your socks and think '70s" with this "instant Bible" that "even atheists" find "fun to sing along with"; "the lite-rock" "hippie classic" is "often overshadowed by its *Hair*-ier cousin", but Stephen Schwartz's retelling of Matthew's gospel is "great for high schools" 'cause it's "tuneful", "youthful" and "inspired", so "prepare ye the way" for a "heartfelt if dated" recording.

Go-Go's, Beauty and the Beat ▥   21 | 18 | 18 | 21
1981, I.R.S.; "We Got the Beat"; www.gogos.com
■ "Pop-punk fusion" is the ticket for this "pioneering" all-female LA band "who are to the Beach Boys what the Bangles are to the Beatles"; girls and guys go-go ga-ga for the "upbeat party mood" and "catchy beats" of this "just fun" No. 1 debut, a "guilty pleasure" that "always lifts your spirits"; "put the top down and go for a drive" – this early '80s "ear candy" can still "make you sing out loud in your car."

Goldfinger (Soundtrack)   24 | 23 | 25 | 23
1964, United Artists; "Goldfinger"
◪ "Delight" Shirley Bassey "belts out" "the unreal theme" "like only she can", while composer "John Barry reaches his peak" on the chart-topping disc for the third film in the 007 series; "if you are able to get only one" of the secret agent's soundtracks, "make it this one" for "an all-time high", but Moneypennys say for the most bang for your buck, "get a Bond compilation" so that "Carly Simon, Louis Armstrong and Duran Duran can join the party."

Gone With the Wind (Soundtrack)   25 | 25 | 26 | 22
1967, MGM; "Main Title"
■ "The South rises again" with "this terrific soundtrack by Hollywood legend, Max Steiner"; "evoking the grandeur and

emotion of one of the greatest films ever", the "sweeping" orchestral music "flows endlessly" through "the bygone antebellum era", the Civil War and the Reconstruction; though carpetbagging critics are "a bit bored" by its more "unremarkable pieces", the main title will make you want to "grab your walking stick or your parasol" and ask "mint julep, anyone?"

Benny Goodman, *B.G. in Hi-Fi*   26 | 26 | 28 | 24
1955, Capitol; "Stompin' at the Savoy"
■ "The true king of swing" and "his licorice stick" "never sounded better" on this album distilling "the essence of the era's legendary band"; his "1938 Carnegie Hall concert" might "have more of the really famous stuff", but this late-dated platter from the "last of the great clarinet guys in jazz" is "yet another essential entry on any list of musical highlights"; jitterbugs twitter that tracks like *Get Happy* and *Stompin' at the Savoy* deliver "the real jump and jive."

The Good, the Bad and the Ugly   26 | 27 | 25 | 23
(Soundtrack)
1968, United Artists; "The Ecstasy of Gold"
■ Composer "Ennio Morricone's finest hour" is high noon on the disc for Sergio Leone's cowboy "classic"; "the ultimate spaghetti Western music" "renders the turbulent emotions beneath the narrative and the stoney facade of the toughs that populate the film"; "you need to see the movie to understand how excellent this soundtrack is", but when you do, the title song's twangy guitars and bells, and *The Ecstasy of Gold*'s kitschy yodelling "will be forever embedded in your consciousness."

Dexter Gordon, *Go!*   27 | 23 | 29 | 25
1962, Blue Note; "Cheese Cake"
■ "Dexter blows like there's no tomorrow", but "Sonny Clark's piano playing is also a highlight" on this "rock-solid pleasure" recorded after a decade of drugs and jail for Gordon; "sophisticated yet fun" with a mix of "bold" bops and "warm" ballads, it's a "prime example of the famous Blue Note sound"; the "premier musician's" "big beefy tenor sax" is "guaranteed to bring a smile to the most hardened cynic" and make them shout 'go!'

Górecki, *Symphony No. 3*   27 | 25 | 28 | 27
1992, Nonesuch; "Second Movement, Lento E Largo"
■ "Who says classical music can't be a bestseller?"; this "dire but beautiful" performance of the "amazingly approachable" 1976 symphony is "intelligently interpreted" by conductor David Zinman and "magnificently" sang by "supple" soprano Dawn Upshaw to "capture the serene majesty of Gorecki's world", which is "heart-rending", but "not overwhelmingly" so; with a "better balance between voice and orchestra than in a concert hall", this is a "crisp, clear recording" of an "extraordinary, ethereal work."

GRATEFUL DEAD, *AMERICAN BEAUTY* 27 | 27 | 27 | 24
1970, Warner Bros.; "Box of Rain"; www.dead.net
■ "Very few studio efforts from the Dead ever really hit the mark, but for a while in the early '70s they couldn't miss", and this, "the charming, woodsy follow-up to *Workingman's Dead*", "hit all the notes: meaningful lyrics, on-key singing and beautiful arrangements" of "great American music mixing folk, blues, country, gospel, bluegrass and a wee bit of LSD"; "striking a balance between their mellow feel and sharper-honed R&R", it's "perhaps the sweetest stop on the long, strange trip."

Grateful Dead, *Live/Dead* 26 | 25 | 26 | 22
1969, Warner Bros.; "Dark Star"; www.dead.net
■ "Not until their fourth album did this band, known for their" "near-mystical", "ultimate acid rock performances", "do the obvious and release a purely live album", and this one "captures their early sound like no other and contains songs that were retired not long after"; "the transcendent set features definitive versions of their most beloved improvisatory tunes segued together" including an "awesome *Fire on the Mountain*", a "searing *Lovelight*" and a "killer version of *Dark Star*."

Grateful Dead, *Steal Your Face* 23 | 24 | 25 | 21
1976, Arista; "U.S. Blues"; www.dead.net
◪ Though some Deadheads say this mid-'70s live album is "full of dance-y tunes" and "worth it just for *U.S. Blues*", most vehemently exclaim "this one pales in comparison to *Europe '72*" and "any number of *Dick's Picks* tapes give a far better picture of a classic show"; all agree, though, that "there was nothing like a Dead concert" – "the albums were merely to relive the live experience."

Grateful Dead, 27 | 26 | 27 | 25
Workingman's Dead
1970, Warner Bros.; "Uncle John's Band"; www.dead.net
■ "The first unplugged rock album" is a "major masterpiece of 20th century music, combining American traditional C&W with contemporary R&R and jazz, and the prophetic lyrics of Robert Hunter, which establishes him as a poet on a par with Bob Dylan"; nailing "the heart and soul" of the band, "this primer on the Dead" includes such signature songs as *Casey Jones* and *Uncle John's Band* and gives a "glimpse of what lay ahead for an entire culture."

David Gray, *White Ladder* 25 | 25 | 24 | 24
1999, ATO/RCA; "Babylon"; www.davidgray.com
■ He "captured my heart and intellect all at once", applaud admirers awed by this UK artist's "biggest commercial success", dubbed "alterna-folk-pop" for its "plaintive melodies", "trancelike beats" and "poignant lyrics" that "make you want to cry or hug everyone"; it "starts with the one-two punch of *Please Forgive Me* and *Babylon*" but

some say "its soul lies in the sadness of the cover of Soft Cell's *Say Hello Wave Goodbye*"; no gray areas here: its "understated brilliance" "leaves you speechless."

Macy Gray, *On How Life Is*   22 | 22 | 22 | 22
1999, Epic; "I Try"; www.macygray.com
■ The "quirky", "gravel voice" of this "sassy, world-weary diva" is "imbued with character and life experience" on a debut album of "funky" "soul-pop" that "moves" "the masses" "physically and emotionally"; "catchy" cuts like *I Try* and *Sex-O-Matic Venus Freak* "stand up against the old Motown and Stax material" on an album that's about "letting go and slipping into the groove."

Grease (Soundtrack) **#1**   26 | 24 | 23 | 25
1978, Polydor; "Summer Nights"; www.greasemovie.com
■ "Grease will always be the word" for "hopelessly devoted" "generations of girls" who "wore out their record players" partying with their own Pink Ladies to this soundtrack; a young, sinewy "Travolta in tight pants", "Olivia Newton-John singing like a bird" and "best thing Stockard Channing" make "pop culture history" as they "whisk us away" to the '50s "teeny bopper" days; the "high-camp" "classic" boasts "summer-loving" "hits" that "will be on karaoke playlists until the end of time."

Al Green, *Greatest Hits*   27 | 26 | 27 | 25
1995, Right Stuff; "Let's Stay Together"; www.algreen.com
■ "Possessed of the sweetest, smoothest voice this side of heaven", the Reverend of soul music delivers such "sultry, sweaty, sexy" songs on this compilation from his early years that you might think it's "too bad he found religion"; grooving to these ballads is like worshiping in the "church of love" where "soaring angelic vocals, gospel voicings and unexpected chord changes" reflect the "seductive" "spirit" of "a man who can sing a Bible passage or the back of a cereal box and move you to tears."

Green Day, *Dookie* **G**   23 | 21 | 21 | 22
1994, Reprise/WEA; "Longview"; www.greenday.com
■ "Billie [Joe Armstrong] and the boys got our heads banging" on this "veritable time capsule of alterna-rock", a "devilish, determined" "beginning-of-an-era" major-label debut that "helped jump-start the "resurgence of punk", bringing it to "masses" of adoring basket cases; combining "killer harmonies" and "melodic zest", this "slammin'" "quintessential middle-school album" is "hard to beat for teen angst with a wry sense of humor."

PATTY GRIFFIN, *LIVING WITH GHOSTS*   29 | 29 | 27 | 26
1996, A&M; "Every Little Bit"; www.pattygriffin.com
■ Voters "immediately connected with" this "true singer-songwriter's" "remarkable stories that get to the heart of being human" on this "stark, beautiful, riveting" debut; a

coffeehouse-honed "demo tape–turned–album" with "organic", "sparse", "stripped-down production" – "just a voice, a guitar" and "Patty's soulful sincerity" – this "wonder" "envelops you from the first moment" with "intensely lyrical, intelligent" "vignettes" and "resonates like nothing else."

Nanci Griffith, *Flyer* #1   24 | 25 | 25 | 24
1994, Elektra; "Flyer"; www.nancigriffith.com
■ "An exciting creative departure" for Austin's "queen of the singer-songwriters", this "surprise hit" features "top-notch guests, including Adam Duritz, the Indigo Girls", Mark Knopfler and members of U2, "which added a new dimension to Nanci's sweet" sound and "down-home lyrics"; her "slightly Southern-accented" voice is "so light and airy you think you are going to float away" yet it's also "full of grit" and tinged with "melancholy", a "hypnotic combination that reaches its pinnacle here."

Vince Guaraldi,   27 | 27 | 28 | 24
A Boy Named Charlie Brown
1964, Fantasy; "Linus and Lucy";
www.vinceguaraldi.com
■ "Capturing the joy, wonder and love" of "long-lost youth" "with a jazzy, hip beat", Vince Guaraldi and his trio get "those who never want to step too far from childhood" "bopping like the *Peanuts* characters" on this "warm and fuzzy" soundtrack to Charles Schultz's original TV special; "it's attached to a cartoon, but it's music of real life", so though it's "corny" compared to the pianist's other platters, "you can't help but smile."

GUNS N' ROSES,   27 | 23 | 26 | 25
APPETITE FOR DESTRUCTION #1
1987, Geffen; "Welcome to the Jungle"
■ "Spotless and fierce from start to finish", "one of the best debut albums of all time" still whets our appetite for the "pure adrenaline rush" of "street rock" in its "most primal form"; "loaded with songs you can't get out of your head", this "masterpiece" "single-handedly" made heavy metal "sleazy and dangerous again"; "Axl and Slash could have been the next Mick and Keith after this triumph" but alas, then came the "feuds and rivalries" – "can't we go back to the jungle, sweet child o' mine?"

Guns n' Roses, *Use Your Illusion I* 22 | 21 | 25 | 24
1991, Geffen; "November Rain"
☑ G n' R disciples are split on whether this "long-awaited" album (released with *UYI II*) is a "superb" half of a "classic" or an "overblown" slice of "unchecked egotism" they should have let die; admirers declare this "daring" disc "exceeded expectations" with "hard-rocking melodies" and Axl's "sexy, screechy vocals" – "from ballads to balls-to-the-wall R&R there's something for everyone"; but

bashers awash in November rain rant it's "equal amounts
brilliant anthems and annoying filler."

Arlo Guthrie, *Alice's Restaurant*   24 | 26 | 21 | 20
1967, Reprise; "Alice's Restaurant Massacree";
www.arlo.net

■ "You can get anything you want on" this "authentic icon's"
"classic anti-war album" best-known for the title-track
"mother of all A.G. story-songs", an "entertaining" 18-
minute "comic tale" about garbage, turkey day, the draft
board and "an officious local cop"; it's "a flashback to the
hippie 1960s" that "every generation loves" insist fans
who "trot it out" "on Thanksgiving for a family listen" – it
"forever brings to mind the film" and the "Vietnam era."

Woody Guthrie,   27 | 29 | 24 | 19
The Greatest Songs of Woody Guthrie
1972, Vanguard; "This Land Is Your Land";
www.woodyguthrie.org

■ "To know folk music you must know Woody" – "it all
starts here" on this "essential" double album "that proves
why" this "grandaddy of them all" "influenced generations
of legendary performers", including friends, sidekicks and
acolytes Ramblin' Jack Elliott, "fave Cisco Houston", the
Weavers, Pete Seeger, Lead Belly, Joan Baez and Odetta, all
featured alongside the "true troubadour"; it's "Americana
personified" from a "compelling" "American icon."

Buddy Guy,   26 | 23 | 28 | 22
The Very Best of Buddy Guy
1992, Rhino; "First Time I Met the Blues"

■ "A great sampler", this anthology collects the "jams and
grooves" of "one of the world's most overlooked guitar
geniuses" culled from various labels, including Chess and
Vanguard, and featuring "extended workouts on *Stone
Crazy* and *First Time I Met the Blues*"; it's "worthy of a late-
night listen", but watch out – it may "emit smoke from your
CD player" because "this guy can wail!"

Guys and Dolls (Revival) **G**   26 | 27 | 25 | 25
1992, RCA; "Adelaide's Lament"

☑ Janes and Johns say "Nathan Lane out-Sinatras Sinatra"
in his "breakout Broadway performance" as Nathan
Detroit, while "priceless" Faith Prince is "the perfect Miss
Adelaide", "hitting a homer" in this revival of a "perfect
blend of music and lyrics and book" based on "Damon
Runyon's gamblers and their world"; even if some Angelos
and Maxies insist it "doesn't hold a candle to the original
soundtrack", they still admit "ya gotta love the show."

Gypsy (Original cast recording) **G**   27 | 27 | 27 | 26
1959, Sony; "Rose's Turn"

■ "Everything's coming up Ethel" on this "disc that
preserves the most challenging role in her career" as "the

stage mother of all time"; "all of Merman's idiosyncrasies become assets" in a "thrilling" show based on the memoirs of daughter/stripper Gypsy Rose Lee; "the remastered CD brings out all the grit of the original", from "the greatest theater overture ever" to the final "nervous breakdown in song" – "without a mike" no less, the lady will "knock your socks off."

H

Hair (Original cast recording) G #1 | 24 | 25 | 22 | 23 |
1968, RCA; "Aquarius"

■ "No shampoo needed to enjoy" the "musical that's head and shoulders above all others" of its kind; "what a piece of work" it was in its time: a "subversive", "hair-storical" "happening" that "captured a cultural moment" and "advanced Broadway to modern times" with "wit" and "raw rock crawling down your spine"; although "flower children might now all be yuppies" "dreaming of when they had hair" and deeming this recording "dated", others find the "great anti-war show" "especially timely" – as in: "send an album to Bush."

Hairspray | 26 | 24 | 25 | 27 |
(Original cast recording)
2002, Sony; "You Can't Stop the Beat"

■ "Dance and hop" and "embrace your grandmother's pink can of Aquanet" to "infectious pop" that "will turn anyone into a hairhopper"; you can't stop the beat of gay caballeros Marc Shaiman and Scott Wittman's "feel-good musical of the century", which "captures the spirit of the '60s" in a "fluffy" fashion; though "hysterically funny" Harvey Fierstein's "croaking" "makes Jack Klugman sound like Perry Como", it "puts a smile on your face" 'cause it positively "out-greases *Grease*."

Hall & Oates, *Rock 'n' Soul, Part 1* | 24 | 24 | 23 | 21 |
1983, RCA Victor; "Sara Smile"; www.hallandoates.com

■ A "guilty pleasure", this duo wrote "some of their best songs before they hit their '80s cheese-rock" period; this "greatest hits proves that when you filter out the chaff, there's fine pop wheat", including "blue-eyed soul" ballads like *Sara Smile* that "show their Philly roots"; "so what if nobody can figure out what John Oates is contributing?" (ok, he plays, sings and produces); just get a load of Darryl Hall's "sing-along" "croon", and know why they charted "more than any group in history."

Herbie Hancock, *Head Hunters* | 26 | 23 | 27 | 26 |
1974, Columbia; "Watermelon Man"; www.herbiehancock.com

☑ "Is it jazz or is it funk, and who cares" anyway when "genius" pianist Herbie Hancock "steps up to the plate" to "enlighten a generation of white boys on what it means to be funky"?; on this "successful crossover effort", "the band is so tight you would swear they're telepathic", and their leader "has never been afraid to take chances", so the "schizo combination" of genres is sure to "shake your bones to the marrow."

Herbie Hancock, *Maiden Voyage*   27 | 27 | 29 | 25

1965, Blue Note; "Maiden Voyage"; www.herbiehancock.com
■ "Herbie's best on Blue Note" is "a cornerstone of any jazz collection"; "just the first four chords" of the "widely praised", "pioneering" platter's title track "put the jazz world in an all-new place", "defining the era and style" of the '60s modal sound with "beautiful melodies and great musicianship"; "those eternal solos are each just perfect", and trumpeter "Freddie Hubbard smokes."

Handel, *Messiah*   28 | 28 | 27 | 26

1991, L'Oiseau Lyre; "Hallelujah Chorus"; www.aam.co.uk
■ It just "wouldn't be Christmas without" this "wonderful" old "holiday" "warhorse", and Christopher Hogwood's "passionate" conducting "brings new life to the large chestnut", while soprano Emma Kirkby "outshines the others" on a "sublime recording" of "crisp beauty" played on "period instruments"; listen and you'll understand "it's more than just the *Hallelujah Chorus*" – "the final two movements should make you cry."

Handel, *Water Music,*   27 | 27 | 26 | 26
Fireworks Music

1991, Philips
■ A "sublimely" "comfortable favorite", conductor John Eliot Gardiner's recording of the *Water Music Suites* and the *Music for Royal Fireworks* – the "toe-tappingest tunes until ragtime" – is a "bright, fresh, joyful celebration" of the "best of baroque", done "with all the old veneer removed"; "it captures the fun and festivities" so well, "if you close your eyes you are transported to Versailles", "firecrackers and fountains" ablaze.

Tim Hardin, *Reason to Believe*   26 | 27 | 24 | 21
(The Best of Tim Hardin)

1981, Polydor; "Reason to Believe"
■ On this "important collection" of "spare, wry, laconic little story-songs", the late "folk legend" Hardin "hurts and haunts the mind with lyrics that cut to the quick" and melodies brimming with "beautiful melancholy"; yes, other singers achieved more success with the songs he wrote than he did (Rod Stewart with the title track and Bobby Darin with *If I Were a Carpenter*) but his "versions really speak to the heart."

Ben Harper, *Burn to Shine*   25 | 27 | 27 | 24

1999, Virgin; "Steal My Kisses"; www.benharper.net
■ "A masterful guitar player" and his "excellent backing band" "cover all bases" on this "brilliant" breakthrough,

delivering an "eclectic, powerful" style that's "part Hendrix, part Marley, all Ben Harper"; no matter "what type of music he tackles", "be it hip-hop, gospel, metal, blues or folk", insiders who want to steal his kisses insist "he can do no wrong."

Emmylou Harris, *Pieces of the Sky*　28 | 26 | 28 | 26
1975, Reprise; "Boulder to Birmingham"; www.emmylou.net
■ "Priceless!" applaud admirers of this "incredibly strong" album that "announced with authority" the arrival of "one of the most adventurous" and "truly great voices in country"; her "pure and honest" sound "acknowledges rock" but remains "faithful to" the genre's rural roots, and even decades later it's still "hard to top the crystal clear elegance" of this "angelic" "musical treasure."

Emmylou Harris, *Wrecking Ball* ⑤　27 | 27 | 27 | 27
1995, Elektra; "Wrecking Ball"; www.emmylou.net
■ Producer "Daniel Lanois pulled off another magic trick, breaking down all the boundaries" with this "transcendent collection" featuring Neil Young, who also penned the title track, Steve Earle and Lucinda Williams; Ball-goers insist that Emmylou, now "one of the icons in alt-country music", has never sounded better"; on one hand "the sweetest sounds you'll ever hear", it's also "a painful set" that "will send you soul-searching" – either way, "you're hooked."

George Harrison,　27 | 26 | 27 | 25
All Things Must Pass 🔢
1971, Apple/Capitol; "My Sweet Lord"
■ "The Silent Beatle's" "creative mark of independence" – "a spiritual, joyful celebration of life" – "meets Phil Spector's Wall of Sound" to create "a transcendental rock & roll romp"; "emerging from the shadows of John and Paul" with "evocative" songs, he "showed he was their equal" ("savin' 'em up, eh, Georgie?"); whether or not they "knew how brilliant he was", one thing is sure: "with a little help from his friends" Eric Clapton, Dave Mason and Ginger Baker", he recorded a "life-affirming" "masterpiece."

PJ Harvey, *Rid of Me*　25 | 27 | 23 | 21
1993, Island; "Rid of Me"; www.pjharvey.net
■ Imagine "Bob Dylan and Patti Smith had a baby and named her Polly Jean!": "what a deeply moving" effort – with "gritty angst and killer riffs", "fierce", "edgy" PJ "rocks from the get-go"; "emotionally sincere and powerful in sound and substance" with "sublime writing", "this album is like having salt rubbed in a wound and liking it"; "getting the Steve Albini production treatment never felt so right."

Richie Havens, *Mixed Bag*　25 | 24 | 25 | 23
1967, Verve/Polydor; "Follow"; www.richiehavens.com
■ A "true song stylist" with a "voice unlike any other folkie", Havens showcases his goods on this mixed bag

that reveals his "gift for making someone else's" tunes "his own" – it's "a must for anyone who lived through Vietnam"; conveying "concern and passion", he tackles his own "heartfelt" *Follow* as well as Dylan's *Just Like a Woman* and the Lennon-McCarthy chestnut *Eleanor Rigby* – yes, "the man who later opened Woodstock rules."

Isaac Hayes, *Hot Buttered Soul* | 27 | 25 | 27 | 25 |
1969, Stax; "Walk on By"; www.isaachayes.com
■ The "influential producer" with the voice of "velvet heat" was "way ahead of his time" in 1969 with this "pure '70s" collection of "extremely lengthy", "full-blown suites" "featuring raps by Hayes and funk workouts courtesy of the Bar-Kays" that "forever changed soul music" by "helping to switch" the conceptual "emphasis from singles to albums"; it's sure to "set you on fire" – "Barry White move over, this is the music to get your girl in the mood."

Isaac Hayes, *Shaft* G #1 | 26 | 24 | 26 | 25 |
1971, Enterprise; "Theme from Shaft"; www.isaachayes.com
■ Wanna be a "badass?" – "get that wah-wah pedal crankin'" and wail along as the "bald-headed, multi-instrumentalist sex machine creates" the "coolest soundtrack" for the "blaxploitation" flick about that namesake "mutha"; one of the "best movie themes of all time" provides the "most distinctive build-up" to a "gritty" "tour de funk" that "ushered in a whole new era" of "innovative, dynamic, rhythmic" sound; "can you dig it?" – it's a "classic" 'cause "ya just don't mess with Shaft."

Hedwig and the Angry Inch | 26 | 27 | 24 | 24 |
(Soundtrack)
2000, Hybrid; "Origin of Love"
■ "In case you were wondering where the next great transsexual rock musical was coming from, here it is"; this "uplifting" "glam opera" manages to be "a more serious *Rocky Horror*" "for the 21st century" and "100% original"; with help from guitarist Bob Mould, "genius" star "John Cameron Mitchell really sells" singer-songwriter Stephen Trask's "incredible songs" "about finding out who you are and where you belong" – you'll "burst into tears", "wondering how best to release your inner wig."

Jascha Heifetz, | 27 | 28 | 28 | 22 |
Beethoven & Mendelssohn: Violin Concertos
1955, RCA; "Beethoven Violin Concerto"
■ Jascha Heifitz's "excellent performance" of possibly "the finest violin concerto ever written" is "a must for fiddlers", and "anyone who wants to hear how warmly" "the technical genius" could play: "it doesn't get any better" than "the master" accompanied by the Boston Symphony Orchestra on a "digital remaster of a hiss-filled analog recording"; the piece is so "unworldly", "this must be how it sounded in Beethoven's inner ear."

JASCHA HEIFETZ, *THE SUPREME*   28 | 27 | 28 | 25
1955, RCA; "Brahms Violin Concerto"

■ "What a combination": Jascha "Heifetz is the master of them all", the Chicago Symphony Orchestra "under Reiner" is "at the top of its game", and Brahms? – he "can do no wrong"; "the violin entrance" in his concerto is one of the "most thrilling moments in classical music", and here it's "played flawlessly" with "excellent imaging" for a "heart-stopping performance" you "never tire of hearing"; on a disc including supreme highlights of the maestro's career, you "could listen to it every day."

Jimi Hendrix, *Band of Gypsys*   25 | 23 | 28 | 21
1970, Capitol; "Machine Gun"; www.jimi-hendrix.com

■ "Maybe the finest live album ever" and "arguably one of the best blues records", this set is "timeless, effortless, beautiful"; recorded at the legendary Fillmore East with Hendrix's old army pal Billy Cox on bass, this is as far from pop as the "undisputed genius of electric guitar" got; "if you really want to hear Jimi stretch out" on his Strat, "get this."

Jimi Hendrix Experience,   28 | 25 | 29 | 24
Are You Experienced?
1967, Reprise/MCA; "Purple Haze"; www.jimi-hendrix.com

■ "The most revolutionary debut album of the era", this "epochal" "milestone" "exploded on the mid-'60s scene like an R&R comet" with "trippy production" and "no sonic precedent"; this "wild, witty" "wow experience" is a "feedback-drenched tour de force" from a "guitar virtuoso" who would be dead three years later – aided by the "inventive" bassist Noel Redding and "superb drummer Mitch Mitchell" who "borrowed from jazz to create a style with funk overtones."

JIMI HENDRIX EXPERIENCE,   28 | 26 | 30 | 26
ELECTRIC LADYLAND 🏆
1968, Reprise/MCA; "Voodoo Chile"; www.jimi-hendrix.com

■ "Limitless facets of bold talent" are showcased on this "high-water mark" that "moves beyond psychedelia", "expanding on blues ideas, stretching into churning jazz themes, yet creating a cohesive vibe"; originally a double album, this "abstract", yet "fully formed" "must-have" "seems to go by in 15 minutes"; "Eddie Kramer produced it so well", "it sounds futuristic today" – still, it's "a bittersweet taste of what was to come", as this "scintillating" guitarist "fell victim to the allure of sex, drugs and R&R."

Don Henley,   24 | 24 | 25 | 25
Building the Perfect Beast 🏆
1984, Geffen; "Boys of Summer"; www.donhenley.com

■ "One of the best lyricists in the music arena", this former Eagle flies high with his second "strong solo effort", flanked by ace musicians, including Randy Newman, Patty Smyth, Belinda Carlisle, Lindsey Buckingham, Benmont Tench and Mike Campbell; "sparkling yet tuneful", this "stellar" beast "doesn't have a flaw" – it's the "perfect summer album" "loved simply" for the hit *The Boys of Summer,* a great top-down-in-the-convertible song" that "evokes memories of sweeter times."

Don Henley,   25 | 25 | 24 | 25
The End of the Innocence 🅖 #1
1989, Geffen; "The End of the Innocence"; www.donhenley.com
■ "The end of the Eagles was not an end to the excellence" for "perceptive" Henley who "continued to soar" with this "coming of age" marker that "gives you chills" as it "looks back at a time that now seems lost"; it's "California rock filtered through a literary sensibility", with "cynicism" and "sharp wordplay" "offset by a dose of romanticism" and many guest appearances, including Axl Rose on *I Will Not Go Quietly* and Bruce Hornsby on the "title track, an anthem of sentimentality."

High Fidelity (Soundtrack)   26 | 23 | 24 | 25
2000, Hollywood; "Let's Get It On "
■ "You feel like you've just gotten a great mix tape from movie hero Rob and his Championship Vinyl gang" with this "eclectic" compilation "epitomizing record collectors everywhere"; a "great book turned into a great movie turned into a great soundtrack" – scratch that, make it a "killer soundtrack" – it manages to include both mainstream hits like Marvin Gaye's *Let's Get It On* with "off-the-beaten-path stuff" like Royal Trux's *Inside Game*; "if only they could have put all the songs in the flick on here."

Faith Hill, *Breathe* 🅖 #1   23 | 22 | 23 | 23
1999, Warner Bros.; "Breathe"; www.faithhill.com
◪ "The lovely Faith" "comes out from the shadow of the Nashville machine" on this Grammy-winning "versatile combo of country and pop", "a crossover smash" that proved she was "more than just a pretty face"; busting "all barriers", Hill "goes uptown with the sultry hit song" and offers a "lovely duet with husband Tim McGraw", prompting Hill-ions to sigh it's "destined to become a romantic classic"; still, a handful huff "she's gone too Hollywood for my taste."

Lauryn Hill,   27 | 26 | 26 | 26
The Miseducation of Lauryn Hill 🅖 #1
1998, Ruffhouse; "Doo Wop (That Thing)"
■ "A showcase" for the "honey voice" of the former Fugee, this Grammy-sweeping solo debut is "damn fine"; "well-crafting" it all, from the "self-assuredness" of *Doo Wop (That Thing)* and the "heartbreak" of *Ex-Factor* to the "joy" of *To Zion,* Hill comes across as "a teacher, lover, mother and fighter" who "brings hip-hoppers over to R&B" and vice versa; though the "spiritual" and "social commentary" can be "preachy", listeners' only real complaint is that "she hasn't produced more" new work.

Robyn Hitchcock,
I Often Dream of Trains

24 | 26 | 23 | 21

1984, Midnight; "Uncorrected Personality Traits"

■ In language akin to a Hitchcock lyric, devotees describe this acoustic set as "a lo-fi beauty that careens between solemn introspection and fungus"; "quirky", "esoteric" but "melodic", this sample of the former Soft Boys' "solo side", as revealed in "a dozen or so incredible tales of trains, trams and furry green atom bowls", spotlights the "off-his-rocker genius" at his "quietest", and some say his "best."

HITSVILLE USA: THE MOTOWN SINGLES COLLECTION 1959-1971 (Compilation)

29 | 28 | 28 | 28

1992, Motown; "Dancing in the Street"

■ A whopping "four CDs of staggering R&B excellence", this "best of the best" will make you feel like you've "died and gone to Motown heaven"; conjuring up baby-boomer nostalgia, songs like Martha and the Vandellas' *Dancing in the Street,* Gladys Knight and the Pips' version of *I Heard It Through the Grapevine* and the Temptations' *The Way You Do the Things You Do* capture "the sound of young America always and forever."

Billie Holiday, *Lady Sings the Blues*

28 | 26 | 28 | 24

1956, Verve; "God Bless the Child";
www.cmgww.com/music/holiday

■ "Speaking to the ache in the soul", this "sad", late-career collection by "the epitome of jazz-blues" singers is perfect "for nursing a broken heart", or breaking it into even smaller bits; for "tragic beauty", Billie is "in a league by herself", but the "coarse" "tenderness" of "Lady Day's voice" "on smack" is so "tortured", you "gotta be in the mood" for "one of the most touching albums ever"; grab the "tissue" and get ready to "cry" from "the emotion of it all."

The Hollies,
The Hollies' Greatest Hits

24 | 22 | 22 | 21

1973, Epic; "Bus Stop"

■ "If you're tired of head-banger music", then turn to Manchester's "powerhouse" of "pure pop perfection" and tune in to hits "with heart" like *Carrie Anne* and *Bus Stop* from a "kinder, gentler era"; "bouncy" with "beautiful harmonies woven around sensitive lyrics", it represents "the best of the British Invasion"; still a few who feel it sounds a "bit samey" insist "they got better later in their career."

Buddy Holly,
The Best of Buddy Holly

27 | 26 | 26 | 22

1999, MCA/Universal; "Peggy Sue";
www.buddyholly.com

■ "A fun, poppy" "collection of the best-known hits" by the "most eclectic, unforgettable rock writer" who was "so much more than just the link between Elvis and the

Beatles": in addition to "great songs, voice, persona and arrangements (though cheesy production)", "he introduced the hiccup and seriously unhip eyewear to rock & roll"; "February 3, 1959, was the day the music died", and "his loss changed the course of American pop" forever.

Holst, *The Planets*   26 | 26 | 26 | 25
1986, Penguin Classics; "Mars, the Bringer of War"; www.osm.ca

■ "The rock opera of the classics", this "spellbinding tone poem" to the solar system has "reverbed" its "influence through every sci-fi soundtrack of the last 50 years"; conductor Charles Dutoit's "dead-on" reading of the 20th-century's "blockbuster" "extravanganza" is "mystical", "dramatic and wonderful", with a "lush sound" and "superb performances" by the Montreal Symphony Orchestra and women of its choir that come through "spectacularly" on the disc's "stunning sonics."

John Lee Hooker, *The Ultimate Collection*   28 | 25 | 27 | 22
1991, Rhino; "Boom Boom"; www.johnleehooker.com

■ "Like a cool breeze on a hot Mississippi night", the "gritty, raw, nasty, emotional and rockin'" sounds from the "pillar of the Delta blues" "draws you in, heals you" and "always gets your booty moving"; one listen and you know "why rockers have used his tunes and licks", such as *Boogie Chillen* and *Boom Boom,* and why we now mourn the loss of "this national treasure."

Lena Horne, *An Evening with Lena Horne* G   26 | 25 | 27 | 25
1994, Blue Note; "The Lady Is a Tramp"

■ "Every one ought to own at least one Horne, and this is the one"; "Lena keeps growing more beautiful with age, as does her voice", and on this date recorded live at The Supper Club in New York when she was "in her 70s, she could still sing almost everyone else under the table", belting "her heart out", with the Count Basie Orchestra making "amazing music" to back up the "swinging lady."

VLADIMIR HOROWITZ, *HOROWITZ IN MOSCOW* G   29 | 27 | 29 | 25
1986, Deutsche Grammophon; "Rachmaninoff Prelude In G Major"

■ "A touching return home for the monster pianist of the 20th century", this 1986 concert – "one of the last and best recordings of this legendary performer" – garners this *Survey*'s top rating for Classical albums, proving that "Horowitz can still do it and more in his 80s"; "we laugh, we cry, we're on the edge of our seats" as "one of the saints" of the genre – now "frail" but still "powerful" – "sublimely" "shows his quieter side", "playing with nuances" and "tugging at heartstrings" for a "historic tour de force."

Whitney Houston,
The Bodyguard G #1

21 | 20 | 22 | 22

1992, Arista; "I Will Always Love You"; www.whitneyhouston.com
◪ The "golden" girl of "vocal acrobatics" slathers on the "sappiness" on this "mega-selling" soundtrack that "kept the movie in the box office"; "if only she could express on screen what she expresses singing", sigh fans hankering for her "stunning cover" of Dolly Parton's *I Will Always Love You* to get them through "dateless nights"; Whitney worshipers scratch tracks by other artists as "filler", while critics of the diva diss her "textbook overemoting."

Whitney Houston,
Whitney Houston #1

23 | 21 | 23 | 23

1985, Arista; "How Will I Know"; www.whitneyhouston.com
■ Sure "crack is whack, but this album is not – what a groundbreaker" Whitney's "stunning debut" was; "a star was born" who "almost had it all": a gospel-trained voice that "could sing the ABCs" and "send chills down your spine", producers who treated her "like the jewel she is" and a record-breaking number of chart-topping hits in a "fresh" R&B style that "made you wanna dance with somebody"; "pure magic" from "the phenom's beginning", it "shows the potential that Whitney has never met."

HOWLIN' WOLF,
MOANIN' IN THE MOONLIGHT

29 | 27 | 28 | 24

1987, Chess; "Red Rooster"; www.howlinwolf.com
■ A "giant of a man" with an "inimitable huge voice and energy" and "a style to match", Wolf was such an "intimidating and ominous" "force", he garners this *Survey*'s Top Blues album – a wonder "that young '60s British rockers" "like the Stones" "even tried to cover him"; one listen to "this double album featuring most of the great hits and the sublime guitar work of Hubert Sumlin" and "you'll see why he was such an influence on so many musicians."

Hüsker Dü, *New Day Rising*

26 | 25 | 24 | 19

1984, SST; "Celebrated Summer"; www.bobmould.com
■ "Never has a punch in the face felt so good" declare diehards who anoint Bob Mould's "glorious" Minneapolis band "The Beatles of punk"; "smart with passion to burn", this "ear-bleeding, pile driver" was "one of *the* definitive albums of college" radio and the "'80s alternative" scene; an "intense" blend of "distorted fury" and "shimmering pop", it's a "kick-ass" "classic" that, no apologies, shows those "flavor-of-the-week bands" "how it's done."

I

Ian & Sylvia, *Northern Journey*

24 | 24 | 24 | 23

1964, Vanguard; "You Were on My Mind"
■ "What beauty they evoked" gush fans of this Canadian husband-and-wife duo, "a great team" who wrote and sang

"folk gems" like *You Were on My Mind*, "which became a pop hit for the group the We Five"; the "long forgotten" couple may have journeyed far from the public eye, but this "yeomanlike" album still stands as an "outstanding" showcase for their "wonderful lyrics" and harmonies.

Janis Ian, *Between the Lines* #1 25 | 26 | 22 | 23
1975, Columbia; "At Seventeen"; www.janisian.com
■ Though she first recorded at age 15, this "ultimate expression of angst", cut eight years later, proved Ian's "breakthrough", thanks to the "intimate" hit *At Seventeen,* "an ode to lost innocence", which "perfectly captures" the turmoil inside "the teenage ugly duckling"; though "not an album to liven up the party", it's "a tour de force" that "showcases" the "strong, fragile, beautiful" voice of "one of the original sensitive young women" singer-songwriters.

Ice Cube, 24 | 24 | 22 | 24
AmeriKKKa's Most Wanted
1990, Priority; "The Nigga Ya Love to Hate"; www.icecube.com
■ A "lyrical masterpiece" by "far-and-away the best rapper" to come out of the rabble-rousing outfit N.W.A, this debut blends the Bomb Squad's blistering "East Coast" production with "West Coast style" to make for a "gangsta version of Public Enemy" on volatile cuts like *The Nigga Ya Love to Hate*; though critics ice its "misguided politics", Cubists call the album "one of the illest ever."

Billy Idol, *Rebel Yell* 21 | 18 | 21 | 21
1983, Chrysalis; "Rebel Yell"; www.billyidol.com
■ The ex–Generation X frontman, with his "spiked hair, sneer and charisma", struck double platinum with this "seminal", "rollicking, rebellious affair" featuring, "oh yeah, baby, killer guitarist Stevie Stevens"; back in the new wave days the golden Idol's "get-you-going" music "made you want to bleach your hair" – while "*Rebel Yell* made you cry more, more, more"; still, a few feel this fantasy-catalyst lacks flesh – "one great song does not a great album make."

India.Arie, *Voyage to India* 25 | 26 | 26 | 24
2002, Motown; "Little Things"; www.indiaarie.com
■ The "smooth-as-silk" voice of this "angelic" singer-songwriter is the "sweet, soulful" vessel for "heartfelt words of wisdom" that voyage "into the crevices of your mind"; fans who were "afraid that her sophomore effort would be overshadowed by the success" of her debut, *Acoustic Soul,* are relieved to have been "wrong"; "empowering", "beautiful" and "sexy", the disc proves this "a breath of fresh air" in R&B is "the real thing."

Indigo Girls, *Indigo Girls* G 26 | 27 | 25 | 23
1989, Epic; "Closer to Fine"; www.indigogirls.com
■ The "spine-tingling harmonies of Emily Saliers and Amy Ray" "speak to your soul" ("these Georgia girls rock!") on

the "accessible folk-pop" duo's "emotionally penetrating" debut that features appearances from R.E.M., Hothouse Flowers and Luka Bloom and the "catchy" "sing-along" single *Closer to Fine*; with "moving" "lyrics that "combine the angst of young adult drama with the idealism of a better tomorrow", it's "great for nights when you're feeling blue."

INXS, *Kick* 　　　23 | 22 | 23 | 24

1987, Atlantic; "Need You Tonight"; www.inxs.com
■ "Is it rock, dance or just a band of fun-lovin' Aussies kickin' it with a new sound altogether?" – however you define it, this Sydney group was "truly a sensation"; "with a funky beat" and "soulful swagger", this "stunning accomplishment", "full of catchy" chart-toppers like *Need You Tonight* and *Devil Inside* highlight the "sexy voice" of "mesmerizing lead singer" Michael Hutchence, who tragically hanged himself in 1997.

Iron Maiden, 　　　24 | 23 | 26 | 22
The Number of the Beast

1982, Capitol; "Run To The Hills"; www.ironmaiden.com
■ "The alpha and omega of metal" full of "spectacular" "twin guitar fury coupled with air-raid siren vocals", this landmark featuring new frontman Bruce Dickinson "put Maiden on the map in the USA"; two decades on, the iron-clad amalgam of "hard, rhythmic riffs" and "supreme bass playing", showcasing the "band in its prime", is still "worth a listen – just to remember the hair."

Chris Isaak, *Heart Shaped World* 　24 | 24 | 26 | 24

1989, Reprise; "Wicked Game"; www.chrisisaak.com
■ "What a hottie" – "brooding" and "seductive", "this generation's Roy Orbison" channels "country, blues and old-fashioned rock & roll" for "the perfect background for a sultry" "beach night" with your "surfer" sweetheart; in a "voice that could melt butter", "the coolest guy in the room" "croons" tunes "full of longing, obsession and love gone wrong" – "check out *Wicked Game*", and the only question you'll have is "how many times can one guy's heart be broken?"

J

Alan Jackson, *A Lot About Livin'* 　26 | 24 | 26 | 25
(And a Little 'Bout Love)

1992, Arista; "Chattahoochee"; www.alanjackson.com
■ *Livin'* lovers laud this third effort as "an excellent representation of the sound and style" of the blond-haired, blue-eyed "country mogul", one of the '90's first to give "C&W a fresh voice"; this "album contributes to his legend" offering up "*Chattahoochie* – what a power song of summer"; his "hot" band "cooks", leaving Jacksonites "ready to chute" that Georgia river "while whistling" his other keeper, *Mercury Blues*.

Jackson 5, *Anthology*   27 | 23 | 25 | 25
1976, Motown; "I Want You Back"

■ Oh, if "Michael could have stayed frozen in time when he was nine" – "in the good old days when they looked like they came from the same family", the five brothers – Jackie, Jermaine, Tito, Marlon and "little" MJ – "were an excellent group, and this collection shows why"; a three-disc retrospective from "innocent times" with "incredible" hits like *I Want You Back*, and *ABC*, plus lesser-known tracks like *Teenage Symphony*, it's guaranteed to "make you want to dance"

Janet Jackson, *janet.* ▣1   25 | 22 | 24 | 25
1993, Virgin; "If"; www.janet-jackson.com

■ "Watch out, world" – this "dynamic performer" "finally sheds her clothes" and comes across as "nasty" and "as sexy as she wants to be", "establishing herself as a mature talented artist" on this "sensually honest" offering; Janet's "voice is in fine shape" and über-producers Jimmy Jam and Terry Lewis "showcase her talent" with "strong grooves" that "make you want to dance", "sultry ballads" and a cache of "catchy" pop tunes.

Janet Jackson,   26 | 24 | 24 | 26
Janet Jackson's Rhythm Nation 1814 ▣1
1989, A&M; "Love Will Never Do (Without You)"

■ Janet "kicks it" with "socially conscious music" on this "essential" album that "set the dance world on its ear" and "still sounds urgent today" rave rhythm nationals who consider the "well-crafted" "breakthrough" her "bridge from nice to naughty"; "every single blows us away" with its "spunk", and all the "brilliant" "rock, R&B and dance-pop" chart-toppers "fit together perfectly"; "what can you say?" – in Ms. Jackson's case, "it's in the genes."

Joe Jackson, *Night and Day*   25 | 26 | 26 | 25
1982, A&M; "Steppin' Out"; www.joejackson.com

■ "Steppin' out" of "angry young man" mode, this "equally sensitive and snide" "reinvented new waver" sounds and "looks sharp" on this "polished, sophisticated" effort jammed with "urbane, lyrical" tales and "well-crafted, impeccably played" melodies; "channeling Cole Porter", this "jazzy", "deftly produced" disc "for more adult tastes" captures "the feel of the big city" through "catchy songs, congas and complex" arrangements.

Michael Jackson, *Bad* ▣ ▣1   22 | 21 | 24 | 25
1987, Epic; "Bad"; www.michaeljackson.com

▨ "Nothing could follow *Thriller* commercially", still this "confident" "colossus" "stands on its own feet" with "rhythm and dancing power"; fans fawn the "legend continues" with a platinum pairing that delivers one of producer "Quincy Jones' finest moments" and places the "true King of Pop" in a "class all his own"; "you expect better" pounce pouters put off by the "duds in the middle" – "in hindsight", this is when "MJ starts losing his touch."

Michael Jackson, *Off the Wall* **①** | 26 | 25 | 26 | 26 |
1979, Epic; "Don't Stop 'Til You Get Enough";
www.michaeljackson.com
■ MJ "makes everybody want to rock with him" on "the album that started it all"; "sweet, soulful singing and emotions" delivered over "smooth" "pop" beats with disco and R&B grooves drove "his ascent into the stratosphere"; this is "the Michael we loved growing up", "before the plastic surgery, the pet monkey, the entourage, when he was just going solo", so there's a "back when" nostalgia to it.

MICHAEL JACKSON, *THRILLER* **G①** | 28 | 26 | 27 | 28 |
1982, Epic; "Billie Jean"; www.michaeljackson.com
■ "I don't care if his nose is falling off", say spectators of the "freaky" MJ circus, this "blockbuster" is "magic"; this *Survey*'s Top Contemporary Pop disc is an innovative "benchmark", "fusing funk, R&B, dance, rock", "pop and soul" into a "masterpiece" "so full of hits, it's ridiculous"; given the "thrill of *Billie Jean*", *Wanna Be Startin' Somethin'* and other cuts, "how could you not sing along"? – "'ma ma se ma ma sa ma ma coo sa', 'nuff said."

The Jam, *The Jam Collection* | 28 | 27 | 24 | 22 |
1996, Polydor; "To Be Someone (Didn't We Have A Nice Time)";
www.thejam.org
■ Perhaps "the greatest British band to completely strike out in the U.S.", this "peer of the Clash" lives again on an "awesome" anthology that moves from "power pop" to "the coming new wave"; UK "national treasure" Paul Weller hitched "a Motown vibe with a punk edge" to "meaningful" lyrics "that reflected the blue-collar life of English youth", providing a sound "that never gets old"; bands like Blur and Pulp "owe the Modfather a big nod in gratitude."

Ahmad Jamal, *At the Pershing:* | 25 | 23 | 27 | 24 |
But Not for Me
1958, Argo; "Poinciana"; www.ahmadjamal.info
■ "Miles Davis admired" this "giant", and it's easy to hear why on this "timeless" live set, one of three recorded at the Pershing during a turning point in the pianist's career; "encapsulating the music at the time", its "sound and rhythms" "opened the ears" of "the masses" to jazz; "later recordings of Jamal doing the same material aren't as fresh as this", poor "miking" and "cafe noise" notwithstanding.

Elmore James, *The Sky Is Crying:* | 28 | 26 | 28 | 22 |
The History of Elmore James
1993, Rhino; "Dust My Broom"
■ "The king of slide guitar", who wrote *Dust My Broom* (based on the Robert Johnson Delta classic), renowned for his "gritty, beautifully raw", "searing, pivotal" style, was a

"touchstone for many blues and rock" fretmen who "came later"; this "great" anthology documents "his passion for playing and singing": "once the white guys heard this, R&R had a new soul"; sadly, "his career was cut tragically short" when he died of a heart attack at age 45 in 1963.

Etta James,   28 | 25 | 27 | 24
The Essential Etta James
1993, MCA/Chess; "At Last"; www.etta-james.com
■ "Raucous, passionate, rowdy and earthy" with a "voice so burning with heartbreak it kills you", the "big, bad Ms. James" "smolders like no other" on this "classic two-CD set" ("no song melts my heart like *At Last*" – "you bet your sweet ass she's essential"); "this is vintage stuff" that "covers the range of her work with style", making you "want to dance or make love all night long."

Jane's Addiction,   25 | 23 | 25 | 24
Ritual de lo Habitual
1990, Warner Bros.; "Three Days"; www.janesaddiction.com
■ Powered by Perry Farrell's "screeching vocals", the "perfect foil" for guitarist Dave Navarro's "art-metal soundscapes", this "enduring" lollapalooza of "tribal rhythms and pure rock" portrayed "the seedy underbelly of LA", revealing the "Hollywood you don't see on the silver screen"; a "sprawling, cohesive masterpiece", this "musical adventure" "set the high-water mark" for "the only alternative band to carry on the epic legacy of Led Zeppelin."

Jean-Michel Jarre, *Oxygene*   25 | 22 | 26 | 25
1977, Dreyfus; "Oxygene, Part IV"; www.jarre.com
■ "Before the terms 'New Age' and 'ambient' came into play, we used to call it 'mood music'", and this "pioneering" "Frenchman with the funky haircut knew how to work" it way back in 1977; "purity personified" on "his synthesizers", Jarre "inspired the world of music to go electronic", creating "timeless, whirling beats" that left "visions of laser light shows in your head" – this "phenomenal" disc is "the one that started it all for so many fans" of techno.

Keith Jarrett, *The Köln Concert*   26 | 24 | 29 | 25
1975, ECM; "Part II C"; www.keithjarrett.net
◪ "Jarrett creates a new piece of music in front of the audience", a "rambling" "journey through many tempos" "sparkling with spontaneous splendor" through to "the finale, *Part II C*, as beautiful and sad a tune as you'll hear"; "dismissed by some as New Age pabulum, it's still one of the most inspired solo piano recordings", and it "could only have been played this way."

Jay-Z, *The Blueprint* 🔢   24 | 24 | 21 | 24
2001, Roc-a-Fella; "Takeover"
◪ Whether it's on the bangin' "party anthem" *Takeover*, the "tearjerker" *Song Cry* or the "damned funny" *Girls,*

Girls, Girls, everyone's "favorite recovering crack dealer from Brooklyn" tells "stories of the streets like no one else" on this "cohesive" "tour de force of bravado"; the "multiplatinum double CD" shows that the "versatile artist" "knows how to put together the flows", even though a handful of hip-hop heads say "his best material is on earlier albums."

Jefferson Airplane, *Surrealistic Pillow*
26 | 25 | 25 | 22

1967, RCA; "White Rabbit"; www.jeffersonairplane.com
■ "Passionate" vocalist Grace Slick joined the "psychedelic San Francisco band" for their second album "bringing great songs with her like *White Rabbit* and *Somebody to Love*" (originally performed with her first band, the Great Society); "one can still get lost in its heavy metalness as she soars on golden voice" ("the clarion call for a generation"), along with "Jorma Kaukonen and Jack Casady rockin'" and "(Marty) Balin and (Paul) Kantner weaving" "brilliant" "tunes that still evoke a smile."

Waylon Jennings, *Honky Tonk Heroes*
27 | 27 | 27 | 26

1973, RCA; "Honky Tonk Heroes"; www.waylon.com
■ "Giving Nashville the finger was never this much fun again" – "they don't make 'em like this anymore" lament lovers of the late legend's stripped-down "excellent" landmark effort, which more or less "defined the outlaw country movement"; it's the "real thing", the "epitome of bad boy music", and it captures the "true essence" of the rambling man's "distinctive voice" and honky tonk 'tude "as he delivers Billy Joe Shaver's well-written songs."

Jesus Christ Superstar (Original cast recording) 🔢
25 | 25 | 23 | 24

1970, MCA; "I Don't Know How to Love Him"
■ The "sublime" "pairing of Andrew Lloyd Weber's powerful music" and "entertaining lyrics" written by Tim Rice was "breathtaking", declare disciples who anoint this "grooving, moving" "masterful concept album" the "granddaddy of Broadway rock operas"; featuring "some of the funkiest bass lines ever" and songs where "every word counted", "this soundtrack evokes all the fire of the musical"; still a few nonbelievers fret it's "a formula, like a Grisham book: not bad, just not all it was cracked up to be."

Jethro Tull, *Aqualung*
26 | 25 | 26 | 23

1971, Chrysalis; "Aqualung"; www.j-tull.com
■ Who "thought a flute could rock this hard"? – "words cannot describe" "the energy, anger, creativity and greatness contained" in every '70s "high school boy's favorite"; led by "captivating" "pied piper" Ian Anderson, whose "lyrics are full of religious and social commentary", these "minstrels" "are extremely talented."

Joan Jett & the Blackhearts, I Love Rock 'n' Roll   22 | 19 | 21 | 20

1981, Blackheart; "I Love Rock 'n' Roll"; www.joanjett.com
■ "It's not going to be anyone's *Sgt. Pepper*" but the former Runaway's platinum seller still stands as "the original tough-girl album"; Jett fliers proclaim this "tough, stripped-back rock-pop" ("fist-pounding in the air is de rigueur"), with its "inspirational anthem" of a title song, "killer screams" and "catchy" cover of Tommy James & the Shondells' *Crimson and Clover,* "essential independent woman listening", proving riot "grrls can do anything."

Antonio Carlos Jobim, Wave   28 | 27 | 28 | 25

1967, A&M; "Wave"
■ "Despite the relatively complicated music, breezy is the only word that captures the ease of this album" – that and "soothing, summery, cheerful, poignant, peaceful, sentimental, wistful" and "sophisticated"; "bossa nova personified", Antonio Carlos Jobim was "a master known by too few", a "perennial favorite" of Brazilian jazz fans who say he "had no superior in songwriting"; on this "gem" and others, he brought "a new sound to the world that continues to influence today."

Billy Joel, Piano Man   27 | 27 | 26 | 24

1974, Columbia; "Piano Man"; www.billyjoelmusic.com
■ "You can almost smell the spilled beer and cigarette smoke" on "the Piano Man's" "first album of consequence", which "launched" and "forever defined his career" ("who can't sing along" with the title track "bar anthem"?); it's "vintage Billy at his best" – the "stirring music and lyrics" "haven't aged one bit" – and if "some of the ballads are getting jukebox play today by kids not born when this came out", it's little wonder, as how could they "not be seduced by the stories he tells"?

Billy Joel, The Stranger   27 | 28 | 27 | 26

1977, Columbia; "Scenes from an Italian Restaurant"; www.billyjoelmusic.com
■ "I love it just the way it is" fawn fans of this "brilliantly produced" "guilty pleasure" of "smart, effective pop" songs that tell "stories of everyday life, love and Catholic girls" with "unabashed romanticism countered by New Yawk charm"; the Long Island "suburban poet" "created so many vivid, relatable characters" on this "sentimental favorite" that there are "no throwaway cuts" – but perhaps "what's stranger is he never had an album this good again."

Elton John, Greatest Hits ▮1   27 | 28 | 27 | 25

1974, MCA; "Your Song"; www.eltonjohn.com
■ "A fantastic starter CD for fans and those who just want the basics of EJ 101", this "gorgeously done" collection showcases the "man-diva's auspicious beginnings" with lyricist Bernie Taupin; "chock-full of likable songs and

incredible melodies" like *Daniel* and *Candle in the Wind* – "everyone knows at least one" – it feels like the "soundtrack to our lives"; "timeless, ageless and indefatigable", the "troubadour for the 20th century" "ain't a Sir for nothin'!"

27 | 27 | 27 | 26

Elton John,
Goodbye Yellow Brick Road ▦
1973, MCA; "Funeral for a Friend/Love Lies Bleeding";
www.eltonjohn.com
■ "Epic is the word to describe" this "flamboyant" "tour de force" that demonstrates "the ease with which John and Taupin could write not only the hit singles, but the outstanding album tracks"; originally a double disc ("we listened till the grooves wore down – remember vinyl?"), "the stunning song cycle" "with no filler" "feels like a mini-movie"; it's "Elton's *White Album*", his "commercial and creative" "apex", and it sure "showed what a piano could do to rock music."

28 | 27 | 28 | 16

Robert Johnson,
The Complete Recordings ▣
1990, Columbia/Legacy; "Cross Road Blues"
■ A "necessity for any collection" and "a primer" for novices, this landmark set features every known recording by the "mysterious Mississippi bluesman who allegedly sold his soul to the devil in exchange for his tremendous talent"; a masterful songwriter, guitarist and singer and the "spiritual father of the Rolling Stones and Eric Clapton", he "sends a chill up your spine": "there's a note in his voice that makes you believe those stories about what happened to him at the crossroads."

28 | 25 | 25 | 23

George Jones,
The Essential George Jones
1994, Epic/Legacy; "He Stopped Loving Her Today"
■ On this double-disc career-spanning collection containing early hits, "lush, loving recordings" of his "finest later" tracks, and collaborations with wife Tammy Wynette, Merle Haggard, Ray Charles and James Taylor, "the Ol' Possum shows why" he's "a country legend" "who's had an influence on every singer" in the genre "to come along after him"; "get out your hankies" – with a "voice as smooth as aged whiskey" he belts out *He Stopped Loving Her Today* – "if you can listen to it without drinking then you're the first."

26 | 24 | 26 | 26

NORAH JONES,
COME AWAY WITH ME ▣ ▦
2002, Blue Note/Capitol; "Come Away with Me";
www.norahjones.com
▨ "She's only how old?" – this "marvelous new voice" "has made a big splash", "sweeping the Grammys", topping the charts and going platinum on her Blue Note debut, "a breath of fresh air" for folks who can't stomach "screaming

rock"; the twentysomething "mistress of laid-back" "soothes away a nasty day" with a "nostalgic sound" as "luxurious as a cashmere wrap"; nevertheless, a "pop" platter "evoking smoky clubs and Old West campfires" alike has hepcats hissing this "fluff" "ain't no jazz."

Rickie Lee Jones, *Rickie Lee Jones*　　26 | 26 | 26 | 24
1979, Warner Bros.; "Chuck E's in Love"; www.rickieleejones.com

■ The beret-wearing, "jazzy Beat" "boho" singer "comes out of the gate smoking" on her "bluesy, laid-back" debut that "radiates cool"; peppered with "late-night themes" about "loving and losing in the city" and "interesting characters", her "beguiling songs" come off like "poetic storytelling", offering "seedy, sad little glimpses of life, much like Tom Waits", while her "incredible voice" ("quirks" and all) reminds some Jones-ians of a "modern Billie Holiday", albeit "with some funk."

Tom Jones,　　　　　　　　　 24 | 22 | 25 | 23
Tom Jones' Greatest Hits
1974, Parrot; "It's Not Unusual"; www.tomjones.com

■ "What's new, pussycat?" – not this guy, but he "still makes you want to be in Vegas every time you hear" these '60s hits; as legions of panty-throwing women confess, "anyone who can keep teen hormones alive for 30 years can't be all bad", but he's "not just a sex symbol – this Welshman can sing"; given his recent comeback, fans "don't underestimate the impact Jones has had on pop, or his way with a ballad" – from *It's Not Unusual* to *Green, Green Grass of Home,* he's a "cocktail party necessity."

Janis Joplin, *Pearl* 🔢1　　　26 | 24 | 23 | 21
1971, Columbia; "Me and Bobby McGee"; www.officialjanis.com

■ For "the 1960s' greatest white blues voice", this posthumous No. 1 album, featuring her hit cover of Kris Kristofferson's *Me and Bobby McGee,* "marked a new mood" that "this generation's Billie Holiday" "didn't live to explore"; "her voice had already been beaten into submission by cigarettes and Southern Comfort", but "few wailed with such soul"; while a handful of holdouts claim Big Brother's "*Cheap Thrills* was her shining moment", both discs "set the cosmos on fire."

Journey, *Escape* 🔢1　　　　22 | 21 | 23 | 22
1981, Columbia; "Open Arms"; www.journeymusic.com

■ "A turning point" in the San Francisco band's career, this "inspirational" album "launched Journey to superstardom", spawned three Top 10 singles, hung on the charts for nearly three years and zoomed to multiplatinum heights thanks to "Steve Perry's captivating voice"; *Don't Stop Believing* and *Open Arms,* "essential '80s power ballads", revive memories of "many underage parties" ("what else were you supposed to make-out to?").

Joy Division, *Closer*
28 | 27 | 25 | 24

1980, Factory; "Isolation"

■ "Beautiful and frightening, the Manchester band's second and final album is a harrowing and emotionally raw testament to the genius (and state of mind) of Ian Curtis", who hanged himself shortly after its completion and just prior to the band's first American tour; the "dark, depressed and innovative" album "saved my life", say some, while others point to its impact on "the subsequent goth movement" – "a paradigm shift for punk music."

Joy Division, *Substance*
26 | 26 | 25 | 23

1988, Qwest; "Love Will Tear Us Apart"

■ "Haunting" and "intense", this double-CD compilation of singles and B sides of the "seminal", "murky, mysterious" late '70s British group features "gloomy", "great songs like *Love Will Tear Us Apart*"; "unappreciated on the world stage", the late vocalist and rock poet Ian Curtis was on a par with Jim Morrison and Kurt Cobain", and his "influential" postpunk band (whose members went on to form New Order) was a "precursor to the angst-laden rock" that followed.

Wynonna Judd, *Wynonna*
24 | 23 | 24 | 24

1992, MCA; "She Is His Only Need"; www.wynonna.com

■ "Who needs Naomi?" Wynonna seems to imply on her debut solo, as she "leaves behind the hokey stylings of the mother-daughter act" the Judds and "stands alone with her big, raunchy voice" (what "great pipes") and big red mane; "it's an excellent country album", offering "stylish, soulful", "memorable tunes" ranging "from bluesy to aching to folksy" – she not only "rocks", she "kicks ass."

The Judds, *Greatest Hits*
26 | 24 | 25 | 24

1988, RCA/Curb; "Grandpa (Tell Me 'Bout the Good Old Days)"

■ The hugely popular "Judds are a magical duo" – "Wynonna's voice melds perfectly with her mother's to make amazing music", as showcased on this "fantastic compilation" of '80s hits, "a must for every contemporary country & western collection"; speaking to working women everywhere, "each song is so good you could cry", especially the "touching, heartfelt" *Grandpa (Tell Me 'Bout the Good Old Days)*.

Jurassic 5, *Power in Numbers*
25 | 25 | 26 | 26

2002, Interscope; "What's Golden"; www.jurassic5.com

■ "Happy hip-hop" with an "old-school flavor", the second major-label release from LA's "favorite mathematically challenged sextet", including four MCs and "two of the best DJs in the business", Cut Chemist and Nu-Mark, bumps with "jazz-influenced samples", "uplifting beats", "scintillating" hooks, "deep statements" and the rich baritone "flow" of standout rapper Chali 2na on "crowd-friendly" cuts that are "funky with a vengeance."

K

Kansas, *Point of Know Return*   22 | 22 | 23 | 22
1977, Kirshner; "Dust in the Wind"; www.kansasband.com
☑ Churning out "ballads in abundance", these "classically trained" "Midwestern icons", wizards who "put the rock in art rock", "solidified their status" with this "surprisingly commercial" multiplatinum "classic"; the "somber hit *Dust in the Wind*" and "the memorable title track" are "proof-positive" of their "unique sound"; but less-enamored listeners lament "the rest blends into obscurity."

KC & the Sunshine Band,   21 | 18 | 21 | 21
The Best of KC & the Sunshine Band
1989, Rhino; "Get Down Tonight"; ww.kcsbonline.com
■ "These songs can get you on the dance floor, drunk or not", so "if your party's going badly", "put your boogie shoes on" your feet, a "smile on your face" and this on your stereo and "enjoy" "reminiscing" to the classic disco beats; "it's amazing how many hits were generated by this band": "*Boogie Man, Shake Your Booty, Get Down Tonight* and so on", "it all comes flooding back" in one "super-funky" flow; hustlers "defy anyone to not shake it till they break it when it's played."

Keb' Mo', *Keb' Mo'*   25 | 24 | 25 | 25
1994, Okeh/550/Epic; "She Just Wants to Dance"; www.kebmo.com
☑ "A rare artist", Kevin Moore "accomplishes what's most hard to do, revitalizing" the "timeless tradition" of "countrified blues" "with witty, creative lyrics" and a "modern approach" that "brings sunshine into your house"; "he understands the masters" – the "spirit of Robert Johnson lives on" in music "sounding like he's in the cotton field with recording equipment"; still, a few purists pout he's a "little too mainstream."

Stan Kenton, *Kenton in Hi-Fi*   26 | 25 | 28 | 25
1956, Capitol; "Intermission Riff"
■ Kenton's "recreation of his music from the 1940s is in many ways better than the original recordings"; the disc "sizzles" with the "pure excitement" of "powerhouse performances" by "mature musicians" on "some of the greatest arrangements on the planet", delivering a "combination of complexity, drive and listenability" by a "true pioneer" of the "atypical big-band" sound.

Alicia Keys, *Songs in A Minor* G #   24 | 25 | 27 | 25
2001, J Records; "Fallin'"; www.aliciakeys.com
☑ "Talent, talent, talent" are three reasons fans "can't wait to hear more" from this young "classical pianist turned diva"; proving Keys "can write, produce and perform beautiful music" with the "versatility" of "a soul seasoned" beyond her 20 years, this "powerful" debut

ranges from "slow", heartfelt R&B ballads like the Grammy-winning *Fallin'* to "up-tempo", hip-hop–influenced numbers like *Girlfriend*; even if some of the cuts are "cheesy", "the more you listen, the more you love" it.

Albert King, *The Ultimate Collection*   28 | 25 | 28 | 23
1993, Rhino; "Born Under a Bad Sign"
■ "The master of the microtone" for whom "the Fender was made", this "underappreciated blues great" is "one of the most imitated guitarists of all time" – "listen to the solo on *Crosscut Saw* that Eric Clapton lifted for Cream's *Strange Brew*"; this double-disc anthology is "an excellent intro to his recordings", documenting his "incredible" talent – "no one else can make so few notes sound so good."

The King and I (Soundtrack) ⊞   27 | 28 | 26 | 25
1956, Angel; "Shall We Dance"
■ "Joy, joy and more joy" awaits in Siam with this "touchingly" "romantic" music "arranged gorgeously for the screen"; the soundtrack "beautifully" "preserves Yul Brynner's Oscar-winning" turn and "the marvelous Marni Nixon" "dubbing Deborah Kerr's voice wonderfully", while "the full power and glory" of the MGM studio orchestra "makes you want to dance" to the "very original" Rodgers and Hammerstein score, "et cetera, et cetera, et cetera."

B.B. King, *Live at the Regal*   28 | 25 | 29 | 23
1965, ABC/MCA; "How Blue Can You Get?"; www.bbking.com
■ "The template for what a blues album should be", this "influential" live set ("arguably the greatest ever") captures a "smokin'" Chicago performance that "is off the scale", with an "audience in obvious ecstasy from the first note on"; "in top form here", the "electrifying" Riley B. King exudes "personal warmth and graciousness" while "working the crowd into a frenzy" – "he makes" "Lucille (at her best)" "talk and still sends chills after all these years."

B.B. King and Eric Clapton,   24 | 22 | 28 | 25
Riding with the King ⏺ ⊞
2000, Reprise/WEA; "Riding with the King"; www.bbking.com; www.claptononline.com
☑ "The student sits back and lets the old master take the lead, but even though B.B. does most of the singing, it is the understated playing of Clapton" and the "back-porch jam session feel" "that makes this CD such a pleasure"; "guitar royalty reigns" on the "dream collaboration", yet a handful fret the set "falls short" due to the inclusion of "some ho-hum stuff" – "and slick production" ("rather listen to the two pals' individual albums").

Carole King, *Really Rosie*   25 | 26 | 25 | 25
1975, Ode; "Chicken Soup with Rice"; www.caroleking.com
■ Even "three-and-a-half-year-olds" get to "feel the earth move under their feet" with "Carole King for the whole

family"; "as much fun as it was 30 years ago", the "brilliant songwriter's" soundtrack to the Maurice Sendak TV special is "deep, adorable and just plain perfect", "in spite of the macabe content" lifted from the author/illustrator's book; "an alternative route for teaching the alphabet", it "makes a clever gift for those endless preschool birthday parties"; so "don't be Pierre, care!"

CAROLE KING, *TAPESTRY* G #1   29 | 29 | 26 | 25
1971, Ode; "So Far Away"; www.caroleking.com
◼ An "almost flawless representation of all that's good about the singer-songwriter movement", this "much-beloved" Grammy-winning "masterpiece" from the "Brill Building graduate" is "indelibly printed on the pop culture consciousness of the '70s" and has "a permanent seat on the all-time-greatest dais"; expect "no bells and whistles", just "powerful" "love-lorn balladry that transcends sap" and feels "like a conversation with an old friend"; this "beautifully woven collection resonates today" – "King is still the queen."

King Crimson,   25 | 24 | 27 | 25
In the Court of the Crimson King
1969, Atlantic; "21st Century Schizoid Man (Including Mirrors)"
◼ This "psychedelic window into the '60s" "simultaneously defined and mastered progressive rock", with songs ranging from the "controlled cacophony" of "apocalyptic" "heavy, metal epics" to "windblown English flute ballads", both "poetic and moving"; Crimson courtiers crown this debut as a "groundbreaking", "seminal work" "far ahead of its time", rife with "pomp, circumstance and bombast – back when those things were cool."

The Kingston Trio,   25 | 23 | 24 | 23
Sold Out/String Along
1992, Capitol; "Raspberries, Strawberries";
www.kingstontrio.com
◼ A "longtime favorite", this trio "popularized a new wave" of urban folk music that "brought fun into that world"; "one of the most listened-to groups" of their time with the "best harmonies" helped pave the way for Joan Baez and even Bob Dylan; strumming their banjos and guitars, they made some of "the most entertaining albums ever" as demonstrated by this single CD, a combination of two albums released in 1960.

The Kinks, *Lola vs. the Powerman* 27 | 27 | 26 | 24
vs. the Money Go-Round
1970, Castle; "Lola"
◼ "What can you say about a band led by" "the Davies boys", "the poet laureate of rock & roll (genius Ray) and the father of heavy-metal guitar" (Dave)?; this "concept album explores the life of a group on the brink of its first success" with "edgy, acerbic, yet tender and quite insightful

songs" "about the ups and downs of stardom"; yeah, these "influential Brits" are "at the peak of their powers here" – and "*Lola* still kicks ass!"

The Kinks, *Something Else* |28| 28 | 25 | 23|
1968, Reprise; "Waterloo Sunset"
■ "While the Summer of Love was going on in San Francisco, the Kinks created an album that sounded more like the Winter of Discontent with this cynical" "jewel in their crown" "that speaks more of everyday existence than the idealism that flourished across the pond"; "all Britpop starts here" – "it influenced everyone from Blur to Jesus Jones" – via the "social satire" and "terrific insight into swingin' London" manifested in "brilliant songs like *Waterloo Sunset.*"

Kiss, *Alive!* |24| 19 | 21 | 23|
1975, Casablanca; "Rock and Roll All Nite"; www.kissonline.net
◪ "A triumph of entertainment" and "attitude", this "definitive" disc (even if it's "not 100% live") "does everything but put you in the front row", "showcasing the excitement and raw energy" that launched the "national phenomenon", back "when we didn't know what they looked like underneath the clown makeup", "before the days of the Kiss koffin, Kiss kondoms and Kiss koffee mugs"; the unkonverted kiss them off as "kontrived."

Kiss Me, Kate |24| 26 | 24 | 22|
(Original cast recording)
1948, Columbia; "Brush Up Your Shakespeare"
■ "Shakespeare would only have been a spear carrier" in Cole Porter's "wickedly funny" skewering of the bard's *Taming of the Shrew*; the composer's "score is delicious", "fabulously" sung by Alfred Drake, who "proves why he was one of the few great Broadway leading men" as he tames "wunderbar" Patricia Morrison and a couple of "hammy" hoodlums; listeners so in love with the show say "thank goodness we have these artists on record."

Kitaro, *Silk Road, Vol. 1* |24| 22 | 25 | 25|
1980, Pony Canyon; "Silk Road"; www.kitaro.net
◪ "The Far East and outer space are together forever" on this first of several far-out soundtracks to a Japanese TV documentary; multi-instrumentalist Kitaro is "as smooth as silk", "nicely weaving Asian sounds into very accessible songs"; space cadets "love" to hear the "water flowing", but earth-bound ears say it's only "excellent in limited doses" 'cause all that synth and "moaning can get to be a bit much."

KLF, *The White Room* |25| 21 | 21 | 25|
1991, Arista; "3 Am Eternal (Live at the S.S.L.)"
■ All aboard for the "last train to trancentral, so let's go!" – "KLF is gonna rock ya" with this "essential" "history

lesson" of "epic" "techno"; "bringing DJ culture to the masses", the "brilliant", "groundbreaking" duo "owned the clubs in '91", and this "one shot at the mainstream" before their high-profile semi-retirement "surprised everyone with some bona fide hits", proving the "dance scene will last"; "getting Tammy Wynette to sing was a stroke of genius" 'cause, as the song she's on says, "she's justified and she's ancient."

LEO KOTTKE, | 28 | 25 | 29 | 25 |
6- AND 12-STRING GUITAR
1972, Takoma; "Vaseline Machine Gun"
■ "Contemporary acoustic guitar starts here" on this "genius" album of solo instrumentals, a "wonderful thing", that "belongs in every fan's collection"; the axeman's "humorous", yet his "astounding" fingerpicking, a combo of folk, blues, pop and classical influences, shows such "serious talent", it's "jaw-dropping"; the "master of the 12-string" "sounds like five guys playing" – move over Jimmy Page, Leo "may be the real god" of fretwork.

Koyaanisqatsi | 25 | 22 | 26 | 25 |
1983, Antilles; "Koyaanisqatsi"; www.philipglass.com
◪ "Since not a single word is spoken" in the "arresting" environmentalist documentary *Koyaanisqatsi*, "Philip Glass' music is critically important" to its viewing, and vice versa – "one needs to watch the movie in order to properly appreciate" its minimalist soundtrack; "hypnotic", "original" and "frustratingly brilliant", the postmodern opus is "classically monotonous, but that's the point."

Kraftwerk, *Computer World* | 26 | 24 | 24 | 26 |
1981, Warner Bros.; "Computer World"; www.kraftwerk.com
■ "There's a reason that every DJ with a clue about music owns a copy of this classic"; a "brilliant album at least a decade ahead of its time", the "prophetic" "catalyst to techno and electro" "manages to be both visionary and wonderfully stupid"; "who knew machine-made bleeps and pings could produce such catchy pop tunes?" – "crisp, playful and melancholy" at once, "full of simple riffs you can't get out of your head", it sounds like "what George Jetson and his family would listen to."

Kraftwerk, *Trans-Europe Express* | 27 | 24 | 25 | 27 |
1977, Capitol; "Trans-Europe Express"; www.kraftwerk.com
■ "The godfathers", the "granddaddies" or "The Beatles" of the genre – no matter how you put it, these German "revolutionists" are the "seminal electronic band", and some musical gearheads say "without them, the category wouldn't exist"; this "amazingly innovative album" from techno's "awkward and shiny" "birth" "still delights" with "symphonic" "soundscapes à la Jarre", "great synth loops" and "driving rhythms" – "kids today could learn a lot from these dapper 'bots."

Diana Krall, *Live in Paris* | 27 | 25 | 28 | 25 |
2002, Verve; "'S Wonderful"; www.dianakrall.com
■ "Don't try to tell your fella 'no'" when this "perfect complement to a romantic evening" is on the stereo; "sultry" songstress Krall puts on her "deepest, soulful voice" and "lets her jazz piano chops shine" "in a live setting" with "incredible backing by band and orchestra" on "wonderfully fresh interpretations of standards" and a few surprises: Diana "doing Joni Mitchell" on *A Case of You*? – "what an awesome combination."

Diana Krall, *The Look of Love* 🄶 | 26 | 25 | 27 | 27 |
2001, Verve; "The Look of Love"; www.dianakrall.com
☑ "You'll need a cold shower if you listen alone" say surveyors "seduced" by the "smoky vocals" and smokin' cover photo; "thoroughly modern diva" Krall delivers the sound and "look of platinum" on this big seller, with "throaty" singing that "puts the torch back in torch songs", "subtle, skilled piano playing" and "lush" production for an album that's "perfect for wine with your lover", even if jazz jurists jibe "if not for her legs, no one would bother."

Alison Krauss, | 28 | 26 | 29 | 26 |
Now That I've Found You
1995, Rounder; "When You Say Nothing at All"
■ "So sweet a voice, so kicking a fiddle", yes, "the female superstar" "of a new bluegrass generation" is a "revelation for both newcomers and devotees" who stomp their feet for this "satisfying" compilation of new and old material; "pure", "fragile" and "other-worldly", her "silky vocals" come on "like velvet" yet "pack power", making "each song a treasure", while her band of "masterful accompanists" heighten the "quietly spectacular" experience.

Lenny Kravitz, | 22 | 20 | 25 | 22 |
Are You Gonna Go My Way?
*1993, Virgin; "Are You Gonna Go My Way?";
www.lennykravitz.com*
☑ A "cool black rocker" that "defines trends, never follows", this "real-deal artist" "sings great, looks great and writes killer" tunes – the "smoothest cat" is "firing on all cylinders" on this "adrenaline-pumping" disc that "has a little bit of everything"; nevertheless, a handful huff his "earlier albums are better" and find that this *Way* sometimes stumbles on "uninspired clichés."

Kris Kristofferson, *Kristofferson* | 25 | 28 | 23 | 24 |
1970, Monument; "Me and Bobby McGee"
■ This is "a bitchin' alt-country", "must-have debut" by one of the outlaw genre's "most important songwriters", whose "eloquent lyrics" and "heartfelt performances" helped Nashville make it through the night and reach "into the modern era"; swooning over his "smoky voice" and "sexy" arrangements, diehards declare tunes like *Me and*

Bobby McGee and "hangover" song *Sunday Mornin' Comin' Down* to be "great poetry" that "changed" the genre.

Kruder & Dorfmeister,   27 | 23 | 25 | 28 |
The K & D Sessions
1998, K7; "Bug Powder Dust"
■ If you "can't think of a record more likely to be enjoyed by parents and their teenagers", you're not alone; "hip-hop, jazz, lounge and great melodies" – "it's all here" on this "gift" of electronica "for ages 15 to 45" to "chill out" "all summer long around the pool with their louche friends", "delving into the layers" of "meticulous" remixing on this "masterpiece of blunted wickedness."

L

Lambert, Hendricks & Ross,   27 | 28 | 28 | 24 |
Sing a Song of Basie
1958, Verve; "Blues Backstage"
■ "There is no one else who can lyricize instrumentals like this voice trio"; "stylish, exuberant, cheerful, spring-like, mannered, playful, freewheeling and complex" all at the same time, their "creative", "overdubbing" presents a "new approach to Basie", making for a "different, funny and enjoyable" listen; "what is vocalese?" – "true jazz aficionados" say "buy this record and find out."

k.d. lang, Ingenue   25 | 25 | 26 | 25 |
1992, Sire; "Constant Craving"; www.kdlang.com
■ With a "voice like liquid smoke", Canada's androgynous crooner can "sing just about any style", and though this pop album still has "a bit of country mixed in with a bit of blues", the "twangy sounds" of her earlier "Patsy Cline"–inspired discs take a backseat to "smooth and sultry" singing over "beautifully produced", "heartbreaking" tunes like *Save Me*; a "languid, lush and luscious" "bathtub album", it's a "torchy delight" fans "constantly crave."

k.d. lang, Shadowland   26 | 25 | 27 | 26 |
1988, Sire; "Busy Being Blue"; www.kdlang.com
■ "Legendary Owen Bradley helps make lang legendary herself" on this "classic" – "channeling Patsy Cline is easy when you work with her producer and have a voice that catches every emotional nuance"; with "an interpretation that's more Western heartache balladry and torch songs than country music", k.d. "transports you to another place and time" – "those clear notes, that longing", that "fluid voice" as "smooth as glass", she "has it all", and with this "terrific song selection" she "takes you over the edge."

Cyndi Lauper, She's So Unusual 24 | 22 | 21 | 23 |
1983, Portrait; "Time After Time"; www.cyndilauper.com
■ "She-bop" with "Betty Boop with a beat" on this "innovative" debut pumping "daring lyrics" for "feminism

without an agenda" beyond "just wanting to have fun"; with "wild looks" and a "powerhouse" voice, this "valley-girl" "juggernaut of the MTV pioneer generation" is "soooooo unusual", but as "good ears not distracted by orange-and-white hair know", "that's what makes her special."

Lawrence of Arabia (Soundtrack)   26 | 26 | 28 | 26
1963, Colpix; "Main Title"

■ "As glorious and expansive as the Arabian sands", "the majestic score" to the "epic" about British soldier T.E. Lawrence "complements the movie precisely"; "outstanding instrumental storytelling" in "soaring themes" "conjures splendid scenes of sky and dunes"; "have a big drink available" for your listen – it might "incite heat rash!"

Led Zeppelin, *Led Zeppelin II* 🔢   27 | 26 | 28 | 26
1969, Atlantic; "Whole Lotta Love"; www.led-zeppelin.com

■ "Down and dirty" and "full of double entendres", this "genre-defining monster" "introduced the first of the band's continuous J.R.R. Tolkien references"; "written and recorded mostly on the road", it displayed "passion", "raw musicianship" and "wisdom that belied their" years, kicking off Jones, Plant, Page and Bonham's "reign as rock gods"; "from the first chords of *Whole Lotta Love*", this "blues-tinged" "classic" "sweeps you off your feet and refuses to put you down [for] a high you still ride after the last note."

LED ZEPPELIN, *LED ZEPPELIN IV*   28 | 27 | 28 | 26
1971, Atlantic; "Stairway To Heaven"; www.led-zeppelin.com

■ "Can folk", "folklore", R&R and "magick" "transport" "you to the land of" "hobbits and heavy metal"? – "hell yeah"; "feel the superhero vibe" of a "confident band" "that captured rhythm, hook, emotion, technical brilliance and big-room production", conjuring up the "mystical" "best of their best"; full of "bombast" and "inhabiting a world of its own" it's almost "a clinic on how to lay down a groove to a hard-rock riff"; "*Stairway to Heaven* is played to death" but you "can't overlook its impact."

Led Zeppelin, *Physical Graffiti* 🔢   27 | 26 | 28 | 27
1975, Swan Song; "Kashmir"; www.led-zeppelin.com

■ "The mighty Led Zep" "covers more territory than most bands would imagine in a lifetime" on this "four-sided opus" that recalls the "summer of '75, when every Camaro" had the "epic" *Kashmir* "blaring from the speakers"; from "*Custard Pie*, which sets the tone with a bounce and a smirk", and "slide guitar raveups (*In My Time of Dying*")) to the shining "rhythmic brilliance" of *The Wanton Song*, "it's bash-and-strut R&R, but it just works."

Peggy Lee, *Spotlight on Peggy Lee*   27 | 26 | 27 | 25
1995, Capitol; "Fever"

■ "A great introduction to Miss Peggy Lee that only scratches the surface of her artistry", this spotlight shines on "standards", including *I've Got the World on a String* and her oft-covered *Fever,* delivered by the singer with a "smooth, sultry sound" "tailor-made for jazz and blues" that seemed to say she had "seen the gutter" and "didn't like it a bit"; though it's missing a few notables like *Is That All There Is,* the collection of tunes from the '50s and '60s tells us that the best isn't necessarily yet to come.

Tom Lehrer,   25 | 29 | 18 | 19
That Was the Year That Was
1965, Reprise; "Vatican Rag"
■ Harvard math professor and "great political comedian" Leher "slashes and burns his way through American foibles and hypocrisies" on one of the "funniest topical albums ever", "lampooning everyone from the army to the Catholic church" and making us "laugh our butts off"; marked by "impeccable timing and supreme cleverness", it's like "an instruction manual on writing satire."

John Lennon, *Imagine* #1   27 | 28 | 25 | 24
1971, Apple/Capitol; "Imagine"
■ "Perhaps his most important recording", this "stirring" album "is a brilliant look at one man's uncompromising view of life", documenting "Lennon's continuous couch trip – self-analysis, love, venom and politics with a backbeat", "demonstrating which Beatle had the brains"; "George Harrison's guitar and Phil Spector's production further elevate" "master provocateur" themes from "peace" (*Imagine,* "one of the greatest antiwar songs" ever) to "skewering Paul McCartney (*How Do You Sleep*)."

John Lennon,   27 | 28 | 26 | 25
The John Lennon Collection
1982, Geffen; "Instant Karma!"
■ "Amazing conversation snippets, stops-and-starts and raw acoustic tracks" are part of this "unusual" box "collection, which ranges from the very good to the transcendent, the political to the homespun – in short, a great summary of the multifaceted" "talent" "post-Beatles"; Lennon "gave the last century's greatest recording and songwriting team" "their edge", "soul, mind and conscience", and his "thoughtful reflections and presence are missed more and more."

John Lennon and Yoko Ono,   21 | 23 | 21 | 22
Double Fantasy G #1
1980, Geffen; "Watching the Wheels"
◪ "Yoko has always been an acquired taste" and remains so for many on this "bittersweet" "farewell kiss", released soon after Lennon's horrific 1980 murder; he's "in prime form" on this "masterful" "record of a wonderful love story", "showing he could still exude greatness without" the Fab Four on his 'n' her tracks that "perfectly balance each other"; but the "turned-off" say oh no to Ono – "it

ought to be called *Single Fantasy*" because "her tracks bog down the album."

Annie Lennox, *Diva*   26 | 26 | 27 | 26
1992, Arista; "Why"; www.annie-lennox.com

■ "You go, girl!" – "fresh from the breakdown of the Eurythmics", the "sultry star" "lives up to the title" of her solo pop debut, "emerging stronger, wittier and edgier"; "vocals, writing, production, album cover, choice of lipstick" – it's "perfection in every way", with a "lush" "synth sheen" and Lennox's "soothing alto holding together" "stories" of "beauty and heartbreak"; "note to other divas: this is how you do it."

Les Misérables   28 | 27 | 27 | 28
(London cast recording) ☐
1985, Relativity; "On My Own"

■ Even "jaded theatergoers" "can't listen without tears in their eyes to this" "bold", "brash", "beautiful" Brit-invasion "crowd-pleaser", the "marvelous", "moving", "mind-blowingly" "masterful" "mega-translation" of Victor Hugo's "timeless" tale of "old France's class wars, struggles and victories"; the highly regarded original London cast, with "Patti LuPone in an extraordinary cameo", "never fails to stir the soul" – "c'est magnifique."

Huey Lewis and the News,   22 | 20 | 21 | 22
Sports ▦
1983, Chrysalis; "Heart of Rock and Roll"; www.hln.org

▨ "Upbeat" and "carefree", this "slice of '80s magic" showcased "Bay Area power pop at its best"; fronted by "hunky Huey", these "old-time rock & rollers" "didn't have a look and didn't need one", thanks to "sing-along songs" that "make up in joie de vivre what they lacked in heft"; but old News isn't good news to a few who recall a "pedestrian" "bar band that should have stayed in the bar."

OTTMAR LIEBERT,   27 | 25 | 28 | 25
NOUVEAU FLAMENCO
1990, Higher Octave; "Barcelona Nights";
www.lunanegra.com

■ It's "the beginning of a new genre" as possibly "the greatest classical Spanish guitarist of our time" "bends tradition in new ways" for the New Age, "trailblazing nouveau flamenco tracks" on the "strongest effort" in a "prolific" decade of recording; "beautifully written and sexy", it "endures hundreds of listenings" for "driving" with the top down or "partying" with a pair of castanets.

Gordon Lightfoot, *Sundown* ▦   25 | 26 | 23 | 22
1974, Reprise; "Sundown"; www.gordonlightfoot.com

▨ The "triple-threat" Canadian "troubadour" "with a one-of-a-kind sound" was "at the peak of his abilities" on this "lyrically amazing", "commercial" success; offering songs like "*Sundown,* a classic", and *Carefree Highway,* it's "perfect listening for laid-back evenings"; still, a few "think it's a shame" that some tunes are a "bit dull", suggesting a "look into *Gord's Gold*" for a cache of pure hits.

Linkin Park, *Hybrid Theory*   24 | 21 | 23 | 25
2000, Warner Bros.; "In the End"; www.linkinpark.com
■ One of the "best bands of the new millennium" fawn followers who feel linked to this LA foursome's "rock-rap crossover"; "concise" and "dynamic", the "stupidly good" hybrid of "hard-edged sounds" and "poplike melodies" feels "fresh and old-school at the same time"; offering an "inventive combination of live and programmed instruments" and "intense lyrics" "about real issues", this "incredible debut" is sure to become "a classic."

The Lion King (Soundtrack) **G #1**   27 | 27 | 27 | 28
1994, Disney; "Circle of Life"
■ "From the majesty of *Circle of Life* to the rockin' *I Just Can't Wait to be King* and the tender *Can You Feel the Love Tonight?,* this "magnificent" Disney "cartoon musical" is "fit for a king"; "infused with African moods and rhythms", "Western pop" stylings and "lyrics that tug at human emotions", songs performed by an all-star cast including "Jeremy Irons, Nathan Lane and Whoopi Goldberg" bring "Elton John's music to a whole new generation" of "kids."

Little Feat, *Feats Don't Fail Me Now*   25 | 25 | 27 | 23
1974, Warner Bros.; "Oh, Atlanta"; www.littlefeat.net
■ Feat frontman Lowell George was "a genius at fusing country and rock" as well as "one of the all-time great slide guitar players", as he proved on this "humorous" and "funky" "fun listen"; "great for shakin' your groove thang" ("my feet never fail me"), this "music for a summer day" is "still immensely enjoyable", even if a handful feel 1978's live album *Waiting for Columbus* is "even better."

The Little Mermaid   25 | 26 | 26 | 26
(Soundtrack) **G**
1990, Disney; "Under the Sea"
■ There's "nothing fishy" about this "real pearl" created by Howard Ashman and Alan Menken for "the first of the new generation of Disney classics"; "perfect on long drives", its "bubblegum" "magic" "captures the curiosity and discovery of the film", "inspiring kids to imagine life in another world" and forget they're strapped in a car seat; "every track" is "bouyed by creativity and panache", particularly *Under the Sea* – "it's calypso, baby!"

Little Richard,   25 | 22 | 24 | 21
The Essential Little Richard
1995, Specialty; "Good Golly Miss Molly"
■ "Nobody let it hang out further" than "the true king", "one of the most insane of early rockers"; the sounds that

"laid the foundation for rock & roll" are captured on this collection of original '50s recordings that "smokes from start to finish" – it blows later Richard remakes away.

Little Shop of Horrors 24 | 24 | 23 | 23
(Original cast recording)
1979, Geffen; "Suddenly, Seymour"
■ A "cute", "campy" "commercial to Ortho-Gro", this "horrifyingly funny" "homage to '50s thrillers", replete with "doo-wop and alien man-eating plants", "ranks high on the sing-along-at-home scale"; "you can tell why Disney grabbed writers Ashman and Menken" when you get a load of *Somewhere That's Green,* while someone who's Greene – Ellen Greene – is "perfect", "bringing humanity to a comic book treatment"; hungry ears beg "feed me, more, more!"

Live, *Throwing Copper* #1 23 | 24 | 23 | 23
1994, Radioactive; "Lightning Crashes"
■ "You can feel the anger and violence in Ed Kowalczyk's voice" as he leads this "talented" group through "powerful, provocative", "spine-tingling" tunes (including an "excellent unlisted track") that "reach into your soul" and "don't let go"; "raw and edgy" with "hard rockin' riffs" and "haunting lyrics", this "emotive", "dynamic sophomore effort" goes "much deeper that most pop."

Living Colour, *Vivid* 22 | 20 | 25 | 22
1988, Epic; "Cult of Personality"
■ "Adventurous" and "barrier-breaking", these "stunning virtuosos" "blew us away" with their Mick Jagger– produced, double-platinum, "seminal black rock" debut; one of the "first successful marriages of funk and metal" with "whirling dervish licks" courtesy of "kick-ass guitarist Vernon Reid", "some serious messages" and the "breakout song *Cult of Personality*", it brings back memories vivid enough for fans to wonder "where did these guys go?"

LL Cool J, *Radio* 25 | 24 | 22 | 23
1985, Def Jam; "Rock the Bells"; www.llcoolj.com
■ Recorded at "a time when personality ruled the mike more than a good sample or fancy production", the debut of this rapper with "tha skillz to pay the billz" is "powerful" and "poetic", with "raw" beats to fan "the bravado and fire" of "fierce", "angst-ridden" verbal barbs on tracks like *I Can't Live Without My Radio* and *I'm Bad*; Mr. 'Ladies Love Cool James' may be "hard as hell", but the popular ballad *I Need Love* was one of the "first hip-hop love songs."

Los Lobos, 26 | 26 | 27 | 23
How Will the Wolf Survive?
1984, Slash/Warner Bros.; "Will the Wolf Survive?"
■ "A great introduction" to one of "America's finest live bands", this "soulful, gritty" major-label debut from East

LA's roots-rock combo demonstrates a "wide range of influences", including "elements of blues, country and Latin" that "blend together seamlessly", making for a potent "mariachi and roadhouse" cocktail – "margaritas, anyone?"

Love, *Forever Changes*   28 27 26 26
1968, Elektra; "Alone Again Or"
■ "Musically cheerful and humorous" yet "lyrically dark, even morbid", this disc conjures "the vibe of the Summer of Love" and the "genius of Arthur Lee"; "intelligent and compelling", the "almost mystic" "masterpiece of folk-pop-flamenco-psychedelia", from one of rock's first integrated groups, is "essential if you want to experience the haze of the '60s" while drinking in sounds still as "fresh as California sunshine."

Lyle Lovett, *Lyle Lovett*   26 28 26 23
1986, MCA; "This Old Porch"
■ "Maybe it's that twang, maybe it's that hair, maybe it's that inimitable voice", whatever it is one thing's fer sure: on his "outstanding debut", featuring the "pure Texas tune *This Old Porch*" co-written with Robert Earl Keen, this "tremendously talented storyteller" with the famous ex-wife delivers a C&W "sound even folks from Jersey can dig"; "sad, smart" and "offbeat" "with a wry sense of humor", "country hasn't seen anybody quite like" him.

Nick Lowe, *Labour of Lust*   26 26 25 25
1979, Columbia; "Cruel to Be Kind"
■ With a "chewy bubblegum center and flavor that lasts and lasts" plus "great guitars from Dave Edmunds and Billy Bremner", this "intelligent" "power-pop" "classic" from the Lowe/Rockpile "combine" is all about "fun, witty rock & roll"; though *Cruel to Be Kind* became a "surprise U.S. hit", this cache of "amazing-to-dance-to", "nicely crafted tunes" was "often overlooked" – it "should have made" the "way-cool" "godfather of the new wave scene" a "household name."

Ray Lynch, *Deep Breakfast*   25 22 25 25
1986, Ray Lynch Productions; "The Oh of Pleasure";
www.raylynch.com
■ Dive deep into your morning Froot Loops with this "great album for Sunday listening"; given frequent airplay, it's often neophytes' "first" "introduction to New Age", but despite its trendiness, it's a "timeless" disc of "inspiring", "soothing", "meditative beauty", making for an "overall fantastic" "escape" for those who 'oh' with pleasure over it.

Shelby Lynne, *I Am Shelby Lynne*   24 24 23 25
2000, Polygram; "Leavin'"; www.shelbylynne.com
■ "After Nashville didn't understand what to do with her", this "underappreciated talent" unleashed her "amazing comeback album", a "career-defining" "breakout" that

"showed everyone who she was"; "sultry, sexy and sensational, Shelby combines rock", "Southern soul" and a sorta "Phil Spector–meets–country" sound into a "powerful" album that, "post-breakup or pre-relationship, is great for thinking and drinking, hurting and flirting."

Lynyrd Skynyrd, *Pronounced Leh-Nerd Skin-Nerd*   25 | 24 | 26 | 22
1973, MCA; "Free Bird"; www.lynyrdskynyrd.com
■ Powered by a "three-guitar jam attack", the "must-have" debut that defined "Southern dirt rock at its finest" is itself defined by "the rock anthem *Free Bird*", "a tribute to the late Duane Allman" that became "the second most overplayed song on the radio"; "all Skynyrd is good Skynyrd", and in fact it's "pronounced a-w-e-s-o-m-e" quip connoisseurs who still consider this "classic band with a unique sound" "phenomenal" ("'nuff said").

Lynyrd Skynyrd, *Second Helping*   25 | 23 | 26 | 23
1974, MCA; "Sweet Home Alabama"; www.lynyrdskynyrd.com
■ "A great follow-up" album, this "influential" effort "grooves from start to finish" with "blues-inspired guitar riffs"; "for 30 minutes, you'll wish you were a Southern boy" as Ronnie Van Zant & co. move from an "intoxicating love dirge" (*I Need You*) and an "overplayed FM classic" (*Sweet Home Alabama*) to an "exploration of fame" (*Don't Ask Me No Questions*) and a "bemused tale of white trash being wined and dined by record label execs" (*Working for MCA*).

M

MADONNA, IMMACULATE COLLECTION   27 | 24 | 24 | 27
1990, Sire; "Like a Prayer"; www.madonna.com
■ "Satisfy every guilty pleasure" with "Madonna's throbbing" "best" on this "provocative" "assemblage of pure pop goodness", "from the mundane (*Holiday*) to the sublime (*Like a Prayer*), from Latin (*La Isla Bonita*) to homage (*Vogue*); the "yummy" "legend" "reinvents herself so often and manages to stay ahead of the curve", and this "must-have" chronicles her "evolution of themes, beats and trends"; as the legions warn: "if you don't like her, we can't be friends – it's a rule."

Madonna, *Like a Virgin* ▥1   24 | 22 | 23 | 24
1984, Sire; "Like a Virgin"; www.madonna.com
■ "What can one say about the goddess of pop" except "this second effort where she began to hone her craft" was "just a hint at what was to come"?; "successfully" "liberating millions of semi-virgins to feel touched for the very first time", "she said 'I am woman: strong, sensual and savvy'" and "it's ok to want and to talk about sex"; some believed this bevvy of "crafty, fluffy songs" would "last as long as bubblegum, only this one got stuck under our heels and has never let go . . . ever."

MADONNA, *RAY OF LIGHT* G #1   26 | 25 | 26 | 27
1998, Maverick; "Ray of Light"; www.madonna.com
■ Madonna worshipers testify that this "lush, sad" and "spiritual", but characteristically "danceable tapestry" from the "evolved" "chameleon" "queen" "changed their lives"; an "ethereal" "trip" into ravedom's "beats, bubbles and burps" guided by "unsurpassable" William Orbit, this "pinnacle" production garnered Ms. Ciccone her first "well-deserved Grammy" for an album and "affirmed that she is a force to be reckoned with" in "Bollywood", "electronica" and "poetics" as well as pop.

Taj Mahal and Ry Cooder,   24 | 22 | 26 | 22
Rising Sons Featuring Taj Mahal and Ry Cooder
1992, Columbia/Legacy; "Corrina, Corrina";
www.taj-mo-roots.com
◪ "The future was clear: these boys could play, even back" in the '60s when this "tribute to American roots" music was recorded; "in retrospect", the "modern blues man" and "another young genius-to-be, Ryland P. Cooder", were akin to a "superband", playing such covers as *Corrina, Corrina* and "obscure material from the land of the devil's music"; while Taj-touters regard it as a "long-lost treasure", some sons say it's "more interesting historically than musically."

Mahler, *Symphony No. 5*   26 | 27 | 27 | 25
1988, Deutsche Grammophon; www.wienerphilharmoniker.at
■ "From the wonderfully rich and dark opening trumpet to the sparkling D major sections", this "big", "thinking man's" classical album "packs a wallop"; conductor Leonard Bernstein is "on fire" for a concert "that sets a new standard in human communication"; "full of emotion and dripping with power", the recording "comes as close as possible to capturing the terror, thunder and awe of the live performance."

The Mamas and the Papas,   25 | 24 | 24 | 23
***If You Can Believe Your Eyes and Ears* #1**
1966, Dunhill; "California Dreamin'"
■ "A sensational blend of four distinct voices" (Mama "Cass Elliott had some set of pipes" . . .), this "exquisite" slice of "harmony heaven" from "one of the definitive '60s pop vocal groups" is "like sunshine on a disc"; born of "the great writing talent of John Phillips and the production of Lou Adler" and "representing the hippie California sound", the "timeless" "tonic for whatever ails you" is so full of hits (like *Monday, Monday*), it's "hard to pick a favorite."

The Mambo Kings (Soundtrack)   27 | 25 | 27 | 26
1992, Elektra; "Beautiful Maria of My Soul"
■ "It's enough to get me out of my wheelchair" gush "ass-shaking" "addicts" in all sorts of circumstances; on the soundtrack that could drive you "to Cuba to study this music", late, great "legends" Tito Puente, great Celia

Cruz "make you wanna dance, preferably with Antonio Banderas"; including the sexy actor himself singing *Beautiful Maria of My Soul,* this platter leads "novices" to "mambo all the way!"

Mame (Original cast recording) **G** | 25 | 25 | 26 | 26 |
1966, Columbia; "If He Walked Into My Life"
■ "Proving that Angela is so much more than *Murder, She Wrote*", this "classy" cast recording "preserves Lansbury's Tony-winning" "tour de force" in the title role, not to mention Bea Arthur's "delightful" "diva" Vera and Jerry Herman's "stylish" score, including the "zesty overture" and the "heartbreaking *If He Walked Into My Life*"; the "lush" CD reissue leaves listeners asking that age-old Hollywood question: "why didn't they cast her in the motion picture?"

Mamma Mia! | 24 | 23 | 24 | 24 |
(Original cast recording)
2000, Polygram; "The Winner Takes It All"
☑ It's "frivolous", "feel-good", "two-for-one" "fun" with "the excellence of a Broadway musical" and "a pop concert of ABBA's best" rolled into a single recording of a show that has "audiences throwing down their canes" to "shimmy" "in the aisles"; while some dancing queens "worship it in the shower" and "rush-hour traffic", others have met their Waterloo, recommending "going right to the source" and buying the original Swedish pop group's *Gold* album instead.

Chuck Mangione, *Feels So Good* | 22 | 21 | 24 | 22 |
1977, A&M; "Feels So Good"; www.chuckmangione.com
☑ "No one ever heard of the flügelhorn before" this "light, cheery album" went double platinum, made Mangione a "'70s jazz" star and "helped launch the career of guitarist Grant Geissman"; "I can hear the title track in my head", and it "really does feel good" gush groupies who "appreciate how much emotion comes out" when Chuck blows; "yakety-yak" crack whackers of this "bland" "pop pap."

Manhattan (Soundtrack) | 28 | 27 | 27 | 27 |
1979, Columbia; "He Loves and She Loves"
■ "Gershwin and Manhattan make magic together" on this "meltingly beautiful" soundtrack of the composer's "greatest hits"; "a perfect selection of extant music" for a modern "black-and-white" "classic", it's made to put the "masses" "in a New York state of mind", so "give it to friends who are leaving the city", or "stay home one rainy Sunday" and "just go with Woody Allen's picks" – "too bad he can't make life choices similar to his choices of song."

Manhattan Transfer, | 25 | 24 | 27 | 25 |
The Best of the Manhattan Transfer
1981, Atlantic; "Birdland"
■ "Extraordinary" "four-part harmonies" on some "bizarre choices of song" make for a "very original" but "tons-of-

fun" early disc of the "tightest" of the Transfer; one of the "best jazz vocal groups ever" delivers "old standards with updated twists", including *Body and Soul,* and avant-garde neo-classics with nostalgic "style", like their "fantastic" version of Weather Report's *Birdland*; you'll "enjoy singing along" with the cool, cool kitties.

Barry Manilow, *Greatest Hits* ◉   24 | 25 | 25 | 24
1978, Arista; "Mandy"; www.barrymanilow.com
■ So, it's "high on the cheese factor, but in a smoked Gouda kind of way": "old and sappy" but "wonderful"; the "amazing songwriter/pianist/performer" "ruled the '70s" with "sentimental", "theatrical" ballads that "stick to the brain"; this out-of-print double LP went triple platinum, but if you can't find it, go for the three separate greatest hits CDs or try *Ultimate Manilow* and take him on a "long drive" – "you'll be hoarse when you arrive", busting "out of the closet" to "say it loud and say it proud: I'm a Barry fan."

Aimee Mann, *Magnolia*   26 | 27 | 25 | 25
2000, Reprise; "Save Me"; www.aimeemann.com
■ The "sophisticated troubadour of angst" isn't the only artist on this "mesmerizing" disc, but the soundtrack to Paul Thomas Anderson's film "was built around Amy's music", displaying "her brilliance as a singer-songwriter" as she pours out a "voice like warm syrup" on "moody, moving" alt-pop/rock tunes, including *Save Me*; "cinematic, dramatic and personal", the CD "takes you on a journey through the psyche" and "pierces your heart."

Aimee Mann, *Whatever*   27 | 28 | 25 | 25
1993, Imago; "Stupid Thing"; www.aimeemann.com
■ The former 'Til Tuesday vocalist "makes up more heartbroken masterpieces before lunch than any ten artists do in their careers" on this "terrific" solo debut, and they're "simply wonderful" – "romantic misery, anger and heartache haven't been this poetic since Shakespeare"; Mann "easily threads provoking lyrics" through "beautiful melodies" and in the process "announces herself as" a "master songwriter" "to be reckoned with."

Mannheim Steamroller,   25 | 23 | 25 | 26
Fresh Aire IV
1981, American Gramaphone; "The Dream"
◪ "One of the best produced albums in the series", the final of the "season"-themed of the *Fresh Aire* discs by this innovative group delivers "some of the clearest synthesizer sounds on record", plus a good dose of the Theramin; "relaxing and invigorating", it "defines what New Age should be" – if you're "in the right mood" mumble malcontents, while radicals rail against its radio play: "if Rush Limbaugh gives them props, they can't be worth the time to listen."

Bob Marley and the Wailers, *Burnin'*
28 | 27 | 28 | 25

1973, Island/Tuff Gong; "Get Up, Stand Up"; www.bobmarley.com
■ With guitarist/vocalist Peter Tosh and percussionist/vocalist Bunny Livingston in the lineup, Bob Marley's "tight group" of Rastafarian reggae warriors "defined an entire genre" with a "socially conscious, uplifting" session that ranges from "gospel to roots to rebel rock"; backed by Chris Blackwell's flawless production, "timeless" tracks like *Get Up, Stand Up* helped make the "genius Trenchtown" "prophet" an "international sensation."

BOB MARLEY AND THE WAILERS, *LEGEND*
29 | 28 | 28 | 26

1984, Island/Tuff Gong; "No Woman No Cry"; www.bobmarley.com
■ A "colossal" "king with a mighty court of followers", the late "father of reggae" "addressed the human spirit, individual power, global politics, life and death" with "relaxing" "island" rhythms that "make your soul dance"; his "excellent musicianship" and "heartfelt" "words continue to affect the world" through songs included on this "greatest hits set of testimonials"; it will "make you want to look deeper into the catalogue" of "one of the most important songwriters of the 20th century."

Dean Martin, *Capitol Collectors Series*
26 | 24 | 26 | 24

1989, Capitol; "That's Amore"
■ "Stir up some martinis, snuggle up with the one you love and relax" as Dino's "smooth-as-silk" voice helps you to "feel suave"; "debonair, charming" and "so calm, like he's singing without any effort at all", the Rat Packer "had a way of putting over a song that has never been captured today"; this "best of the best of the king of cool" proves "no one can top Dean, not even Frank", who "claimed Martin was the better singer" – "now, that's *amore!*"

Mary Poppins (Soundtrack) G #1
26 | 26 | 25 | 25

1964, Disney; "Feed the Birds"
■ "You have to sing along" with Julie Andrews "in her vocal prime" as "everyone's dream nanny" and the "delightful" Dick Van Dyke as her "charming chimney-sweeping buddy" on this classic Disney soundtrack; "lighthearted and spirited" "with fantastic hooks", the "enchanting" tunes go down like "a spoonful of sugar", and since "everyone likes trying to belt with an accent", the "whole family" finds the disc "supercalifragilisticexpialidocious."

Massive Attack, *Blue Lines*
27 | 24 | 26 | 27

1991, Virgin; "Unfinished Sympathy"; www.massiveattack.com
■ "Out of the blue", this "boundary breaker" from "Bristol's finest paved the way" for "the trip-hop craze"; Massive

Attack's "massive" debut is "an introspective album that also packs some mighty grooves", with "moments of heart-stopping beauty" that "blur the lines between soul, hip-hop and electronica"; "smooth rapping by Tricky, great background vocals by Horace Andy and Shara Nelson's "sexy" singing are "perfect for making out, chilling out" or "a summer night's walk."

MASSIVE ATTACK, *PROTECTION*   28 │ 25 │ 27 │ 27
1994, Virgin; "Protection"; www.massiveattack.com
■ "Massive Attack prove their ingenuity" on their second effort, scoring this *Survey*'s top rating for Electronica, as well as Everything But the Girl's "brilliant" Tracey Thorn for a "silky-smooth cameo" on the title track, "one of the sexiest songs ever"; a "masterwork of trip-hop" made of "magical", "liquid virtuosity", this "ambient, wicked" disc "cemented the movement"; snobs sniff that "the only bad outcome is that now everybody claims to be a long-term fan."

Matchbox 20, *Yourself or Someone Like You*   23 │ 23 │ 22 │ 23
1997, Lava; "Push"; www.matchbox20.com
◪ "A heartfelt", "infinitely listenable album", this "catchy" collection, featuring "hot" frontman Rob Thomas' "poignant" lyrics and "smooth, sultry", "soulful" vocals, makes "good cruising music" you "want to play over and over again", maintain Match-makers; but fence-sitters quibble it's "half killer, half filler" while dissenters deride it as "corporate rock, spoon-fed to the masses."

Johnny Mathis, *Johnny's Greatest Hits* 🔢   27 │ 25 │ 27 │ 25
1958, Columbia; "Chances Are"; www.johnnymathis.com
■ "If you're feeling low", the "pure velvet" voice of "Johnny will make you feel right"; the singer that "saved more teen dances than any other on platter" crooned the tunes in "that player in the Oldsmobile as you parked on lover's lane", and "slow dancing" to "gorgeous" "'50s" songs like *Chances Are* "is still the best way to spend a quiet, romantic evening"; this greatest hits "should be called greatest hots", not only because it's so sexy but because it stayed on the charts for over a decade.

Matrix (Soundtrack)   24 │ 20 │ 23 │ 25
1999, Maverick; "Spybreak!"
■ "Red pill or blue pill, this album kicks ass"; "standout tracks include Ministry's *Bad Blood,* the excellent *Prime Audio Soup* by Meat Beat Manifesto" and for "a nice variation", the Propellerheads' jazzy *Spybreak!* amid "hip", "harsh" hard rock and "phenomenal" techno that "makes you want to do some martial arts magic"; "stronger than the flick", the soundtrack "pumps you full of energy and gets you ready to face the urban jungle" – in other words, "whoa!!!!"

DAVE MATTHEWS BAND, *CRASH*   24 | 24 | 26 | 25
1996, RCA; "Crash"; www.dmband.com
■ Dave Matthews, a "genius" who "makes everyone
swoon" with his "irresistible voice" and his "talented,
nearly perfect" band, "crashed onto the pop/rock map",
debuting high on the charts with this Grammy-winner;
"staying true to his roots with jams such as *Tripping Billies*
and *Two Step*" while spotlighting "stunning arrangements"
and "jazzy, carefree beats you never tire of", he "seduces
your senses and leaves you with a tingling feeling."

Dave Matthews Band,   25 | 25 | 26 | 24
Live at Red Rocks 8.15.95
1997, Bama Rags/RCA; "Seek Up"; www.dmband.com
■ "Listening to this" "excellent live" double disc, the first
that attempted to "eliminate bootlegs" by "capturing the
jam band's show while it was still thrilling and they were
new", you "forget you're in your car, and you begin to think"
you're at this "amazing venue" with these "top-notch
musicians"; from "Dave Matthews' wonderful vocals to
Carter Beauford, who's unreal on drums to Leroi Moore, who
cuts loose on the sax", "every member shines through."

Dave Matthews Band,   25 | 25 | 27 | 25
Under the Table and Dreaming
1994, RCA; "Ants Marching"; www.dmband.com
■ "Talk about a gateway album" – it was obvious "DMB
wouldn't be a little secret anymore among its large
underground following" with this "infectious" "crown
jewel"; boasting "genius musicianship" and a "masterful
mix of styles", the "funky, jamming songs" fused jazz, rock
and country with Dave's vocals – "he could sing the
alphabet to me and it would still sound great" – and exhaled
a "breath of fresh air into the '90s rock scene" that helped
"define the soul of Generations X and Y."

Maxwell,   27 | 26 | 28 | 27
Maxwell's Urban Hang Suite
1996, Columbia; "Ascension (Don't Ever Wonder)";
www.musze.com
■ "Step 1: put it on; step 2: take it off . . . take it all off" and
kick a little sumthin' sumthin' with this "contemporary and
subtly smooth" "panty dropper", the debut album by "one of
the sexiest voices in R&B"; "charming and disarming", he's
"as beautiful as his music", which has the "unbelievable
horns" and "neo-funk-soul" grooves to "take everyone
back to the days when Marvin Gaye was the epitome"; in
other words, "mmmm . . ."

John Mayall, *Bluesbreakers:*   26 | 22 | 28 | 21
John Mayall with Eric Clapton
1965, London; "Hideaway"
■ "The great British bluesmaster" (whose talents include
"guitar, harp, songwriting and musical direction") "led

youngster EC" (fresh from the Yardbirds) "to nirvana" when he "plugged a Les Paul into a Marshall combo amp, defying his age" and "bridging the gap between rock and blues"; admirers assert it's "the guitar album by which many others are measured" – from "the opening strains of *All Your Love* you'll be hooked on this gem."

John Mayer, *Room for Squares*   24 | 26 | 25 | 24
2001, Columbia; "Your Body Is a Wonderland";
www.johnmayer.com

☑ Pinch his "cute" cheeks – this "folksy" "teenybopper" "fave" displays "sincerity", combining "solid acoustic guitar" and "magical lyrics" for a "promising" "soft-rock" debut; "each song is like a conversation" between "insecure" "25-year-olds" mulling over the "quarter-life crisis", though most "crushes on the guy have nothing to do with his insight"; even if the dismayed diss the "Dave Matthews imitator", the kid is sure to "better with age."

Curtis Mayfield, *Superfly* ▉**1**   28 | 29 | 29 | 27
1972, Curtom; "Freddie's Dead"

■ "No wonder this is a staple for hip-hop sampling" – "the baddest" brother around "explores the dark streets, full of hustlers, pushers and pimps" on "hands-down one of the most important funk/soul records to be made"; high on howling horns, churning grooves and wah-wah guitar, the "kick-ass" "milestone in black music" "bests its movie by a country mile"; so, skip the "cheesy" blaxploitation flick and "wear out the album" 'cause it's "cool, real cool."

Yo-Yo Ma, Edgar Meyer, Mark   25 | 22 | 27 | 27
O'Connor, *Appalachia Waltz*
1996, Sony Classical; "Appalachia Waltz"

■ "Laying classical music on its ear" amid the "bluegrass" down on the "farm", these "masters of different genres" have created "an exquisite amalgam of sound" that makes stateside music lovers "feel American to the depths of their souls"; fiddler Mark O'Connor "uplifts", bassist Edgar Meyer is "unbelievable" and Yo-Yo Ma is "not just a cellist anymore", "crossing over" with a "fresh", "fabulous mix" that is "great for both brunch and brown-hour cocktails."

Martina McBride,   25 | 24 | 26 | 24
The Way That I Am
1993, RCA; "Independence Day";
www.martina-mcbride.com

■ "For any woman who just ended a relationship", the songs on this "wonderful country album" provide a "powerful healing effect that empowers you to stand tall", especially after listening to "her all-time best", *Independence Day*; a "phenomenal hit" about a "battered woman breaking free", it's "sung with conviction and raw power" and, like the rest of this "fine album", is marked by her "muscular voice, feminist lyrics" and "soaring delivery."

Les McCann/Eddie Harris, 26 24 27 24
Swiss Movement
1969, Atlantic; "Cold Duck Time"; www.eddieharris.com
■ "Yee-ha!" – "electrified" saxophonist Harris and pianist
McCann dazzle the Montreux Festival audience with this
"ethereal" "synthesis of jazz and funk" on a "magical
night" of "pure fun" in Switzerland in oh-so-1969; "some
of the best sound engineering for a live album" makes it
a "classic" that "defies superlatives", particularly on
the 30th anniversary reissue.

MC 5, *Kick Out the Jams* 26 21 22 16
1969, Elektra; "Kick Out the Jams"
■ This "revolutionary" Detroit band – "an early precursor
of '70s punk" – released a few independent singles but
"could never capture the power of their shows until this
full-length debut" was recorded live at the Grande Ballroom;
the "ferocious" "call to arms" is "a guaranteed neighbor
complaint starter" but also shows that "politics and hard
rock can mix and mix well" – yeah, the "Motor City Five
had it all figured out more than 30 years ago."

Kate & Anna McGarrigle, 27 27 27 25
Kate & Anna McGarrigle
1976, Warner Bros.; "Heart Like a Wheel";
www.mcgarrigles.com
■ "Have you ever heard better harmonies" than on this
"phenomenal" debut from the "talented" Canadian sisters
whose "loyal fan base bespeaks their enduring appeal"?;
pairing "fresh", "pithy folk instrumentation" with "quirky",
"emotional" lyrics told "from a woman's point of view",
like *Heart Like a Wheel*, the single Linda Ronstadt covered
a few years earlier, they create "haunting", "wispy"
songs made for listening – this is "intelligent" music that
"stays with you."

Tim McGraw, 25 24 25 25
Not a Moment Too Soon ⧉
1994, Curb; "Don't Take the Girl"; www.timmcgraw.com
◩ "There's nothing pop" about "McGraw's breakthrough
album" of "laugh, cry and feel-good" songs, which "keeps
to his roots" ("his pining is so heartfelt") – this "when
country-was-still-country" "good stuff" "shows the promise
of what was to come" from the future Mr. Faith Hill; still, a
handful retort that this "mixed bag" hat-act comes off
as "very clichéd."

Loreena McKennitt, 25 25 25 26
The Book of Secrets
1997, Warner Bros.; "Highwayman"; www.quinlanroad.com
■ "Modern, misty music at its best" applaud admirers
who compare this "truly gifted" Canadian songstress'
"haunting", "hypnotic" sound to an "intoxicating drug that

calms and soothes your soul"; open her "mysterious" *Book* and dive into the "dizzying" "mix of cultures", with "top-notch" performers interpreting stories and influences ranging from Siberia to Ireland; this is a "rainy-afternoon soundtrack" that's "different and refreshing."

Brian McKnight, *Anytime*   24 | 26 | 25 | 25
1997, Mercury; "Anytime"; www.brian-mcknight.com
■ "Soulful", "wonderful ballads" like the heart-wrenching title track permeate the third release of one of R&B's most "romantic" vocalists who "showcases his talent as a songwriter", producer and "excellent" keyboardist; "no one can write better bridges" to "set the mood" for breakups and make-ups than this "modern-day Luther Vandross."

Brian McKnight, *Back at One*   25 | 25 | 25 | 25
1999, Motown; "Back At One"; www.brian-mcknight.com
■ The "genuine", "soothing lyrics" of this cool R&B crooner stand out on a "gospel-inspired" album of "beautiful", PG-rated songs about "love" and loneliness; picking up the bass guitar and "stepping up" to the role of arranger for his fourth effort, the "impressive" singer/songwriter proves that "his music just keeps getting better."

SARAH MCLACHLAN,   27 | 27 | 26 | 27
FUMBLING TOWARDS ECSTASY 🔳#1
1993, Arista; "Possession"; www.sarahmclachlan.com
■ "Dim the lights, light a candle and listen" to the "deeply introspective" breakthrough album ("a $16 version of a therapist") from this Canadian "channeler of feelings" with the "weepingly gorgeous" voice – it's "the pinnacle of bedroom music for the intellectual set"; "sumptuous" and "darkly erotic", from the "title track, about throwing fear to the wind while falling in love", to the stalker tale, *Possession*, it makes "the hairs on the back of your neck rise."

Sarah McLachlan, *Surfacing* 🔳#1   26 | 26 | 26 | 26
1997, Arista; "Angel"; www.sarahmclachlan.com
■ "Once again, Sarah turns out a work of art" "proving that *Fumbling Towards Ecstasy* was no fluke"; "get ready to have your world rocked, gently", with this "moody" CD, which, along with Lilith Fair, "made her a household name"; dealing with "everything from drug addiction (*Angel*) to faith (*Witness*)", "her songs are pointed yet soothing to the soul" and, with "that silky voice", it's no mystery why they'll "ring in your mind forever."

Don McLean, *American Pie*   23 | 26 | 21 | 20
1971, United Artists; "American Pie"; www.don-mclean.com
■ "All those people of every age singing *American Pie* can't be wrong" about the "classic" status of this singer-songwriter's "11-minute opus to American pop culture"; "the official anthem for a generation lost in space", the "all-time sing-along" "transcends any literal reference to

a historic moment" – and even "brings back memories" for those born after its "early '70s heyday"; it's "great populist writing", especially coupled with the "hidden gem" *Vincent (Starry Starry Night)*, so "cut me another slice."

Meat Loaf, *Bat out of Hell*   25 | 25 | 24 | 25
1977, Epic; "Paradise by the Dashboard Light"
■ "An epic story of teenage lust", this "motor-vatin'" "roadtrip"-worthy "rock opera" is driven by "racing rhythms" and Todd Rundgren's "bombastic" production; "brassy, brash and over the top", this "meatloaf and potatoes of any collection" "brought dramatic performance" to light through the "poignant, funny" songs of Jim Steinman and the "showmanship" of Meat Loaf, this genre's "Andrew Lloyd Webber and Tim Rice."

Meet Me in St. Louis (Soundtrack)   26 | 26 | 26 | 24
1944, MGM; "Have Yourself a Merry Little Christmas"
■ "Clang, clang, clang went the trolley", and zing, zing, zing go your heartstrings when you listen to this "charming" soundtrack "from when movies had songs" as a matter of course; "you can't help smiling" or crying at the "fantastic" Judy Garland "at her most touching" – her *Have Yourself a Merry Little Christmas* is both "joyous and heartbreaking", particularly on the "better" Rhino reissue.

John Cougar Mellencamp,   22 | 22 | 22 | 21
American Fool
1982, Riva; "Jack and Diane"; www.mellencamp.com
■ The Coug "hit the heartland big time with this career-launching album", a "feel-good", "raw and real" "rock & roller" that "sounds like it was recorded in the back of a pickup truck"; he really "showed his maverick ability" with "sterling" hits like *Hurts So Good* and *Jack and Diane* ("if you don't know the words" to this "you're either lying or have been living under a rock").

John Cougar Mellencamp,   26 | 26 | 24 | 23
Scarecrow
1985, Riva; "Small Town"; www.mellencamp.com
■ "His songwriting was solid before", but "Mellencamp (née Cougar) came of age" on this "thematic breakthrough" that takes an "affectionate, often melancholic look at the Midwest", "spotlighting social issues without sacrificing" its "roots rock" sound; deftly "balancing plight-of-the-farmer anthems (*Rain on the Scarecrow*)", "poignant, personally felt tracks" (*Small Town*) and "party pop tunes (*R.O.C.K. in the USA*), it's "message music at its best."

Sergio Mendes & Brasil '66,   25 | 23 | 25 | 23
Fool on the Hill
1968, A&M; "Fool on the Hill"
■ "You will be swinging your hips before you know it", say fortysomething scenesters who "ran home every day from

school as kids just to hear the smooth female voices" serve up those "swirling harmonies against a salsa/samba beat" on this "kool" lounge "treat" featuring "purely Rio" "updates" of the Beatles and Simon & Garfunkel; "cutting-edge for its time" and totally "groovy now", it's "the ultimate cocktail party CD."

Natalie Merchant, *Tigerlilly*   23 | 24 | 23 | 23
1995, Elektra; "Wonder"; www.nataliemerchant.com
■ "Soft, blue and a bit melancholy", this singer-songwriter's "exquisite first solo effort" is "proof she was the one indispensible Maniac in 10,000"; "sultry and sexy", "her unique voice is a gift", adding "nuance and power" to a collection of "immensely satisfying" "winners", from the radio hit *Carnival* to *River,* a tribute to the late actor Phoenix.

Jo Dee Messina, *I'm Alright*   25 | 23 | 23 | 23
1998, Curb; "I'm Alright"; www.jodeemessina.com
■ With her "polished second outing", produced by Tim McGraw, this flame-haired New Englander "definitely struck a chord", proving she is more than alright with country and pop audiences by way of "sassy songs that make you want to get up and dance"; often "upbeat", "like Katrina and the Waves but with a twang", "she can wrap her voice around a ballad too."

METALLICA, *MASTER OF PUPPETS*   27 | 25 | 28 | 24
1986, Elektra; "Master of Puppets"; www.metallica.com
■ "The masters of crunch" (including "the late bass virtuoso Cliff Burton") were at the "creative peak" of "their thrash period" when they created this "flawless" "sonic assault" that helped "establish metal as an intelligent, credible form of rock"; combining "aggression and composition" with "classical complexity", this "thunderous and beautiful" breakthrough "makes you want to jump around and head-bang till you have whiplash."

Metallica, *Metallica* Ⓖ #1   25 | 24 | 27 | 26
1991, Elektra; "Enter Sandman"; www.metallica.com
■ "More tuneful" and "radio friendly" than "James Hetfield and crew's" earlier efforts, this Grammy-winning "monster", "dubbed the black album", brought "snarling" "metal to the mainstream" with "haunting melodies" like *Nothing Else Matters,* which showed a softer side", and "flawless production" from Bob Rock; while "old-school fans sometimes" believe its "acoustic guitar" and "symphonic orchestration" "signaled the end of the rough and rowdy mighty" era, even they admit it's "a good introduction for those a bit intimidated by the genre."

THE METERS, *FUNKIFY YOUR LIFE:*   28 | 24 | 29 | 24
THE METERS ANTHOLOGY
1995, Rhino; "Cissy Strut"
■ "You can't funkify your life without" this "no-frills" double-disc "benchmark" from the "originators of the New

Orleans scene"; the "Neville clan" and company "pack quite a punch into their early instrumentals", with George Porter's "percolating" "bass riffs" underscoring classics like *Cissy Strut*; "the cleverly simplistic", "tight" beats "rival those of James Brown" on a retrospective that "means a party", though bayou-boosters agree there is "no substitute for seeing them live."

Pat Metheny, *Pat Metheny Group*   27   26   28   26
1978, ECM; "Phase Dance"
■ "Groupies" "jump for joy", "inspired" by the "ethereal energy" of the "swirling, tuneful, improvised jazz" of the Group's first disc; with a "guitar strung to his heart", Metheny employs an "excellent" "combination of technical gifts and soul" to set "the standard by which other fusion artists are measured", and the "delicate interplay" between the "seminal" strummer and keyboardist Lyle Mays makes this "dreamy" disc "worth listening to over and over again."

Miami Vice (Soundtrack) #1   24   21   24   24
1985, MCA; "In the Air Tonight"
■ "Jan Hammer's decision to give some characters their own theme dramatically enhanced the attraction" of "the first music video masquerading as a TV show"; his score might provide "the closest tie-in to a series since *Peter Gunn*", which is fitting because the "haunting" music "helped the plot" of a detective show as cool as its predecessor; Phil Collins, Chaka Khan and a host of '80s pop stars quicken the "solid album" – "just watch out if you're driving!"

George Michael, *Faith* G #   24   22   23   24
1987, Columbia; "Faith"; www.georgemichael.com
■ Everyone's favorite filthy "father figure" "went from bubblegum to credible crooner" on this "addictively sexy" post-Wham! Grammy-winner, which "defined the '80s" but "doesn't sound dated"; before "the whole bathroom incident" with the long arm of the law, George Michael put out some "near-perfect pop confections", both "danceable" and "soulful" becoming the first white solo artist to top the R&B charts with "one of those CDs that keeps you going an extra mile at the gym."

Bette Midler, *Beaches*   24   24   25   24
1989, Atlantic; "Wind Beneath My Wings"
■ "Admit it, ladies: you danced to *Wind Beneath My Wings* with your dad at your wedding", and why not?; the Grammy-winning anchor to the Divine Miss M's "financial success" of a "sappy film" is just one track she "nails with such beauty" that she "breaks your heart"; with "vocals as smooth as silk" and "amazing power and emotion", Bette belts out a soundtrack that makes you "laugh, cry and play it over and over"; did she ever know that she's our hero, ask "fans of Midler"?

Midnight Oil, *Diesel and Dust*   25 | 25 | 23 | 24
1988, Columbia; "Beds Are Burning"; www.midnightoil.com
■ "Activism never rocked so hard" as on this "all-time Oils' classic" of "accurate and pointed" "socially conscious" "anthems" about "the plight of the Aborigines, the destruction of natural resources and humanity's general need to screw up the world"; with its "unmistakable Aussie surf-punk influence" and "big, bald" and "scary" law student–turned–frontman Peter Garrett, this "hard-hitting" "rally" hit a "high-water mark in America" – it was simply "too good to be denied."

Charles Mingus, *Mingus Ah Um*   28 | 28 | 28 | 25
1959, Columbia; "Better Git It in Your Soul"; www.mingusmingusmingus.com
■ "The word 'rapturous' doesn't begin to express the bliss to be found" on this "life-affirming" disc from "the master of jazz bass and post-bop composition"; a "genius on all levels", Mingus leads a "great band", including sax players John Handy and Booker Ervin, on "multilayered orchestrations" for a "spiritual experience" "with an attitude"; "exuberant to an almost ridiculous degree", this album "might be his best, and that's saying a lot" because the dude was "just sooo coool."

Liza Minnelli, *Liza with a "Z"*   27 | 26 | 25 | 26
1972, Columbia; "Ring Them Bells"
■ You better "ring them bells" for this "Z-riffic" recording of Liza live "at the absolute peak of her career"; "like her mother, she is very inconsistent", but "before life wore her down", she was "a first-rate entertainer", pulling off "one delight after another" "with panache" in this "full-of-energy", "fun" collaboration with Fosse, Kander, Ebb and an "audience that's having a great time."

Kylie Minogue, *Fever*   24 | 20 | 22 | 25
2002, Capitol; "Can't Get You Out of My Head"; www.kylie.com
■ "Who knew this is what would become of the *Locomotion* girl?"; "from hopeless little Aussie to the mistress of the club floor", "almost 20 years" after her first surprise hit, the "hot" actress-turned-diva "comes into her own", dishing out a "disco revival" that "showcases her foremost strength: having fun" "with none of the teen-cult guilt"; "dance-pop candy for a brave new decade", it might be "ultimately meaningless", "but it makes you move."

JONI MITCHELL, *BLUE*   29 | 29 | 27 | 26
1971, Reprise; "A Case of You"; www.jonimitchell.com
■ "Longing never sounded so gorgeous" as on this "legendary", "chillingly beautiful" "tapestry" that "set the standards for the singer-songwriter/confessional genre"; "lonely odes from Europe?", "love songs where the protagonist admits fault but is too strong for any man? – it's

all here", "sung with power and harmony" – not to mention "a vocal range to die for" – prompting the Blue-clued to chorus, "I could drink a case of Joni and still be on my feet."

JONI MITCHELL, *COURT AND SPARK* 28 | 28 | 27 | 26 |
1974, Asylum; "Help Me"; www.jonimitchell.com
■ "The starting point in your Joni infatuation" is this "very LA" "masterwork", a "perfect blend of jazz and pop" that's her "most radio-friendly" release, and "one of the defining albums of the 1970s"; "all hail the high priestess": with "accessible but stylistically challenging arrangements", a "crystal clear voice", "top-notch lyrics" that "demonstrate love found and lost", "acerbic wit and remarkable insight into human nature", she "takes you to a place of wonder."

Joni Mitchell, *Hejira* 27 | 27 | 27 | 27 |
1976, Asylum; "Coyote"; www.jonimitchell.com
■ The former folkie "hits the road" on this "dreamy, jazz-inflected" "spiritual journey", and with Weather Report bassist Jaco Pastorius and drummer Larry Carlton "riding shotgun", "the musicianship is raised to dizzying heights"; gliding through this "cathartic, ethereal wandering" she "revels in vapor trails and irascible bluesmen", spinning "the odd lyric" that "haunts your sleep" and songs that "wrap you in warmth and melody"; "utterly unique, spare and delicious", it's "another bull's-eye for Joni."

Moby, *Play* 26 | 23 | 25 | 27 |
1999, Elektra; "Porcelain"; www.moby-online.com
■ "If you haven't heard it, you've been living in a cave" – "varied, tight, sexy, original and intelligent", this "orgy" of "everything from gospel to electronica" is "head-to-toe fabulous" and has been head-to-toe licensed; "though it's hard to listen to without remembering which commercial you first heard each song in", "every track has so many layers and is blended together so artfully", its "beauty" can "still make you cry."

Moby Grape, *Moby Grape* 24 | 22 | 23 | 21 |
1967, CBS; "Omaha"
■ "Can you smell the weed?" quip Grape fans who fondly recall this "too-short-lived" Summer of Lover as "one of the most perfect debuts"; this "influential" outfit from "San Francisco led the way" with a "stunning mix of country, blues and rock & roll", "tight songwriting" and "beautiful harmonies" stoked by Jerry Miller, who some fans rank "along with Clapton and Hendrix as one of the best guitarists of that era."

The Modern Lovers, 25 | 26 | 22 | 19 |
The Modern Lovers
1976, Beserkley/Rhino; "Roadrunner"
■ "Inspired, Velvet Underground–style songs from Jonathan Richman's first" group, including the "bare-bones rock" of

Girlfriend, Pablo Picasso and *Roadrunner,* make this "protopunk" outfit an early proponent of "seminal teen angst"; sure, the "cute" frontman went on to become a "funny, dorky" "folkie", Dave Robinson co-founded the Cars and Jerry Harrison joined the Talking Heads, but infatuated fans feel this "infectious" "band before its time" just "didn't get enough credit."

Thelonious Monk, *Monk's Dream*   27 | 27 | 28 | 24

1962, Columbia; "Monk's Dream"

☑ "As distinctive as anyone", Thelonious Monk was "a truly original" pianist and composer who spent some time being "misunderstood", but once his "sparse", "eccentric" style caught on, he became "a huge influence on all who followed"; "rollicking, wry, poignant and just amazing", this "bright, accessible" "stuff from his Columbia years" is "what they mean by virtuoso", even if aficionados would rate "a half dozen other" discs from the "master" "ahead of this one."

Wes Montgomery,   28 | 25 | 29 | 24
Incredible Jazz Guitar of Wes Montgomery

1960, Riverside; "West Coast Blues";
www.cmgww.com/music/montgomery

■ "You mean there's only one guy playing" the axe on this disc? – "demonstrating why he was undeniably worthy of the accolades" in his relatively short career, "Wes makes the guitar gently weep" "with beautiful, muted octave melodies" on *Polka Dots and Moonbeams* and inspires you to "get out the beer and the shots" on *West Coast Blues*; simply put, "what's not to like?"

Moody Blues,   25 | 24 | 26 | 26
This is the Moody Blues

1974, Threshold; "Nights in White Satin";
www.moodyblues.co.uk

☑ "Beautiful melodies, wondrous harmonies, heartfelt lyrics", "orchestral textures" – this "fabulous" double-disc "treasure" from the British band's "second coming" shows they "can do it all"; "creative and mood-provoking", this "class act" "set new trends in its time" and they're "still wonderful"; still, a few peeved purists implore "get the individual concept albums" instead.

Morcheeba, *Big Calm*   26 | 24 | 26 | 26
1998, Sire; "Part of the Process"; www.morcheeba.net

■ "After a long, hard day at work", "just sit back" and get a big calm on "without any controlled substances" as singer Skye's "silken breath whispers along your skin", "soothing troubles away" on this "amazing exercise in trip-hop chill-out with a gangsta edge"; full of "sexy, smooth" "mood music", it's also got "a fair amount of tunes to pump you up" – the "perfect" combination for an "entertaining", "romantic evening."

Lee Morgan, *The Sidewinder*   27 | 26 | 29 | 25
1964, Blue Note; "The Sidewinder"

■ "Bop till you drop! Lee is on top" for this "hard-swinging, blues-based jazz" album; Bob Cranshaw delivers "a study in upright bass playing" on the "addictive" hit title track, and trumpeter "Morgan and tenor man Joe Henderson are joined at the hip throughout" for a disc that's both "challenging" and "infectiously catchy"; "upbeat and enthusiastic", it's a "classic" from a "wonderful" musician who "died too young."

Alanis Morissette,   24 | 25 | 22 | 24
Jagged Little Pill G #1
1995, Maverick; "You Oughta Know"; www.alanis.com

■ "Gotta love the bitterness" that's all over this "mall-pop songstress"–turned–"angry rocker chick's" Grammy-winning breakthrough – "a defining disc for her generation" that's full of "guts" and "edge"; you oughta know by now it's "an inside look into the minds and moods of young women" who've been "jilted and scorned", and it's "all about taking power back from others"; every teenage girl who owned it says "she's not annoying, damn it! she's me, circa 1995!"

Morphine, *Cure for Pain*   24 | 23 | 24 | 22
1993, Rykodisc; "Cure for Pain"; www.morphine3.com

■ The "totally unique instrumentation" of this "bare minimum but awesome" Boston trio – "a two-string slide bass, drums and a Roland Kirk-ish sax attack" – created a "sultry" album full of "ultrahip", "fascinating rock-jazz" "that still hasn't been successfully imitated"; sadly, frontman Mark Sandman's "haunting yet so beautiful" voice was stilled forever in 1999, when he suffered a fatal heart attack onstage in Rome.

VAN MORRISON, *ASTRAL WEEKS*   29 | 28 | 28 | 26
1968, Warner Bros.; "Madame George"

■ "After being released from a Bang Records contract, Morrison exhibited a spurt of creativity, putting forth three outstanding Celtic-soul albums", "beginning with this startling blend of jazz, rock and folk", "a mystical journey" rife with "orchestral arrangements" and "unorthodox phrasing"; "surrounded by great musicians", "Van the Man" cuts loose – "it's the sound of joy and sadness, wrapped in a human voice, echoed by flute, bass and fiddle."

VAN MORRISON, *MOONDANCE*   28 | 28 | 27 | 25
1970, Warner Bros.; "Moondance"

■ "Earthier and more accessible than *Astral Weeks*", this "charming ode to romance" is the "ultimate hookup" disc, brimming with "warmth and depth", "fantastic jazz-style accompaniment" and "exultant vocals"; such "pastoral hippie poetry" "swoon" the smitten who fall for lyrics that "speak from the heart", "beautifully manifested in tracks like *Into the Mystic, Caravan*" and the title track; "filled with whimsy and enchantment, it puts you under a shady oak tree on a sunny June afternoon."

Morrissey, *Viva Hate*   24 | 25 | 23 | 23

1988, Sire; "Suedehead"; www.morrissey-solo.com
☑ The first post-Smiths album by Manchester's "king of mope rock" is a work of "wrist-splitting excellence" and "probably the best of Moz's solo efforts", declare diehards who angst along to his "captivatingly self-centered, maudlin pop songs" full of "delicious, mostly sarcastic lyrics", "delivered in a lilting, lovely voice"; sure he's a "depressed teen's best friend", but the "music is hypnotizing" and the choruses are "catchy"; but a few faithful to earlier days quip "where's Johnny Marr when you need him?"

Mos Def, *Black on Both Sides*   26 | 29 | 24 | 25

1999, Rawkus; "Ms. Fat Booty"
■ Hip-hop's "renaissance man" is "gifted" with the "smooth flow" to "make you laugh, raise a fist and cry" on his "socially important" solo debut that is as "lyrically intelligent" as it is "musically captivating"; "honest", "complex" poetry laces the jazz-, rock- and funk-driven beats on tunes like the libidinous *Ms. Fat Booty,* which is "melodic" and "soulful", yet bodacious enough for "bumping in the car."

Mos Def and Talib Kweli, *Black Star*   27 | 28 | 24 | 25

1998, Rawkus; "RE: DEFinition"; www.mosdefinitely.com
■ "Lyrically stunning, sensitive and moving", these "innovative" Marcus Garvey–inspired "poets" from Brooklyn "prove conscious rap is alive and well" with their brand of "intelligent hip-hop with heart and soul"; the smoothed-out, Native Tongues–style beat to *RE: DEFinition* helps make the album "a backpackers' classic" that "will not only get you to bob your head but take you on a journey through your cerebral cortex."

Mott the Hoople, *All the Young Dudes*   25 | 22 | 23 | 21

1972, Columbia; "All the Young Dudes"
■ Vocalist Ian Hunter and guitarist Mick Ralphs' "precursor to punk" flourished under David Bowie's glammy production style, resulting in a "smarter, more tuneful album than their previous outings"; "sexy, rocking fun", from the Duke's "fresh" "favorite" title track to "the definitive version" of the Velvets' *Sweet Jane*, this "classic" deftly demonstrates "where Oasis got their ideas."

Bob Mould, *Workbook*   24 | 25 | 25 | 21

1989, Workbook; "Wishing Well"; www.bobmould.com
■ Perhaps "the most engaging collection" of the ex–Hüsker Dü frontman's solo career, this "deliberate departure" proved that "even guitar shredders" can "turn down the

amps and let the pain shine through"; "exposing raw regret, loss and other primal emotions", this "acoustic-driven" album of "deep lyrics" and "catchy hooks" "closes the door" on Mould's former Minneapolis trio and "opens the next to a decade-plus of reverence from the world's indie punks."

Moulin Rouge! (Soundtrack)   25 | 23 | 25 | 27
2001, Interscope; "Come What May";
www.clubmoulinrouge.com

■ "Yes, these are their real voices", and they prove to be "surprisingly strong, if a tad overdone"; "Ewan McGregor and Nicole Kidman perform amazingly for actors, not musicians", on this "crazy, catchy, clever" compilation of "pop culture plagiarism" from "genius" Baz Luhrmann's musical about boho Paris; "the songs aren't new", but their "terrific presentation" is: Beck covers Bowie, Bowie covers Nat King Cole and Fat Boy Slim conjures a cancan for a "spectacular spectacular" that's "surprisingly addictive."

MOZART, DON GIOVANNI   29 | 29 | 28 | 26
1959, EMI; "Madamina, Il Catalogo E Questo";
www.philharmonia.co.uk

■ The "revolutionary" Mozart's "most perfect opera" is "what stories should be: long, complex, intertwined and extremely beautiful", "replete with personal anguish" and, yup, "always fun"; conductor Maria Giulini "gives the dramatic momentum" to "the ultimate Joan Sutherland" performance for "the ultimate *Don Giovanni*"; "the balance of singers, orchestra and pacing is perfect", and though it's "now remastered", "even the antiquated technology seems to fit" the original recording.

MOZART,   29 | 29 | 28 | 28
PIANO CONCERTOS NOS. 19-23
1985, Philips; "Piano Concerto No. 20"

■ Pianist Mitsuko Uchida "is incapable of playing anything but great Mozart" as this "eminently worthwhile" set attests: "her technique, color and depth is unquestionably terrific" and "she found a fine match in the English Chamber Orchestra", led by conductor Jeffrey Tate; these concertos make "fine background music for afternoon tea", as just like those little crustless sandwiches, they "explore a multitude of ideas within the restraints of form."

Mozart, Requiem   28 | 29 | 27 | 27
1987, Philips; "Dies Irae"; www.monteverdi.co.uk

◪ Mozart's "beautiful" "last piece" "makes you wonder" if he meant to "write his own requiem"; this "reverential" "emotion-soaked" recording is "angst-riddled but riveting", with "strings masterfully complementing vocals" under John Eliot Gardner's "textured but ponderous" conducting; though some fans feel "the traditional text, period instruments, faster tempi and solo singing make it a must", less emotive ears find it "big on drama, light on the spritual."

Mozart, *Symphonies Nos. 35–41*   28 | 29 | 27 | 26
1966, Deutsche Grammophon; "Jupiter Symphony";
www.berliner-philharmoniker.de
☑ "Without dispute, Nos. 35–41 make life worth living",
and listeners immersed in a "love affair" with Karl Böhm's
"fabulous" renditions of these "masterpieces" call them
"almost essential recordings"; nontraditionalists look to
other versions, tsking that this conductor's "heavy hand"
"hasn't aged well" and booing "big-band Mozart at
its most bland."

MUPPET MOVIE (Soundtrack) G   28 | 27 | 23 | 25
1979, Atlantic; "The Rainbow Connection"
■ "Why aren't there more songs about rainbows?" – find
the answer in Jim Henson's "absolutely classic" soundtrack,
which "captures the essence" of the "amazing" Muppets
as Kermit and friends journey from the swamp to the big
city; though the crew got their start on *Sesame Street,* the
album "is not just for kids" as "sweet tracks" like *I'm Going
Back There*" "aren't mindless or reductionist"; hands down,
it wins the prize for "best work by pieces of felt, ever."

Anne Murray, *Greatest Hits*   25 | 25 | 26 | 24
1980, Capitol; "Snowbird"; www.annemurray.com
■ "You want enjoyable? you want singable? you want
comfortable? you want Anne"; the "consistently excellent"
pop "crooner" with the "knack for phrasing" and the
"wonderful, mellow voice" lets the *Snowbird* fly along with
the rest of "her biggest and best-charting hits" on this
"beautiful" collection that "brings back fond memories" of
the '70s' lite years.

The Music from Peter Gunn   28 | 27 | 29 | 25
(Soundtrack) G #1
1959, RCA Victor; "Peter Gunn Theme"
■ The rhythms on this orchestral soundtrack are as "ice-
cold" as the martinis favored by the private dick on its hit
series; with "jazz so cool it's hot", "Henry Mancini's score
made an average show into exciting TV", "perfectly
evoking the '50s" vibe of smoky clubs and swingin' pads;
listening to this "great music", nostalgists get all noir over
the end of the Eisenhower years, "crying just thinking about
what's been lost."

The Music Man (Soundtrack)   26 | 26 | 27 | 26
1962, Warner Bros.; "76 Trombones"
■ "Mom and apple pie have nothing on this" "good bit of
old-fashioned hokum", a "guilty pleasure" for the fans of
the "boisterous and loud" "family musical" with Robert
Preston as the "ultimate" Professor Harold Hill, and "babe
of all babes" Shirley Jones "lighting, up the room with great
voices"; folks from "Gary, Indiana" and everywhere else
say "*76 Trombones* never sounded so good" as on the
"glorious, full-of-vinegar" soundtrack.

Mussorgsky,   28 | 27 | 28 | 26
Pictures at an Exhibition
1964, Sony Classical; "The Great Gate of Kiev"
■ "Wonderful for getting children interested in classical music", Mussorgsky's "whimsical, stirring, sentimental" composition "translates into any idiom": "originally written for solo piano, it rocks with ELP", gets "jazzed" up by Allyn Ferguson and "sounds great" on this "moving, beautiful interpretation" by the Cleveland Orchestra under George Szell "at his best"; "boisterous, joyous, yet introspective", this "delightful" disc "may be definitive."

My Bloody Valentine, Loveless   25 | 23 | 26 | 26
1991, Sire; "Soon"
■ "It's impossible to determine how many bands were influenced" by this "surreal" "sonic masterpiece", "layered like an oil painting" with its "brilliantly fuzzy", "ethereal" "wall of guitars" set against "wispy female vocals"; "representing the shoegazer movement at the height of power", these "swirling" "waves of sound" take listeners to "a sensual and occasionally sinister place"; it's like the "aural equivalent of an acid trip" – "it doesn't matter that you can't make out the lyrics."

MY FAIR LADY   29 | 29 | 28 | 27
(Original cast recording) **#1**
1956, Columbia; "I Could Have Danced All Night"
■ Voted the No. 1 Musical in this *Survey*, "the fairest of all ladies" features "twenty-year-old revelation" Julie Andrews and her "glorious voice and emotional range" that make the "loverly" Lerner and Loewe score "soar" for the "gold-standard" of "*Pygmalion* take-off", with the "expressive", "excellent", "effortlessly charming" Rex Harrison pulling the strings; "musical theater is at its peak" on a "literate masterpiece" "that makes you want to sing all night."

The Pink Panther (Soundtrack) **G**   26 | 26 | 27 | 25
1964, RCA Victor; "Pink Panther Theme"
■ "Sipping gimlets" "with a smile on your face" is "a must" "purr" panthers pouncing on this "peppy" "period piece"; "instantly recognizable on any inhabited planet", just about "the most famous of movie themes" establishes the "prevalence" of that pink cartoon feline and Peter Sellars' Inspector Clouseau "in the social subconscious"; it's "ultimate Mancini", a "seamless collection of '60s sophistication" from the composer who "owned" the era.

N

Nas, Illmatic   28 | 29 | 25 | 26
1994, Columbia; "NY State of Mind"; www.stillmatic.com
■ No rapper "depicts life growing up in the New York City ghetto" like this "straight-up" "urban poet", whose "raw",

"allusion"-filled rhymes "dance around" beats crafted by a "dream team" including Large Professor, Pete Rock, Q-Tip and DJ Premier; "sensitive yet manly", the son of jazzman Olu Dara delivers one of "the best debuts" by any MC, "redefining East Coast hip-hop" in under forty minutes; as for this "lyrical assassin's" *NY State of Mind,* "let's just say it isn't Billy Joel's."

Oliver Nelson, *Blues & the Abstract Truth* 28 28 28 27
1961, Impulse!; "Stolen Moments"
■ "Wonderful ensemble writing", "blues clichés made fresh" and "the best title of any jazz album" – "it all comes together" on this "all-star" "gem"; "the contrast between Nelson's melodic style and Eric Dolphy's conversational" flute and tenor sax "creates a thing of rare beauty", enhanced by trumpeter Freddie Hubbard and pianist Bill Evans; "connoisseurs" concur "they caught magic in a bottle the day it was recorded."

Willie Nelson, *Red Headed Stranger* #1 28 28 28 27
1975, Columbia; "Blue Eyes Crying in the Rain"
■ "Fire one up and listen" as this laid-back cowboy spins "a remarkable, threadbare tale of love, loss and murder" on a "true concept album" about a "preacher who kills his wife and goes on the run"; supporters spread the gospel that it's not just "a quintessential outlaw recording" but "perhaps the greatest country album" ever with a "spare" style that "changed the way C&W was played"; considered "daring" in '75, it's "as real as it comes" today.

Willie Nelson, *Stardust* #1 27 26 26 26
1978, Columbia; "Stardust"
■ On this "legendary" "departure from the traditional Willie", "America's gentle troubadour" "puts his one-of-a-kind touch on old pop standards", finding "common ground between outlaw country" and "mellow", "classic stuff" by Berlin, Carmichael, Gershwin and Ellington; "sweet" and "simple", more bow tie than bandana, "each song is turned and twisted until it's his own" and, paired with the "production talents of Booker T. Jones", "sets a romantic mood" that appeals to "a whole new audience."

Randy Newman, *Little Criminals* 25 28 24 23
1977, Warner Bros.; "Short People"; www.randynewman.com
■ "Sarcasm reaches new heights in the lyrics" of this "always witty, always on target" "cerebral" album, which represents "clever Randy" before he became "Hollywood Randy"; there's a "scary amount of good songs here", many of which "spoof on everything considered holy" – no doubt some petite people "never recovered" from the "sly", "controversial *Short People*" – just a small example of his "twisted and comical look at life."

New Order, Power, Corruption & Lies

27 | 27 | 26 | 26

1983, Qwest; "Blue Monday"

■ "The innocence of youth" "tinged with the angst of Ian Curtis' suicide makes this pastiche of styles a masterpiece" from the artists that formed New Order following their Joy Division band member's death; an "amazing meld of new wave", "manic-depressive dance music", "synthesized beats" and "powerful, blooming harmonies", it's a "seminal album" from the 1980s' "prototypical electronica band."

New Order, Substance

27 | 25 | 25 | 26

1987, Qwest; "Bizarre Love Triangle"

■ "Once you know their history" ("wherein a former mope rock group rises from the ashes and does something really radical: performs dance music"), they're "much more interesting to listen to", but your experience "won't have any substance without this" "blueprint" to the tale; the "riveting archipelago" of "synth-alterna-pop" and "real emotions" collects "their greatest radio singles", B-side "gems" and "borderline Joy Division" tracks "to introduce you to the elder statespersons of electronica."

Stevie Nicks, Bella Donna 🔢1

25 | 26 | 25 | 25

1981, Modern; "Edge of Seventeen"; www.nicksfix.com

■ Fleetwood Mac's "smoky voiced" bella donna "rocks solo" on this "shining" "country/pop/rock" debut album, "surrounding herself with excellent musicians" including Don Henley and Tom Petty, while "proving her power as an artist"; tracks like *Edge of Seventeen* show that if the "prolific songwriter" "wasn't a singer, she could be a poet", but "the album is a classic for the cover alone": Stevie, dove perched on forearm, "casts a magical spell" worthy of Rhiannon.

A Night at Studio 54

24 | 20 | 23 | 23

(Compilation) ⊙

1979, Casablanca; "I Love the Nightlife (Disco Round)"

■ Shake your groove thing with one of the '70s' "best party albums" from the era's most infamous glitterfest; whether you like to "push push in the bush" or go where you can hang out with all the boys, this "perfect time capsule of disco classics and cheese", from Alicia Bridges' *I Love the Nightlife* to the Village People's *Y.M.C.A.*, will "inspire you to quit your job and open a club – before you remember that they ended up in jail."

Harry Nilsson, Nilsson Schmilsson

26 | 26 | 25 | 24

1971, RCA Victor; "Without You";
www.harrynilsson.com

■ "Dim the lights and hang with your honey", but first, slip on this "whimsical, dark", "quirky" record, featuring Nilsson's *Without You,* a tearjerker that "really yanks on the heart" making this album of "not-so-mindless pop" his most commercially successful; "an icon", "humorous" Harry also proved to be a "magnificent storyteller" and "all-time great vocalist", capable of "sharing many moods" and "styles" – no wonder he's "sadly missed."

Nine Inch Nails,   25 | 25 | 25 | 28
The Downward Spiral
1994, Nothing/Interscope; "Closer"; www.nin.com
■ "You can hear the pain and raw emotion in every song" on this "difficult", "intense", "scary" "masterpiece" that "documents one guy at his lowest moment, and then some"; frontman Trent Reznor's "dark genius" "brought industrial dance music roaring into mainstream America", proving that "textured, thoughtful" "S&M for the soul", "raucous enough" to "peel paint off the walls", is "not just for people with chipped black fingernails" – it "achingly speaks to anyone who listens."

Nirvana, *In Utero* #1   26 | 26 | 25 | 25
1993, DGC; "All Apologies"
■ This "perfect marriage of punk rage and Cobain's often repressed pop instincts" "brilliantly displayed how far creativity and a few chords can get you", though it was "sadly the swan song" for Seattle's "driving force behind grunge"; a "bare look into Kurt's tortured self", "the raw, scratchy" tracks, including "*Scentless Apprentice,* a blast of jagged noise", and "beautiful, inspiring *All Apologies*", "sound more like demos" with "all three members in top form as pile-driving instrumentalists."

NIRVANA, *NEVERMIND* #1   28 | 27 | 26 | 26
1991, Geffen; "Smells Like Teen Spirit"
■ "Washing away the musical sins" of "hair-band hell", this "earth-shattering" "masterpiece by the undisputed kings of grunge" "ushered in a revolution"; Cobain's "jagged-enough-to-cut" guitar, "painfully intense lyrics" and vocals "that would shred most larynxes" are "backed by Krist Novoselic's chunky bass lines" and Dave Grohl's "thunderous drumming" – "an amazing combination of punk power, angst and pop hooks" that "delivers emotion without posturing"; "Kurt brings you so far into his world you see the demons singing him to sleep."

THE NITTY GRITTY DIRT BAND,   29 | 27 | 29 | 27
WILL THE CIRCLE BE UNBROKEN
1972, United Artists; "Will the Circle Be Unbroken";
www.nittygritty.com
■ Decades "before *O Brother, Where Art Thou?*", this *Survey*'s top-rated Country & Western album, a three-disc "landmark", "pulled out all the bells and whistles", "bringing folk and hill music to the masses" by pairing young Dirt Band pickers with a "breathtaking supporting cast of traditional C&W stars", including Roy Acuff, Maybelle Carter and Doc Watson; giving "new life to old material", the bluegrass

"classic" is "a great scrapbook of Americana" that "stands the test of time."

No Doubt, *Rock Steady* | 23 | 21 | 23 | 24 |
2001, Interscope; "Hella Good"; www.nodoubt.com
■ "Gwen . . . need we say more?" – "witty" frontwoman Stefani "casts a spell on everyone", including "excellent artists" like Prince, Sly & Robbie and Lady Saw who guest star on this "sensual", "eclectic" "groovy party" disc with a "dancehall reggae vibe"; you can't help but "bop around to *Hey Baby*", "bask in the beautiful *Underneath it All*" or "rock out to *Hella Good*", "pop confections" that are "every girl's anthems for love and loss."

No Doubt, *Tragic Kingdom* 🔢 | 23 | 23 | 23 | 24 |
1996, Trauma/Interscope; "Don't Speak"; www.nodoubt.com
■ The "fun, funky" major-label debut of "SoCal ska-rock" from "the Blondie of the new millennium", this "energetic", "entertaining" breakthrough established lead singer Stefani as perhaps "the sexiest woman in rock" who could "kick some serious musical ass"; close listeners consider the "quirky, smart" "classic" "the ultimate breakup album", suggesting it "should have been called *Gwen's Diary*."

Notorious B.I.G., *Life After Death* 🔢 | 27 | 26 | 24 | 27 |
1997, Bad Boy; "Hypnotize"
■ "A fittingly creepy swan song" by a street "Shakespeare" many consider the "greatest rapper of all time", this double disc displays the late Brooklyn-born MC at "his freshest and fiercest" on a "combo of ballads, party anthems and hard-core thug beats" boosted by Sean Combs' slick production; with his "smooth flow", razorlike "enunciation" and "unbelievable rhymes", "the man could spit lyrics like no other" – "it is too bad hip-hop has lost him."

Notorious B.I.G., *Ready to Die* | 27 | 27 | 25 | 26 |
1994, Bad Boy; "Juicy"
■ The "grandaddy of gangsta rap's" debut is credited with saving "New York hip-hop" with its "grimy, devastatingly true vision" of "the street hustling" lifestyle, "delivered with skill, precision and humor" by an "unparalleled storyteller" backed by Puff's "hardcore" beats; "from the pavement to the clubs, it was Biggie's time, and we were all feeling" this lyrical "genius who knew his way around a sixteen-bar verse."

NUGGETS: ORIGINAL ARTYFACTS | 29 | 25 | 21 | 21 |
FROM THE FIRST PSYCHEDELIC ERA 1965-1968
(Compilation)
1998, Rhino; "Open My Eyes"
■ A "plethora of lost gems" compiled by Patti Smith Group guitarist Lenny Kaye, the "amazing" 1972 original was a "must-have for anyone" of the psychedelic- "rock persuasion"; expanding on the "influential" producer's

concept, Rhino's four-CD reissue is "even better", with the likes of The Sonics and The Kingsmen revealing "where today's garage bands got their ideas"; these acts "may not have been the best musicians around but the feeling and power put this collection over the top."

N.W.A, *Straight Outta Compton*   27 | 25 | 22 | 25
1989, Ruthless; "Straight Outta Compton"

■ This "quintessential gangsta rap album" is a "high-octane" production by a "tremendous lineup" of future stars who "caught the music world in a drive-by"; Ice Cube, Eazy-E, Dr. Dre, MC Ren and DJ Yella give a "brutal slap in the face" with the "dark, revolutionary" title track and *Fuck tha Police,* which speak "strong street" about poverty and racism in the "LA ghettos"; "not since the Sex Pistols' *Never Mind the Bollocks* have so many kids scared their parents with one album."

Laura Nyro,   27 | 28 | 25 | 24
Eli and the Thirteenth Confession
1968, Columbia; "Stoned Soul Picnic"; www.lauranyro.com

■ "Sit up and say 'wow'" to the "late singer-songwriting genius' influential early masterpiece", which, "full of tremendous spirit, both exhausting and exhilarating", just "seems to get better every day"; "it's almost criminal that her songs are better known by other people's" interpretations of them – "go back to the source" of The 5th Dimension's *Stoned Soul Picnic* and Three Dog Night's *Eli's Comin'* and rediscover "the originals" of "a pioneer."

O

Paul Oakenfold, *Tranceport*   25 | 20 | 25 | 26
1997, Kinetic; "Someone"

■ Get "swept off to danceland" when "one of the best DJs of all time" "brings Ibiza to your living room" with a "seamless listening experience" of house remixes; "a good starter" for "glowstick" virgins, this "trippy" "trance intro" "makes everyone a rock star", particularly its creator who "brilliantly made a brand name for himself while not writing one original tune"; a few feel "he has sold out, but this album reminds you of how important he once was."

Oasis,   23 | 22 | 22 | 23
(What's the Story) Morning Glory?
1995, Epic; "Wonderwall"; www.oasisnet.com

■ "Say what you want about" the Gallagher brothers "ripping off The Beatles" (ok, "excellent stealing"), this "powerhouse" sophomore album "rocks", "end of story"; the "songs are flat-out infectious" with "melodies that capture their passion", "sneering arrogance and good chops", showing the Mancunians at "their creative peak"; "bad attitudes, drugs, R&R, Union Jacks and sibling rivalry" – yup, it's "quintessential Britpop."

O Brother, Where Art Thou? ⎹ 26 ⎸ 25 ⎸ 26 ⎸ 25 ⎹
(Soundtrack) **G #1**
2001, Mercury; "Man of Constant Sorrow"
■ "O, brother", "get high on bluegrass" with this "great throwback to pickin', grinnin'", "fiddling" and "knee-slappin'", the "obscenely successful" soundtrack to the Cohen Brothers' down-home *Odyssey*; "bringing a traditional music revival to the big screen and across the land", "catchy" tunes by Dan Tyminski and other artists are so "chock-full of ol'-timey fun" that "even the hardest-core urban listener can find joy in" them.

Phil Ochs, ⎹ 26 ⎸ 27 ⎸ 21 ⎸ 20 ⎹
I Ain't a'Marchin' Anymore
1965, Carthage; "Draft Dodger Rag"
■ A "great American patriot" as well as one of this country's "premier folk artists", "thinking man's liberal" Ochs "captured the spirit of a generation" with this "poetic triumph for peace" that was many peoples' "first intro to the anti-Vietnam war movement"; "tapping into the political fervor of the '60s", he comes off as "more Bob Dylan than Dylan himself" and as a result, "takes protest music to the next level", "touching the heart, soul and mind."

Sinéad O'Connor, ⎹ 23 ⎸ 25 ⎸ 22 ⎸ 22 ⎹
I Do Not Want What I Haven't Got **G**
1990, Ensign; "Nothing Compares 2 U";
www.sinead-oconnor.com
■ "With the voice of an angel and a devil's fury", Sinéad belted out this chart-topper of "emotion and drama without the baggage that has plagued her music since"; it's like "a winter day: cold, stark and beautiful", with "funky music supporting" lyrics to "haunt romantic hearts with tales of ghosts, lovers and loss"; "whatever her head looks like or whatever her politics", her "revolutionary" version of Prince's *Nothing Compares 2 U* is "one of the best examples of a cover improving on the original."

Oklahoma! (Soundtrack) **#1** ⎹ 27 ⎸ 27 ⎸ 27 ⎸ 25 ⎹
1955, Capitol; "Oklahoma!"
■ "Oh, what a beautiful soundtrack" featuring Shirley Jones "showing off her strong soprano" in her screen debut, "terrific" Gordon McCrae and an "unsurpassed" supporting cast in the "cowboy" "daddy of modern musicals"; a "superb" score by Rodgers and Hammerstein, "lush Hollywood orchestrations" and a "rousing" "story of Midwestern romance" make you "ready to homestead" along with those "strong women" on screen, or "at least", "eat corn on the cob" and "sing along."

Olive, *Extra Virgin* ⎹ 24 ⎸ 22 ⎸ 23 ⎸ 25 ⎹
1997, RCA; "You're Not Alone"
■ "While most trip-hop efforts were overrated and underwhelming, Olive delivers on the marriage's promise",

serving up a "lovely album" with "odd, funky beats" and a "sexy vibe" totaling "dance music at it's fiercest"; the "wonderful vocals, production and songwriting" "set the mood" to "motivate" "while sweating on the Stairmaster", the club floor or in the sack.

Oliver! (Soundtrack)   25 | 26 | 24 | 25
1968, RCA; "As Long as He Needs Me"
■ Songs, glorious songs abound in this "gem" of a soundtrack "exploring the adventures of young Oliver"; "no matter how hard you fight it, you will find yourself humming along" to a "witty", "captivating" score bouyed by "masterful arrangements and orchestrations" and "superb" performances by Georgia Brown and Ron Moody; it's "a rare instance where the soundtrack is better than the cast album."

The Orb,   27 | 22 | 25 | 27
Adventures Beyond the Ultraworld
1991, Island; "Little Fluffy Clouds"; www.theorb.com
■ "It's hard to believe this two-hour journey into space was made by human beings", but it was; climb "one of the genre's supporting pillars" and rest upon the *Little Fluffy Clouds* in this "waking dream" of "electronic trance at its best"; melting synths, trippy dialogue and chanting into one "brilliant" puddle, it's an "indispensible" "ambient house classic" of "auditory fugue states" for a "neo-hippie" chill out.

Roy Orbison, *The All-Time Greatest*   27 | 25 | 27 | 24
Hits of Roy Orbison, Volume One
1993, Monument; "Crying"
■ Although "never given the credit due until after his death" in 1988, this "great" "rockabilly star" possessed the "transcendent", "irreplaceable" "voice of an angel" that "spanned the octaves", but he was also a "masterful" songwriter who co-wrote many of his "soaring", "operatic" hits, including *Oh, Pretty Woman* ("only Roy could pull off that growl"), *Crying* and *Blue Bayou*; no wonder "every guy that can sing wishes he could sing like" this "extraordinary talent."

Orchestral Manoeuvers in the Dark,   24 | 22 | 24 | 24
The Best of OMD
1988, A&M; "If You Leave"; www.omd.uk.com
■ By "one of the bands the 1980s would have been very different without", this greatest hits collection is "like a chunk of Gruyère": "it ages well", remaining "curiously appealing" in a "pleasant and cheesy" way; "filled with love ballads" and "upbeat dance tunes" with "enough hooks to be made into two songs" each, the disc gives "listeners a chance to hear the hits and be exposed to those that didn't make it" "onto the *Pretty in Pink* soundtrack."

Orff, *Carmina Burana*   27 │ 26 │ 27 │ 25

1967, Deutsche Grammophon; "O Fortuna";
www.deutsche-oper.berlin.de

■ "Orff's magnum opus" is "bawdy, rousing" and classical
fans say it "beats Led Zeppelin hands down", so no wonder
"everyone who's listened gets hooked" – "who wouldn't
love an album that contains Latin drinking songs?"; "the
art of the profane does not get any better" than Eugen
Jochum's "gold standard", which the composer himself
gave his blessing to; it's "great to have sex to", so go
ahead – "shake the rafters."

Beth Orton, *Central Reservation*   26 │ 25 │ 24 │ 24

1999, Heavenly/Arista; "Central Reservation";
www.bethorton.mu

■ "A cohesive flow of emotion, wit and intellect" runs
through this singer-songwriter's "moody, mysterious"
sophomore release, a "brilliant" "genre-busting fusion of
folk and electronica"; "wispy and sexy", her "unique"
"voice sounds so fresh against the arrangements" as she
sings about "longing and lust"; "you can feel her ache" on
"ethereal" tracks like *Pass in Time,* with legendary "Terry
Callier providing beautiful backing" and the Ben Watt
remix of the title track, a "chill-out" favorite.

Ozzy Osbourne, *Blizzard of Ozz*   25 │ 22 │ 25 │ 22

1980, Jet; "Crazy Train"; www.ozzy.com

■ Long "before the MTV show, the house, the kids and the
drug-induced fog", the former Black Sabbath frontman
made an "amazing comeback" with this "absolutely
essential" "piece of heavy-metal history" packed with
"great arrangements" and "hooks aplenty"; "while Ozzy
writes magic", the "late, great" guitarist Randy Rhodes
"literally blew the doors off", "providing the spark that
made this album" "rule."

Outkast, *Aquemini*   26 │ 26 │ 26 │ 27

1998, LaFace; "Rosa Parks"; www.outkast.com

■ "Projecting the rap style called Dirty South", this Atlanta
duo "sounds nothing like its contemporaries", "redefining"
hip-hop with "socially conscious" lyrics, "earthy melodies
and a down-home, front-porch vibrance" on "zenithal
dance songs and smoke-induced ditties" brimming with
"blues, soul, thoughtfulness and complexity"; the disc is
"simultaneously revolutionary and funky as hell."

Outkast, *Stankonia*   27 │ 26 │ 26 │ 27

2000, LaFace; "B.O.B."; www.outkast.com

■ Appealing "to the vapid radio listener, the most keeping-
it-real thug, a dancer at the club and the harshest music
critic", this "benchmark" incorporates "hardcore rock",
"funk roots" and "extraterrestrial phantasm" into a
"sonically astonishing" production with the "energy to
stop Superman"; from the "pimp" "satire" of *So Fresh, So*

Clean to the "cacophony" of *B.O.B.*, Dre and Big Boi "turned tons of white dorks onto Southern-fried hip-hop" – "damn if they don't make you want to shake your ass!"

P

Charlie Parker, *Jazz at Massey Hall*   28 | 26 | 29 | 19
1953, Debut; "Salt Peanuts";
www.cmgww.com/music/parker
■ "Who said 'blame Canada'", and how could they when it's home to the hall where the "greatest live jazz performance of all time" took place?; "Dizzy Gillespie on trumpet, Parker on alto, Bud Powell on piano, Charles Mingus on bass and Max Roach on drums" – "it doesn't get any better" than this "summit meeting of the titans" playing "off the scale" during their "last hurrah together"; though the original "sound is weak", on remasters, you can clearly hear Bird's "masterful, extended bebop solos."

CHARLIE PARKER, *YARDBIRD SUITE:*   29 | 26 | 29 | 23
THE ULTIMATE COLLECTION
1997, Rhino; "Parker's Mood";
www.cmgww.com/music/parker
■ "If an Airstream trailer, a fedora, a gin martini and a Jackson Pollock could play the alt sax, they'd surely sound" like "classic Bird"; "jazz's greatest soloist" was "good enough to overshadow all who came before and after", "changing the music forever", and Rhino's "brilliant" two-disc compilation of 1945–1952 recordings by "the king of bebop" is "essential" listening; "Mozart would have loved it", so you should too.

Graham Parker,   26 | 27 | 25 | 24
Squeezing Out Sparks
1979, Arista; "Discovering Japan"; www.grahamparker.net
■ One of the "kings of cynicism", this "articulate, rockin'" English singer-songwriter "hit a peak" with his "taut, acerbic, probing" lyrics on perhaps "one of the finest albums of the new wave era"; brimming with "biting sarcasm", "brilliant songwriting" and an "energy only matched at a Springsteen concert", its "awesome" power was heightened by Jack Nitzsche's production and the "superb intensity" of his backup band, the Rumour; "it's mystifying" that he "did not get to be a big star."

Parliament, *Mothership Connection*   26 | 23 | 26 | 23
1976, Casablanca; "Mothership Connection (Star Child)";
www.georgeclinton.com
■ "George Clinton, Bootsy Collins and the cat with the diaper on" "revolutionized" funk, "establishing it as an artistic statement", all the while "creating some of the best party tunes ever written"; the modern musical mothership arrived the day this album landed to deliver the "key to the gates of contemporary pop" and "hip-hop", so earthlings

should "run, don't walk, and buy it" to "shake their asses off" to its historic, "transcendent space-grooves."

Alan Parsons Project, *I Robot* 24 | 23 | 25 | 27 |
1977, Arista; "I Wouldn't Want to Be Like You"
■ "The engineer of *Dark Side of the Moon* did his own thing here" with collaborator Eric Woolfson and "it was indeed a project"; "something original, fusing an orchestra", progressive rock and "pop laced with science-fiction themes", "this work of studio art" was "totally radical for its time", with "cinematic, crisp, clear production" and "slick musicianship" – in sum, "good head music" that was "ponderous man, ponderous."

Gram Parsons, *Grievous Angel* 28 | 29 | 27 | 23 |
1974, Reprise; "Return of the Grievous Angel"
■ "The father of alt-country" conveys a "breathtaking lyricism" with "tales of hard drinking, love gone sour and salvation on the prairie" on this "beautiful" posthumous release; the "visionary pioneer's" "magnificent" duets with Emmylou Harris blazed a "heavenly" trail of "true American music" taken up by Son Volt, "Wilco and Lucinda Williams, his legacies"; "listen to Parsons' haunting voice" on "songs that would make Hank Williams proud" and "weep for his untimely death."

Dolly Parton, *Coat of Many Colors* 26 | 27 | 26 | 23 |
1971, RCA; "Coat of Many Colors"
■ Country music's "queen mother" "takes a trip down memory lane" on this "semi-autobiographical album", "replete with ballads of heartbreak" like the "centerpiece title track", a "triumphant tale sung with subtlety", but she also "punctuates the set with moments of humor and life affirmations"; though "physically one of the most deliciously artificial music stars ever, her writing and singing have a purity" that says "there's way more to Dolly than those wigs and breasts."

Dolly Parton, Linda Ronstadt & 25 | 25 | 27 | 26 |
Emmylou Harris, *Trio* 🄖
1987, Warner Bros.; "Telling Me Lies"
■ Three of country and pop music's "greatest voices" create a "seminal work of refined brilliance" that features "exquisite harmonies" and "a glorious array of songs", from the traditional (*Rosewood Casket*) to the original (*The Pain of Loving You*); "the beautiful ladies" are backed by a "who's who of" "acoustic" "experts" who "further urge direct emotional communication."

Mandy Patinkin, *Mandy Patinkin* 26 | 24 | 28 | 25 |
1989, Columbia; "Rock-A-Bye Your Baby with a Dixie Melody"
■ "Just stop now, open up your body and hand over your soul – you have no choice" because "the man kidnaps you", taking you "to heights unknown" with the "intensity"

and "idiosyncracy" of his "honey-coated voice"; the "glorious" Broadway singer "paired with top-notch tunes" "is unbeatable" on this eponymous disc, so whether you spend Sunday in the park with George or fly over the rainbow, you'll "listen to it over and over" thinking "whoever I marry, it's got to be a tenor."

Pavement,   26 | 25 | 24 | 22
Crooked Rain, Crooked Rain
1994, Matador; "Cut Your Hair";
www.pavementtherockband.com

■ "Holy Malkmus!" – frontman Stephen and company, the "poster band for indie rock", got "slicker" and "more accessible" on this "delightful, escapist" sophomore set that "mines gold sounds", thanks to "better studio production"; while the "greatest" group "nobody knows" offers "more tuneful and structured songs" like the "radio-friendly" *Cut Your Hair,* they still "provide plenty of quirky", "inventive lyrics" that reveal a "way with words."

Pavement, *Slanted and Enchanted*   27 | 27 | 24 | 21
1992, Matador; "Summer Babe (Winter Version)";
www.pavementtherockband.com

■ "You want witty and pithy?" this "classic of Gen-X proportions" that marked the "marriage of pop and low-fi" production weaves a "spell characterized by clever lyrics" and "catchy, off-kilter melodies" – "sketchy songs that fall together in abstract harmonies" offset by a "devil-may-care slacker attitude"; reissued in 2002 with "500% better sound" and a bonus disc, this "indie prerequisite" once "launched a thousand alternative rock ships."

PEARL JAM, *TEN*   27 | 26 | 26 | 25
1991, Epic; "Black"; www.pearljam.com

■ "A landmark that tore through the gloom of Seattle grunge for the coming of a new day in rock", this debut "differentiated the group from like-minded acts through harder riffs and a darker edge tempered with a craftier, more narrative lyrical style"; it's "packed with anthemic tunes and a few ballads" (including "*Jeremy,* the song of a generation") and features the "dual guitar attack of Gossard and McCready" and "Vedder's commanding", "gravelly" "baritone vocals."

Pearl Jam, *Vitalogy* 🔢   23 | 23 | 25 | 24
1994, Epic; "Better Man"; www.pearljam.com

◪ At its "most scorching and scathing", the group's third album, marked by "phenomenal songwriting and powerful execution", is the "sound of a garage band on fire" returning to "their punk roots"; "it opens with three acerbic songs, making up in fury what they lack in melody, but it's not until the haunting ballad *Nothingman,* that a true classic appears"; still, a few feel while "it's worthy of accolades, it's not as gripping as prior releases."

Pearl Jam, *Vs.* 🏆1
1993, Epic; "Rearviewmirror"; www.pearljam.com

25 | 25 | 26 | 24

■ "Featuring a more unpolished but sonically purer production than their debut", this "mind-blowing" follow-up to *Ten* "comes roaring out of the gate" proving "there's still an abundance of rage and angst in PJ's tank", "with the furious duo of *Go* and *Animal,* before the acoustic groove of the hit *Daughter* provides some breathing room"; "raw, loud and angry", it offers some of their "finest stuff, front to back", including "*Leash,* which seems to sum up the band's feelings behind the grunge movement."

A Perfect Circle, *Mer de Noms*
2000, Virgin; "3 Libras"; www.aperfectcircle.com

24 | 24 | 26 | 25

■ "It seems like anything Tool's Maynard James Keenan touches turns to gold", or make that platinum, thanks to this collaborative debut featuring the "all-star lineup" of former Tool guitar tech Billy Howerdel, G n' R session man Josh Freese and Primus drummer Tim 'Herb' Alexander; a "swirling mix of rising and falling melodies", this "deep, complex", "disturbingly beautiful" alt-metal "entices the ears" with "emotional force."

Peter, Paul & Mary, *Peter, Paul & Mary* 🏆1
1962, Warner Bros.; "If I Had a Hammer"; www.peterpaulandmary.com

26 | 26 | 25 | 24

■ "You always feel centered and at home with" these "crossover" "superstars" whose "crystal clear approach" ("their voices blend like magic") "opened up the world of folk music" on this "prime time" 1962 debut; "one of the forces of the era" later on, they only hint at a "deeper social agenda" here with their cover of Pete Seeger's *Where Have all the Flowers Gone?* and *If I Had a Hammer,* "emotionally powerful" tunes that remain summer "camp songs today."

Oscar Peterson, *On the Town*
1958, Verve; "Moonlight in Vermont"; www.oscarpeterson.com

28 | 25 | 29 | 23

■ "Caressing the piano, caressing your ears", this "master" of the many notes is "better with one hand than most with two", and on this late-'50s live date with "exciting" bassist Ray Brown and guitarist Herb Ellis, he "never lets you down"; you can get it remastered and extended today, but also try to catch Peterson's "fine" fingers in person because "the old standby" "continues to be great."

Pet Shop Boys, *Very*
1993, Capitol; "Go West"; www.petshopboys.co.uk

25 | 25 | 24 | 26

■ "To keep you pumping, but suavely", the former "bards of London's jaded club scene" "wrote about love and loss" while "exploring newer and more creative hooks", delivering "ironic lyrics" and "real emotion carried by beautiful melodies"; with "coming-out tales, class commentary and a camp classic redone with a hopeful eye towards an AIDS-free future", all set to a beat you can "dance your ass off to", this "mind-blowing" disc is "always very, well, er . . . very."

Tom Petty and the Heartbreakers, *Damn the Torpedoes*   25 | 26 | 25 | 24

1979, MCA; "Refugee"; www.tompetty.com
■ "Full speed ahead" for "perfect American R&R" – showing "true rock integrity", this "unbeatably" "solid", Jimmy Iovine-produced breakthrough put the guys from Gainesville "over the top"; featuring such "classics" as *Refugee, Here Comes My Girl* and *Don't Do Me Like That*, it's a "damn good record", and a blast "from start to finish."

Tom Petty, *Full Moon Fever*   25 | 25 | 26 | 24

1989, MCA; "Free Fallin'"; www.tompetty.com
■ "One wouldn't think that Jeff Lynne's Beatle-inspired production would meld at all with Petty's down-and-dirty guitar rock, yet this album led to some of the best work either has created"; it includes "terrific contributions from the Heartbreakers and Wilbury pals" George Harrison and Roy Orbison and "a great series of anthems best heard in summer with the windows down": the "raveup *Running Down a Dream*" and the "irresistibly catchy" *Free Falling.*

Tom Petty & the Heartbreakers, *Greatest Hits*   27 | 26 | 26 | 25

1993, MCA; "American Girl"; www.tompetty.com
■ A "gold mine from more than 25 years" of a stellar career, this CD "hits the essence" of this "bona fide all-American R&R star", "satisfying all, from the most hard-core Pettyite to the casual listener"; though "the songs have different moods and tempos", they represent "the best of his roots rock with a glimpse of what he calls psychedelic hillbilly music" to "get you in the mood to go out" and "howl at the moon."

Liz Phair, *Exile in Guyville*   25 | 27 | 21 | 21

1993, Matador; "Fuck and Run"
■ "Everyone's favorite indie 'it' girl proved that real talent is having something to say" in a "blunt way" on her "ambitious" debut, a "bad" babe's "bible" that came off like "a feminist shock to the system"; "basement production", "empowering chick music" and Liz's "life coalesced into a concept album of impeccable brilliance", "capturing the poignancy behind modern promiscuity"; "a song-by-song answer to the Stones' *Exile On Main Street*", it "kicks ass" "with the swagger of Mick Jagger."

THE PHANTOM OF THE OPERA   26 | 25 | 27 | 27

(Original cast recording)
1986, Polydor; "The Music of the Night";
www.thephantomoftheopera.com
☑ The music of a knight – Sir Andrew Lloyd Webber – "is the music of seduction" and "memory"; "draining and

energizing at once", these "stupendous" "songs can be hummed for days", along with "phenomenal" Phantom Michael Crawford and "superb" Sarah Brightman "before she went cuckoo"; "taken to soaring, even schmaltzy, heights", the soundtrack can even "make alpha-males cry", though some would prefer not to "unmask" performances that "grate on their nerves."

Pharcyde,
26 | 25 | 24 | 24

Bizarre Ride II the Pharcyde
1992, Delicious Vinyl; "Passing Me By";
www.thepharcyde.com
■ Take a "psychedelic ride" with this "goofy slice of genius from left field", a "hysterical" but "unpretentious" debut by a crew of "hip West Coast non-gangstas"; "zany and lyrically entertaining" with jazzy beats, it's both "excellent for parties" and for "cruising around town when you have nowhere to go"; the group might have "come from phar, but they reign you in" with their "contagious enthusiasm."

Phish, *A Live One*
24 | 22 | 27 | 23

1995, Elektra; "Bouncing Around the Room"
■ "A great place to start for new phans", this "clearly recorded" "dream set" offers the "ultimate summer jam band experience" "after the Dead" and a "great sampling" of live "musicianship at its phinest"; its phantastic sound, "created through years of touring and dedication", "is perfect for back-porch lounging or driving with the windows down in your beat-up Chevy"; still a phew pheel it "does not do justice", phinding "you can only listen to Phish" in concert.

Edith Piaf, *La Vie En Rose*
28 | 27 | 26 | 23

1974, Columbia; "La Vie En Rose"
■ "France claimed her, but this little Sparrow belongs to the world"; the "vibrating voice in Edith's chest" was like a stick of "dynamite", exploding into "dreamy", "draining" songs that will have you "crying at the anguish and pain she conveys"; a *chanson* "icon" who "immortalized" tunes like the title track, she's "one of the great landmarks of the 20th century", and "anything by her is worth owning."

PINK FLOYD,
29 | 27 | 28 | 29

DARK SIDE OF THE MOON 🔢
1973, Capitol; "Time"; www.pinkfloyd.com
■ "No college experience is complete without" this "watershed" "masterpiece" with the *Wizard of Oz* on mute – it's "what headphones were created for"; "dim the lights and take a trip" "to the other side" for an "auditory story best enjoyed in one sitting", a "wall of complex sound" that reached "sonic perfection", "set the gold standard for prog rock" and remains "astonishing when heard today"; "any album that sustained" 741 weeks on the charts "has to have done something right."

PINK FLOYD, *THE WALL* 🅖 #1 | 27 | 27 | 27 | 28 |
1979, EMI; "Comfortably Numb"; www.pinkfloyd.com
◼ "Rock opera meets seminal songwriting" on this "brilliant but alienating" "magnum opus", a double-album "journey through the tortured mind of a star losing touch with his audience"; a "bold, forceful move forward", this "cathartic crown jewel" earned Pink Floyd their third U.S. No. 1; "such music from the depths of despair" revealed "Roger Waters at his insane best", and it "gave every stoner kid a passport to another reality"; still, a handful of Wall-bangers find it "patchy" and "pretentious."

Pink Floyd, *Wish You Were Here* #1 | 28 | 27 | 28 | 28 |
1975, Columbia; "Wish You Were Here"; www.pinkfloyd.com
◼ "A stirring, eloquent tribute" to former member Syd Barrett, this "cohesive symphony" of "bluesy space-rock" was Floyd's hit follow-up to *Dark Side of the Moon* and perhaps their "most affecting" album; sure, its fabled predecessor "was on the charts for most of the Mesozoic era", but some say this "consummate" "classic" "actually holds together better" by virtue of "nakedly emotional" songwriting and "crystalline" instrumentals that form its "jazzy, trippy moodscapes."

P!nk, *M!ssundaztood* | 22 | 22 | 21 | 24 |
2002, Arista; "Just Like a Pill"; www.pinkspage.com
◼ "The "pretty girl who can kick your a**" "eludes the sophomore slump" on this "gutsy" album of "raw white-chick R&B/rock" pulsing with "over-the-top, catchy" "dance" songs (*Get the Party Started*) and "unconventional ballads" (*Just Like a Pill*); "you go, girl!" gush groupies gaga over her "fierce lyrics", even though "disappointed" discologists dis "marketing ploy" "songs sounding like ninth-grade journal entries" from an "anti-Britney punk rocker."

Pixies, *Surfer Rosa* | 27 | 26 | 25 | 24 |
1988, 4AD/Elektra; "Where Is My Mind?"
◼ With "catchy pop melodies, surf guitar leads" and frontman Black Francis (later known as Frank Black) "shattering glass at the top of his lungs", "Kurt Cobain's favorite band" plotted "the blueprint for the grunge movement", making waves with an "angry, funny, noisy" album of "quirky" tunes "rendered in rocking lo-fi fashion"; though "a favorite for sing-along angst", insiders also call it "a windup to their masterpiece", the "start-to-finish perfect *Doolittle*."

The Pogues, | 26 | 25 | 24 | 22 |
If I Should Fall from Grace with God
1988, Island; "Fairytale of New York"
◼ "When Irish trad and punk rock share a hookup" the "vital" result is "Shane McGowan and company at their best" on a "bracingly intelligent, funny and tragic" album "full of mud and majesty" that "moves from drunken

swagger to aching beauty"; on *Fairytale of New York*, his "bittersweet" duet with the late Kirsty MacColl, the frontman "sets the standard" of alcohol-fueled "delivery counterbalanced by superb musicianship."

The Pointer Sisters, *Break Out*   24 | 22 | 24 | 23
1983, Planet; "Jump (for My Love)";
www.thepointersistersfans.com
■ The trio of gospel-trained siblings from Oakland, CA, "ruled the airwaves" for a short time in the early '80s with "their bubbly hybrid of pop and R&B" displayed on this "kitschy classic" of "irrepressible dance tunes" like *Jump (For My Love)* and *I'm So Excited* that are at once "sexy, fun, romantic and carefree"; it's a back-when "party" platter pulsing with "pure" if "lightweight" "energy."

The Police, *Outlandos d'Amour*   25 | 24 | 25 | 22
1979, A&M; "Roxanne"; www.sting.com
■ "Super songs" and an "enthusiastic" "freshness" are the hallmarks of this "compelling debut" by "the best trio ever", "truly original thinkers and musicians" whose "merger of styles (reggae, punk, rock)" "hints at future greatness" years "before Sting became a New Age guru"; "bursting with energy", songs like *Roxanne* and *Can't Stand Losing You* proved "hugely influential" and can still be "heard in movies, TV and rap samples today."

The Police, *Synchronicity* G #1   26 | 26 | 27 | 26
1983, A&M; "Every Breath You Take"; www.sting.com
■ Featuring the "achingly obsessive" No. 1 hit *Every Breath You Take* and lyrics that are "alternately bizarre and thought-provoking", this "mesmerizing", "complex" disc practically "ranks with *Abbey Road* as one of rock's best finales" – "nothing like leaving at the top"; the band's "charisma was unsurpassed", and this "fitting swan song" cops to "pop near-masterpiece" status, showing their "willingness to experiment" – until "Sting went on to become a successful lounge singer."

Iggy Pop, *Lust for Life*   25 | 23 | 22 | 21
1977, Virgin; "Lust for Life"; www.iggypop.com
■ "The godfather" and ("grandfather) of punk" "hooks up with the Thin White Duke" (aka David Bowie wearing the producer's hat) "with resounding success" on this "ultimate combination"; a few fans frown at the title track – "one of the greatest R&R" anthems – being used in a Carnival Cruises ad, but it made a "great" *Trainspotting* track, and all agree this "manifesto" represents "Iggy at his apogee" singing with "reckless abandon, flying without a net."

Portishead, *Dummy*   27 | 26 | 26 | 28
1994, Go!; "Glory Box"; www.portishead.co.uk
■ "Succumb" to the "sinister, doomed romanticism" of a "spooky spy soundtrack to a film that never was" with this

"noir" "blueprint for breakups", "rainy days" and other "angsty moods"; "as beautiful and dirty as your first stripper", the "dark" debut "threw down the gauntlet for atmospheric trip-hop"; Beth Gibbons' "haunting vocals" in "an exacting chemistry" with Geoff Barrow's "seductive" grooves plus "background tracks" "crackling on vinyl" make for a "homey feel" – if "you suffer from depression."

Elvis Presley, *Elvis' Golden Records* | 27 | 25 | 26 | 25 |
1958, RCA Victor; "Jailhouse Rock"; www.elvis.com

■ "When anyone anywhere talks about popular music the conversation begins and ends with Presley" laud loyalists who wonder "how can you not have the King in your collection?", especially this set that "sums up his great" "early gold records"; representing the "birth of rock & roll", "the definitive Elvis on RCA" is "better than sliced bread."

ELVIS PRESLEY, *ELVIS (TV SPECIAL)* | 28 | 25 | 26 | 25 |
1968, RCA Victor; "If I Can Dream"; www.elvis.com

■ "After years of cheesy movies, the King returned to the stage" with this "brilliant performance that includes a stripped-down jam session" "in the round" "with old pals Scotty Moore and DJ Fontana", and ends with "*If I Can Dream,* almost frightening in its intensity"; "funny and exciting", "he reigns" throughout "a mélange of rock, gospel, country, blues and out-and-out corn" that's almost "an aural metaphor for the man himself" – "the '50s rebel, the '60s crooner, the '70s Vegas icon, they're all here."

Elvis Presley, *From Elvis in Memphis* | 26 | 25 | 27 | 26 |
1969, RCA Victor; "In the Ghetto"; www.elvis.com

■ "A bunch of covers never sounded so good" and Elvis' "mature" "voice never sounded grittier" than on this "thoughtful selection" of "Southern soul", showing that "he could still make powerful and meaningful music after nearly a decade of largely insipid soundtracks"; his "most passionate performances" mark a "link between his early skinny years and later fat ones."

The Pretenders, *Learning to Crawl* | 24 | 24 | 24 | 22 |
1984, Sire; "Back on the Chain Gang"; www.pretendersband.com

■ "Following the death of two original members [bassist Pete Farndon and guitarist James Honeyman-Scott] came this album about pain, aging and survival – these themes make for the best art, and this work stands up because of it"; the "original badass rocker", "Chrissie Hynde is sexy, cool and seductive", and this "brilliant work", full of "enduring songs" like *Back on the Chain Gang* and *Middle of the Road*, "bristles with primo energy."

The Pretenders, *The Pretenders* | 27 | 26 | 25 | 24 |
1980, Sire; "Brass in Pocket"; www.pretendersband.com

■ On "one of the greatest debuts" and "edgiest postpunk pop albums" "of all time", "tough-but-vulnerable" "Chrissie

Hynde breaks new ground", "taking no prisoners with her biting, hard-edged", "no-nonsense rawk"; featuring "the band's best lineup" (including "James Honeyman-Scott's wonderful guitar style") and her "inspired" vocals, "swagger" and "snarlin' f—you attitude", the "true original" still "sounds sassy" 'n' brassy.

Pretty in Pink (Soundtrack)   24 | 23 | 23 | 23
1986, A&M; "Pretty in Pink"
■ The soundtrack that "makes you want to put on a skinny tie and Members Only jacket" and ask a "big-haired" "girl dressed like Molly Ringwald" to the "high school prom" is "excellent for remembering the '80s"; this "brat pack" nostalgiafest offers a "quintessential distillation of teenage angst, filtered through the synth/new wave/pop" of "the John Hughes generation": The Smiths, OMD, Suzanne Vega and the Psychedelic Furs keep you "hopping and bopping" like Duckie.

Pretty Woman (Soundtrack)   22 | 21 | 22 | 22
1990, EMI; "Oh, Pretty Woman"
◪ "Wanna be a hooker, work it, own it?" – then get a load of this "fun romp of a soundtrack" "for that extra boost of energy during your day" hustling the streets of Beverly Hills; as "delightful" as "all of Julia Roberts' adventures in the movie", the "very '80s/early '90s" compilation scored "several big hits": "romantics" "fell in love with Lauren Wood's *Fallen*", and "Roy [Orbison] hit it on the head with his classic" title track; it's "great" to "exercise to", whether you're getting paid for it or not.

Louis Prima, *Zooma Zooma:*   25 | 22 | 25 | 23
The Best Of Louis Prima
1990, Rhino; "Just a Gigolo/I Ain't Got Nobody";
www.louisprima.com
■ "You must be dead if this album doesn't get you dancing around your living room", but watch out for spillage because "you need a cocktail every time"; as toe-tappin' old-timers testify, "modern acts can't put a patch on" this "great blend" of "feel-good" '50s "party" "pop with a lot of comedy" from the "entertaining" trumpeter/singer's Capitol years; with "outstanding vocalist" Keely Smith "cooking" on the medleys, "boy, is it good on a rainy day."

Prince, *1999*   27 | 27 | 27 | 27
1982, Warner Bros.; "Little Red Corvette";
www.npgmc.com
■ "The torch was passed from James Brown, Sly Stone and George Clinton" to this "freaky", "multitalented musican" for "a nonstop party" that "changed the face of pop music in the '80s"; the double "tour de force" is "crammed" with "sex appeal", "danceable" "hooks", wicked "guitar licks", splashes of "rock, soul" and "Minneapolis funk", "innovative" but tight production and a "Y2K" anthem of a

title track; "who can resist a short little girlie-man in high-heeled boots" that can "write his ass off"?

Prince, *Purple Rain* Ⓖ #1   27 | 27 | 28 | 26
1984, Warner Bros.; "When Doves Cry"; www.npgmc.com
■ Forget the "lousy" movie – "His Purple Majesty" was in "top form" on this "snapshot" of the era of "neon socks and rubber bracelets"; it's "not your father's R&R" as the "master musician" takes listeners on a "sublime" "sex" romp featuring "nasty" lyrics and "incredible guitar" "delivered with ecstatic frenzy" over "raunchy" R&B and funk; how can "any '80s child deny" that they still "ooze [with] excitement" when they hear the "stone-cold classic"?

Prince, *Sign 'O' the Times*   27 | 28 | 28 | 27
1987, Paisley Park; "Adore"; www.npgmc.com
■ "Every song is sonically" "a world in itself" on a "glorious double album" that some consider Prince "at his creative peak", blending "funky-ass" riffs, "straight-ahead rock", "swinging pop" and "sweet", passionate" R&B; whether he's making "social commentary", "channeling God" or waxing his "weird sense of humor", this "deceptively simple" "embarrassment of riches" "takes you to the highest heights, lowest lows and everywhere in between."

JOHN PRINE, *JOHN PRINE*   28 | 29 | 24 | 24
1971, Atlantic; "Hello in There"
■ "Witty and wise", this "American original" is at "his most raw and genuine" on this "stellar debut" rated this *Survey*'s Top Folk album; he "reviews the human condition in every state, from ecstasy to despair" and in the process devises "a new kind of working-class folk-pop"; "songs like *Sam Stone* will seem fresh in 100 years" – hell, "even his cheesiest tongue-in-cheek tunes tell us more about life than volumes of prose" – little wonder this "master of the storytelling leaves you wanting more."

Procol Harum, *Procol Harum*   24 | 24 | 26 | 22
1967, Deram; "Whiter Shade of Pale"
■ "One of the best British rock bands of the '60s", this Robin Trower–led quintet served up a "sleeper debut" featuring "the first melding of rock and classical"; backed by "solid musicianship", their "big orchestral sound" combines "Bach's melodies" and the "superb imagery" of "Keith Reid's poetry", and while there's "not a bad note", for most of their harem "it's all about" that "one major-league hit *Whiter Shade of Pale*."

The Prodigy, *Music for the Jilted Generation*   25 | 22 | 24 | 25
1995, Mute; "No Good (Start the Dance)"; www.theprodigy.org
■ "The Prodigy get their revenge on short-sighted critics who wrote them off as a novelty act", as well as on anti-dance lawmakers on this "raw" "groundbreaker"; "testing

the boundaries for sound and style", the group demolishes "the electronica and punk barriers", "remaining true to their rave roots and yet hinting at the big-beat excitement to come" on a disc of "progressive craftsmanship."

Public Enemy, *Fear of a Black Planet* 27 | 27 | 24 | 26

1990, Def Jam; "Fight the Power"; www.publicenemy.com
■ The "take-no-prisoners", "make-no-apologies" attitude of one of hip-hop's most "incendiary" and "important albums of the 1990s" "stirred the waters of American culture"; mixing "heavy", "dynamic" beats by the Bomb Squad, Chuck D's "breathless", "political" raps and Flavor Flav's "antics", its "hard, funky, unforgettable" joints "could bring the black militant out in David Duke"; "*Fight the Power,* indeed."

PUBLIC ENEMY, *IT TAKES A NATION* 29 | 29 | 26 | 27
OF MILLIONS TO HOLD US BACK

1988, Def Jam; "Bring the Noise"; www.publicenemy.com
■ "A call to arms", the *Survey*'s No. 1 Hip-Hop disc was "light years ahead" of its time, "having as much influence on rock" as on rap; DJ Terminator X and a "chaotic production" stir up "funky", "hard-core beats" for "Chuck D's fiery rants and Flavor Flav's lighthearted asides" on "electrifying songs" like *Bring the Noise*; "more dense than a bundt cake, but with a bitter icing", the "militant" "noisefest" "will make you want to stand up and party for your right to fight."

Puccini, *La Bohème* Ⓖ 28 | 28 | 28 | 28

1987, London; "Che Gelida Manina";
www.berliner-philharmoniker.de
■ No, Puccini did not "steal the story from *Rent*" – it's vice versa, and there's "not an extraneous note" to muddle the "sexy", "wonderfully tragic" "goings-on"; for "intelligence and delicacy", "soap opera" buffs "can't forget" when tenor Luciani Pavarotti and soprano Mirella Freni "were young, beautiful and in perfect voice", and conductor Herbert von Karajan was at his "finest hour"; "this recording can bring even the most hard-boiled cynic to tears."

Puccini, *Tosca* 27 | 26 | 28 | 25

1953, EMI; "Vissi D'arte"
■ "La Callas lives for art and love", baritone Tito "Gobbi ranks as the best of all Scarpias" and tenor Giuseppe di Stefano is "in really good voice" in "one of the greatest casts ever assembled for one of the war horses of opera", "transformed" by conductor Victor de Sabata's "genius"; the only thing left to say about the "supreme example" of the "splendid, emotionally exasperating" "classic" is "what, you don't have this one?"

Pulp Fiction (Soundtrack) 25 | 22 | 23 | 25

1994, MCA; "Girl, You'll Be a Woman Soon"
■ "Quentin Tarantino knows how to assemble" songs for a "fantastic flick", "using music to heighten mood"; "moving

from groovy dance tunes and funk to soft, lacy ballads" and "camp surfer songs" "interspersed with entertaining dialogue", the disc "can make the movie replay so perfectly, it's frightening", or as fanatics riff, "I love this album, pumpkin . . . I love this album too, honey bunny . . . everybody be cool, this is a soundtrack!"

Q

Queen, *Classic Queen*
27 | 26 | 27 | 26

1992, Hollywood; "Bohemian Rhapsody";
www.queenonline.com
■ "As per the title: classic" – this "great collection" "scratches the surface of the group's artistry" featuring "later material with key" early "anthems" like *Bohemian Rhapsody* , plus the Bowie collaboration *Under Pressure* "tossed in"; "Freddie Mercury had one of the most distinctive, outstanding voices ever", yet the "operatic rock" "band was not appreciated until after his death"; "they had unbelievable range", and guitarist Brian May "makes playing seem so effortless", "it gives you chills."

Queen, *News of the World*
25 | 25 | 27 | 25

1977, Elektra; "We Are the Champions"; www.queenonline.com
■ "From the classic stadium chant *We Will Rock You*" and the "famous *We Are the Champions*" to the "punk smackdown of *Sheer Heart Attack*", this is an "awesome" "album that any collection of great '70s R&R cannot be without"; "it's cohesive but covers an eclectic range of styles" and stands as perhaps the "powerhouse group's" "most introspective and emotional work, made all the better by Freddie's" "phenomenally" "strong vocals."

Queens of the Stone Age, *Songs for the Deaf*
24 | 23 | 27 | 26

2002, Interscope; "No One Knows"; www.qotsa.com
■ The Queens' loyalists crown this "awesome album" "the most precise, imaginative metal of the 21st century": "a perfect mix of raunchy guitar riffage and brilliant musicianship" from an "immensely talented" lineup featuring Foo Fighter frontman Dave Grohl, "currently the best drummer" in the genre, and ex–Screaming Trees vocalist Mark Lanegan; "they're fun and they know how to rock out" with "a creative sound" – a band with "a brain broke into the mix" – what a "gift from heaven."

Queensryche, *Empire*
24 | 25 | 26 | 25

1990, EMI; "Silent Lucidity"; www.queensryche.com
◩ "The thinking metal band's commercial peak" may have been "the best concept album of the 1990s", a "polished" release that conveys the Seattle group's "uncanny ability to tell a story in each song" through "excellent guitar work" and singer Geoff Tate's "stellar vocals"; nevertheless, longtime loyalists label it an "interesting interlude between

their two best works", decreeing its predecessor, *Operation Mindcrime* their "definitive album."

R

Rachmaninoff, *Concerto No. 2: Rhapsody on a Theme of Paganini* | 28 | 28 | 27 | 25 |
1951, RCA

■ "An emotional force wrapping centuries of history into one piece", Rachmaninoff's concerto "takes you away from everyday existence to another plane", and "all one can say" about pianist William Kappel's "virtuosic" performance of it is "wow"; "technically dazzling" "but not overly flamboyant", his playing is an "inspiration", and "engineers have done a good job remastering this recording" from vinyl's "golden age."

Radiohead, *The Bends* | 28 | 27 | 28 | 27 |
1995, Capitol; "Fake Plastic Trees"; www.radiohead.com

■ "*OK Computer* was the critics' darling", but this "radio-friendly Radiohead" album is "equally gripping" reveal revelers, quipping "this was when we learned they weren't a bunch of *Creep*s"; tying together "dark electro-folk-rock" and "Yorke's heartbreaking vocals", it offered "enough to keep us future forward thinkers satisfied and enough guitar chunkiness to convert the masses" – a heady blend of "gorgeously depressing" "candy for intelligent ears."

RADIOHEAD, *OK COMPUTER* G | 28 | 27 | 28 | 28 |
1997, Capitol; "Paranoid Android"; www.radiohead.com

■ A revolutionary "political" concept disc with "atmosphere by the bucketload" this "utter masterpiece" "screams of modern alienation" with "profound landscapes of sound and surprising twists"; "every song is given enigmatic characteristics, with Thom Yorke's haunting melodies" and "piercing wail" "inducing you into a sonic dream from which you never want to wake up" – "think prog-rock for a new millennium – this is not your father's Yes album."

Raffi, *Baby Beluga* | 23 | 23 | 21 | 23 |
1980, Rounder; "Baby Beluga"; www.raffinews.com

■ "Who doesn't like whales in the deep blue sea?" – parents had better because kids will "sing *Baby Beluga* more times than the ABC song"; full of "catchy tunes with a message", this "solid" album opens with the marine mammals' squeaks and features songs about them and other animals; even today, "you can't escape the power" of "the Pied Piper" – "as a two-year-old would say, 'more please!'"

Rage Against the Machine, *Rage Against the Machine* #1 | 25 | 25 | 26 | 23 |
1993, Epic; "Killing in the Name"; www.ratm.com

■ "The zeitgeist of post-riot LA" was "perfectly captured" in all its "seething aggression" on this "blisteringly angry" and "politically dead-on" debut that "paved the way for rap-rock bands of today", even if "they cannot come close to what Rage did"; "if teen angst could grow up" it would aspire to this "agitprop pop" "that screams revolution."

Bonnie Raitt, *Luck of the Draw*   26 | 26 | 27 | 26
1991, Capitol; "I Can't Make You Love Me"; www.bonnieraitt.com

■ This "good ol' gal" proves "she's got the pipes and the soul" to "wail and rock and cry" "soul-tugging ballads" of "heartache", "and she ain't half bad on the guitar either", on her follow-up to *Nick of Time*, "a journey through the spectrum of human emotions" that "gives you strength when you feel alone"; "she's been around the block, you can hear it in her voice" – it's an "intoxicating sound" that "makes the blues not such a bad place to be."

Bonnie Raitt, *Nick of Time* G #1   27 | 26 | 27 | 26
1989, Capitol; "Nick of Time"; www.bonnieraitt.com

■ "Overlooked for far too long", "smoky-voiced Raitt" returns from the brink of obscurity with this "great Don Was–produced comeback" that proved to be her smash "breakthrough"; one of the "best slide guitarists in the business", she's also a "classy lady with a classic voice" who belts out "tunes guys only wish they could do so well"; offering a "little bit of country" plus "blues and sex in a one-stop package", it's an "accessible" "rock album for grown-ups" that proves artists "improve with age."

The Ramones, *Ramones*   28 | 23 | 20 | 21
1976, Sire; "Blitzkrieg Bop"; www.ramones.com

■ "The standard-bearers for punk", the "unassuming mop-haired guys" from Forest Hills "brought pop sensibilities to their hard-nosed street attitude" and, with "buzzsaw guitars", produced "perfect three-chord, two-and-a-half minute blitzes" that were "stupid, simplistic, inspired!"; "you can almost smell the Bowery" as they whip through "30 minutes or so" of "unrelenting, humorous and catchy" tunes about "the Ice Capades, shock troopers, chainsaw massacres and more."

The Ramones, *Ramones Mania*   28 | 24 | 22 | 22
1988, Sire; "I Wanna Be Sedated"; www.ramones.com

■ "The beauty of this release is that it holds the high points of the band's 20-plus-year history on a single disc, thanks to the brevity of the songs": "70 minutes played so fast you can listen to it in half an hour, the seminal DIY ethos of punk is here"; oh yeah, "they started it all and blew prog-rock out of the water."

Rancid, *And Out Come the Wolves*   24 | 22 | 24 | 23
1995, Epitaph; "Ruby Soho"; www.rancidrancid.com

■ Latter-day punk protagonists declare that "Rancid's finest statement" is "as close to the Clash as you can get", with Tim Armstrong's "grunty, snarling voice delivering lyrics over" "savage guitar riffs", "reggae beats and nihilism", creating a "distinct sound"; the band's career brush with record company big guns "fuels the subject matter" – once "Green Day and the Offspring became hot commodities, the wolves, i.e. the major labels, nearly had them", but "they stayed with indie Epitaph."

Ravel, *Boléro*

26 | 26 | 27 | 26

1980, Decca; "Bolero"; www.osm.ca

■ "Who can forget Bo Derek walking down the beach" to this "atmospheric and heavenly" classical music?; but "the movie, *10*", is not the only reason the piece "just stays with you forever and ever" – listening to it "transports you to another place, like ancient Egypt" or wherever you consider to be "sexy as hell"; on this two-disc set, it's paired with other Ravel "classics", including the "charming" *La Valse,* a tribute to the composer's own dying era.

Reality Bites (Soundtrack)

22 | 20 | 21 | 21

1994, RCA; "Stay"

■ "Life in your twenties is crazy, and love sucks", but this "Gen-Xer must-have" "sure doesn't bite"; "what *Pretty in Pink* did for the '80s, this did for the '90s": the "amazing" "mix of artists" "defines a generation", "bringing back memories" of "the horrible grunge look" with "Lisa Loeb's breakout hit" *Stay,* Crowded House, mid-career U2 and Lenny Kravitz at his height; it's "great cruising-with-the-top-down material."

Otis Redding, The Otis Redding Story

28 | 26 | 28 | 24

1987, Atlantic; "Dock of the Bay"; www.otisredding.com

■ "What woman wouldn't find herself doing a slow hip groove" as "sweet Otis transports her to another soulful place in time"?; this "classic" compilation "shows the depth" of "one of the sexiest men alive" on rockin' hits like *Hard to Handle* and sweet ballads like *I've Been Loving You Too Long*; you "can sit on the dock all day and listen" to "the pain" in the voice of a "huge talent" who "died too young."

Red Hot Chili Peppers, Blood Sugar Sex Magik

26 | 24 | 26 | 26

1991, Warner Bros.; "Under The Bridge"; www.redhotchilipeppers.com

■ "The epitome of funk-rock" and perhaps "their most soulful, organic, coherent album" yet, this "breakout" CD became the Peppers' first top-ten entry, certifying their "maturation into a very diverse, talented unit"; it's "beautifully layered" with "great production values", courtesy of Rick Rubin, on a "gaggle of good songs", ranging from the "heartfelt" *Under the Bridge,* a recount of frontman Anthony Kiedis' drug addiction, to *Give It Away*, which "no party is complete without."

Red Hot Chili Peppers, *By the Way*   23 | 23 | 25 | 25

2002, WEA; "By The Way"; www.redhotchilipeppers.com

◪ "Just when you thought they couldn't get any better", "their most melodic", "accessible" "set to date" appeared and "elevated RHCP's standards"; the "mellowed" band leaves the "funky spice" behind for "more introspective" lyrics, "stellar guitar work" and a "less aggressive" sound, making a "great jump into more listener-friendly territory"; still, a few fans aren't as hot on it, lamenting that it sounds like "echoes rather than cutting-edge new music."

Red Hot Chili Peppers, *Californication*   24 | 23 | 25 | 24

1999, Warner Bros.; "Californication"; www.redhotchilipeppers.com

■ "The Chilis come back in a big way with a record" that reveals a "palpable, laid-back California feel", a "departure enough to update their sound", but still stay "true" to their "hip, funky rhythm" roots, courtesy of the returning original guitarist John Frusciante; "something happened here: it's less raw, but more amazing", with "familiar rollicking funk and punk songs going back-to-back with reflective ballads and gripping rockers" – yeah, the "revived Peppers show why they kick ass."

Lou Reed, *Transformer*   26 | 27 | 24 | 23

1972, RCA; "Walk on the Wild Side"; www.loureed.com

■ An "amazing transition from the Velvet Underground", this "defining moment in glam rock" jammed with "great melodies" is "funny, wasted, brilliant" and "far ahead of its time"; David Bowie's "glossy, detailed production" – best heard on a 2002 reissue – "added charm" to Reed's songs administering "electroshock therapy for the masses" with the "poetically beautiful" *Walk on the Wild Side* – ya "can't help but hum 'doot, da doot, da doot.'"

R.E.M., *AUTOMATIC FOR THE PEOPLE*   26 | 27 | 26 | 26

1992, Warner Bros.; "Nightswimming"; www.remhq.com

■ "There is not a weak track on this humdinger", "a lush, gorgeous album that defies genre and comparison"; "full of beautiful elegies, sweet sentiments and even some political venom", it's "an artfully arranged masterpiece of loneliness, rage and guarded optimism, on which Michael Stipe offers his shoulder for millions to cry on"; just as "captivating": "inspired string arrangements by John Paul Jones" and "Peter Buck's quest to record every guitar sound possible."

R.E.M., *Murmur*   28 | 26 | 25 | 23

1983, I.R.S.; "Radio Free Europe"; www.remhq.com

■ This "brilliant" full-length debut introduced the "young, uninhibited" Athens, Georgia, band's "spooky, enigmatic yet catchy" "Southern, gothic-inspired jangle pop, which practically spawned the term 'college rock'" and still "casts an enchanting spell" with its "depth, grit, insight and melodic comfort"; "smothered, cryptic lyrics" and "indecipherable" vocals (what an "appropriately named album") from Michael Stipe added to the band's mystique: "a perfect combo of kudzu and Rickenbacker!"

RENT (Original cast recording)   25 | 24 | 24 | 25
1996, Dreamworks; "Seasons of Love"

◪ "Ten-thousand kisses for the late Jonathan Larson" for taking "a step forward" with his "hip", "high-energy" "Gen-X musical", which "deals with real issues" like AIDS and "captures the essence of East Village bohemian life"; the recording of the "raw", "raucous", "refreshingly different" reimagining of *La Bohème* "reaches to the bone" so "teenagers everywhere" "cry as well as sing along", even if oldsters say the "bunch of drug addicts" making "a bunch of noise" "should have been evicted."

THE REPLACEMENTS, *LET IT BE* 28 | 28 | 22 | 21
1984, Twin/Tone; "Unsatisfied"

■ "The coming-out party for Minneapolis' best rock band (and there have been many)", this "superlative combo of heart and snarl" shows "Paul Westerberg starting to shine as an incredible songwriter – the "sharp lyrics and stick-in-your-brain tunes" are "funny, angry, desperate, raucous and smart all at the same time"; from "the biting angst of *Sixteen Blue* and *Answering Machine* to *Unsatisfied,* one of the greatest" ballads, "he sang them with DIY intensity."

The Replacements, *Tim* 28 | 28 | 24 | 21
1985, Sire; "Here Comes a Regular"

■ "Introspective power thrash and catchy pop tunes collide beautifully on this major-label breakthrough produced by former Ramones drummer Tommy Erdelyi"; finding frontman "Westerberg at his frustrated best", this "seminal album" is "wild and fun but a bit sad" – *Here Comes a Regular* perfectly captures "boozy" Minneapolis, "then the center of alternative music"; "too lazy to be punks, too loud to be singer-songwriters", the 'Mats taught "Nirvana and Pearl Jam everything" they knew.

Reservoir Dogs (Soundtrack) 24 | 22 | 24 | 24
1995, MCA; "Stuck in the Middle With You"

■ The "super sounds of the '70s keep on truckin'" with this "guys'-late-night-out"-at-the-"bar" disc, a soundtrack "just as rough and mesmerizing" as its "gritty" film, which may have kept these songs from "otherwise fading from the social consciousness"; "blast it on a road trip" and "enjoy" even "Steven Wright's annoying narration" – "just don't cut off someone's ear during *Stuck in the Middle with You.*"

Lionel Richie, *Can't Slow Down* 🅖 🏵 24 | 24 | 24 | 24
1983, Motown; "Hello"

■ "Lionel had a way with catch phrases and hooks", and "there's no denying that he wrote some incredible songs", mostly those "you want to hear when you are with the one you love"; he was in his "prime" on his second post-Commodores pop/R&B effort, topping the charts and acing the Grammys with a "great Motown voice" on "high-scoring ballads" like *Hello,* plus "good dancing music" to make you fiesta "all night long."

The Righteous Brothers, *Anthology 1962-1974*   26 | 25 | 25 | 24
1989, Rhino; "You've Lost That Lovin' Feeling"
■ "Blue-eyed soul", "white soul" ... "forget the labels" – "this is just plain old great singing" from the Caucasian doo-wop duo; men who "grew up in the '60s slow-danced with their favorite girl" to the "perfect [Phil] Spector–produced track", *You've Lost That Loving Feeling,* "wanting to croon like one of these guys"; "isn't *Unchained Melody* due for another rebirth?" – "there's a *Ghost* of a chance it could chart yet again" as it still "makes people cry."

LeAnn Rimes, *Blue*   22 | 21 | 23 | 22
1996, Curb; "Blue"; www.rimestimes.com
☑ "What a spectacular voice from this young girl", gush fans of the "thrilling" singer's "freshman album" – she sounds "eerily like" a "reincarnation of Patsy Cline" on the Grammy-winning title track written decades ago with the late, legendary crooner in mind; while a few feel she "sometimes picks the wrong songs", they're still true blue because she's "not like any 13-year-old you've ever heard."

Rimsky-Korsakov, *Scheherazade*   28 | 27 | 29 | 25
1960, RCA; "Scheherazade's Theme"
■ "Scheharazade swings!" – this Russian "masterpiece" based on "tales from the gypsy" is "brilliantly interpreted" by "fabulous Fritz" Reiner and the Chicago Symphony Orchestra "at their peak"; "so rich, so beautiful", "so very romantic", it's "another audiophile favorite", in part because "it's the best-engineered of the conductor's great series for RCA", and "the Stravinsky coupling", *Song of the Nightingale,* is itself a "real treat."

Smokey Robinson, *Anthology*   27 | 26 | 27 | 25
1986, Motown; "Tears of a Clown"; www.smokeyrobinson.net
■ "Silken soul at its best", "this compilation is packed with beautifully written", passionately sung, "outstandingly produced" harmonies "that will take you back to days gone by"; in a high-pitched, "smokin'" voice as "unique as the songs he wrote", the Miracles' "brilliant" leader delivers classic love tunes like *Tears of a Clown,* which "practically define a generation of pop music."

The Roches, *The Roches*   26 | 25 | 26 | 24
1979, Warner Bros.; "Hammond Song"
■ The "incredible talents of Maggie, Terre and Suzzy" Roche "shine on this" Robert Fripp–produced "delightful

introduction" to "a cappella girl group nonpareil"; "the songs sparkle with wit and heartbreak all at once" ("these sisters must have quirkiness as a family trait") and "oh those harmonies!" – so "perfect" they "could make an angel chorus hang up their music books."

Rocky (Soundtrack)
25 | 22 | 25 | 24

1977, United Artists; "Gonna Fly Now"

■ "Yo, Adrian, ain't nobody gonna sit still when this comes on", but they might hit the mat 'cause "Bill Conti's score is so uplifting and emotional, it packs a punch"; the "knockout" theme song to Sylvester Stallone's "golden" gloved boxing blockbuster "still symbolizes victory over all odds", helping to "make *Rocky* a champ in cinemas around the world"; "if this doesn't inspire you" to go "work out", "you don't have a pulse."

Rocky Horror Picture Show (Soundtrack)
24 | 24 | 21 | 23

1978, Ode; "Time Warp"; www.rockyhorror.com

■ "Damnit, Janet, this is one fine soundtrack" – "it's rock, it's kitsch, it's Tim Curry" at his "finest moment" as the sweet transvestite from Transylvania on the disc for this "threw-toast"-at-the-screen-"who-knows-how-many-times-at-midnight", "camp-gone-wild" "coming-of-age milestone"; "offbeat is putting it mildly, but it works", so "get in costume, crank up the music", "put those hands on your hips" and "it's just a jump to the left and a step to the right. "

Kenny Rogers, *The Gambler*
25 | 26 | 24 | 24

1978, United Artists; "The Gambler";
www.kennyrogers.net

■ "Master of the story song", this "crossover country singer" "brought a new pop-oriented audience" to the genre, thanks in good part to this collection's title track, "one of the most classic and well-known songs" of its time; "if occasionally too corny", he still "brings tears to your eyes" and proves himself a "remarkable" raconteur – few wind up folding, in fact, as "everyone knows this album is one to hold."

The Rolling Stones, *Beggar's Banquet*
28 | 27 | 28 | 27

1968, London/Abkco; "Sympathy for the Devil";
www.rollingstones.com

■ "The perfect blend of depravity, blues", "full-tilt R&R" and country, this "masterpiece" marked "the end of the Brian Jones era" and the beginning "of a string of great releases that document the glimmer twins [Jagger and Richards] in their prime"; *Sympathy for the Devil, Salt of the Earth* and *Prodigal Son* "defined a specific point in time", but it "wasn't always a happy party" as this "disillusioned soundtrack for a society coming apart" illustrates.

THE ROLLING STONES,   28 | 28 | 28 | 26
EXILE ON MAIN STREET #1
1972, Rolling Stones/Atlantic; "Tumbling Dice";
www.rollingstones.com
■ "Gritty, grimy, glorious" – "it doesn't get any Stonesier"
than this "sprawling" "killer" "recorded during Keith's heroin
days in a castle in the South of France"; the "perfect soup"
captures them at their "most elegantly wasted, translating
their sex-and-drugs lifestyle into some of the raunchiest
R&R" offset by "horns aplenty" and pal "Gram Parsons,
who strongly influenced their flirtations with C&W" (*Sweet
Virginia, Torn and Frayed*) – "you can almost smell the Jack
Daniels coming through."

The Rolling Stones, ***Some Girls*** #1   26 | 26 | 27 | 26
1978, Rolling Stones/Atlantic; "Miss You";
www.rollingstones.com
■ "The Stones deflect punk's attack" and "show off their
muscles in the middle of" the Studio 54 era with this
"naughty rock" "comeback featuring Ron Wood on guitar";
"if the down and dirty lyrics" of this "homage to NYC"
"don't detract from your listening pleasure, then you're in
for a good time" with such "sly, slinky songs" as the title
track, "*Miss You* (a "disco-y" attempt), "*When the Whip
Comes Down* (pure energy)", "*Far Away Eyes* (a larf")" and
"*Shattered* ("the best ever written about Manhattan").

The Rolling Stones, ***Sticky Fingers*** #1   28 | 27 | 28 | 26
1971, Rolling Stones/Atlantic; "Brown Sugar";
www.rollingstones.com
■ A "celebration of unabashed hedonism as the band soars
on the fiery lead guitar work of Mick Taylor", this "Anglo-
blooze with a sexual swagger" features "nasty classics
Brown Sugar and *Bitch,* the non-saccharine sweetness of
Wild Horses", "the droll, country silliness of *Dead Flowers*",
"the Santana-ish raveup of *Can't You Hear Me Knockin'* "
and "*Sister Morphine,* an almost tactile experience of a
drug overdose"; it's like "you've been to the wildest party
of all time and lived to tell the tale."

Sonny Rollins, ***Saxophone Colossus***   28 | 26 | 29 | 25
1956, Prestige; "St. Thomas"
■ "Colossus is an apt title" for this "masterpiece" by a
"legendary" "monster of the instrument"; including Rollins'
popular, "beautifully melodic calypso riff", *St. Thomas,* and
a "swinging rendition of *Moritat*" (better known as *Mack
the Knife*), with "some monumental improvisations" and a
"mature, smooth sound" throughout, the disc is "so emotive
and vibrant", it might just "spoil you for other saxophonists."

Romeo + Juliet (Soundtrack)   24 | 23 | 23 | 26
1996, Capitol; "Kissing You"
■ "Before there was *Moulin Rouge,* there was this" "other
great Baz Luhrmann soundtrack", "a spectacular mix" of

"piano and pop", electronica and alt-rock "perfectly suited to" a "modern-day version" of the Bard's tragic love story; *#1 Crush* "by Garbage is the most haunting of all songs", Cassandra Wilson's *Kissing You* is "really moving" and cuts by Radiohead, Everclear and others are "not to be missed."

Linda Ronstadt,   26 | 25 | 24 | 24
Heart Like a Wheel 🔢
1974, Capitol; "You're No Good"
■ It's "easy to see what then-governor Jerry Brown saw in her" – Linda Ronstadt "was so cute in her hot pants you didn't realize how talented she was", but this chart-topping pop-rock disc "put her on the map"; the "superbly" "natural" "voice of the California '70s" "jumps from the speakers and wraps the songs around you" in a style that is nonetheless "mellow" on a "heartbreakingly beautiful album" that, with the help of a whole lot of her friends, is "100% good."

The Roots, *Phrenology*   26 | 24 | 27 | 25
2002, MCA; "The Seed (2.0)"; www.okayplayer.com/roots
◪ Mixing old-school "wisdom" with "live instrumentation", hip-hop's "brilliant" house band "experiments more than ever" on this album of "adventurous" tunes like *The Seed (2.0)*, which features guitar and vocals by Cody ChesnuTT; rooters rave the Philly crew is "to rap what Radiohead is to rock – innovators who keep getting better with time" – still, some get their digs in on a disc that's "not their best."

Mstislav Rostropovich, *Dvořák:*   28 | 26 | 29 | 24
Cello Concerto; Tchaikovsky: Rococo Variations
1968, Deutsche Grammophon; "Dvořák Cello Concerto"; www.berliner-philharmoniker.de
■ "Nobody does Dvořák like Rostropovich", one of "the premier cellists of the 20th century"; "lyrical and muscular at once, the musicianship is paired perfectly with the music", conducted by Herbert von Karajan for a "riveting, suave, majestic and atmospheric" recording with a "more-than-satisfactory sound" quality; the Tchaikovsky *Rococo Variations* coupling" "is a finely played bonus."

Roxy Music, *Avalon*   27 | 25 | 26 | 27
1982, Warner Bros.; "Avalon"
■ "How did people get laid before this came out?" – "if you can't close the deal" with this "seduction album", "move on"; with "layers of lush", "suave", "fantastically produced" "soundscapes", the band's "swan song showcases Bryan Ferry's panache" and "haunting lyrics" "while maintaining the instrumental flair of their oeuvre"; "smooth as butter", "it takes you to a magical place, far away."

Roxy Music, *For Your Pleasure*   27 | 25 | 27 | 26
1972, Atlantic; "In Every Dream Home a Heartache"
■ "Following their eponymous debut, this sophomore outing was a true winner": "Ferry's singing is miraculously

good", Eno's "cutting-edge, avant-garde" synths are "strange and wonderful" and "the drumming of the great Paul Thompson is, well, great"; "the art deco of rock", the "trailblazing" album was "radically different than anything else" and "10 years ahead of its time" – "after hearing it, everyone wanted to *Do the Strand.*"

Todd Rundgren, *Something/Anything?*   26 | 26 | 26 | 26

1972, Bearsville; "Hello It's Me"; www.tr-i.com

■ "Pop obsessive one-man band" and "whiz-kid" Rundgren, a "restless creator never content to do the same thing twice", sang and played every track on three out of four sides of this "inspired", "experimental", "diverse" double album; better yet, he wrote "brilliant, enduring songs" like *Hello, It's Me,* "in the ranks of Brian Wilson", and the result is a "truckload" of "pure pop bliss."

Run-D.M.C., *Raising Hell*   28 | 27 | 25 | 26

1986, Profile; "Peter Piper"

■ "Off-da-hook" party anthems abound on the "holy grail" of contemporary black music, overflowing with "wicked" wordplay and the "deft turntable work of the late, great Jam Master Jay"; "the Beatles" of "head bobbing" built a "bridge to rock" with tracks like the "classic" *Peter Piper* and the Joe Perry- and Steven Tyler-backed remake of Aerosmith's *Walk This Way,* which "single-handedly forced MTV to play rap videos", "sending hip-hop crashing into the living rooms of white America."

Rush, *Moving Pictures*   27 | 27 | 29 | 26

1981, Mercury; "Tom Sawyer"; www.rush.com

■ "The Canadian power trio's signature", this "precocious teenage boy's guide through high school hell" "combined great songwriting" with "technical prowess", "thrusting Rush into the mainstream"; "while staples like *Tom Sawyer* and *Limelight* are the stars here, the entire album is worth listening to" for its "damn fine mix of juicy pop nuggets and longer progressive epics" laced with "cerebral lyrics."

Rush, *2112*   25 | 25 | 28 | 25

1976, Mercury; "2112"; www.rush.com

■ "Waving in the metaphysical Rush", side one of "the only sci-fi opera put to vinyl" is devoted to the title track, a "blissfully overblown" "25-minute opus", inspired by Ayn Rand's novels, in which "great literature and great rock collide"; fueled by Geddy Lee's "howls", this "conceptual" album "takes you to other planets" and "into oblivion"; it was "thinking man's metal – or so we thought in 1976."

Tom Rush, *The Circle Game*   25 | 27 | 24 | 21

1968, Elektra; "The Circle Game"; www.tomrush.com

■ Showcasing a "warm, bluesy style" and a voice that could "melt anyone's heart", this "treasure" proved to be the "folky" singer-songwriter's "breakthrough"; the Joni Mitchell–penned "title cut alone makes it worth the price", though Rush's own songs are also "classic" – keep his "wonderful ballad *No Regrets*" around for listening on "lonely, late nights."

S

Sade, *Diamond Life*   27 | 25 | 26 | 26
1985, Portrait; "Smooth Operator"; www.sadeusa.com
■ "Singing like a goddess and looking like a vixen", the "sultry" Nigerian-born "queen of romance" serves up "sensual" sounds "to put you in the mood" for "silk sheets, soft caresses" and a "romantic dinner with candles"; her "velvety" vocals complement the "luscious", "jazzy" production, creating "the soundtrack for baby-making"; fans wax poetic, "if the moon had a voice and a backup band, Sade would be it."

Santana, *Abraxas* #1   27 | 25 | 28 | 25
1970, Columbia; "Black Magic Woman";
www.santana.com
■ "This is where it all began – the quintessential" "Latin-rock milestone" "laid the groundwork" with "moody, mystical arrangements (*Singing Winds, Crying Beasts*), soaring guitar solos (*Samba Pa Ti*), funky beats (*Oye Como Va*)", "superb production" and "the best big percussion section in the business"; "Carlos created a rhythm and zone few artists have since equaled – it's "pulse-pounding, get-on-your-feet-and-move music", and it "makes a devil out of you."

Santana, *Shaman* #1   24 | 23 | 27 | 25
2002, Arista; "The Game of Love"; www.santana.com
■ "Carlos and the boys continue to produce interesting collaborative work" on this "rockin'" disc "showing that *Supernatural* was not a fluke"; from Macy Gray to Nickelback singer Chad Kroeger to Placido Domingo to Seal and "especially Michelle Branch", featured on Grammy-winning *The Game of Love,* "each guest artist shines"; "this is a set of duets for anyone's tastes", proving the "soaring guitarist" "hasn't lost his edge after all these years."

Santana, *Supernatural* G #1   26 | 24 | 28 | 27
1999, Arista; "Smooth"; www.santana.com
■ A "superbly done collabfest" – the "Latin-rock fusion master" "knows how to engineer a comeback" and a No.1 hit, "giving the limelight to" "fresh new stars" and a few old hands; "all of the songs play to the strengths of guest artists, whether they're Lauryn Hill, Eric Clapton", Everlast, Dave Matthews or, of course, "Rob Thomas (all the way!)" on *Smooth,* culminating in a "stunning mix of styles that melds with Carlos' searing guitar riffs" – "he only gets better with age."

Satie, *Gymnopédies, Gnossiennes* 　26　27　28　24
1983, EMI; "Trois Gymnopédies "

■ The "sublime, spacey, mysterious, hypnotic" music of the "bewitching" lead "satirist of Les Six", an "elegant, wistful, fin-de-siècle" group of classical composers, "will haunt you for days"; pianist Aldo Ciccolini, "the one who finally made Satie famous", offers these "tuneful, lovely" yet "offbeat" miniatures in "lilting, atmospheric" interpretations for a disc of "pure enchantment."

Joe Satriani, *Surfing with the Alien* 　26　21　29　23
1987, Relativity; "Surfing with the Alien";
www.satriani.com

■ A paragon of six-string "dexterity and speed", this "virtuoso" with "incredible vision" "caught the wave" and came up with "probably the most diverse and technically proficient instrumental guitar album ever"; "when metal meets melody", this "wizard's" "effortless" fretwork "conveys deep emotion", conjuring up "seductive, powerful, soulful" "music to cruise the highway by."

Boz Scaggs, *Silk Degrees* 　26　24　25　24
1976, Columbia; "Lido Shuffle"; www.bozscaggs.com

■ "In 1976 you could walk across any college campus and hear this" "alternative for white kids who wanted to be funky without diving into disco", but the "champagne-rock" "jewel" has outlived its time with *Lowdown*'s rep as a rap sample fave; "every song is good" on a "slick, sophisticated pop album that paid the bills" for Boz; his "distinctive voice" and "jazzy" grooves on cuts like *Lido Shuffle* still sound "smooth" on "summer evenings" – "what a cool dude!"

Diane Schuur, *Diane Schuur &* 　24　24　25　26
The Count Basie Orchestra 🄶
1987, GRP; "Everyday"

◩ "Schurr invigorates every tune with heart and angst", and with the "astounding support" of the "hard-swinging Basie band", she's "the best she's ever sounded" on one of the "finest examples of emotion meeting composition", "stunningly arranged by Orchestra alumni Frank Foster"; still, the jazz jury's split on this one: groupies go gaga for the "great lady's" "golden" voice, but naysayers needle Deedles, dishing "she simply cannot sing."

Jill Scott, *Who Is Jill Scott?* 　27　27　26　25
Words and Sounds Vol. 1
2000, Hidden Beach; "A Long Walk"; www.jillscottonline.com

■ "Is it poetry, is it rap or something in between?" – "not sure, but damn", this Philly "queen" "can sing"; with a voice "like buttah", "sexy" "grooves" and "original" words, the "fresh, new talent" "blows you away" on a debut disc on "the softer side of neosoul"; "mellow" and "empowering" all at once, she makes female fans "proud to be women", garnering the title of "our modern-day Nina Simone."

Seal, *Seal* 25 | 23 | 24 | 25
1994, ZTT; "Kiss From a Rose"

■ Seal's "got the goods" on his second self-titled effort, "the one that put him on the map" with the "sultry" *Batman Forever* single, *Kiss From a Rose*; "bountiful" in "soulful pop" with the Brit's "sexy, sexy, sexy voice" laid over "lush" melodies on "reflective" ballads and "easy-listening" dance numbers, the music "sparked almost as much discussion as the origin of his scars", the legacy of discoid lupus; "crank it up on your Bose" "on a rainy night with that special someone" and wonder "where did this guy go?"

Pete Seeger, *We Shall Overcome* 26 | 27 | 24 | 22
1963, Columbia; "We Shall Overcome"

■ "Where would folk music be without Pete?" ponder proles, pols and plebs overcome by the singing ("voice like a bell"), choice of music (it "covered the world"), audience interaction ("one man leading thousands in song") and message ("world peace and social justice") on this "fine pioneer's" 1963 Carnegie Hall concert, now available in full on a 1989 reissue on two CDs; his "delivery has reached the hearts of young and old for decades."

Bob Seger & The Silver Bullet Band, *Against the Wind* 🎵 23 | 24 | 24 | 23
1980, Capitol; "Against the Wind"

☑ "No singer converts loss into triumph as relentlessly" as this "original" "American idol" from Detroit who "nails it" on a "consistent" collection, a No. 1 "record that made him a household name"; "we were all younger" back when the "traveling soul" sang "about his journey", still, cynics snipe "how many songs does he have where he remembers something that happened 10 years before he wrote it?"

Bob Seger & The Silver Bullet Band, *Night Moves* 26 | 25 | 25 | 24
1976, Capitol; "Night Moves"

■ "Seger arrives" armed with "blue-collar" "Motor City rock at its best" on this heartland "classic", featuring the title hit plus "lesser-known gems" rife with "bittersweet nostalgia"; "a hometown boy who knows how to rev up a crowd" and much "more than the guy on the Chevy ads", he's a voice of "rare grit" and a "supreme songwriter you suspect has been listening to your thoughts."

Sesame Street, *Platinum, All-Time Favorites* 27 | 27 | 23 | 25
1995, Sony Wonder; "I Love Trash"; pbskids.org/sesame

■ "Any album with *Put Down the Duckie* is a classic" proclaim "parents who grew up on *Sesame Street*" and still "love hearing songs from 30 years ago" along with "very clever" tracks from more recent years; this "definitive" disc from "the very best early childhood TV show" is "fun for long car rides" 'cause it "keeps the little ones happy", and "young and old can sing along" – "you'd have to be a cold, cold person to not join in on *I Love Trash.*"

The Sex Pistols, | 26 | 22 | 16 | 19 |
Never Mind the Bollocks Here's the Sex Pistols
1977, Warner Bros.; "God Save the Queen"
■ "Be afraid, be very afraid" ... "from the harsh reality of the lyrics to the throbbing melodies spit from the guitar", this "historically significant", "quintessential punk album" – "loud, snotty and angry" "youthful anarchy in all its glory" – "defined a new genre of music and culture" and "instantly made many popular bands obsolete"; with "hard-rock production that other bands would kill for", "radical" Johnny Rotten and the lads created a "phenomenon" that "lives up to the hype."

Tupac Shakur, *All Eyez on Me* **#1** | 27 | 27 | 25 | 25 |
1996, Death Row; "California Love (Rmx)"; www.2paclegacy.com
■ Fresh out of "prison" and giving off "rare light in the dark world of gangsta rap", "one of the greatest lyricists" comes across as a "genius" "poet" in his thuggish but "moving" "message and persona"; this "much-anticipated" double album is a "spirited and appealing" "combo of hard-core beats and party anthems", like the remix of the No. 1 single *California Love*; "it's too bad he's not around anymore to hit us with more of his" "mad rappering skills and hot beats."

Tupac Shakur, *Greatest Hits* **#1** | 28 | 28 | 26 | 26 |
1998, Interscope; "I Get Around"; www.2paclegacy.com
■ "With all the Tupac CDs out there, it's good to have nearly all of his best on these two discs"; "a necessary collection" in the hip-hop canon that contrasts the slain rapper's "most heartfelt lyrics with some of his most violent themes", the "posthumous album" "captures" "complex", "unparalleled writing" "just a step away from that of John Donne" backed by a booming production; this "distinctive voice" "will continue to be influential to all hip-hop artists" for years to come.

Michelle Shocked, | 24 | 24 | 23 | 22 |
Short Sharp Shocked
1988, Mercury; "Anchorage"; www.michelleshocked.com
■ A "gem from the late '80s" anti-folk-"rock revival", this "raw, raw, raw" album stands as "an intelligent political statement from a talented" singer-songwriter just on the rise; the former squatter, skateboard punk and protest veteran (the evidence is on the album cover) is on the "top list of great angry young women", and every "snappy" song she sings, including her hit *Anchorage,* is a "winner."

Wayne Shorter, *Speak No Evil* | 27 | 27 | 29 | 26 |
1964, Blue Note; "Speak No Evil"
■ "Can't speak no evil about Wayne Shorter" – on yet "another album that defines an era/genre/style", arguably

"the finest jazz composer of the late 20th century" lays down "spellbinding" originals and covers with an "explosive force" "that shows off his talents" as a musician; in 1964, the "groundbreaking saxman" was at the "peak of his creative form", "with an incredible band" to back him and the "good, if primal, recording quality" of the Blue Note label to wrap it up.

Show Boat (Studio)   26 | 27 | 25 | 25
1989, Angel Classics; "Ol' Man River"

■ A "classic score gets star treatment" in this three-disc show boat, "a wonderful remake that includes all the songs ever included in performances" and then some; "fabulous" but "frequently deleted material" speaks to producer John McGlinn's "reverence" for the "groundbreaking musical", and though the operatic vocals of "fabulous" Frederica Von Stade and "poignant" Teresa Stratas "may be too good" not to "overshadow the words", "the historical importance of this complete recording overwhelms any quibbles."

Side by Side by Sondheim   25 | 27 | 24 | 23
(London cast recording)
1976, RCA; "Could I Leave You?"

■ "Isn't it warm, isn't it cozy" listening to the revue of the composer's "career through the mid-'70s"?; the "delicious" disc preserves a show that "cemented Sondheim's popular reputation" "when he needed help", "leaving us to revel in his genius" as "three of London's best musical performers" wow with "witty", "wonderful", "fresh interpretations of early standbys" and previously "unheard" songs; "wonder what would happen if they tried a sequel?"

Sigur Rós, 'Agaetis Byrjun   28 | 25 | 27 | 28
2000, Fatcat; "Svefn G Englar"; www.sigur-ros.com

■ "It's an Icelandic thing you can't understand . . . no, literally, it is" – Reykjavik's top export sings "in a fictional language" mixed with their native tongue over "haunting" music that "brings tears to the eyes"; it "sounds like elf hymns in the forest" or "whalelike wanderings that build to crescendo" – whatever it is, the "raucously uplifting strings" are arranged "more beautifully than on any other rock record."

Horace Silver, Song for My Father   26 | 26 | 27 | 24
1964, Blue Note; "Song for My Father"

■ "And you thought Steely Dan came up with that *Rikki Don't Lose That Number* vamp" – actually, it was cribbed from the title track of this disc from the "pinnacle of an outstanding career"; "one of the finest hard-bop dates ever recorded" is "typical of Silver's approach", with its "tight blues, swing and funk beats" "giving a great idea of what the classic Blue Note sound is all about"; kitsch queens call it "ultra-campy", but that's their kudos to a "most enjoyable" listen.

Carly Simon, *No Secrets* 24 | 25 | 24 | 23
1972, Elektra; "You're So Vain"; www.carlysimon.com
■ It's "no secret" that this "sexy, soulful" record represents "prolific" "Carly at her peak"; "great then, classic now", her "unique, evocative voice" "handles some fine material" like *The Right Thing to Do,* her duet with then-partner James Taylor, and her "deeply personal" signature *You're So Vain* – and whether they think that tune is about them or not, perhaps "today's pop divas could learn" something "from Simon's carefully crafted songs."

PAUL SIMON, *GRACELAND* G 28 | 28 | 28 | 28
1986, Warner Bros.; "Diamonds on the Soles of her Shoes"; www.paulsimon.com
■ "Simon's crowning achievement in a career of musical highs", this "gutsy, graceful" "groundbreaker" and this *Survey*'s top-rated World Music album brought global sounds "to a new audience"; "mining African rhythms" for "transcendent, durable bliss", this "landmark" introduced the "upbeat sounds" of Ladysmith Black Mambazo on "wildly creative songs"; "freshened" by the experience, "he loosens up lyrically and musically", and as a result, nearly every song on this Grammy-winner "oozes with joy."

Paul Simon, 25 | 27 | 26 | 25
There Goes Rhymin' Simon
1973, Columbia; "Kodachrome"; www.paulsimon.com
■ "Paul hits it on the sweet spot" with this "impressive" combination of folk, gospel, rock and R&B that "marked his real emergence as a solo artist, following his eponymous" first effort; though it's often "overshadowed by the earlier" albums with Art "and the later *Graceland*", its "complex rhythms and great lyrics" about color film and a mother's love make it a "priceless" "American classic."

Simon & Garfunkel, 28 | 29 | 27 | 26
***Bridge over Troubled Water* G #1**
1970, Columbia; "Bridge over Troubled Water"; www.artgarfunkel.com, www.paulsimon.com
■ Their vocals "a seamless blend", these "talented", "classy guys" pulled together a final "gift to mankind" that "spoke eloquently to their generation" and is sure to "thrill little girls and English teachers for the next 100 years"; it may have turned out to be the "swan song to a beautiful collaboration" between Paul's "intuitive, thoughtful" lyrics and Art's "awesome" tenor, "but at least they finished on top" with armfuls of Grammys – "what a way to go out."

Simon & Garfunkel, *The Graduate* 27 | 28 | 27 | 25
(Soundtrack) **G #1**
1968, Columbia; "Mrs. Robinson"; www.artgarfunkel.com, www.paulsimon.com
■ "A masterpiece of its time", this "album redefined what it meant to be a soundtrack", "fitting flawlessly with" the

"landmark film" and "making it all the better"; Simon & Garfunkel's "amazingly written and performed" folk-rock tunes "touch on subjects that other artists shied away from", "commenting on the generation gap" at "the beginning of the era" of the late '60s; amid *Mrs. Robinson* and *Scarborough Fair* are David Grusin's instrumentals, which may be "cheesy", but they "set the tone" of Benjamin's parents' cocktail culture.

Simon & Garfunkel,   <u>28</u> <u>29</u> <u>27</u> <u>26</u>
Parsley, Sage, Rosemary and Thyme
1966, Columbia; "Scarborough Fair/Canticle";
www.artgarfunkel.com, www.paulsimon.com
■ "New York's golden boys" "really hit their stride" on their third album, which is "topical, intelligent and, as always, filled with" "perfect harmonies" ("was anything ever so sweet?"); the folk-rock songs "speak of their time" ("a splendid trip down memory lane") but remain "quite relevant today" (they "never escape one's soul") – it's no wonder "an entire generation followed the duo to Scarborough Fair" and beyond.

Nina Simone, *Wild Is the Wind/*   <u>28</u> <u>27</u> <u>28</u> <u>23</u>
High Priestess of Soul
1990, Philips; "Wild Is the Wind"
■ "What a voice!" – it's "not perfect, but perfectly able to convey emotion", and "when it breaks, so does your heart"; with an "intense musicianship" "full of truth, pain" and "anger", this "important artist" delivers "deep, dark" ballads like the title track and scathing protest tunes like *Four Women* on this double CD combining of two 1966 LPs; no wonder they called her the High Priestess of Soul: "nobody sings the blues like Nina Simone."

Frank Sinatra, *Duets*   <u>21</u> <u>24</u> <u>23</u> <u>23</u>
1993, Capitol; "I've Got You Under My Skin";
www.franksinatra.com
◪ "A fine capper to an awesome legacy" according to Frank's lifelong lovers, this "great idea of mixing Sinatra with younger contemporaries", from Babs to Bono, is "lots of fun" fashioned to "wow fans of a whole new generation"; it worked, going multiplatinum, but did it sell just as a "curiosity"?; the Chairman "was not even in the room with his duet partners" when he "phoned in" his vocals for the "canned" collection, but it's "a bit like a train wreck – you're compelled to listen" anyway.

FRANK SINATRA,   <u>29</u> <u>28</u> <u>28</u> <u>27</u>
IN THE WEE SMALL HOURS
1954, Capitol; "In the Wee Small Hours";
www.franksinatra.com
■ Ol' Blue Eyes' Reprise "mid-years show how he could wrap around a lyric and make it his" with this "noir" "concept disc" of "sublime performances that convey

love, romance, loneliness and melancholy" from the man with "the world's greatest diction"; "if you want to cry, here's one to do it with" – just "kick back in a comfy chair with a pipe", and drink in these "classic torch songs" for "the best tonic for a love gone bad."

FRANK SINATRA, *ONLY THE LONELY* 28 | 27 | 28 | 28
1958, Capitol; "One for My Baby";
www.franksinatra.com
■ "Frank sings for all the lonely people", showing off "his most intimate" side on this "heartbreaking work of sadness and loss", "one of the greatest blues albums by a white guy"; Nelson Riddle lays down possibly his "finest arrangements" on tunes like the "eerie" *Blues in the Night* for "a beautiful voice with great interpretation" on the "completely perfect companion for the end of a romance"; "wow!" – "feeling low can be so good!"

Frank Sinatra, *Sinatra Reprise:* 28 | 27 | 28 | 26
The Very Good Years
1991, Reprise; "Fly Me to the Moon";
www.franksinatra.com
■ "No collection is complete without this" "very good overview of the years at Reprise" (Frank's own label, with his mug spinning on every disc) by the "big, bad king" of "crooning"; the disc "is like a magnet to steel – it draws you in and won't let you go", "flying you to the moon" with "the softer sounds that made Sinatra great"; it's "a staple for anyone wooing a woman" because "the ladies will flock" to "strangers in the night" when "one of the sexiest voices of all times" sings.

Frank Sinatra, 28 | 27 | 28 | 27
Songs for Swingin' Lovers
1956, Capitol; "You Make Me Feel So Young";
www.franksinatra.com
■ The "upbeat companion to *Wee Small Hours*", this too-marvelous-for-words "cream of the crop" recorded when Frank was "swingin' at his peak" is full of "joy and mastery", "each word sung with the meaning and supreme cockiness" that only the Chairman of the Board could deliver; Nelson Riddle's "phenomenal arrangements shine but still show off the undeniable character of Sinatra's voice" "at his happiest" – if this "make-out" "gem" "doesn't make you amorous, nothing will."

Singin' in the Rain (Soundtrack) 28 | 28 | 27 | 26
1952, MGM; "Singin' in the Rain"
■ "If you're in the rain and don't care if you're wet, chances are you're dancing to the title song" of this "gloriously" "corny" soundtrack as it plays in your head; "arguably the best MGM musical" "still shines after fifty years" on the "superior" "expanded Rhino version" that captures Gene Kelly's "raspy" voice, Donald O'Connor's "snappy charm"

and Debbie Reynolds' "rich" and "peppy" screen debut;
now, "get out your umbrella" and "wow" 'em in the puddles.

Singles (Soundtrack)   26 | 24 | 25 | 24
1992, Epic; "State of Love and Trust"

■ This sonic "snapshot" of "the Seattle sound" "completely
capturing the tone of the early 1990s" grunge scene
"chronicles musicians that shaped the way we hear today":
Pearl Jam, Alice in Chains, Soundgarden, Mudhoney and
Screaming Trees; "Cameron Crowe is a genius", "putting
songs front and center" to "remain favorites long after the
flannel shirts have been donated to charity."

Siouxsie & the Banshees,   24 | 22 | 24 | 22
Kaleidoscope
1980, Polydor; "Christine"

◪ "The goth princess" and her Banshees blend "punk
philosophy with feminist fury and animal-rights ideology"
on this disc released after a changing of the guard, with
John McKay and Kenny Morris exiting and former Sex Pistol
Steve Jones and Magazine's John McGeoch climbing
onboard; the result is "genius" gush a few, but most
Siouxsie swooners say it's "not as good as later albums."

Slayer, *Reign in Blood*   25 | 22 | 25 | 25
1986, Def Jam; "Angel of Death"; www.diabolus.net

■ "Fast, brutal and virtually without melody", this Rick
Rubin–produced "must-have" seethes with "sheer ferocity";
with its "frenetic guitar riffs" and "overall Satanic vibe" it's
"the bible of thrash-death metal" beside which "everything
else pales in comparison"; diehards swear on a freshly
dug grave that "rarely has anything so dark been so life-
affirming", noting that "the best, shortest masterpiece" in
the genre clocks in "under 30 minutes."

Sleepless in Seattle   24 | 24 | 25 | 25
(Soundtrack) **#1**
1993, Epic Soundtrax; "As Time Goes By"

■ "A girl's best friend on a dateless Friday night" might just
be this "sweet", "sentimental" soundtrack of "feel-good"
"popular tunes from the American songbook", including
"gorgeous, jazzy" numbers by Nat King Cole, Jimmy
Durante and Louis Armstrong; "choked-up" "romantics"
rave that the "dreamy" disc "can stay in your carousel for
years", while even cynics say the "yummy" mix "made a
trite story bearable."

Slick Rick,   26 | 26 | 23 | 25
The Great Adventures of Slick Rick
1989, Def Jam; "Children's Story"

■ "Could anything put a smile to your face like a Slick
Rick disc? – "a true storyteller" with "a sense of humor"
and the "illest flow", this London-born "rap pioneer" with
the trademark "gold chains" honed his "original", British-

tinged voice and "masterful rhymes" stateside to produce a "classic" debut album that includes the epic party joint *Children's Story*, which helped him become "one of the most sampled voices in hip-hop."

Sly & the Family Stone, *Greatest Hits* #1
| 27 | 25 | 26 | 24 |

1970, Epic; "Stand!"

■ "Sly Stone's crazy brilliance is all over" this anthology of "crossover music" that's so "killer" it can start a "party" the size of "Woodstock", with Larry Graham's rich, slap-"happy" "bass lines" steering the stew of "psychedelic soul" (*Stand!*), "energizing funk" (*Thank You Falettinme Be Mice Elf Agin*) and space-aged "rock" (*I Want to Take You Higher*); "be careful when you turn it up": "as fresh as the day they put them down", these "kick-ass" beats could "break some windows."

Smashing Pumpkins, *Mellon Collie and the Infinite Sadness* #1
| 24 | 24 | 25 | 25 |

1995, Virgin; "1979"

◪ "You have to admire" a band "with the guts to try a double album in the '90s" – the "kicker is they pulled it off" on this "sprawling", "impeccably produced" multiplatinum "masterwork" that makes up for its "lack of a cohesive concept" with a "folder of emotions"; "Billy Corgan digs deep and breaks new ground" with each "blistering rocker and vulnerable lullaby" evoking a "distinct mood"; still, some sigh the "bombastic" work "would have been stronger if whittled down to a single disc."

Smashing Pumpkins, *Siamese Dream*
| 26 | 25 | 26 | 25 |

1993, Virgin; "Today"

■ "A sonic joyride", this "boundary-breaking" sophomore "monster" "provided a soft, fuzzy balance to Seattle grunge" that's still "perfect for the headphones-obsessed adolescent within us all"; "beautifully orchestrated and produced", with "exquisite guitar riffs" and "heartfelt lyrics" – all (save drums) performed by the head Pumpkin – it's a "passion play in which Billy Corgan is crowned king of alternative rock", "before the slickness set in and the rawness dissipated."

Smetana, *Má Vlast*
| 28 | 27 | 28 | 25 |

1990, Supraphon; "Die Moldau"

■ "With an outpouring of emotion" "after decades of self-exile", conductor Rafael Kubelik "marks his return" to the philharmonic of his native country with a "powerful performance" of "a deeply felt piece" evoking "national pride"; "there's a lot more to it than" the "engaging, enchanting" *Moldau* – when you hear the "lovely musical poetry" so "warmly" and "soulfully played" clear through, you realize that "no one does Smetana as passionately as the Czechs!"

Elliot Smith, *XO*   25 | 27 | 25 | 23
1998, DreamWorks; "Waltz #2"
■ "He's the singer-songwriter equivalent of a favorite pair of slippers", gush fans – "you want to share a fire with him" and relax with his "oh-so-intuitive" songs; this "stirring" follow-up to Smith's *Good Will Hunting* outing "sparkles with amazing lyrics" and "soul-wrenching" numbers – it's "misery in the form of beautiful songs", and "the lowest of the lows have never sounded so simple or sweet"; go on, "reach for a whiskey and a cigarette" with a "sad smile on your face."

Patti Smith, *Easter*   25 | 27 | 22 | 22
1978, Arista; "Because the Night"; www.gungho2000.com
■ "The poetess of punk" is "at her peak in every way" on this "emotionally taut and driving" "classic" that shows "why she was such a cult figure"; it's a "masterful undertaking, melding raw energy into accessible, melodic tones", and with the help of Springsteen producer Jimmy Iovine, it "leaned toward a more commercial sound" and reaped this "true artist" her hit *Because the Night,* co-written by the Boss himself.

Patti Smith, *Horses*   27 | 28 | 25 | 23
1975, Arista; "Gloria"; www.gungho2000.com
■ "One of the best albums of the New York pre-punk scene", this "prophetic" "watershed" debut triggered a "tidal shift in thought that allowed poets with ideas to participate in a world inhabited by The Eagles and ELP"; "rock had gone big hair and Patti brought big attitude", merging lyrics that "slam danced" with "flailing guitars" and "fiery determination" – she even turned Van Morrison's "*Gloria* from a male-dominated song into something with no gender, just power."

The Smiths, *The Queen Is Dead*   28 | 27 | 26 | 25
1986, Sire; "There Is a Light that Never Goes Out"
■ "The stars aligned" for "king of mope" Morrissey and Johnny Marr on this "landmark recording", with the latter's "jangly, layered", "swirling guitars" ("heaven on the ears") and "Spectoresque production" forming a "happy counterpoint" for the former's "neurotic, dark, wry lyrics"; it's "absolute bliss meets a razor blade" – with "angst for all" from the "boys who spawned a nation of imitators" mimicking an "irreverent", "literary bent that could only be born in the UK."

Snoop Dogg, *Doggystyle* 🔲1   26 | 24 | 24 | 25
1993, Death Row; "Gin and Juice"; www.snoopdogg.com
■ "Controversial" "sexual humor" never sounded so "great" as on the solo debut from "Dr. Dre's crazy-ass protégé", who (thanks to his work on *The Chronic*) was already "the biggest rap star of the '90s" "when this album dropped"; the Dogg's "liquidy, mellow, hilarious" flow

swims through "the Doctor's" "laid-back", "smoked-out", "G-funk" beats with lazy precision; "lewd and crude", "soulful and unnerving", the "superior production" helped bring "West Coast gangsta cool" to the masses.

Phoebe Snow, *Phoebe Snow* 　26 | 25 | 26 | 23

1974, Shelter; "Poetry Man"; www.phoebesnow.com
■ Back in '74, this genre-crossing pop-soul-jazz singer-songwriter-poet seemed to "come from out of nowhere", "delivering a treasure" in the form of this "lovely first album"; with a voice that's "mellow", "earthy" and full of "unique" swoops and swirls, she wowed fans with songs like *Poetry Man,* the biggest radio hit of her career.

Sonic Youth, *Daydream Nation* 　26 | 25 | 26 | 22

1988, Blast-first Enigma; "Teenage Riot"; www.sonicyouth.com
■ Like the line from *Hey Joni* instructs, "'forget the past and just say yes'" to this "touchstone" of "truly modern psychedelia" on which "noise, melody and unfettered expression coalesce in a dynamic wall of sound" that "seamlessly flows together as one full piece"; "less dissonant and harsh" than this "truly important" New York group's earlier works, the "brilliant, alternative benchmark of the '80s" perhaps "spawned more bands than the Velvet Underground did in the '60s."

Soundgarden, *Superunknown* 🔢 25 | 23 | 26 | 26

1994, A&M; "Black Hole Sun"
■ "One of the pillars" of the Seattle scene, this "young, fresh band" "transcended its grunge trappings" with a "full-tilt howl" that reached No. 1 and, thanks to songs that "ranged from straight-ahead hard rock to Middle Eastern–tinged ballads", "left a lasting mark"; "dark and full of angst", they "had the perfect chemistry", earmarked by "wailing god" Chris Cornell's "incredibly powerful" vocals; look out, "this is the big daddy coming through, louder than love."

The Sound of Music 　28 | 28 | 28 | 27

(Soundtrack) 🅖 🔢
1965, RCA Victor; "Edelweiss"
■ "The hills are definitely alive" "with the sound of Julie Andrews", "pitch perfect" and "clear as a bell", as she "wraps herself around" the "magical writing" of Rodgers and Hammerstein, "transporting us to Maria's Alps"; "one of our favorite things", this "moving", "mass-appeal" "masterpiece" is a "cultural icon" full of "sweet" "songs we all know by heart" to "bring out the karaoke in everyone" – "Austria never had a better proponent for tourism!"

South Pacific 　27 | 27 | 26 | 25

(Original cast recording)
1949, Sony; "Some Enchanted Evening"
■ Rodgers-and-Hammerstein heads are "happy"-talking about this "high point in musical theater" from the "golden

age" "before they butchered the delightful gem into movie form"; the "tuneful take on Michener's *Tales of the South Pacific*" is a "melodic feast" including "some enchanted" songs sung by "superb" Mary Martin and "dreamy" Ezio Pinza ("one man to leave in your hair"); it isn't only "hummable" – "condemning prejudice but not preachy", it "still speaks to today."

The Specials, *The Specials*   25 | 23 | 22 | 21
1979, Chrysalis; "A Message to You Rudy"
■ "You can't help but dance" to this "definitive" debut by the band that spearheaded England's postpunk revival of Jamaican ska; on this "fan-skankin'-tastic" Elvis Costello–produced disc, Terry Hall and the guys applied "a good message and a great" "rock-steady beat" to "black-and-white issues during a racially charged time", and every song, from *A Message to You Rudy* to the teenage pregnancy rant *Too Much, Too Young*, is a "classic."

The Spinners, *A One of a Kind*   25 | 24 | 25 | 26
Love Affair: The Anthology
1991, Atlantic; "They Just Can't Stop It (The Games People Play)"
■ "Get ready to have your feet tapping and your car shakin'" to the "excellent harmonies" of a "prototypical" vocal group "that spanned several musical eras" from the "doo-wop" of *That's What Girls Are Made For* to "funked-out" soul of *Games People Play*; "two CDs of greatest hits may be too many, but one just wouldn't cut it" for such "utterly essential music."

Dusty Springfield,   27 | 25 | 26 | 26
Dusty in Memphis
1969, Atlantic; "Son of a Preacher Man";
www.dustyspringfield.co.uk
■ "How did a British white woman have so much soul?" – everything about the "divine" Dusty said "look beneath the surface, and you'll find so much" happening; on "funky yet ornate arrangements", the "glorious" growler lays down "smoky vocals that make every cut" on this "masterwork" "full of moodiness"; the "sublime" *Son of a Preacher Man* not only "taught female rockers how to sing", it remains "the best make-out music for those who love kitsch."

BRUCE SPRINGSTEEN,   27 | 27 | 27 | 27
BORN IN THE USA 🔢
1984, Columbia; "Born in the USA";
www.brucespringsteen.net
■ "The indisputable Boss and the boys" "hit on all cylinders" with this "insanely popular" "supernova"; the "poppy hits" "obscured" the "master storyteller's" "dark themes" of "unflinching social commentary": "loneliness and betrayal" in "working-class America", conveyed with a "blue-collar swagger impossible to resist"; the "iconic record" spun off seven top-ten singles, including the "most misinterpreted"

title track, the "harsh" "lament of a Vietnam vet" Reaganites misconstrued "as flag-waving patriotism."

BRUCE SPRINGSTEEN, *BORN TO RUN* | 29 | 29 | 29 | 27 |
1975, Columbia; "Thunder Road"; www.brucespringsteen.net
■ A "classic from the first drum beat", this "cinematic vision of American teenage romanticism" that "changed the face of R&R and the role of the singer-songwriter" was voted the *Survey*'s Most Popular, as well as Top Rock recording; with this "epic" "song cycle", perhaps "never equaled in scope", the Boss delivers "towering ambition", "utter desperation" and "passion by the truckload", "providing tremendous views from the Joisey shore about girls, cars and the promise of the endless Saturday night."

BRUCE SPRINGSTEEN, *BRUCE SPRINGSTEEN & THE E STREET BAND LIVE/1975-85* ⃣1 | 28 | 29 | 29 | 26 |
1986, Columbia; "Rosalita"; www.brucespringsteen.net
◪ "A goody bag of hits" that shot to No.1, this "three-and-a-half-hour marathon" captured the "humor, energy, spirit, passion, sweat" and "magic" of "rock's bard" and "greatest live performer" in early to mid-career, "untainted by the weight of superstardom"; "while it's a good glimpse inside the world of Bruce shows", diehards deem the song selection "too dependent on the *Born in the USA* era", claiming "nothing compares to seeing him" on stage.

BRUCE SPRINGSTEEN, *DARKNESS ON THE EDGE OF TOWN* | 29 | 29 | 28 | 26 |
1978, Columbia; "Badlands"; www.brucespringsteen.net
■ "After a three-year absence imposed by legal battles with his former manager", Bruce returned with a "blistering tour de force" that "really showed off his band"; though the "production is a little rough", this "cathartic record" is "tight" and "direct" with "some of his most resonant songs"; "turning to the troubles of adulthood", it offered a "brooding, stark version of life for his characters" and yet "hope shines through – 'I believe in a promised land', indeed."

BRUCE SPRINGSTEEN, *THE RISING* ⃣1 | 27 | 28 | 28 | 28 |
2002, Columbia; "The Rising"; www.brucespringsteen.net
■ "A fitting rebirth for the E Street Band" and a "magnificent return to form" for their leader, this "poignant", "riveting" post-9/11 "time capsule" may have been "snubbed by the Grammys" but it "succeeds both as a rock album and as a healing", "non-jingoistic" "meditation on one of our nation's darkest days" that's neither "patriotic dribble or emotional exploitation"; it's "therapy for the blues" and the Boss was perhaps "the only one who could legitimately provide it."

Squeeze, *Singles 45's and Under* | 26 | 26 | 24 | 23 |
1983, A&M; "Tempted"; www.squeezefan.com
■ "Squeezing in" "the essential tracks from the heyday" of "the best singles band of the '80s", this "defining album"

"skims the cream off an alternately brilliant and vapid career"; ranging from the "pithy pop" of *Black Coffee in Bed* to the sweaty longing of *Tempted*", the collection of "masterful new wave tunes" places Chris Difford and Glenn Tillbrook "among the best songwriting teams of the later 20th century" and makes a "perfect gym companion."

A Star Is Born (Soundtrack)   25 | 25 | 26 | 24
1955, Columbia; "The Man That Got Away"
■ "There's still a tear or two hiding" in this "heartaching" "Judy Garland triumph", a "fabulous soundtrack" featuring the star "at top form"; "worth it for *The Man That Got Away*" and the Gershwin/Arlen score alone, the album that "enhanced and cemented" the diva's "legend" "is more than a memory" now that it's been reissued with bonus tracks; catty fans hiss "the Streisand remake is a pale imitation."

Star Wars (Soundtrack) 🄶   27 | 26 | 28 | 27
1977, RCA Victor; "Main Title"; www.starwars.com
■ "A long time ago in a galaxy [not so] far away, John Williams returned us to a symphonic movie score, and we are grateful"; the "groundbreaking", "heart-pumping" soundtrack to George Lucas' opus has been "enormously influential", introducing science-fiction cinema to a "classical romanticism" that conveys "the largeness of space" and delivering a main title that has "become part of the lexicon of our culture" – "the force" is with it indeed.

Steely Dan, *Aja* 🄶   27 | 27 | 28 | 27
1977, ABC; "Deacon Blues"; www.steelydan.com
■ "In the pre–new wave wasteland" of '77, Walter Becker and Donald Fagen created this "mini-film without pictures" by way of "brilliant lyrics and musicianship"; this "incredible kismet of talent" "reached the pinnacle of their jazz-pop studio perfection" on this "funky", "slickly" produced "evergreen" that "still sounds like tomorrow"; back then "you felt mature listening" to these "radio-phobic, long-form tunes" made of "aural velvet."

Steely Dan, *Can't Buy a Thrill*   26 | 26 | 28 | 25
1972, MCA; "Do It Again"; www.steelydan.com
☑ "Fans of Dan" say "the seeds of something spectacular" were planted on their "smart, snappy, stylish" debut, which announced "these dudes have some serious talent"; "reeling in the riffs, awesome guitar work" and "Latino rhythms", "they brought class to '70s rock", and "no one else sounded remotely like them"; still, a few waverers feel later efforts "*Pretzel Logic* and *Katy Lied* are vastly superior."

Steely Dan, *The Royal Scam*   26 | 25 | 28 | 27
1976, ABC; "Kid Charlemagne"; www.steelydan.com
■ Becker and Fagen spin "a web of lyrical cynicism" in nine "dark", "intriguing" songs "about divorce, mass murder, immigration troubles, condom use and life on other planets"

set to "some of the greatest jazz-rock guitar lines ever recorded (thanks to Larry Carlton)"; the "perfect mix between earlier, edgier stuff and later, too-slick" recordings brings back memories of a "wonderfully misspent youth."

Stereolab,   27 | 25 | 27 | 27
Emperor Tomato Ketchup
1996, Elektra; "Cybele's Reverie"; www.stereolab.co.uk
■ "Trippy, spacey, looped-out" – in other words, "a great amalgam of out-there styles, past and present" – this fourth full-length release from the experimental "kings of modern rock-electronica" is "damn good", perhaps even their most "complex, multilayered record to date"; the *Ketchup*-crazy say it's "music for relaxing", but you can also "play it in the bedroom for a rompin' good time."

Steve Miller Band,   22 | 21 | 22 | 22
Greatest Hits 1974-78
1978, Capitol; "The Joker"; www.stevemillerband.com
◪ "No matter your age", this multiplatinum "blast from the past" "probably evokes" "memories of college keg parties"; filled with "catchy", "easy-to-sing-along-to" tunes, this "classic summer rock" collection makes you "stand up and dance"; but dissenters steamed by overkill kvetch that "it would be a masterpiece" if only "most every fan hadn't heard every single five-million times."

Cat Stevens, *Tea for the Tillerman*   25 | 25 | 23 | 23
1971, A&M; "Father and Son"; www.yusufislam.org.uk
◪ "Perfect to curl up with on a rainy day", this "fine, thoughtful album "brings back memories of a gentler time" when "hippiedom ruled and Cat was a favored son"; a "lost teller of tales", he wrote "wistful melodies punctuated by playful tunes, leaping from *Wild World* to the melancholy *Sad Lisa*"; while some wonder why he left music to "become a Muslim cleric at the height of his career", cynics suspect "the clues were all here" in this "icky treacle."

Rod Stewart,   26 | 25 | 25 | 24
Every Picture Tells a Story
1971, Mercury; "Maggie May"
■ Back when "he didn't need to ask if we thought he was sexy", "Rod the Mod" "used to matter" and his first No. 1 album is "historical proof"; on this "sparsely produced", "brilliant" breakthrough, the "gravel-voiced" Brit "struts his stuff", bringing "character" to the chart-topping B side, *Maggie May,* the "title track, a miracle" and "sandpaper soulful" covers of Tim Hardin and the Temptations; Ron Wood "adds his inimitable guitar licks and songwriting."

St. Germain, *Tourist*   24 | 20 | 23 | 26
2000, Blue Note; "Rose Rouge"
■ "Jazz meets lounge meets techno in this amazing blend of different genres" from the French house music outfit;

"excellent for a country drive or swanky cocktails", its "stunning tracks" were "playing everywhere in Paris in 2000"; "throw it on at your next party", "set the groove of the mood" and get "hooked" on the "hypnotic" "fun."

The Sting (Soundtrack) #1　　27 | 27 | 27 | 26
1974, MCA; "The Entertainer"

■ Marvin Hamlisch "single-handedly brought Scott Joplin and ragtime to new heights", "reintroducing the public" to the nearly forgotten music of the jazz predecessor and pianist on this soundtrack to the charming Robert Redford/ Paul Newman crook flick; "setting the beat for the hit movie", this "fine selection of classics" aced the charts and scored a top-ten single with a "historical" cut that, as its name claims, is "still quite entertaining."

Sting,　　25 | 26 | 27 | 26
The Dream of the Blue Turtles
1985, A&M; "Russians"; www.sting.com

■ "It took nerve to leave The Police after *Synchronicity*", but the former frontman took a "brave first step" and "didn't miss a beat", pulling together this "lush" collection of "jazz-inflected pop" that proved he wasn't "just a pretty blonde"; "Branford Marsalis, Kenny Kirkland and drummer Omar Hakim helped to create a masterful blend of pop and world rhythms" "crafted around Sting's socially relevant lyrics" on songs that "made activists out of teenaged girls."

Sting, *Ten Summoner's Tales* ☉　　25 | 25 | 26 | 26
1993, A&M; "Fields of Gold"; www.sting.com

■ "Finally an all-out pop album from" the onetime Police-man fawn fans who feel Mr. Sumner "has the Midas touch" "when it comes to creating clever", "cosmic" material (he "takes my breath away"); so "dreamy" with "superb arrangements", "first-rate musicians", "haunting melodies" and a "wonderful mix of styles", this "strong collection" showcases "Sting at his most serene" and "least pompous."

The Stone Roses, *The Stone Roses*　　27 | 24 | 26 | 25
1989, Silvertone; "I Wanna Be Adored"

■ "It had a hook, it had a melody, it had all of England in a rage", and while it may "not be the seismic masterpiece the UK thinks it is", this "always enjoyable" debut "changed millions' take on indie music in a nanosecond"; "jangly, funky, rhythmic, folky" and "trippy", it was "the first great example of Britpop", providing "the key to the 'Madchester' scene"; then legal battles and "egos got in the way", and they "never ascended these heights again."

Stone Temple Pilots, *Core*　　23 | 22 | 23 | 23
1993, Atlantic; "Plush"; www.stonetemplepilots.com

■ This "intense, mesmerizing debut" flies high fawn fans who rise to defend the "critically dismissed" STP as much more than "Pearl Jam lite"; "unfairly derided", "these dudes were a rockin' grunge"-metal act, and this multiplatinum, Grammy-winning "classic", containing "catchy songs that touch all bases" and "forceful melodies that make it excellent for a road trip", "hits you between the eyes."

The Stooges, *Funhouse*

| 27 | 23 | 20 | 19 |

1970, Elektra; "TV Eye"

■ This second LP "may not be their best songwriting", but "weak Stooges is still better than most"; "the album everyone should own but no one does" is an "all-out musical explosion" that plays "loud at any volume" like "one long heavy track"; proto-punkster "Iggy makes it fun to wallow in the dirt", and it "still sounds as fresh and mind-blowing as it did when it first came out."

The Stooges, *The Stooges*

| 25 | 21 | 19 | 18 |

1969, Elektra; "I Wanna Be Your Dog"

■ "If you were a teen in the '70s, the following happened: you bought this" "groundbreaking" album "and formed a punk band"; on this "seminal Detroit" disc that "started it all", "Iggy rules", snarling out the frequently covered *I Wanna Be Your Dog*; "'raw' is overused these days, but there's no other way to describe" the "bad production", yet it has "the attitude to transport you to another world."

George Strait, Does Fort Worth Ever Cross Your Mind

| 26 | 27 | 27 | 26 |

1984, MCA; "Does Fort Worth Ever Cross Your Mind"; www.georgestrait.com

■ "Strait up, some of the best country music" around applaud admirers who "like the honky-tonk" and Western swing–revival style Nashville's "reigning king" delivers on this "strong album" from his first decade as a neo-traditionalist newcomer; "his songs paint a picture of a simpler time and place", which may be why so many fans holler "everything George does is gold."

Richard Strauss, *Also Sprach Zarathustra* G

| 26 | 26 | 26 | 24 |

1954, RCA; "Also Sprach Zarathustra"

■ Though "the famous opening fanfare from the movie *2001: A Space Odyssey* is electrifying", "have you ever listened to the second minute?"; play this classical disc beyond the initial "cliché", and the "overwhelming" recording is "sure to grab your attention"; "Reiner was a great Strauss interpreter", and on the "superb reissue" of this "classic from the dawn of the stereo era", you might even be able to discern "the deep organ pipe" from "your furniture buzzing."

Stravinsky, *Petrushka, Le Sacre du Printemps* G

| 26 | 29 | 27 | 24 |

1960, CBS Masterworks; "The Rite of Spring"

■ "Primitive essence" to the "end of the world" – the great Russian "master speaks" of it all, leading the Columbia

Symphony through the "raw vortices of layered classical chaos" in "superb, modern" readings of two of his "chilling, shattering" compositions; "beautiful" and "blindingly cool to this day", Stravinsky's "extraordinarily complex music" is "not just risky but successful" – "you can hear the earth renewing itself in the spring", or see *Fantasia*'s Disney dinosaurs marching in your mind's eye.

Barbra Streisand,   24 | 25 | 24 | 24
Back to Broadway #1
1993, Columbia; "Children Will Listen";
www.barbrastreisand.com
■ "Of all the genres Streisand has tried, she's most at home with wonderful Broadway classics" by composers like Rodgers and Hammerstein, Sondheim and Gershwin; "no one else has the ability to make these songs sound the way the writers anticipated them" better than the "diva playing a diva", with "exquisite vocals" and "unbelievable control" on the follow-up to her first hit show tune album; yet "another Barbra disc to debut at No. 1 on the charts", this one's "on the money."

Barbra Streisand,   28 | 27 | 29 | 27
The Barbra Streisand Album G
1963, Columbia; "Happy Days Are Here Again";
www.barbrastreisand.com
■ "Hear why Streisand became a star" on this "dazzling" Grammy winner, a "stunning debut" released when she was a mere 20 years old; "cute as a button and belting her heart out", the "young Babs" "actually sounds excited about singing" "a mix of exquisite choices" like *Happy Days Are Here Again* and *Cry Me a River*; she's so "fresh" that "classy" arranger Peter Matz found no need to "rely on huge productions to back her up."

Barbra Streisand,   26 | 26 | 27 | 26
The Broadway Album G #1
1985, Columbia; "Somewhere"; www.barbrastreisand.com
■ "When a multiawarded diva like Barbra does a Broadway album, it goes down like buttah"; the Great White Way's "eternal baby" "returns to her roots, and what a great homecoming" it is: "brassy and bold", Babs is "in her element", delivering tunes like *Somewhere* "at the peak of her interpretive skills", "encompassing the wide range of feelings of which she is capable" for a "masterful accomplishment" that will give you "the chills."

Barbra Streisand, Memories   25 | 24 | 26 | 25
1981, Columbia; "Memory"; www.barbrastreisand.com
◪ "Memories are made of this kind of music": "classic", "wonderful" and "just so romantic", sung by "one of the best female vocalists ever"; the "strong" "album bridges the gap between ballads" like *Memory* and "songs that reach out to a younger audience", including her duet with

Donna Summer on *No More Tears*; nevertheless, though the "exalted" diva might be "incapable of making a bad record", this "compilation" released on the heels of a greatest hits smacks of "product for product's sake."

The Strokes, *Is This It*   22 | 20 | 21 | 20 |
2001, RCA; "Last Night"; www.thestrokes.com
A "pop version of the Velvet Underground" with "totally 21st-century lyrics", this debut from the "well-connected", "much-hyped" band "got the dirty" garage "sound down without trying too hard"; with its "tight rhythm section" and "hummable melodies", it's a "toe-tapping good time" that radiates a "great 'I don't give a damn' attitude"; even those on the down-Stroke concede it's "mostly the rehashing of NYC rock of an earlier era, but hey, it's damn fun."

Styx, *The Grand Illusion*   22 | 22 | 23 | 23 |
1977, A&M; "Come Sail Away"; www.styxworld.com
"The keyboards! The synthesizers! The hair!" – "gather round, kids, this is what arena rock used to sound" and look like; the "first of four platinum albums" from the Chicago band, featuring new guitarist/vocalist Tommy Shaw, this "texturally rich", "theatrical" effort "lives up to its grand billing"; but cynics throw styx suggesting this "pompous work" of "bombast" be called *The Grand Delusion.*

Sublime, *Sublime*   25 | 23 | 24 | 22 |
1996, MCA/Gasoline Alley; "Santeria"
The Long Beach trio "had the potential to be one of the biggest acts around" until singer-guitarist Bradley Nowell died of a drug overdose in 1996, but he left behind this "awesome album" of "informed stoner rock" that "deftly combines punk, rap" and ska and embodies "the addictive sound of SoCal life"; for a more sublime experience, "check out *40 Oz. to Freedom*" suggest a few fans.

Sugar, *Copper Blue*   25 | 24 | 24 | 22 |
1992, Rykodisc; "If I Can't Change Your Mind";
www.bobmould.com
After fronting Hüsker Dü, then going solo, "genius" "Bob Mould puts this band together" and "strikes again", "continuing his unbelievable track record of making great music"; a "relentless aural attack of hard-driving power pop", this "spectacular" debut is "gritty at the right points, poignant at others"; a collection of "dense tracks with unforgettable hooks", particularly the "amazing *If I Can't Change Your Mind*", it "must be listened to at the highest volume you can withstand."

DONNA SUMMER,   27 | 23 | 25 | 25 |
THE DANCE COLLECTION
1987, Polygram; "MacArthur Park Suite"
"Dancey, dazzling, decadent and distinctively Donna", this "DJ's dream" of a disc "defines an era", dishing up

"super-extended versions" of all her "hot stuff" from the '70s as it was "played in the clubs at the time"; "for car rides with your girlfriends", partying with your posse and boogeying in front of your bedroom mirror all by your lonesome, it's "essential listening" from the "ultimate diva ripping a fit."

Sunday in the Park with George   25 | 25 | 26 | 24
(Original cast recording) **G**
1984, RCA Victor; "Move On"
■ "You can hear the chemistry" between "intense" Mandy Patinkin and "Bernadette Peters at her expressive best" in Sondheim's "Pulitzer winner"; with a "deeply moving" first half offering "a brilliant glimpse of the world of [painter] Georges Seurat" and an "anticlimactic", "tacked-on" Act Two set in the "modern money-loving art scene", the show itself "seems like it could have been a one-act", but "cutting wordplay" and "fabulous" singing help the album "surpass the actual production."

The Sundays,   24 | 24 | 23 | 23
Reading, Writing and Arithmetic
1990, DGC; "Here's Where the Story Ends"
■ Harriet Wheeler's "angelic voice" "alone is worth the price of admission" to this "dreamy, ethereal" debut; "so soothing, so relaxing", so "beautiful for a rainy day", this "lovely" "jangly guitar pop" platter is "Brit-chick rock at its finest"; yes, it's "as charming as England itself", but that's not where the story ends – some say it's so influential that perhaps "the Cranberries should pay them their royalties."

Supertramp,   23 | 23 | 23 | 24
Breakfast in America **#1**
1979, A&M; "The Logical Song"; www.supertramp.com
◪ A multiplatinum, Grammy-toting "guilty pleasure", this "great sing-along" album was "chock-full of witty, charming, urbane hits", "like *Take the Long Way Home, The Logical Song* and the title track, that propelled" this "super fun" act to "superstar status" ; but a vocal minority tramples on the Tramps, attesting that while it was "staggeringly popular", "fluffy writing with little or no meaning" "sounds pretty tired by now."

The Supremes, *Anthology*   26 | 24 | 24 | 25
1995, Motown; "Someday We'll Be Together"
■ A definitive "Motown collection" by "the only female group to score a dozen No. 1 hits", "this one's for all the Supremes fanatics out there" and then some; it's "hard to imagine the '60s without" the "pure gold sound" of Diana Ross, Mary Wilson and Florence Ballard on "fine", fabulous, "fun pop" chesnuts like *Someday We'll Be Together* and *Stop! In the Name of Love*, and even today, "these girls still rule!"

SWEENEY TODD: THE DEMON BARBER OF FLEET STREET

29 | 29 | 28 | 28

(Original cast recording) ⑤
1979, RCA; "A Little Priest"; www.sondheim.com

■ "You'll eat up" this "deliciously demonic", "darkly humorous", "Grand Guignol" "half opera/half musical" of "cannibalism and revenge" performed by "glowering", "ghoulish" Len Cariou and "daft and dangerous" Angela Lansbury; "since there's little dialogue" in Sondheim's "macabre" "masterpiece", you get "a complete theatrical experience" when you "turn the lights out and listen" to the recording of this "bloody good show."

Matthew Sweet, *Girlfriend*

26 | 25 | 25 | 24

1991, Zoo; "Girlfriend"; www.matthewsweet.com

■ "Fifteen knockout tunes", "killer licks", "classic riffs" from guitarists Richard Lloyd, Robert Quine and Lloyd Cole "and a voice that lives up to his surname" make Sweet's third album a "kick-ass" hunk of "perfectly crafted" R&R; "as raucous as a drunken sorority girl, as soothing as a lullaby to your baby daughter", this "modern masterpiece" pours "every aspect of romance" into "toe-tapping, head-bopping" melodies that "single-handedly ignited the power-pop revival of the 1990s."

Swingers (Soundtrack)

24 | 23 | 26 | 25

1996, Hollywood; "You're Nobody Till Somebody Loves You"

■ "Have a martini", then "slap some polish on" "your spectator shoes and get Lindy Hopping" to "cool, hot, jazzy" joints from "retro-hip" artists like Dean Martin; "a convincing blend of old and new bands", including some "funk", this soundtrack was "key in the revival of swing and lounge", leading the night-owls of LA and beyond to "wanna be vintage"; "oozing sex, smarm and blind ambition", the album "is so money and it doesn't even know it."

System of a Down, *Toxicity* 🔢1

25 | 24 | 25 | 25

1999, American; "Aerials"; www.systemofadown.com

■ "Another breathtaker", this sophomore effort from the SoCal foursome represents just "about the only hope for nü-metal"; "musically revolutionary" on themes and moods "ranging from the politically charged to the sexually depraved to the hauntingly melodic", the System's "chemistry is compelling" – they're "charismatic, tight and goofy enough to pull it all together and make powerful, danceable" hardcore rock.

T

Talking Heads, *Remain in Light*

27 | 27 | 26 | 26

1980, Sire; "Once in a Lifetime"

■ "A creative high point" for "one of the most prolific bands to emerge from the '70s punk scene", this "groundbreaker" may be "the best art-rock album ever"; producer "Brian Eno is all over this one" – think "Euro-funk meets chic New York new wave in a good way" – as "David Byrne's edgy lyrics do a spastic dance" over "a bizarre combination of African polyrhythms, electronica" and guest star "Adrian Belew's screaming guitar"; *Once in a Lifetime* says it all: this "collection is so good it hurts."

Talking Heads, *Speaking in Tongues* 27 | 26 | 26 | 25
1983, Sire; "Burning Down the House"
■ "More accessible than *Remain In Light*", the Heads' "happiest" and highest-charting album "is their crowning pop moment, with all the fire of their earlier work"; "there's not a dud" among the "smart, quirky jams" that come on "like Funkadelic with a nervous twitch"; "can you sit still listening to" this "powerful stuff"? "hell no, as David Byrne's electric energy permeates every song", especially the favorite *Burning Down the House.*

Art Tatum, 27 | 25 | 29 | 23
Tatum Group Masterpieces, Vol. 1
1954, Verve; "Undecided"
■ "God is on this CD", working miracles through the "flowery, flying fingers" of this "true keyboard genius" – "the first time you hear it, it will blow you away", and "you'll barely believe that Tatum was human"; with "ultra-talented musicians" Benny Carter on sax and Louie Bellson on drums backing him up in "astonishly fine" style, the "unrivaled" pianist graces the ivories with "jaw-dropping virtuosity."

JAMES TAYLOR, *GREATEST HITS* 27 | 28 | 26 | 25
1976, Warner Bros.; "Fire and Rain"; www.jamestaylor.com
■ "Like your favorite pair of jeans", this "early stuff" is "always comfy to put on and hang out with", as the "soft-rock" "troubadour for a generation" has "one of the sweetest", "friendliest", "most beguiling" "voices in the world"; his "seemingly simple songs say just what you feel" and "warm you like cognac", so "if this collection doesn't automatically transport you to summer, you're not listening."

James Taylor, *October Road* 24 | 24 | 26 | 25
2002, Sony; "October Road"; www.jamestaylor.com
■ "Welcome back" says fans of the Boston-born singer-songwriter, who is "as mellow as ever" on his 15th studio album, his first in five years; there are clearly elements of "classic James" on songs like *Caroline I See You* and *My Traveling Star,* and his "voice and lyrics are still both soothing and provocative" – the faithful fawn he "can't turn out a bad album" and, in fact, "just keeps getting better."

James Taylor, *Sweet Baby James* 27 | 28 | 26 | 25
1970, Warner Bros.; "Sweet Baby James"; www.jamestaylor.com
■ With its "heart-wrenching", "confessional style" this "folk-rock classic" not only "made JT a household name"

and practically a "patron saint", it "set the standard for sensitive '70s singer-songwriters"; a "great chronicler of his generation" "with an easy voice" that's "far older than his age", he brings acoustic ballads like *Fire and Rain* and *Country Roads* into the arms of "the R&R crowd" – yeah, it's "overplayed", but it's "sweet through and through."

Tears for Fears,   22 | 22 | 22 | 23
Songs from the Big Chair ⬛**1**
1985, Mercury; "Everybody Wants to Rule the World"
■ The "tunes are timeless" and "the musicianship is on a very high plane" on this "nearly forgotten masterpiece of the '80s" by the "melodic duo" of Roland Orzabal and Curt Smith; encompassing "the band's best and biggest hits", it includes their singles "*Everybody Wants to Rule the World* – how prophetic" – and *Shout*, "a wonderful, emotional" work exuding "deep passion."

Susan Tedeschi, *Just Won't Burn*   24 | 22 | 25 | 24
1998, Tone-Cool; "It Hurts So Bad"; www.susantedeschi.com
■ "Where did a petite girl" from a Boston suburb "get that kind of voice and that kind of guitar prowess?" marvel admirers who compare her "throaty", "blazing vocals" and "red-hot blues" style to Janis Joplin and Bonnie Raitt; with her take on such tracks as *It Hurts So Bad* and John Prine's *Angel from Montgomery,* all agree "she plays a mean lead" that "captures the soul" of the genre.

Television, *Marquee Moon*   27 | 25 | 26 | 23
1977, Elektra; "Marquee Moon"
■ "Tell those Strokes fans to listen" to what is "probably one of the most influential rock records": a "sinuous, entrancing and gorgeous" debut – "the finest album of the class of CBGB's 1977" – from the "great American proto-punk" outfit that "embodied the scruffy artiness of New York's" downtown scene; plunge into the "guitar nirvana" of Richard Lloyd and "unsung hero Tom Verlaine" – it's "still enough to make any decent person's eyes cross."

The Temptations, *Greatest Hits*   27 | 27 | 27 | 26
1966, Motown; "My Girl"; www.thetemptations.com
■ "As long as you're not tired of hearing the songs on the radio", this "classic" brings back "wonderful memories" of "riding in the car with mom with *Baby, I Need Your Loving* playing in full bass", "every voice dripping with honey"; "five-part harmonies", "dance moves and looks", the Temps "had it all", including hits like *My Girl*, which "crossed racial barriers during the civil rights era" – "cool, man."

10,000 Maniacs, *In My Tribe*   23 | 24 | 22 | 21
1987, Elektra; "Like the Weather"; www.maniacs.com
■ Serving up "adventure and social consciousness" "from start to finish", this "must-have" marries Natalie Merchant's "dreamy" voice with "perfectly jangly guitars"; on topics

ranging from child abuse to war, the songs are "literate", "meaningful" and "conveyed with such urgency and intimacy" you may want to have the "lyrics in hand to fully appreciate them"; P.S. look for the "original pressing that still includes Cat Steven's *Peace Train*."

They Might Be Giants, *Flood*   25 | 26 | 23 | 24
1990, Elektra; "Birdhouse in Your Soul"; www.tmbg.com
■ "An off-the-wall collection by the masters of the eclectic", the major-label debut of the two Johns, "Brooklyn's ambassadors of love", is a "nonsensical, wacky, insightful" "cavalcade of hilarious snippets"; an "unrivaled mood-lifter" – "how can you be sad listening to *Birdhouse in Your Soul,* a song about a night-light?" – it may be "the most accessible of a series of strange and wonderful albums."

They Might Be Giants, *NO!* 🔢   27 | 28 | 27 | 28
2002, Idlewild/Rounder; "Bed Bed Bed"; www.tmbg.com
■ "Adults without children" "buy this after hearing it on NPR" because it's "one of the few kids' albums that parents can groove to on their own"; though "some tracks require a mature mind for maximum understanding", its "quirky" songs tell tykes "so much about life, with fun questions like 'where do they make balloons'?"; you "won't go crazy when your child wants to listen to it again" say sophisticates who sigh "may we never see another purple dinosaur."

Thievery Corporation,   26 | 23 | 25 | 28
The Mirror Conspiracy
2000, ESL; "Lebanese Blonde"; www.eslmusic.com
■ "Cosmopolitan" conspirators who thought the "trip-hop" trio was their "little secret" better guess again: "spinning Middle Eastern–inspired mixes into incredible spy-techno", "down-tempo beats", "the best thing to come out of DC" "understands the universal language of music, teaching the rest of us to speak it" on a disc that's so "stylish and swank", it's "now de rigueur for W Hotel lobbies", "cocktail parties" and "more individual seductions" "worldwide."

This Is Spinal Tap (Soundtrack)   23 | 26 | 18 | 20
1984, Polydor; "Big Bottom"; www.spinaltap.com
■ Director Rob Reiner's "rockumentary spoof" that "mocks and pays homage to hair metal" with the "over-the-top" story of a '70s band facing its '80s decline spawned this "brilliant send-up" that "could pass for a legit Judas Priest–type" offering; a remastered CD of "the best fake album by a fake band ever" includes two versions of *Christmas With the Devil* but not the film highlight, *Lick My Love Pump.*

Marlo Thomas and Friends,   25 | 25 | 21 | 22
Free to Be . . . You & Me
1972, Arista; "William's Doll"
◪ "Woo-hoo, feminism!" – "one of the faves" of "kids of the '70s'" "touchy-feely" childhoods was Marlo Thomas'

"attention-grabbing", "self-esteem"–boosting soundtrack about loving and knowing yourself; with "the different voices" and songs performed by stars from Diana Ross to Mel Brooks, "it's a definite classic" for "throwback" "sing-along fun", but now that "some of what it preaches has become accepted wisdom", the "sophisticated kids of today" may find it "corny."

Richard & Linda Thompson, Shoot Out the Lights

28 | 29 | 29 | 26

1982, Hannibal; "Wall of Death"

■ "Much has been made of the fact that" vocalist Linda and guitarist-songwriter Richard's last and most "fierce" album was a "portrait of their marriage falling apart", but in the end "it's irrelevant" – what matters is that they "made great art" with this "stirring, emotional album", "so intense and intelligent it hurts"; "voyeuristic and fascinating", with "impassioned lyrics", "dark humor" and "phenomenal" fretwork that "defies description", it's a "masterpiece, any way you cut it."

Richard Thompson, Rumor and Sigh

26 | 27 | 27 | 23

1991, Capitol; "1952 Vincent Black Lightning"

■ "Twisted love songs" are the modus vivendi of this "guitar genius and misanthrope" – a founding member of pioneer UK folk-rock band Fairport Convention and a "brilliant", "underappreciated" "rare bird, with talent to burn"; "there's more to Thompson than just the motorcycle song [*1952 Vincent Black Lightning*] but it's one heck of a song", in fact, "he doesn't disappoint with" this outing, mixing "jaw-dropping" guitar work with "sly lyrics."

Three Dog Night, The Best of Three Dog Night

23 | 22 | 21 | 21

1989, MCA; "Joy to the World"; www.threedognight.com

◨ A "fun flashback", this "catchy, kitschy" "bunch of hits" from the "excellent interpreters of great, unknown material written by Randy Newman, Hoyt Axton, Laura Nyro and Paul Williams" "brings back memories of junior high" and "long car trip" sing-alongs; though bashers bark at ditties like *Joy to the World* ("abysmal bombast"), denouncing this three-part-harmony trio as the "epitome of schlock-rock", one thing's certain: "These Dogs had their day in the '70s."

The Three Tenors, The Three Tenors in Concert

22 | 21 | 23 | 23

1990, Decca; "Nessun Dorma"

◨ "The opera equivalent of the NBA slam-dunk competition" is the "unparalleled collaboration" between these "three fat guys who sing better than most"; the "outstanding" "sound of Luciano Pavarotti and Plàcido Domingo", the "engagement" and "energy" of José Carreras and the "great chemistry" among the trio make this "outing" from "the phenomenon's beginning" the "only" one "to own"; "before they became overly commercial", there was "no denying the excitement."

Titanic (Soundtrack) #1   23 | 22 | 24 | 24
1997, Sony Classical; "My Heart Will Go On"; www.titanicmovie.com

◪ "The Titanic may have sunk, but this blockbuster soundtrack still has steam", most of it coming from the powerhouse lungs of Celine Dion, who "more than defined the film" with *My Heart Will Go On*; the rest of the "haunting", "masterful" work is a "lush, romantic" instrumental score that "creates the feeling of the lumbering ship on its fateful journey" so well that some "cry", "thinking of blue, floating people"; dry cynics say "yuck" – "I wish they'd never found that damn boat."

TLC, CrazySexyCool Ⓖ   25 | 23 | 23 | 25
1994, LaFace; "Creep"; www.cybertlc.com

■ The "chemistry" between these "three very talented ladies" – T-Boz, Chilli and the late Lisa 'Left Eye' Lopes "ripping" the raps – is in full swing on their "refreshing" follow-up of "imaginative", "sing-along" singles like *Creep, Red Light Special* and *Waterfalls* that are fueled by the R&B trio's "fresh" vocals, sassy "attitude", "originality" and hip-hop beats; like the title says, this disc is as "crazy, sexy, cool" as the artists themselves.

Tool, Aenima   27 | 26 | 27 | 27
1996, Volcano; "Aenima"; www.toolband.com

■ A "lyrical apocalypse merged with driving drum tracks and surging guitars", this "modern concept album" shows that "dark doesn't always mean loud" and "metal doesn't mean anti-melody" with "songs that mutate before you"; thanks to the "operatic voice" of Maynard James Keenan and the band's blend of "cerebral words and ingenious musicianship", this "piece of art" may be "the best music for the marriage of heart and mind since Pink Floyd."

Top Gun (Soundtrack) #1   25 | 22 | 23 | 24
1986, Columbia; "Danger Zone"

■ You don't have to be George W. Bush to get to know what it's like to "fly a high-performance jet fighter" just like Tom Cruise; take off with the "sheer joy" of this "pumped-up" soundtrack to the "classic '80s" "action/romance film"; from Kenny Loggins' "kickin'" *Danger Zone* to the "super-sexy" "ballad from Berlin, *Take My Breath Away*", this "great driving" disc "has everything: love, excitement, fun, seriousness" and, yes, the "cheese" that tastes of the era.

Traffic, John Barleycorn Must Die   26 | 25 | 27 | 24
1970, Island; "Glad"

■ "Jazz and rock are successfully united" on a "very eclectic album, ranging from folk ballads to swing jams";

"Steve Winwood, Jim Capaldi and Chris Wood made magic" with "haunting, evocative songs" that "stretched their boundaries and showed what musical chops they had"; "anyone who was there will be brought back to that era with" *Glad* and *Freedom Rider* on an "obvious classic" that's "fun to listen to."

Trainspotting (Soundtrack)　　26 | 22 | 24 | 25
1996, Capitol; "Born Slippy"

■ A "fabulous adrenaline ride", this "mostly halcyon soundtrack to the classic heroin flick" about a crew of Scottish druggies "mixes straight electronica" with Iggy Pop, Lou Reed, "speed and Quaaludes" for a potent hit "of that European feel" that makes "Anglophiles" and audiophiles sink "into the carpet" and "fall in love with modern British rock all over again."

Travis, *The Invisible Band*　　24 | 24 | 24 | 23
2001, Independiente; "Sing"; www.travisonline.com

◪ "Worthy of praise by an American audience" as well as fans across the pond "who adore them", this band writes "serene", "simple yet poignant" songs marked by "amazingly heartfelt lyrics", as on this "shimmering, beautiful album that represents all that's right with Britpop"; touters tut it "may not be as good" as *The Man Who,* their first effort, but it's like "the big daddy to Coldplay", and it "gets better with every listen."

Randy Travis, *Storms of Life*　　27 | 27 | 27 | 25
1986, Warner Bros.; "On the Other Hand"; www.randy-travis.com

■ On his "first and best" album, this "true country" singer stormed Nashville with a "deep baritone" smooth and warm enough to "melt a snowman", sending Travisites into a tailspin with his "touching" tunes "written with feeling"; this "must-have" debut "almost single-handedly reinvigorated" the genre, helping to "bring the traditional back" to C&W and, in the process, "changed the rules for many artists who followed."

T. Rex, *Electric Warrior*　　26 | 22 | 24 | 25
1971, Reprise; "Bang a Gong (Get It On)"

■ Both "irresistible and trashy", "sexy and sultry", this "playful" breakthrough from the English group founded and fronted by the late Marc Bolan, "the guy who invented glam rock", "doesn't take itself too seriously"; "essential listening for any fan of straightforward, electrifying R&R", it includes "songs about cars and girls", like *Jeepster* and, most notably, *Bang a Gong (Get It On)*, their only U.S. hit.

A Tribe Called Quest,　　28 | 28 | 27 | 27
The Low End Theory
1991, Jive; "Scenario"; www.atcq.com

■ "Introducing millions to hip-hop", the "gifted" "non-gangstas" "from Linden Boulevard" "go the distance" with this "funny, fresh and funky" follow-up pulsing with "sharp wordplay and jazzy grooves"; from the "low-key" *Check the Rhime* to the rambunctious *Scenario*, which "led to the breakout of Busta Rhymes", "you end up dancing and educated all at once"; without it, most "posses" "would still be rockin' gold rope chains and velour track suits."

A Tribe Called Quest, *People's* Instinctive Travels and the Paths of Rhythm
27 | 27 | 25 | 26

1990, Jive; "Bonita Applebum"; www.atcq.com
■ "Can they kick it? yes, they can!" – this "harbinger of change" from one of the "pioneer" crews of "take-it-easy" rap delivers "happy, smooth, danceable fun"; "sly humor" steers Q-Tip and Phife's "slammin'" lyrics on joints like the feel-good love song *Bonita Applebaum,* while the "sick set of jazz samples" and "revolutionary" messages still "hold up" today.

Tricky, *Maxinquaye*
27 | 26 | 26 | 28

1995, Island; "Overcome"; www.trickyonline.com
■ If you "can't figure out if you're turned on, terrified, anxious" or "stoned to the bone", you're probably listening to Tricky's "cryptically beautiful" "breakout from Massive Attack"; a "stellar" solo disc of "brooding atmospherics" "capturing reggae, dub, rock, punk, jazz" and electronica, it "was deadly original when it hit the streets"; the rapper's "gravelly vocals" and Martine Topley-Bird's singing "stay with you long after the buzz has worn off" – just "don't quote any of the lyrics to your shrink."

Ike and Tina Turner, *Proud Mary:* The Best of Ike and Tina Turner
24 | 22 | 23 | 23

1991, EMI; "Proud Mary"
◪ Behind the music was the devastating marital abuse that led to the breakup of these "R&B rockers"; yet, the "tragic duo" managed to cut some "masterpieces" together: with "boundless energy", soulful vocals, groovy instrumentation and the "recently problem"-ridden Phil Spector providing "great production", "these beats have stood the test of time"; if the collection is "patchy", classics like *River Deep, Mountain High* and *Proud Mary* are "very nice indeed."

Tina Turner, *Private Dancer*
26 | 24 | 26 | 25

1984, Capitol; "Private Dancer"; www.tina-turner.com
■ "What a comeback from what a woman" – Tina Turner "introduces the legs to a new generation" with this "fabulous" adult spin on her pop-rock 'tude; with "beauty" and "talent to spare", the "red-hot" "lady" is "in rare form" for "lyrical, melodic, hard-driving" songs like the title track and the Grammy-winning *What's Love Got to Do With It,* "making this one of the most celebrated albums of the '80s" as well as the "triumph of a true survivor."

Shania Twain, *Come on Over*   23 | 21 | 23 | 25
1997, Mercury; "From This Moment On";
www.shania-twain.com

☑ "Country queen or pop princess? who cares when the songs are this much fun?" – just "try not to sing along with tantalizing Twain" when you spin this "feel-good" CD that "solidified her stance as an outstanding crossover artist"; perhaps she's "no Patsy", but she exhibits "extraordinary energy", "daring to be sexy" and "rocking the C&W world" with her "chick music" – c'mon, who can resist "the ultimate invitation" she issues in the title track?

Twin Peaks (Soundtrack)   25 | 23 | 25 | 25
1990, Warner Bros.; "Falling"

■ "Haunting" and "unsettling, just like the show itself", this "spooky", "late-night" selection "captures the weirdness and cleverness of David Lynch to a tee" while standing on its "moody, mysterious" own; "atmospheric" instrumentals by the "unique crafter Angelo Badalamenti", with "eerie vocals from Julee Cruise", "play like a dream of a time and place not quite understood"; "don't think of it as a soundtrack" – "think of it as a really trippy album – *really* trippy" – and just "drift with it."

2001: A Space Odyssey   26 | 24 | 26 | 25
(Soundtrack)
1968, MGM; "Also Sprach Zarathustra"

■ "A great CD test for any sound system", this "space-y" selection "will blow you away" as well as your speakers; Gyorgy Ligeti's "elegant" "classical score" "perfectly" "matches" Stanley Kubrick's "futuristic movie", "expressing the uncertainty and mystery of a world in flux"; this "baby-boomer must-have" "brought Strauss [both Johann II and Richard] to the masses", and they'll "never hear *The Blue Danube* the same" again.

U

Uncle Tupelo, *No Depression*   26 | 26 | 24 | 21
1990, Rockville; "Whiskey Bottle"

■ Jeff Tweedy (now of Wilco) and Jay Farrar (who later formed Son Volt) come on "like Hank Williams on speed" and, as a result, "songs about booze and guns have never been" so "beautifully rendered"; a "hybrid of sweet sounds" that "cleverly" blended punk and C&W, this "progenitor" "spawned an entire genre" of alt-country (or "y'all-ternative"); Tupelo touters tsk that "*Anodyne* is the one to get", but there's no denying "it all started here."

Underworld, *Beaucoup Fish*   24 | 22 | 25 | 27
1998, V2; "Moaner"; www.v2music.com/underworld

☑ Settle yourself in for "a thrilling ride through the binary roller coaster" with this "bouncy", "brilliantly produced

techno beauty", Underworld's "most rave-tastic album";
given "Kool Karl's motormouth vocals, Rick Smith's knob-
twiddling" and Darren Emerson's final contribution before
his "solo DJ career", beaucoup fans find it "doesn't dull"
after any amount of listens; still, critical clubbers find it
"less bubbly and drabber than" "their earlier discs."

U2, *ACHTUNG BABY* G #1   27 | 26 | 27 | 27
1991, Island; "One"; www.u2.com

■ "One of three U2 albums that changed rock", this
"crowning achievement" signified their "daring rebirth";
it's "a masterpiece in every way: no filler, no junk, just"
"gorgeously dark soundscapes" that take the "plunge into
electronica" and "brim with the excitement of a better
today"; a "slinky, sexy, angsty" disc that "celebrates the
postmodern age of fragmentation, irony and superficiality",
from the "hyper-danceable *Mysterious Ways* to the "poetic"
One – "this baby's got it all."

U2, *THE JOSHUA TREE* G #1   28 | 28 | 28 | 27
1987, Island; "With or Without You"; www.u2.com

■ "An astonishingly" "magical mix", this diamond-certified
Grammy winner, with its "stark black-and-white cover
photography" showing Bono and the boys "looking like
missionaries", "shifted them from raw, angry Irish boys to
polished pop-rock icons" "at the height of their powers";
"ambition and spirituality combined" to "timeless and
vital" effect on an "incredible guitar-driven piece of art"
from "a band firing on all cylinders, showing the world the
possibilities of faith, hope, love and doubt."

U2, *War*   26 | 26 | 26 | 24
1983, Polygram; "Sunday Bloody Sunday"; www.u2.com

■ An "urgent, anthemic record" that catches the Dubliners
"on the cusp of moving from postpunk wonders to arena
rockers", this "stunner" seething with "passion and
conviction" "dominated the college radio airwaves";
"sure it was strident" and "preachy" but it was also a
"great commentary on Irish troubles" "that meant the
world to you" thanks to songs like "*Sunday Bloody Sunday*
and *New Year's Day*, which captured the zeitgeist of the
Thatcher-Reagan era perfectly."

V

Van Cliburn, *Tchaikovsky: Piano*   27 | 28 | 27 | 25
Concerto No. 1; Rachmaninoff:
Piano Concerto No. 2 G
1958, RCA

◪ "Yes, children, there really was a day when a classical
pianist got a ticker-tape parade in NYC" – learn "why Van
Cliburn was the first American to win the Moscow piano
competition" with this "beautifully produced" "classic"
recorded on the heels of the "drama and delight" of that

"historic" event; the young musician's "talents shine" with "confidence", so while "he never made it" to the level of "Argerich, Gilels and others", that's "not bad for a kid."

LUTHER VANDROSS,   27 | 26 | 27 | 27
THE BEST OF LUTHER VANDROSS
1989, Epic; "A House Is Not a Home"; www.luthervandross.com
■ "Grab the Riunite and dim the lights" because the *Survey*'s top-rated R&B album is laden with "music to swoon by"; "anyone in love should live" for "spine-tingling" "favorites" like *A House Is Not a Home* and *Here and Now* from the "silky voice" of "romance" who "caresses your body and mind" "like a hot bubble bath on a cold evening"; "spell 'smooth' L-U-T-H-E-R" because, "ooh, this man can sing."

Vangelis, *Chariots of Fire* 🔢1   26 | 25 | 26 | 25
1981, Polydor; "Titles"
■ "Before there was Yanni, there was Vangelis", and in 1981, his music took off at a sprint, "bursting into popularity with this soundtrack" to the film about the 1924 British Olympic track-and-fielders; teaming synths and rhythm boxes for "incredible orchestration", the winner scored "a breakthrough for electronica"; whether you're "getting pumped to run" or have "sex", the title theme is a "must for athletes" on the streets and in the sheets.

Van Halen, *1984 (MCMLXXXIV)*   25 | 21 | 27 | 24
1984, Warner Bros.; "Jump"; www.van-halen.com
■ On this "insanely good" "monster" seller, "the last real Van Halen album" with "David Lee Roth, the only VH singer that matters", and "virtuoso" Eddie Van Halen, who "validated shredder guitar rock", "America's best party band" made "awesome R&R" that "filled the void left by Aerosmith while they were in rehab"; a "kick-ass" "classic", it featured the No.1 single *Jump* and "mind-blowing" *Hot for Teacher* that "made us all look at our instructors differently."

Van Halen, *Van Halen*   26 | 22 | 28 | 24
1978, Warner Bros.; "Ain't Talkin' 'Bout Love";
www.van-halen.com
■ "The ultimate in bad-boy rock & roll", this "rowdy, rambunctious" record "started their legacy off with a bang" and "helped get heavy metal out of its plodding stage"; guided by singer David Lee Roth "at his most obnoxiously great", "every song begs you to stand up, scream along with the lyrics, air guitar and bang your head"; *Eruption* elevates Eddie Van Halen to the status of "a god" – "copied by many, surpassed by none, he's an influence upon all."

Sarah Vaughan,   28 | 27 | 28 | 24
Sarah Vaughan With Clifford Brown
1954, EmArcy; "Lullaby of Birdland"
■ "A young Sassy shows off" her "thick and sexy voice" "elevated by the presence of Clifford Brown", "a classic

bop trumpeter who died too young"; *Lullabye of Birdland, April in Paris* and other "vividly interpreted songs" display a "near-perfect merging of minds" for a "sublime" session; "Sarah Vaughan was so smart and Brownie so inventive", "how could it miss?"

Stevie Ray Vaughan & Double Trouble, *Greatest Hits*   **27 | 24 | 29 | 25**
1995, Epic; "Pride and Joy";
www.srvdoubletrouble.com
■ This anthology of "gems" is an "excellent showcase of the talent that was tragically taken away from us in a helicopter crash in 1990": "an absolutely scintillating musician", SRV ("the master of the pentatonic scale") "synthesized numerous influences into a potent attack" with a "scorchin'" "guitar technique that astonished"; "you can hear his mentors in his playing, yet he had his own style" and was "respected by elder statesmen of the blues" and "youngbloods" alike.

Suzanne Vega, *Solitude Standing*   **25 | 27 | 24 | 22**
1987, A&M; "Luka"; www.vega.net
■ With her debut and this "timely, inspirational" follow-up, the "gifted New York City singer-songwriter" who helped "make folk cool" "provided a foundation" for fellow "greats" such as Shawn Colvin and Tracy Chapman; "keeping to her storytelling roots", she "crafted the heartfelt", disturbing *Luka*, a tale of child abuse with "honest", stirring "turns of phrase", along with the "refreshingly original" *Tom's Diner*, "simple melodies that wouldn't leave your head for weeks."

Velvet Underground, *The Velvet Underground and Nico*   **28 | 27 | 25 | 22**
1967, Verve; "Heroin"
■ "As important for what it spawned as for what it is", this "perverse, infectious" debut from "one of the first bands to celebrate the dark side of the human spirit" took a "drug-infused dive into the avant-garde" and became "the blueprint for everyone from The Modern Lovers to R.E.M. to Yo La Tengo"; "a gritty but sonically soothing amalgam of Lou Reed's poetry" ("*Heroin* is as harrowing as it should be"), "John Cale's unique viola and Nico's haunting voice", its "charm is in its rough edges."

Verdi, *Aida*   **26 | 28 | 27 | 26**
1974, EMI; "Celeste Aida"
■ The *Aida* that "Elton John will never match", this "great recording" of "Verdi's masterpiece" – an opera that will "always be a celebrated hymn to freedom and civilization" – is the "crown jewel" among many versions; "what a combo" with the "young Domingo and the mature Caballé" "at their peaks" led by Ricardo Muti, whose conducting is "full of life and fury"; "bring on the elephants!"

Violent Femmes, *Violent Femmes*   25 | 24 | 22 | 21 |
1983, Slash; "Blister in the Sun"; www.vfemmes.com

■ "Quirky, whining perfection", the Femmes' "first and best album" of "punk rock with acoustic guitars" sold over a million copies without significant radio or MTV airplay; "if you're looking for teenage angst, listen no further" – the "recording that made nice kids feel naughty" resonates with the "desperate intensity" of "sexual frustration"; maybe "Gordon Gano can't sing, the performance is marginal, the songs rudimentary" – but thanks to "wads of humor" "it all comes together."

Vivaldi, *The Four Seasons* G   26 | 28 | 26 | 26 |
2000, Sony Classical; "Spring"

◪ Go to "a Swiss mountaintop" "in your mind" with this "enchanting" classical "masterpiece" "expressing man's awe of nature"; just the "tempo" for everything from "jogging" to "relaxation" inside while an "intense storm" blows, it's "an evergreen for renewed enjoyment every listen"; Guiliano Carmignola, Andrea Marcon and the Venice Baroque Orchestra give a "good", if "too breathlessly brilliant" performance of a composition that's "even better than Frankie Valli's group" of the same name.

Andreas Vollenweider, *Down to the Moon* G   24 | 21 | 26 | 24 |
1986, Columbia; "Down to the Moon"

■ "Ah, memories"; you "loved it when you first heard it" back in the New Age '80s, when this disc climbed the charts and made its creator a sensation, while today it's just plain "fun"; Vollenweider amplifies and updates the classical harp, plucking out a "colorful, elative" album that "flows so well that it's impossible to imagine how it could be improved upon."

W

Wagner, *Der Ring des Nibelungen*   28 | 29 | 28 | 27 |
1958, Decca; "Die Walkure"

■ "Eighteen hours of fun, fun, fun" gasp "opera audiophiles" overdosing on this "landmark" version of the "complex, magnificent" *Ring Cycle*, the "pinnacle" of classical epics, available in a hefty 14-CD set; conductor Georg Solti and an "all-star cast" "eclipse other performances", "capturing the music as never before by adding sound effects that Wagner dreamed of"; it's the "next best thing to hearing it live."

Rufus Wainwright, *Poses*   27 | 27 | 25 | 26 |
2001, DreamWorks; "Cigarettes and Chocolate Milk"; www.rufuswainwright.com

■ Folksinger Loudon's "genius son" matches "21st-century production" with "sophisticated" "Cole Porter–esque lyrics" and a "soaring tenor" ("the male Stevie Nicks?") on an "achingly beautiful" sophomore release spilling over with "universal beauty"; with "flamboyance, on-his-sleeve heartbreak", "wry, sensitive lyrics, charm and humanity", it's "the soul pourings of a sickeningly creative mind" and as "addictive as *Cigarettes and Chocolate Milk*."

Tom Waits, *Rain Dogs* 28 | 28 | 26 | 25
1985, Island; "Downtown Train"; www.tomwaits.com
■ In a "rough poetic voice" that's "halfway between innocent croon and bourbon-soaked" "growls", Waits pulls together a "blend of rock, jazz", blues and "macabre cabaret" that's "the epitome of a West Coast guy capturing New York cool"; his "musicianship is phenomenal as he experiments with drums and pianos" (Marc Ribot and Keith Richards "contribute to its greatness"), while his "oddball characters" lure you into the "dark", absurd "land of Tom."

Tom Waits, *Small Change* 27 | 29 | 24 | 24
1976, Asylum; "Tom Traubert's Blues";
www.tomwaits.com
■ This "devastatingly lovely" album offers the "straight-no-chaser, wrong-side-of-the-tracks, sandpaper-voiced Waits" "before he got arty" and experimental; "raw, emotional and powerful", "the unsung troubadour of a Beat generation gone bad" "blows through the songs like a traveling medicine man" ("he really Damons the Runyon"), "each character springing to life" to "become your friend" – so "pour yourself a gin and tonic and let the words envelope you."

Fats Waller, *Ain't Misbehavin'* 26 | 26 | 27 | 23
1995, ASV/Living Era; "Ain't Misbehavin'"
■ Someone's gotta prove that "jazz can be fun", and "no one does it better" than "the original Fat man"; the "king of the stride piano" of the 1930s does his share of misbehavin', serving up "sassy songs" with "memorable tunes and even more memorable lyrics", but "behind the comic facade" lurks his "great musicianship"; in other words, this compilation "has it all", and "anyone who says they love the genre should own it."

Wallflowers, 21 | 22 | 21 | 21
Bringing Down the Horse
1996, Interscope; "One Headlight";
www.wallflowers.com
☑ Frontman Jakob Dylan may be "easier to understand and much better to look at" than Bob, but "you can clearly see" on his band's multiplatinum disc that "he picked up his father's talent"; "touching" tunes, "strong lyrics and catchy beats created promise" for followers who feel it flowers with "passion and power"; but a handful feel it's "unremarkable" and find his songwriting "pales in comparison to his revered" dad's.

War, *War's Greatest Hits*   24 | 23 | 25 | 24
1976, United Artists; "Low Rider"
■ "You may be amazed at how many of these tunes you know and love" concur connoisseurs who consider this "Cali funk" outfit "one of the greatest Afro-Latino groups" to ever record; "there's enough variety here to entertain everyone" and make you "appreciate how good they were", from "classics" such as *Cisco Kid* and *The World is a Ghetto* to "loose grooves" like the "fun *Low Rider.*"

Dionne Warwick, *The Dionne*   26 | 27 | 26 | 27
Warwick Collection: Her All-Time Greatest Hits
1989, Rhino; "Walk On By"
■ "The only way to hear Burt Bacharach and Hal David's masterpieces" is to listen to this "single best overview" of the definitive days of a diva who was "perfectly in sync" with the songs; "only Ms. Warwick could have navigated" the "difficult time signatures and chord progressions" of *I'll Never Fall in Love Again* or *Walk On By* "with such ease"; "super arrangements with terrific string and horn lines" complement Dee's "unique phrasing."

Grover Washington Jr.,   26 | 24 | 28 | 26
Winelight ⑤
1980, Elektra; "Just the Two of Us"; www.protectthedream.com
◪ "Grover made great cool jazz before it became a dirty name", so even if the disc sounds "cheesy" today, it's still "cherished" as an "R&B"-inflected "classic"; Bill Withers' vocals are "comfy as a pair of favorite slippers" on the hit track *Just the Two of Us,* "punctuated by Washington's sexy sax riffs", and the "slick", "soulful" sound throughout makes it a "great mood album" for a "romantic" rendezvous.

The Waterboys,   26 | 26 | 25 | 24
Fisherman's Blues
1988, Chrysalis; "Fisherman's Blues";
www.mikescottwaterboys.com
■ "Like life itself" this "amazing, elegant blend of rock and traditional Irish folk" "offers a full range of emotions that lifts the spirits and tears out the heart"; the "pure poetic beauty, grace" and "drama" of leader Mike Scott's "songs of joy and melancholy" win over respondents who "fall head-over-heels over" a "rollicking title track too infectious to describe" and the "great fiddling" that "makes your heart yearn for the old" Emerald Isle.

Muddy Waters,   28 | 27 | 28 | 23
The Best of Muddy Waters
1958, Chess; "Mannish Boy"; www.muddywaters.com
■ "Despite his Delta roots" this "true innovator" "helped make Chicago's" sound (where he was first recorded by folklorist Alan Lomax in 1947), "becoming the undisputed champion of the electric blues" who was "untouchable in

his prime"; "raw, powerful and serene", "he's a triple-threat performer" with a "nuanced vocal delivery" that "could take a phrase and squeeze out all the feelings that were there", "soulful" guitar playing and "authoritative" songwriting.

Weather Report, *Weather Report* 　25 | 25 | 26 | 25
1971, Columbia; "Orange Lady"
◪ "The weather's always fine when this is playing", say sunny suppliants soaking up "one of the earliest exposures to electronic jazz", a "harbinger of excellence" from the "outstanding" quintet; on their debut, "one-of-a-kind" keyboardist Joe Zawinul, saxman Wayne Shorter and the other "awesome" "talents" "cover the world" in beams of "funk fusion"; not all barometers rise, though: some meteorologists mash the music as plain "bad."

The Weavers,　　　　　　　28 | 26 | 26 | 23
The Weavers at Carnegie Hall
1956, Vanguard; "Goodnight Irene"
■ Cut live in 1955 after the allegedly "rabble-rousing" group had been blacklisted, this "landmark" "return from exile" "marks the birth of the modern folk era", bringing songs like *Kisses Sweeter Than Wine* and Lead Belly's *Goodnight Irene* "into the mainstream"; Pete Seeger and company's "joyful music" is "politically committed" – a "bridge between generations" that "should be required listening" for anyone considering "becoming Republican."

Ween, *Chocolate and Cheese* 　26 | 26 | 26 | 25
1994, Elektra; "Freedom of '76"; www.ween.com
■ Dean and Gene Ween "finally get it right" on this "hilarious and musically outstanding" set that "sprawls all over the genre map with confidence", from Philly soul (*Freedom of '76*) to lounge rock (*Take Me Away*); tastemakers reveal that while it's "unfortunately underrated in their canon" this "'college fave' should be listened to by any adventurous music fan", deeming it "the best album for those new" to the wacky duo.

Weezer, *Weezer* 🔢　　　26 | 25 | 24 | 24
1994, DGC; "Buddy Holly"
■ "The *real* revenge of the nerds", fronted by Rivers Cuomo, "the Fonz of geek rock", brought the "emo sound into the spotlight" and – thanks to "revolutionary videos" for *Undone (The Sweater Song)* and *Buddy Holly* – "increased V-neck sweater sales"; with Ric Ocasek steering production, "Beach Boys harmonies met grunge" on this "super hook-happy" debut (aka *The Blue Album*), a "succulent feast" of post-grunge pop "that never loses its flavor."

Gillian Welch, *Revival* 　27 | 27 | 28 | 28
1996, Almo Sounds; "Orphan Girl"; www.gillianwelch.com
■ What a "revelation" – "*Revival* revived my faith in country music" applaud supporters smitten by the "pared-down,

neo-traditional" "non-spritely side of modern bluegrass" Welch and partner David Rawlings offer on this "hauntingly beautiful", T Bone Burnett–produced debut; capturing the "poignant", "sweet" essence of "original folk music of rural" Appalachia, "the lyrics and music sound like they were written 70 years ago"; no moonshine required – this is "powerful stuff."

JUNIOR WELLS, *HOODOO MAN BLUES* 28 | 25 | 28 | 23
1965, Delmark; "Snatch It Back and Hold It"
■ "Call it what you wanna – I call it genius, baby", and this "phenomenal album by any standard" shows Junior "at his best"; "his sly vocals interspersed with his smoky harp solos" are "raw, rude, nasty", "exciting and scary" – "he has such a presence" – and accompanied by his longtime Chicago-based partner, Buddy Guy, whose "fab guitar playing" "crackles", "all backed by a funky shuffle", "this album has a real after-hours club feel to it."

WEST SIDE STORY 28 | 28 | 27 | 26
(Original cast recording) **G**
1957, Sony; "Tonight"
■ "There aren't points high enough for the 1998 remaster of this great soundtrack", which "vividly" captures the "landmark" from "a duo never duplicated": Leonard Bernstein and Stephen Sondheim; "Shakespeare does get around, even in disguise", in this "modern" *Romeo and Juliet,* a story that's "as relevant now as it was" in the 1500s and 1950s; "amazing vocals" from Carole Lawrence, Larry Kert and "rockin' Chita" Rivera plus a "suite of symphonic dances" make it a "cool" listen "from womb to tomb."

Wham!, *Make It Big* 🔢 21 | 19 | 19 | 20
1984, Columbia; "Careless Whisper"
◪ "Who wants a steady diet of serious all the time", anyway? – "perfect non-thinking" Britpop, this "light, breezy album" is so "catchy" that "even the elevator muzak version makes you hum"; it "may have been fluff", but in the '80s, "everyone was singing" its "lively" songs, mimicking "George Michael's great voice" and having "goofy fun"; there's "no skill in those sound-beat machines" point out snobs who beg "please, shoot me before you go-go."

When Harry Met Sally 25 | 25 | 27 | 24
(Soundtrack) **G** 🔢
1989, Columbia; "It Had to Be You";
www.mgm.com/whenharrymetsally
■ "Harry Connick, Jr.'s voice could make any woman weak-kneed", so "have what she's having" and get a load of the singer/pianist's "big break" that "introduced a new generation" to the "vocal classics from the '50s"; "get a babysitter" and settle in for a "love affair" with the neo-"crooner's" "snazzy" "revamps" of "old standards" – "great dinner music", it's "as good as Sally's sandwich."

Barry White, *All-Time Greatest Hits* 27 | 25 | 26 | 26
1994, Mercury; "Can't Get Enough of Your Love, Babe"
■ "One of the sexiest voices on earth" passed away in
2003, and this "ultimate compilation" is a fitting way to
remember him; with "more soul than all the shoes in your
closet", the "velvety", baritone "king of mood music" lays
down "positive vibes" for "romance" on *Can't Get Enough
of Your Love, Babe* and other "songs any man needs
to swing with the ladies"; "ooohhh, baby" – when the
"master of seduction" sounds his "mandatory booty call",
it's "futile to resist."

The White Stripes, 24 | 23 | 22 | 22
White Blood Cells
2001, V2; "Fell in Love with a Girl"; www.whitestripes.com
☑ "You'll hear a million influences" in the "witty lyrics" and
"bluesy" sounds of Detroit duo Jack and Meg White's
"garage rock redefined" as they "create sonic textures of
surprising depth and beauty" with just electric guitar and
drums; "crammed with hard-crunching punk rock tunes and
sweet little ditties", it's "the most exciting development
since Nirvana", even if a few cynics snipe it's "for people
whose parents don't own Cream albums."

The Who, *Tommy* 28 | 28 | 28 | 27
1969, Decca; "Pinball Wizard"
■ "The whole is twice as great as the sum of the parts" on
this "ultimate rock opera" that "blends pop culture, Freud
and Dickensian melodrama in one kick-ass album"; what
"phenomenal songwriting, musicianship and storytelling" –
"nothing compares to those opening guitar twangs of
Pinball Wizard"; a few feel composer Peter Townshend's
"reach exceeded his grasp" but *Tommy* touters contend
"the fury blazes through" as the band "breaks down barriers
between R&R and musical theater."

THE WHO, *WHO'S NEXT* 29 | 28 | 29 | 27
1971, MCA; "Won't Get Fooled Again"
■ "The apotheosis of adolescent angst mixed with adult
wisdom", this "straight-out-of-the-box classic" created
from "leftovers from an unfinished rock opera" is, "ironically,
Pete Townshend's greatest achievement"; "from the
opening synth of *Baba O'Riley* to the final power chord of
Won't Get Fooled Again", every "epic" tune "stands on its
own", spotlighting "lyrics full of primal urgency" proving
that while they "made their big leap to hard R&R" they
"never lost sight of the fundamentals of pop."

Wilco, *Summerteeth* 26 | 27 | 26 | 26
1999, Reprise; "She's a Jar"; www.wilcoworld.net
■ Jeff Tweedy and company "move further away from Uncle
Tupelo's alt-country sound to create their own legacy"
with "pop arrangements that argue that sometimes feeling
bad feels good"; "simultaneously uplifting and unsettling"

it "lays the groundwork for their masterpiece, *Yankee Hotel Foxtrot*", and "grows better with each listen"; "think *Pet Sounds*–era Beach Boys meets vintage ELO" – "chewy, sweet and gorgeous" with "far-out effects and lyrics as raw and hot as a rug burn."

Wilco, *Yankee Hotel Foxtrot*   28 | 27 | 27 | 28
2002, Nonesuch; "Jesus, Etc."; www.wilcoworld.net
■ Sure, it's "an underdog story", but "forget the backroom record company dealings" and just concentrate on this "landmark of pop"; "thick with musical ideas" that pioneer "new frontiers in sound" and lyrics that deal "with everyday life in an extraordinary manner", it's "essential listening"; by "contorting the alt-country genre" and melding "experimental landscapes with simple folk-styled songs", Wilco conjures up equal parts "rainy-day Pink Floyd" and "the country soul of Gram Parsons."

Hank Williams, *40 Greatest Hits*   28 | 28 | 26 | 23
1978, Polydor; "I'm So Lonesome I Could Cry";
www.hankwilliams.com
■ "First there was Hank, the rest come second" agree honky-tonkin' diehards who say this collection of '40s and '50s recordings from the "granddaddy" of "modern country" (who "died too young" at age 29) "should be handed out in hospitals to every newborn"; when it comes to the "definition of C&W", "he wrote the book" – he "put his heart and soul into his music" and "lived his songs, which is why they sound so good" and "satisfying" and why Williams remains "immortal."

Lucinda Williams, *Lucinda Williams*   27 | 29 | 26 | 25
1988, Rough Trade; "Passionate Kisses";
www.lucindawilliams.com
■ "A critic's darling who actually deserves" the accolades – "does anyone sing better about bad love than Lucinda?" – "country's current brightest light" delivers "incredibly literate" songs in a "beautifully gritty", "tough but vulnerable voice" on "this blues-flavored record"; "moody" and "real", it "evokes human experiences" like "loneliness, despair, desire and hope" to reveal a "writing genius" "like Tennessee Williams'", making it a "must-have for anyone who's known hurt and survival."

Cassandra Wilson, *New Moon Daughter* 🄶   25 | 24 | 27 | 27
1995, Blue Note; "Last Train to Clarksville";
www.cassandrawilson.com
■ Cassandra Wilson takes that "sweet jazz sound" and "turns a pop tune into something haunting" on this "beautiful collision of genres", a "mellow, moody and magnificent masterpiece" by a "distinctive" artist with an "incredible whiskey voice" and "a unique sense of arrangement and interpretation"; as "the melancholy

beauty of *Harvest Moon*" and other tunes "bring tears to your eyes", you too might agree that she could be "the replacement for Billie, Ella and Sarah in our era."

Wings, *Band on the Run* #1   25 24 25 25
1973, Capitol; "Band on the Run"; www.paulmccartney.com
■ Paul McCartney "proves himself a fab instrumentalist" and "songwriter with talent that far surpasses his cute Beatles image" on this "fresh", "fun" and "still listenable" disc that flocks of fans feel is "the only album that comes close to his legacy" with "the lads"; "recorded under duress" in Nigeria, this multiplatinum No. 1 "is an unmitigated" "catchy pleasure" thanks to the title hit, *Helen Wheels* and *Jet,* chart-topping tunes that "make it work incredibly well for parties and long drives."

George Winston, *Autumn*   26 24 27 25
1980, Windham Hill; "Colors/Dance"; www.georgewinston.com
■ "Imagine yourself amidst the swirling leaves and changing colors" of the namesake season, and you'll "get to the heart of what George Winston is about"; the pianist's first season-themed album is a "stellar effort" in "reflective music", with "mood-altering sublime pieces" "forged" for "meditating"; slip it on and "forget about the outside world" – or get "misty eyed" and commune with it, if the view from your window looks anything like "fall in New England."

Johnny Winter, *Johnny Winter*   24 22 27 22
1969, Columbia; "Good Morning Little Schoolgirl";
www.johnnywinter.net
■ "A forgotten gem" showcases the Texas albino playing "excellent electric blues slide guitar" "with rock infusion" and a "number of guests", including brother Edgar on piano and sax, Willie Dixon on bass and Big Walter Horton on harmonica; "they broke the mold" with this "unique performer": "his last name should've been *Hot* not Winter."

Steve Winwood, *Arc of a Diver*   23 22 25 22
1981, Island; "While You See a Chance";
www.stevewinwood. com
■ Traffic's "boy wonder grows up", reemerging on the "blue-eyed soul" vanguard with this "nice album" of soft-rock hits; the "extremely talented" Winwood delivers "interesting lyrics" over funky pop instrumentation he performs primarily himself for an "original sound" on tunes like *When You See a Chance*; "ok, so your kids will hate it, but if you were in college" at the turn of the '80s, this "damn good stuff" "will bring back a flood of memories."

The Wizard of Oz (Soundtrack)   28 28 27 26
1939, MGM; "Over the Rainbow"
■ "Only the Wicked Witch of the West" wouldn't "thrill" to this soundtrack featuring "incredible" "Judy Garland at

her best" leading us down the yellow brick road to "sheer enjoyment"; "we're off to see this movie over and over again" in our minds when we listen to Rhino's 1995 two-volume set of "music and spoken word" that captures the "unbeatable", "heartfelt" Harold Arlen/Yip Harburg score that "is as much a legacy as the film" itself.

STEVIE WONDER, *INNERVISIONS* Ⓖ 29 | 28 | 29 | 28
1973, Tamla; "Living for the City";
www.steviewonder.net
■ In a "creative surge" at his "'70s prime", soul music's ultimate prodigy "perfectly blends the political and the personal", setting a "standard of excellence" for "sheer diversity" with "sweet singing, precision playing" and "beautiful" use of synthesizers supporting "genius" pop songwriting; "the hesitant rhythms of *Too High,* the social commentary of *Living for the City* and the funk exuberance of *Higher Ground*" "flow" together like "liquid gold."

Stevie Wonder, 28 | 28 | 29 | 28
Songs in the Key of Life Ⓖ #1
1976, Tamla; "Sir Duke"; www.steviewonder.net
■ "Pop and soul meld perfectly" on a "sprawling, indulgent" and "utterly brilliant" double "explosion" of "inspiring" songs that "stand as a testament to the hope and dreams of the '70s"; jazz "big guns" Herbie Hancock, George Benson and Eddie 'Bongo' Brown lay down a "stylistic cornucopia" of Latin-tinged grooves for one of the "best writers in the biz" to sing "powerfully" yet "soothingly" about Duke Ellington, "political" issues, "the miracle of birth" and everything else; it'll "blow you away."

Stevie Wonder, *Talking Book* #1 28 | 28 | 29 | 28
1972, Tamla; "Superstition"; www.steviewonder.net
■ "The greatest one-man band" in soul gets help from rock guitarist Jeff Beck, sax man David Sanborn, vocalist Deniece Williams and a host of others on an "exultant" album of "winners", from "pretty ballads" like *You Are the Sunshine of My Life* to "funk-filled" dance tunes like *Superstition* and "message songs" like *Big Brother* "that capture the times and yet are universal"; genre-defying, the disc "evokes Stevie's pure joy and enthusiasm."

Woodstock (Soundtrack) #1 26 | 24 | 26 | 22
1970, Cotillion; "Star Spangled Banner"
■ "A historical document on vinyl" from "the most famous rock concert in the world", this album was "recorded live, with accompanying weather, sound glitches" and warnings about brown acid; "cockeyed, flawed" and "invaluable for no other reason than as a reflection of the times" "when R&R could change the world", the "landmark" "grab bag" contains "some schlock" ("Sha Na Na?!") but also "amazing performances" like Jimi Hendrix's "noisy, drugged-out version of *The Star Spangled Banner.*"

Wu-Tang Clan,   28 | 27 | 26 | 27
Enter the Wu-Tang (36 Chambers)
1993, Loud; "C.R.E.A.M."
■ "Never had a group sounded so hard-core and lyrically skilled at once" as on the debut from the nine Staten Island rhyme-slingers that "turned the hip-hop and musical world on its head" with "mad master" RZA's "raw, dirty", "flawless beats" and old-school, pass-the-mike MC-ing thick with NYC gang "slang" and martial arts mysticism – "it's amazing what hungry rappers can do when provoked."

Tammy Wynette,   26 | 24 | 24 | 24
Stand by Your Man G
1969, Epic; "Stand by Your Man"
■ "This is what C&W is supposed to sound like" insist women and men alike who stand by "Ms. Teardrops" (aka the First Lady of Country Music) and this platinum-selling hit, which they deem her "finest album"; the showpiece title track remains "one of the best vocal performances" of the genre "ever done", wherein this "honky-tonk angel taught us all" just how much "a voice could cry."

X

X, Wild Gift   26 | 27 | 23 | 21
1981, Slash; "White Girl"
■ Exene and John Doe stir up a "heady brew" on this "genuine" "killer" "classic", a "perfect combination of poetry and music, Beat and punk" with a twinge of country twang; "embodying the trash of LA", "the songs are absolute gems", all-in-all a mixture so "great" "no one else has done it again" quite like this.

XTC, Drums and Wires   26 | 26 | 25 | 24
1979, Geffen; "Making Plans for Nigel"
■ When guitarist Dave Gregory joined the "quirky UK" combo, "Andy Partridge and Colin Moulding came up with their best batch" of pop-punk songs and "put it all together" on this "superb", "high-energy, fun" album that packs a "lyrical punch"; "alternately spastic and reflective" with "traces of herky jerky new wave", this "seminal ear candy" "achieves the tight sound that they worked toward" on two prior releases.

Y

Trisha Yearwood, Hearts in Armor   26 | 24 | 27 | 25
1992, MCA; "Walkaway Joe"; www.trishayearwood.com
■ "Abandonment never sounded so glorious" as it does on this Georgia native and frequent Garth collaborator's second album, a hit-filled showcase for her "mellifluous", "pure country voice", underscored by "great backups from Don Henley and Emmylou Harris"; "Yearwood's achy-

breaky album" is "much more quiet" than many she's done and "contains the best selection of ballads" "you can't help but sing along to."

Yes, *Fragile* | 25 | 24 | 28 | 25 |
1972, Atlantic; "Roundabout"; www.yesworld.com
■ On this "classically influenced" "theater-of-the-mind tour de force", this "talented bunch" "boldly ventured where no band had gone before"; they created "the art-rock gold standard", "a new progressive sound" that "seamlessly integrated lush orchestral arrangements with the then-latest, greatest electronic music" and "broke the mold"; from the "ethereal voice of Jon Anderson" to Rick Wakeman's keyboards, Yes-men (and women) insist it's an "aural wonder."

Dwight Yoakam, *Guitars, Cadillacs, Etc., Etc.* | 26 | 26 | 27 | 25 |
1986, Reprise; "Guitars, Cadillacs"; www.dwightyoakam.net
■ "Honky-tonk throwback Yoakam comes out roaring" on his "fun" debut, which not only marked "the beginning of a long, outstanding career of well-performed, well-produced music" but also helped "reawaken the dead country scene"; having lived the LA life, he proves he "can kick it Bakersfield-style" with or without Music City's assistance, while his duet with Maria McKee on *Bury Me* and cover of June Carter's *Ring of Fire* leave loyalists hollering "Nashville be damned", "this album cooks."

Dwight Yoakam, *This Time* | 27 | 27 | 28 | 27 |
1995, Reprise; "Fast as You"; www.dwightyoakam.net
■ "A country star" who "stretches the boundaries while keeping the twang intact", Dwight proves it on this "fabulous compilation of C&W, swing and fun"; while he breathes "new life into the genre" by way of "tight jeans, tight lyrics (loose women)", his "great wailing voice and delivery take me back to the King, as in Hank Williams" – how could he ever "top this one"?

Lester Young, *With the Oscar Peterson Trio* | 26 | 24 | 28 | 24 |
1952, Norgran; "It Takes Two to Tango"
■ "Prez is ably backed by Peterson" and his trio on this "special, inspired album" that finds "two masters still in their prime", despite the saxophonist's failing health; Young blows "such a soft tone", and "Oscar sure can tickle the ivories", and for no other reason, the disc is "worth it for Lester's only recorded vocal" on the "very cool" and bawdy *It Takes Two to Tango.*

Neil Young, *After the Gold Rush* | 27 | 28 | 26 | 24 |
1970, Reprise; "After the Gold Rush"; www.neilyoung.com
■ The former Buffalo Springfield singer-guitarist was "not fully mature, like Athena from Zeus' head", when he

released his third solo effort, a "folk-rock masterpiece" of "biting ennui" that "still has the sound of hope" and "sets the tone for greatness to come"; with each song "a tight, well-written gem", "from the introspective *I Believe in You* to the incendiary *Southern Man*, "neither time nor repeated listenings have dulled its impact."

Neil Young, *Harvest* #1   27 | 27 | 26 | 24

1972, Reprise; "Heart of Gold"; www.neilyoung.com
■ "The solitary troubadour is at his most elegiac" on his only No. 1 album, and it includes his only No. 1 hit, *Heart of Gold*, as well as "*The Needle and the Damage Done,* one of the most poignant songs about drug addiction ever recorded"; along with David Crosby, Linda Ronstadt, Stephen Stills, James Taylor and the London Symphony Orchestra, Neil's "haunting voice rocks" this "sublime" collection of "country-tinged rock" that "feels like a visit from an old friend every time" you put it on.

Neil Young & Crazy Horse,   28 | 27 | 27 | 24
Rust Never Sleeps

1979, Reprise; "Powderfinger"; www.neilyoung.com
■ "Effectively straddling" different styles – "the acoustic first side featuring Nicolette Larson" "complements the vitriol of the electric side" with Crazy Horse – this "tribute to the rowdy punk scene of the late '70s" "gave Neil back his street cred" as America's leading "iconoclast folk-rocker"; "some of the lyrics are pure haiku" ('it's better to burn out than it is to rust') that became a "philosophy and a rallying cry."

Neil Young, *Tonight's the Night*   26 | 27 | 25 | 23

1975, Reprise; "Tonight's the Night"; www.neilyoung.com
■ A "harrowing" "masterpiece of dissolution and despair", Young's "dark, dirty and incredibly powerful" musical eulogy for roadie Bruce Berry after the latter's fatal heroin overdose may be "the most depressing record ever made"; "woozy and stumbling, full of pain and hurt", this is the "sound of a world not making sense"; "a catharsis for Neil and his band", it remains that "rare thing in rock: an honest attempt to deal with death."

Z

Frank Zappa, *Apostrophe*   27 | 27 | 28 | 26

1974, Discreet; "Apostrophe"; www.frankzappa.com
☑ "The most commercial album from this "scrambled genius" may not be his zenith, but "his mediocre is better than many others' best"; revealing his "avant-garde leanings" and "compositional competence", the "most underrated guitarist ever" "retains his art-rock integrity" while "deftly joining the absurd" with "kick-ass riffs" for a "witty" workout; it's "slightly more accessible", but like all of his "intellectual music", it's an "acquired taste."

Warren Zevon, *Excitable Boy*   26 | 28 | 25 | 24
1978, Asylum; "Werewolves of London";
www.warrenzevon.com

■ "Forget the Eagles – the Excitable Boy, Mr. Bad Example himself, takes the cake and rubs it all over his chest" on this "acidic" release that represents "LA with a bitter twist" à la "Lou Reed West"; a "wildly creative work" rife with werewolves, headless gunmen and wanna-be mercenaries, delivered with "sardonic wit and a rough snarl", it "brought him to the forefront of the California singer-songwriter class" and nearly "catapulted him to stardom."

The Zombies, *Odessey and Oracle*   28 | 26 | 26 | 26
1968, Rhino; "Time of the Season"

■ "An absolute gem", this "iconic representation of London psychedelia", released in the U.S. after the band broke up, practically "gives *Sgt. Pepper* a run for its money" thanks to "gorgeous arrangements" and singer Colin Blunstone's "exceedingly beautiful voice"; while "it's all about" the "huge hit *Time of the Season*" for some, the Zombified declare the entire "lost classic" is "as good as anything by The Beatles, The Beach Boys, The Who, The Stones or The Kinks", and with "each passing year, its legend grows."

ZZ Top, *Eliminator*   24 | 20 | 24 | 24
1983, Warner Bros.; "Legs"; www.zztop.com

■ "The hard-driving" "bearded ones" "provided a much-needed shot of fun in the early '80s", "spicing up their blues-rock" with actual "lyrics and music, not atonal noise"; a diamond-certified "true road-trip classic", this "slick Texas boogie-woogie" "gets your blood moving", laying bare the band's "enormous pop ambition" with such radio and MTV hits as "*Gimme All Your Lovin'*", "*Sharp Dressed Man*" and "*Legs*" – "how can you sit still?"

Indexes

Indexes list the best of many within each category.

GENRES

Blues

Mose Allison, *Your Mind Is on Vacation*
Mike Bloomfield, *Super Session*
Clarence "Gatemouth" Brown, *Texas Swing*
Buckwheat Zydeco, *On a Night Like This*
Paul Butterfield, *East-West*
Tracy Chapman, *New Beginning*
Ray Charles, *Anthology*
Albert Collins, *Ice Pickin'*
Albert Collins, Johnny Copeland and Robert Cray, *Showdown!*
Robert Cray, *Strong Persuader*
Buddy Guy, *The Very Best*
John Lee Hooker, *Ultimate Collection*
Howlin' Wolf, *Moanin' in the Moonlight*
Elmore James, *The Sky Is Crying*
Etta James, *The Essential*
Robert Johnson, *Complete Recordings*
Keb' Mo', *Keb' Mo'*
Albert King, *Ultimate Collection*
B.B. King, *Live at the Regal*
B.B. King and Eric Clapton, *Riding with the King*
Taj Mahal/Ry Cooder, *Rising Sons*
John Mayall, *Bluesbreakers*
Susan Tedeschi, *Just Won't Burn*
Stevie Ray Vaughan, *Greatest Hits*
Muddy Waters, *The Best*
Junior Wells, *Hoodoo Man Blues*
Johnny Winter, *Johnny Winter*

Classical

Adams, *The Chairman Dances*
Anonymous 4, *An English Ladymass*
Apocalypse Now
Martha Argerich, *Début Recital*
J.S. Bach, *Brandenburg Concertos*
J.S. Bach, *Mass in B minor*
J.S. Bach, *Six Unaccomp. Cello Suites*
J.S. Bach, *State of Wonder*
Barber, *Adagio for Strings; Violin Concerto*
Bartók, *Concerto for Orchestra*
Bartók, *6 String Quartets*
Beethoven, *Piano Concertos 3 & 5*
Beethoven, *Piano Sonatas 8, 13 & 14*
Beethoven, *Symphonies 5 & 7*
Beethoven, *Symphony No. 9*
Beethoven, *Violin Sonatas 9 & 5*
Berlioz, *Symphonie Fantastique*
Bizet, *Carmen Suites; L'Arlesienne Suites*

Brahms, *Symphony No. 4*
Sarah Brightman, *Time to Say Goodbye*
Maria Callas, *The Very Best*
Chopin, *Nocturnes*
Aaron Copland, *Appalachian Spring*
Gershwin, *Rhapsody in Blue*
Philip Glass, *Glassworks*
Górecki, *Symphony No. 3*
Handel, *Messiah*
Handel, *Water Music*
Jascha Heifetz, *Beethoven & Mendelssohn: Violin Concertos*
Jascha Heifetz, *The Supreme*
Holst, *The Planets*
Vladimir Horowitz, *in Moscow*
Mahler, *Symphony No. 5*
Yo-Yo Ma, etc., *Appalachia Waltz*
Mozart, *Don Giovanni*
Mozart, *Piano Concertos 19-23*
Mozart, *Requiem*
Mozart, *Symphonies 35–41*
Mussorgsky, *Pictures at an Exhibition*
Orff, *Carmina Burana*
Puccini, *La Bohème*
Puccini, *Tosca*
Rachmaninoff, *Concerto No. 2*
Ravel, *Boléro*
Rimsky-Korsakov, *Scheherazade*
Mstislav Rostropovich, *Dvorák; Tchaikovsky*
Satie, *Gymnopédies, Gnossiennes*
Smetana, *Má Vlast*
Richard Strauss, *Also Sprach Zarathustra*
Stravinsky, *Petrushka*
The Three Tenors, *The Three Tenors in Concert*
2001: A Space Odyssey
Van Cliburn, *Tchaikovsky; Rachmaninoff*
Verdi, *Aida*
Vivaldi, *The Four Seasons*
Wagner, *Der Ring des Nibelungen*

Country & Western

Alabama, *Mountain Music*
Clint Black, *Killin' Time*
Brooks & Dunn, *Brand New Man*
Garth Brooks, *No Fences*
Garth Brooks, *Ropin' the Wind*
Glen Campbell, *Wichita Lineman*
Mary Chapin Carpenter, *Shooting Straight in the Dark*
Johnny Cash, *American Recordings*
Johnny Cash, *At Folsom Prison*
Johnny Cash, *The Essential*

Rosanne Cash, *Interiors*
Patsy Cline, *Greatest Hits*
Charlie Daniels Band, *Fire on the Mountain*
Iris DeMent, *My Life*
Dixie Chicks, *Home*
Dixie Chicks, *Wide Open Spaces*
Bob Dylan, *Nashville Skyline*
Steve Earle, *Guitar Town*
Vince Gill, *When I Call Your Name*
Nanci Griffith, *Flyer*
Emmylou Harris, *Pieces of the Sky*
Emmylou Harris, *Wrecking Ball*
Faith Hill, *Breathe*
Alan Jackson, *A Lot About Livin'*
Waylon Jennings, *Honky Tonk Heroes*
George Jones, *The Essential*
Wynonna Judd, *Wynonna*
The Judds, *Greatest Hits*
Alison Krauss, *Now That I've Found You*
Kris Kristofferson, *Kristofferson*
k.d. lang, *Shadowland*
Lyle Lovett, *Lyle Lovett*
Shelby Lynne, *I Am Shelby Lynne*
Martina McBride, *The Way That I Am*
Tim McGraw, *Not a Moment Too Soon*
Jo Dee Messina, *I'm Alright*
Willie Nelson, *Red Headed Stranger*
Willie Nelson, *Stardust*
The Nitty Gritty Dirt Band, *Will the Circle Be Unbroken*
O Brother, Where Art Thou?
Gram Parsons, *Grievous Angel*
Dolly Parton, *Coat of Many Colors*
Dolly Parton, Linda Ronstadt & Emmylou Harris, *Trio*
LeAnn Rimes, *Blue*
Kenny Rogers, *The Gambler*
George Strait, *Does Fort Worth Ever Cross Your Mind*
Randy Travis, *Storms of Life*
Shania Twain, *Come on Over*
Gillian Welch, *Revival*
Wilco, *Summerteeth*
Wilco, *Yankee Hotel Foxtrot*
Hank Williams, *40 Greatest Hits*
Lucinda Williams, *Lucinda Williams*
Tammy Wynette, *Stand by Your Man*
Trisha Yearwood, *Hearts in Armor*
Dwight Yoakam, *Guitars, Cadillacs*
Dwight Yoakam, *This Time*

Dance

ABBA, *Gold/Greatest Hits*
AWB (Average White Band), *AWB*
Basement Jaxx, *Rooty*
The Bee Gees, *Children of the World*

The Bee Gees, *Saturday Night Fever*
Björk, *Debut*
The Chemical Brothers, *Dig Your Own Hole*
Chic, *Dance Dance Dance*
The Crystal Method, *Vegas*
Deee-Lite, *World Clique*
En Vogue, *Funky Divas*
Erasure, *Erasure Pop!*
Everything But the Girl, *Walking Wounded*
Fatboy Slim, *You've Come a Long Way, Baby*
Flashdance
Frankie Goes to Hollywood, *Welcome to the Pleasuredome*
INXS, *Kick*
Michael Jackson, *Bad*
Michael Jackson, *Off the Wall*
Michael Jackson, *Thriller*
KC/Sunshine Band, *The Best*
Madonna, *Immaculate Collection*
Madonna, *Like a Virgin*
Madonna, *Ray of Light*
Kylie Minogue, *Fever*
New Order, *Substance*
A Night at Studio 54
Paul Oakenfold, *Tranceport*
Olive, *Extra Virgin*
Parliament, *Mothership Connection*
Pet Shop Boys, *Very*
Donna Summer, *Dance Collection*

Electronica

Air, *Moon Safari*
Aphex Twin, *Selected Ambient Works*
Björk, *Selmasongs*
The Chemical Brothers, *Dig Your Own Hole*
The Crystal Method, *Vegas*
Daft Punk, *Discovery*
Daft Punk, *Homework*
Depeche Mode, *Music for the Masses*
Depeche Mode, *Violator*
Sasha & John Digweed, *Northern Exposure 2: East Coast Edition*
DJ Shadow, *Endtroducing . . .*
Enigma, *MCMXC A.D.*
Everything But the Girl, *Walking Wounded*
Fatboy Slim, *You've Come a Long Way, Baby*
Jean-Michel Jarre, *Oxygene*
Joy Division, *Closer*
KLF, *The White Room*
Kraftwerk, *Computer World*
Kraftwerk, *Trans-Europe Express*
Kruder & Dorfmeister, *K & D Sessions*

Mos Def, *Black on Both Sides*
Mos Def and Talib Kweli, *Black Star*
Nas, *Illmatic*
Notorious B.I.G., *Life After Death*
Notorious B.I.G., *Ready to Die*
N.W.A, *Straight Outta Compton*
Outkast, *Aquemini*
Outkast, *Stankonia*
Pharcyde, *Bizarre Ride*
Public Enemy, *Fear of a Black Planet*
Public Enemy, *It Takes a Nation*
The Roots, *Phrenology*
Run-D.M.C., *Raising Hell*
Tupac Shakur, *All Eyez on Me*
Tupac Shakur, *Greatest Hits*
Slick Rick, *The Great Adventures*
Snoop Dogg, *Doggystyle*
A Tribe Called Quest, *Low End Theory*
A Tribe Called Quest, *People's Instinctive Travels*
Wu-Tang Clan, *Enter the Wu-Tang*

Jazz

Cannonball Adderley, *Somethin' Else*
Mose Allison, *Your Mind Is on Vacation*
Herb Alpert/Tijuana Brass, *Whipped Cream and Other Delights*
Louis Armstrong, *Hello, Dolly!*
Chet Baker, *Chet Baker Sings*
Basie Count, *The Complete Atomic Basie*
Jeff Beck, *Blow by Blow*
George Benson, *Breezin'*
Art Blakey, *Moanin'*
Clifford Brown, *Memorial Album*
Dave Brubeck, *Time Out*
June Christy, *Something Cool*
Stanley Clarke, *School Days*
Rosemary Clooney, *Sings the Music of Cole Porter*
Natalie Cole, *Unforgettable*
Nat King Cole, *Nat King Cole Story*
Nat King Cole and George Shearing, *Nat King Cole Sings/George Shearing Plays*
Ornette Coleman, *Shape of Jazz to Come*
John Coltrane, *Blue Train*
John Coltrane, *A Love Supreme*
Chick Corea, *Return to Forever*
Miles Davis, *Bitches Brew*
Miles Davis, *Kind of Blue*
Miles Davis, *Miles Ahead*
Miles Davis with Gil Evans, *Porgy and Bess*
Miles Davis with Gil Evans, *Sketches of Spain*
Blossom Dearie, *Blossom Dearie*

Eric Dolphy, *Out to Lunch!*
Duke Ellington with John Coltrane, *Duke Ellington & John Coltrane*
Bill Evans, *Waltz for Debby*
Ella Fitzgerald, *Best of the Songbooks*
Ella Fitzgerald, *Complete Ella in Berlin*
Erroll Garner, *Concert by the Sea*
Stan Getz, *Getz/Gilberto*
Dizzy Gillespie, *At Newport*
Benny Goodman, *B.G. in Hi-Fi*
Dexter Gordon, *Go!*
Vince Guaraldi, *A Boy Named Charlie Brown*
Herbie Hancock, *Head Hunters*
Herbie Hancock, *Maiden Voyage*
Billie Holiday, *Lady Sings the Blues*
Lena Horne, *An Evening with*
Ahmad Jamal, *At the Pershing*
Keith Jarrett, *The Köln Concert*
Antonio Carlos Jobim, *Wave*
Norah Jones, *Come Away with Me*
Stan Kenton, *Kenton in Hi-Fi*
Diana Krall, *Live in Paris*
Diana Krall, *The Look of Love*
Lambert, Hendricks & Ross, *Sing a Song of Basie*
Peggy Lee, *Spotlight on Peggy Lee*
Chuck Mangione, *Feels So Good*
Les McCann/Eddie Harris, *Swiss Movement*
Sergio Mendes, *Fool on the Hill*
Pat Metheny, *Pat Metheny Group*
Charles Mingus, *Mingus Ah Um*
Joni Mitchell, *Hejira*
Thelonious Monk, *Monk's Dream*
Wes Montgomery, *Incredible Jazz Guitar of Wes Montgomery*
Lee Morgan, *The Sidewinder*
Oliver Nelson, *Blues/Abstract Truth*
Charlie Parker, *Jazz at Massey Hall*
Charlie Parker, *Yardbird Suite*
Oscar Peterson, *On the Town*
Sonny Rollins, *Saxophone Colossus*
Diane Schuur, *Diane Schuur & The Count Basie Orchestra*
Wayne Shorter, *Speak No Evil*
Horace Silver, *Song for My Father*
Nina Simone, *Wild Is the Wind*
The Sting
Art Tatum, *Tatum Group Masterpieces, Vol. 1*
Sarah Vaughan, *Sarah Vaughan With Clifford Brown*
Fats Waller, *Ain't Misbehavin'*
Grover Washington Jr., *Winelight*
Weather Report, *Weather Report*
When Harry Met Sally

Cassandra Wilson, *New Moon Daughter*
Lester Young, *With the Oscar Peterson Trio*

Kids

Annie
Beauty and the Beast
Best of Schoolhouse Rock
Jerry Garcia/David Grisman, *Not for Kids Only*
Carole King, *Really Rosie*
The Lion King
The Little Mermaid
Mary Poppins
Muppet Movie
Raffi, *Baby Beluga*
Sesame Street, *Platinum*
They Might Be Giants, *NO!*
Marlo Thomas and Friends, *Free to Be . . . You & Me*

Lounge

Air, *Moon Safari*
Herb Alpert/Tijuana Brass, *Whipped Cream and Other Delights*
Burt Bacharach, *Greatest Hits*
Tony Bennett, *Playin' With My Friends*
The Good, the Bad and the Ugly
Tom Jones, *Tom Jones' Greatest Hits*
Dean Martin, *Capitol Collectors*
Sergio Mendes, *Fool on the Hill*
St. Germain, *Tourist*
Swingers
Thievery Corporation, *The Mirror Conspiracy*

Musicals

Ain't Misbehavin'
A Little Night Music
Annie
Annie Get Your Gun
Anything Goes
Candide
A Chorus Line
Company
Crazy for You
Damn Yankees
Dreamgirls
Evita
Fiddler on the Roof
Follies in Concert
Godspell
Guys and Dolls
Gypsy
Hair
Hairspray
Jesus Christ Superstar
Kiss Me, Kate
Les Misérables

Little Shop of Horrors
Mame
Mamma Mia!
My Fair Lady
The Phantom of the Opera
Rent
Show Boat
Side by Side by Sondheim
South Pacific
Sunday in the Park with George
Sweeney Todd
West Side Story

New Age

Deep Forest, *Deep Forest*
Enigma, *MCMXC A.D.*
Enya, *Watermark*
Philip Glass, *Glassworks*
Jean-Michel Jarre, *Oxygene*
Kitaro, *Silk Road, Vol. 1*
Leo Kottke, *6- and 12-String Guitar*
Koyaanisqatsi
Ottmar Liebert, *Nouveau Flamenco*
Ray Lynch, *Deep Breakfast*
Mannheim Steamroller, *Fresh Aire IV*
Loreena McKennitt, *Book of Secrets*
Vangelis, *Chariots of Fire*
Andreas Vollenweider, *Down to the Moon*
George Winston, *Autumn*

Pop Vocals, Contemporary

ABBA, *Gold/Greatest Hits*
Marc Anthony, *Marc Anthony*
The Association, *Greatest Hits*
The Bee Gees, *Children of the World*
Toni Braxton, *Secrets*
The Carpenters, *The Singles*
Phil Collins, *No Jacket Required*
Crowded House, *Crowded House*
Terence Trent D'Arby, *Introducing*
Neil Diamond, *The Jazz Singer*
Dido, *No Angel*
Celine Dion, *Let's Talk About Love*
Duran Duran, *Duran Duran*
Duran Duran, *Rio*
Gloria Estefan, *Greatest Hits*
The 5th Dimension, *Greatest Hits on Earth*
Roberta Flack, *Softly With These Songs*
Macy Gray, *On How Life Is*
Hall & Oates, *Rock 'n' Soul, Part 1*
Whitney Houston, *The Bodyguard*
Whitney Houston, *Whitney Houston*
Chris Isaak, *Heart Shaped World*
Janet Jackson, *janet.*
Janet Jackson, *Janet Jackson's Rhythm Nation 1814*
Michael Jackson, *Bad*
Michael Jackson, *Off the Wall*

Michael Jackson, *Thriller*
Billy Joel, *The Stranger*
Norah Jones, *Come Away with Me*
Alicia Keys, *Songs in A Minor*
Carole King, *Tapestry*
Cyndi Lauper, *She's So Unusual*
Annie Lennox, *Diva*
Madonna, *Immaculate Collection*
Madonna, *Like a Virgin*
Madonna, *Ray of Light*
Barry Manilow, *Greatest Hits*
John Mayer, *Room for Squares*
George Michael, *Faith*
Stevie Nicks, *Bella Donna*
Harry Nilsson, *Nilsson Schmilsson*
Laura Nyro, *Eli and the Thirteenth Confession*
Sinéad O'Connor, *I Do Not Want What I Haven't Got*
P!nk, *M!ssundaztood*
Lionel Richie, *Can't Slow Down*
Linda Ronstadt, *Heart Like a Wheel*
Sade, *Diamond Life*
Boz Scaggs, *Silk Degrees*
Seal, *Seal*
Dusty Springfield, *Dusty in Memphis*
Sting, *The Dream of the Blue Turtles*
Sting, *Ten Summoner's Tales*
Tina Turner, *Private Dancer*
Wham!, *Make It Big*
Steve Winwood, *Arc of a Diver*
Stevie Wonder, *Innervisions*
Stevie Wonder, *Songs/Key of Life*
Stevie Wonder, *Talking Book*

Pop Vocals, Traditional

Paul Anka, *Paul Anka Sings*
Burt Bacharach, *Greatest Hits*
Harry Belafonte, *Calypso*
Harry Belafonte and Lena Horne, *Porgy and Bess*
Tony Bennett, *I Left My Heart in San Francisco*
Tony Bennett, *Playin' With My Friends*
Sarah Brightman, *Time to Say Goodbye*
Rosemary Clooney, *Sings the Music of Cole Porter*
Natalie Cole, *Unforgettable*
Nat King Cole, *Nat King Cole Story*
Bing Crosby, *A Merry Christmas with Bing Crosby and The Andrews Sisters*
Linda Eder, *It's No Secret Anymore*
Ella Fitzgerald, *Best of the Songbooks*
Ella Fitzgerald, *Complete Ella in Berlin*
Judy Garland, *Judy at Carnegie Hall*

Tom Jones, *Tom Jones' Greatest Hits*
Diana Krall, *Live in Paris*
Diana Krall, *The Look of Love*
k.d. lang, *Ingenue*
Peggy Lee, *Spotlight on Peggy Lee*
Manhattan Transfer, *The Best*
Dean Martin, *Capitol Collectors*
Johnny Mathis, *Johnny's Greatest*
Bette Midler, *Beaches*
Liza Minnelli, *Liza with a "Z"*
Anne Murray, *Greatest Hits*
Mandy Patinkin, *Mandy Patinkin*
Edith Piaf, *La Vie En Rose*
Louis Prima, *Zooma Zooma*
Frank Sinatra, *Duets*
Frank Sinatra, *In the Wee Small Hours*
Frank Sinatra, *Only the Lonely*
Frank Sinatra, *Sinatra Reprise*
Frank Sinatra, *Songs for Swingin' Lovers*
Barbra Streisand, *Back to B'way*
Barbra Streisand, *The Barbra Streisand Album*
Barbra Streisand, *The Broadway Album*
Barbra Streisand, *Memories*
Sarah Vaughan, *Sarah Vaughan With Clifford Brown*
Dionne Warwick, *The Dionne Warwick Collection*

R&B

Boyz II Men, *Boyz II Men, II*
Aaliyah, *Aaliyah*
Erykah Badu, *Baduizm*
Anita Baker, *Rapture*
Mary J. Blige, *My Life*
Mary J. Blige, *No More Drama*
Mary J. Blige, *What's the 411?*
Boyz II Men, *Cooleyhighharmony*
Toni Braxton, *Secrets*
D'Angelo, *Brown Sugar*
D'Angelo, *Voodoo*
Terence Trent D'Arby, *Introducing*
Earth, Wind & Fire, *That's the Way of the World*
En Vogue, *Born to Sing*
En Vogue, *Funky Divas*
Macy Gray, *On How Life Is*
Lauryn Hill, *The Miseducation*
Whitney Houston, *Whitney Houston*
India.Arie, *Voyage to India*
Janet Jackson, *janet.*
Janet Jackson, *Janet Jackson's Rhythm Nation 1814*
Alicia Keys, *Songs in A Minor*
Little Richard, *The Essential*
Maxwell, *Urban Hang Suite*
Brian McKnight, *Anytime*

Genre Index

Brian McKnight, *Back at One*
The Pointer Sisters, *Break Out*
Prince, *1999*
Prince, *Sign 'O' the Times*
Lionel Richie, *Can't Slow Down*
Jill Scott, *Who Is Jill Scott?*
The Temptations, *Greatest Hits*
TLC, *CrazySexyCool*
Luther Vandross, *The Best*
Barry White, *All-Time Greatest Hits*

Reggae

Burning Spear, *Marcus Garvey*
Jimmy Cliff, *The Harder They Come*
Bob Marley and the Wailers, *Burnin'*
Bob Marley and the Wailers, *Legend*

Rock

AC/DC, *Back in Black*
AC/DC, *Highway to Hell*
Ryan Adams, *Gold*
Aerosmith, *Pump*
Aerosmith, *Toys in the Attic*
Alice in Chains, *Dirt*
The Allman Brothers, *Eat a Peach*
America, *History*
American Graffiti
Bad Brains, *I Against I*
Bad Company, *Bad Company*
The Band, *The Band*
Barenaked Ladies, *Stunt*
Bauhaus, *Mask*
The Beach Boys, *Pet Sounds*
The Beatles, *Abbey Road*
The Beatles, *The Beatles 1962-1966*
The Beatles, *Revolver*
The Beatles, *Rubber Soul*
The Beatles, *Sgt. Pepper*
The Beatles, *The White Album*
Beck, *Odelay*
Jeff Beck, *Blow by Blow*
Belle & Sebastian, *If You're Feeling Sinister*
Pat Benatar, *Crimes of Passion*
Ben Folds Five, *Ben Folds Five*
Chuck Berry, *The Great Twenty-Eight*
The B-52's, *The B-52's*
Big Brother and the Holding Company, *Cheap Thrills*
Big Star, *Sister Lovers/Third*
Björk, *Debut*
Black Flag, *Damaged*
Black Sabbath, *Paranoid*
Blondie, *Parallel Lines*
Blood, Sweat and Tears, *Blood, Sweat and Tears*
Bon Jovi, *New Jersey*
Bon Jovi, *Slippery When Wet*
Boston, *Boston*
David Bowie, *Changesbowie*

David Bowie, *Heroes*
David Bowie, *Station to Station*
David Bowie, *Ziggy Stardust*
Billy Bragg & Wilco, *Mermaid Ave.*
The Breakfast Club
Tim Buckley, *Happy Sad*
Buckwheat Zydeco, *On a Night Like This*
Buffalo Springfield, *Buffalo Springfield Again*
Kate Bush, *Hounds of Love*
Buzzcocks, *Singles Going Steady*
The Byrds, *Fifth Dimension*
Captain Beefheart, *Safe as Milk*
The Cars, *The Cars*
Nick Cave/Bad Seeds, *From Her to Eternity*
Cheap Trick, *Live at Budokan*
Chicago, *Chicago IX: Greatest Hits*
Eric Clapton, *Slowhand*
Eric Clapton, *Unplugged*
The Clash, *The Clash*
The Clash, *London Calling*
Joe Cocker, *With a Little Help from My Friends*
Cocteau Twins, *Heaven or Las Vegas*
Coldplay, *Parachutes*
Coldplay, *A Rush of Blood to the Head*
Lloyd Cole/Commotions, *Rattlesnakes*
Shawn Colvin, *A Few Small Repairs*
Alice Cooper, *Greatest Hits*
Elvis Costello, *My Aim Is True*
Elvis Costello, *This Year's Model*
Counting Crows, *August and Everything After*
The Cramps, *Songs the Lord Taught Us*
Cream, *Disraeli Gears*
Creedence Clearwater Revival, *Chronicle*
Jim Croce, *I Got a Name*
Crosby, Stills & Nash, *Crosby, Stills & Nash*
Crosby, Stills, Nash & Young, *Déjà Vu*
Crosby, Stills, Nash & Young, *Four Way Street*
Sheryl Crow, *Tuesday Night Music Club*
Crowded House, *Crowded House*
The Cure, *Boys Don't Cry*
Charlie Daniels Band, *Fire on the Mountain*
Dead Kennedys, *Fresh Fruit for Rotting Vegetables*
Deep Purple, *Machine Head*
Def Leppard, *Hysteria*
Def Leppard, *Pyromania*

Genre Index

R.E.M., *Automatic for the People*
R.E.M., *Murmur*
The Replacements, *Let It Be*
The Replacements, *Tim*
The Righteous Brothers, *Anthology*
Rolling Stones, *Beggar's Banquet*
Rolling Stones, *Exile on Main Street*
Rolling Stones, *Some Girls*
Rolling Stones, *Sticky Fingers*
Linda Ronstadt, *Heart Like a Wheel*
Roxy Music, *Avalon*
Roxy Music, *For Your Pleasure*
Todd Rundgren, *Something/ Anything?*
Rush, *Moving Pictures*
Rush, *2112*
Santana, *Abraxas*
Santana, *Shaman*
Santana, *Supernatural*
Joe Satriani, *Surfing with the Alien*
Bob Seger & The Silver Bullet Band, *Against the Wind*
Bob Seger & The Silver Bullet Band, *Night Moves*
The Sex Pistols, *Never Mind the Bollocks Here's the Sex Pistols*
Sigur Rós, *'Agaetis Byrjun*
Squeeze, *Singles 45's and Under*
Siouxsie & the Banshees, *Kaleidoscope*
Slayer, *Reign in Blood*
Smashing Pumpkins, *Mellon Collie and the Infinite Sadness*
Smashing Pumpkins, *Siamese Dream*
Elliot Smith, *XO*
Patti Smith, *Easter*
Patti Smith, *Horses*
The Smiths, *The Queen Is Dead*
Sonic Youth, *Daydream Nation*
Soundgarden, *Superunknown*
The Specials, *The Specials*
Bruce Springsteen, *Born in the USA*
Bruce Springsteen, *Born to Run*
Bruce Springsteen, *Bruce Springsteen & the E Street Band Live/1975-85*
Bruce Springsteen, *Darkness on the Edge of Town*
Bruce Springsteen, *The Rising*
Steely Dan, *Aja*
Steely Dan, *Can't Buy a Thrill*
Steely Dan, *The Royal Scam*
Stereolab, *Emperor Tomato Ketchup*
Steve Miller Band, *Greatest Hits*
Rod Stewart, *Every Picture Tells a Story*
Sting, *The Dream of the Blue Turtles*
Sting, *Ten Summoner's Tales*
The Stone Roses, *The Stone Roses*
Stone Temple Pilots, *Core*

The Stooges, *Funhouse*
The Stooges, *The Stooges*
The Strokes, *Is This It*
Styx, *The Grand Illusion*
Sublime, *Sublime*
Sugar, *Copper Blue*
Supertramp, *Breakfast in America*
Matthew Sweet, *Girlfriend*
System of a Down, *Toxicity*
Talking Heads, *Remain in Light*
Talking Heads, *Speaking in Tongues*
James Taylor, *Greatest Hits*
Tears for Fears, *Songs from the Big Chair*
Television, *Marquee Moon*
10,000 Maniacs, *In My Tribe*
Sundays, *Reading, Writing and Arithmetic*
They Might Be Giants, *Flood*
They Might Be Giants, *NO!*
This Is Spinal Tap
Richard Thompson, *Rumor and Sigh*
Three Dog Night, *The Best*
Tool, *Aenima*
Traffic, *John Barleycorn Must Die*
Travis, *The Invisible Band*
T. Rex, *Electric Warrior*
Tina Turner, *Private Dancer*
Uncle Tupelo, *No Depression*
U2, *Achtung Baby*
U2, *The Joshua Tree*
U2, *War*
Van Halen, *1984 (MCMLXXXIV)*
Van Halen, *Van Halen*
Velvet Underground, *The Velvet Underground and Nico*
Violent Femmes, *Violent Femmes*
Wallflowers, *Bringing Down the Horse*
Waterboys, *Fisherman's Blues*
Ween, *Chocolate and Cheese*
Weezer, *Weezer*
White Stripes, *White Blood Cells*
The Who, *Tommy*
The Who, *Who's Next*
Wilco, *Summerteeth*
Wilco, *Yankee Hotel Foxtrot*
Wings, *Band on the Run*
Johnny Winter, *Johnny Winter*
Steve Winwood, *Arc of a Diver*
Woodstock
X, *Wild Gift*
XTC, *Drums and Wires*
Yes, *Fragile*
Neil Young, *After the Gold Rush*
Neil Young, *Harvest*
Neil Young & Crazy Horse, *Rust Never Sleeps*
Neil Young, *Tonight's the Night*
Frank Zappa, *Apostrophe*
The Zombies, *Odessey and Oracle*
ZZ Top, *Eliminator*

Singer-Songwriter

Ryan Adams, *Gold*
Tori Amos, *Little Earthquakes*
Joan Baez, *Diamonds & Rust*
David Bromberg, *David Bromberg*
Jackson Browne, *Running on Empty*
Jackson Browne, *Saturate Before Using*
Jeff Buckley, *Grace*
Tim Buckley, *Happy Sad*
Jimmy Buffett, *Songs You Know by Heart*
Mary Chapin Carpenter, *Shooting Straight in the Dark*
Harry Chapin, *Verities & Balderdash*
Tracy Chapman, *New Beginning*
Tracy Chapman, *Tracy Chapman*
Leonard Cohen, *I'm Your Man*
Leonard Cohen, *The Songs*
Judy Collins, *Wildflowers*
Shawn Colvin, *A Few Small Repairs*
Jim Croce, *I Got a Name*
Iris DeMent, *My Life*
John Denver, *Greatest Hits*
Ani DiFranco, *Living in Clip*
Donovan, *Donovan's Greatest Hits*
Nick Drake, *Bryter Later*
Nick Drake, *Pink Moon*
Bob Dylan, *Blonde on Blonde*
Bob Dylan, *Blood on the Tracks*
Melissa Etheridge, *Yes I Am*
Marianne Faithfull, *Broken English*
Roberta Flack, *Softly With These Songs*
Dan Fogelberg, *Phoenix*
David Gray, *White Ladder*
Patty Griffin, *Living with Ghosts*
Nanci Griffith, *Flyer*
Arlo Guthrie, *Alice's Restaurant*
Woody Guthrie, *The Greatest Songs*
Tim Hardin, *Reason to Believe*
PJ Harvey, *Rid of Me*
Richie Havens, *Mixed Bag*
Janis Ian, *Between the Lines*
India.Arie, *Voyage to India*
Billy Joel, *Piano Man*
Elton John, *Greatest Hits*
Elton John, *Goodbye Yellow Brick Rd.*
Rickie Lee Jones, *Rickie Lee Jones*
Carole King, *Tapestry*
Tom Lehrer, *That Was the Year That Was*
Gordon Lightfoot, *Sundown*
Lyle Lovett, *Lyle Lovett*
Shelby Lynne, *I Am Shelby Lynne*
Aimee Mann, *Magnolia*
Aimee Mann, *Whatever*
John Mayer, *Room for Squares*

Kate & Anna McGarrigle, *Kate & Anna McGarrigle*
Sarah McLachlan, *Fumbling Towards Ecstasy*
Sarah McLachlan, *Surfacing*
Don McLean, *American Pie*
Natalie Merchant, *Tigerlilly*
Joni Mitchell, *Blue*
Joni Mitchell, *Court and Spark*
Joni Mitchell, *Hejira*
Alanis Morissette, *Jagged Little Pill*
Van Morrison, *Astral Weeks*
Van Morrison, *Moondance*
Randy Newman, *Little Criminals*
Harry Nilsson, *Nilsson Schmilsson*
Laura Nyro, *Eli and the Thirteenth Confession*
Phil Ochs, *I Ain't a 'Marchin' Anymore*
Beth Orton, *Central Reservation*
Graham Parker, *Squeezing Out Sparks*
Gram Parsons, *Grievous Angel*
John Prine, *John Prine*
Bonnie Raitt, *Luck of the Draw*
Bonnie Raitt, *Nick of Time*
The Roches, *The Roches*
Todd Rundgren, *Something/Anything?*
Tom Rush, *The Circle Game*
Jill Scott, *Who Is Jill Scott?*
Michelle Shocked, *Short Sharp Shocked*
Carly Simon, *No Secrets*
Paul Simon, *Graceland*
Paul Simon, *There Goes Rhymin' Simon*
Simon & Garfunkel, *Bridge over Troubled Water*
Simon & Garfunkel, *The Graduate*
Simon & Garfunkel, *Parsley, Sage, Rosemary and Thyme*
Elliot Smith, *XO*
Phoebe Snow, *Phoebe Snow*
Cat Stevens, *Tea for the Tillerman*
James Taylor, *Greatest Hits*
James Taylor, *October Road*
James Taylor, *Sweet Baby James*
Richard & Linda Thompson, *Shoot Out the Lights*
Richard Thompson, *Rumor and Sigh*
Suzanne Vega, *Solitude Standing*
Rufus Wainwright, *Poses*
Tom Waits, *Rain Dogs*
Tom Waits, *Small Change*
Gillian Welch, *Revival*
Lucinda Williams, *Lucinda Williams*
Neil Young, *After the Gold Rush*
Neil Young, *Harvest*
Neil Young, *Tonight's the Night*
Warren Zevon, *Excitable Boy*

Soul

The Blues Brothers
James Brown, *Live at the Apollo*
James Brown, *Sex Machine*
Solomon Burke, *Don't Give Up On Me*
Ray Charles, *Anthology*
The Commitments
Sam Cooke, *The Man and his Music*
The Drifters, *All-Time Greatest Hits*
The 5th Dimension, *Greatest Hits on Earth*
The Four Tops, *Anthology*
Aretha Franklin, *Lady Soul*
Aretha Franklin, *Queen of Soul*
Marvin Gaye, *Anthology*
Marvin Gaye, *What's Going On*
Al Green, *Greatest Hits*
Isaac Hayes, *Shaft*
Hitsville USA: The Motown Singles
Jackson 5, *Anthology*
Etta James, *The Essential*
Curtis Mayfield, *Superfly*
Otis Redding, *The Otis Redding Story*
The Righteous Brothers, *Anthology*
Smokey Robinson, *Anthology*
Sly & the Family Stone, *Greatest Hits*
The Spinners, *A One of a Kind Love Affair: The Anthology*
The Supremes, *Anthology*
The Temptations, *Greatest Hits*
Ike and Tina Turner, *Proud Mary*
Dionne Warwick, *The Dionne Warwick Collection*
Stevie Wonder, *Innervisions*
Stevie Wonder, *Songs/Key of Life*
Stevie Wonder, *Talking Book*

Soundtracks

Aladdin
Amélie
American Graffiti
An American in Paris
Animal House
Apocalypse Now
Beauty and the Beast
The Bee Gees, *Saturday Night Fever*
The Big Chill
Björk, *Selmasongs*
The Blues Brothers
Breakfast at Tiffany's
The Breakfast Club
Buena Vista Social Club
Bye Bye Birdie
Cabaret
Camelot
Carousel
Jimmy Cliff, *The Harder They Come*
Close Encounters of the Third Kind

The Commitments
The Crow
Neil Diamond, *The Jazz Singer*
Dirty Dancing
Dr. Zhivago
Easy Rider
8 Mile
E.T. The Extra-Terrestrial
Fame
Flashdance
Footloose
Forrest Gump
Funny Girl
Peter Gabriel, *Passion*
Gigi
The Godfather
Goldfinger
Gone With the Wind
The Good, the Bad and the Ugly
Grease
Vince Guaraldi, *A Boy Named Charlie Brown*
Isaac Hayes, *Shaft*
Hedwig and the Angry Inch
High Fidelity
Whitney Houston, *The Bodyguard*
The King and I
Carole King, *Really Rosie*
Koyaanisqatsi
Lawrence of Arabia
The Lion King
The Little Mermaid
The Mambo Kings
Manhattan
Aimee Mann, *Magnolia*
Mary Poppins
Matrix
Curtis Mayfield, *Superfly*
Meet Me in St. Louis
Miami Vice
Bette Midler, *Beaches*
Liza Minnelli, *Liza with a "Z"*
Moulin Rouge!
Muppet Movie
The Music from Peter Gunn
The Music Man
O Brother, Where Art Thou?
Oklahoma!
Oliver!
The Pink Panther
Pretty in Pink
Pretty Woman
Prince, *Purple Rain*
Pulp Fiction
Reality Bites
Reservoir Dogs
Rocky
Rocky Horror Picture Show
Romeo + Juliet
Sesame Street, *Platinum*
Simon & Garfunkel, *The Graduate*

Singin' in the Rain
Singles
Sleepless in Seattle
The Sound of Music
A Star Is Born
Star Wars
The Sting
Swingers
This Is Spinal Tap
Titanic
Top Gun
Trainspotting
Twin Peaks
2001: A Space Odyssey
Vangelis, Chariots of Fire
When Harry Met Sally
The Wizard of Oz
Woodstock

World

Afro-Celt Sound System, Sound Magic Volume 1
Amélie
Harry Belafonte, Calypso
Buena Vista Social Club
Manu Chao, Clandestino
The Chieftains, Long Black Veil
Deep Forest, Deep Forest
Enya, Watermark
Cesaria Evora, Miss Perfumado
Peter Gabriel, Passion
Gipsy Kings, Gipsy Kings
Ottmar Liebert, Nouveau Flamenco
The Mambo Kings
Loreena McKennitt, Book of Secrets
Edith Piaf, La Vie En Rose
Paul Simon, Graceland

DECADES

1940s and Before

Annie Get Your Gun
Bing Crosby, *A Merry Christmas with Bing Crosby and The Andrews Sisters*
Gone With the Wind
Robert Johnson, *The Complete Recordings*
Kiss Me, Kate
Meet Me in St. Louis
Charlie Parker, *Yardbird Suite*
Edith Piaf, *La Vie En Rose*
South Pacific
Fats Waller, *Ain't Misbehavin'*
The Wizard of Oz

1950s

Cannonball Adderley, *Somethin' Else*
An American in Paris
Paul Anka, *Paul Anka Sings*
J.S. Bach, *State of Wonder*
Chet Baker, *Chet Baker Sings*
Bartók, *Concerto for Orchestra*
Basie Count, *The Complete Atomic Basie*
Harry Belafonte and Lena Horne, *Porgy and Bess*
Chuck Berry, *The Great Twenty-Eight*
Art Blakey, *Moanin'*
Clifford Brown, *Memorial Album*
Dave Brubeck, *Time Out*
Maria Callas, *The Very Best*
Candide
Carousel
June Christy, *Something Cool*
Ornette Coleman, *Shape of Jazz to Come*
Nat King Cole, *Nat King Cole Story*
John Coltrane, *Blue Train*
Damn Yankees
Miles Davis, *Kind of Blue*
Miles Davis, *Miles Ahead*
Miles Davis with Gil Evans, *Porgy and Bess*
Miles Davis with Gil Evans, *Sketches of Spain*
Blossom Dearie, *Blossom Dearie*
Bo Diddley, *The Chess Box*
Fats Domino, *My Blue Heaven*
The Drifters, *All-Time Greatest Hits*
Everly Brothers, *Cadence Classics*
Ella Fitzgerald, *Best of the Songbooks*
Erroll Garner, *Concert by the Sea*
Gershwin, *Rhapsody in Blue*

Gigi
Dizzy Gillespie, *At Newport*
Benny Goodman, *B.G. in Hi-Fi*
Gypsy
Jascha Heifetz, *Beethoven & Mendelssohn: Violin Concertos*
Jascha Heifetz, *The Supreme*
Billie Holiday, *Lady Sings the Blues*
Buddy Holly, *The Best*
John Lee Hooker, *Ultimate Collection*
Howlin' Wolf, *Moanin' in the Moonlight*
Ahmad Jamal, *At the Pershing*
Elmore James, *The Sky Is Crying*
Stan Kenton, *Kenton in Hi-Fi*
The King and I
Lambert, Hendricks & Ross, *Sing a Song of Basie*
Peggy Lee, *Spotlight on Peggy Lee*
Little Richard, *The Essential*
Dean Martin, *Capitol Collectors*
Charles Mingus, *Mingus Ah Um*
Mozart, *Don Giovanni*
Mozart, *Symphonies 35–41*
The Music from Peter Gunn
My Fair Lady
Oklahoma!
Charlie Parker, *Jazz at Massey Hall*
Oscar Peterson, *On the Town*
Elvis Presley, *Elvis' Golden Records*
Louis Prima, *Zooma Zooma*
Puccini, *Tosca*
Rachmaninoff, *Concerto No. 2*
Sonny Rollins, *Saxophone Colossus*
Frank Sinatra, *In the Wee Small Hours*
Frank Sinatra, *Only the Lonely*
Frank Sinatra, *Sinatra Reprise*
Frank Sinatra, *Songs for Swingin' Lovers*
Singin' in the Rain
A Star Is Born
Richard Strauss, *Also Sprach Zarathustra*
Art Tatum, *Tatum Group Masterpieces, Vol. 1*
Van Cliburn, *Tchaikovsky; Rachmaninoff*
Sarah Vaughan, *Sarah Vaughan With Clifford Brown*
Wagner, *Der Ring des Nibelungen*
Muddy Waters, *The Best*
West Side Story
Hank Williams, *40 Greatest Hits*
Lester Young, *With the Oscar Peterson Trio*

1960s

Herb Alpert/Tijuana Brass, *Whipped Cream and Other Delights*
Martha Argerich, *Début Recital*
Louis Armstrong, *Hello, Dolly!*
The Association, *Greatest Hits*
Burt Bacharach, *Greatest Hits*
Joan Baez, *Joan Baez*
The Band, *The Band*
Barber, *Adagio for Strings; Violin Concerto*
The Beach Boys, *Pet Sounds*
The Beatles, *Abbey Road*
The Beatles, *The Beatles 1962-1966*
The Beatles, *Revolver*
The Beatles, *Rubber Soul*
The Beatles, *Sgt. Pepper*
The Beatles, *The White Album*
The Bee Gees, *Children of the World*
Beethoven, *Piano Concertos 3 & 5*
Beethoven, *Symphony No. 9*
Harry Belafonte, *Calypso*
Tony Bennett, *I Left My Heart in San Francisco*
Big Brother and the Holding Company, *Cheap Thrills*
Bizet, *Carmen Suites; L'Arlesienne Suites*
Blood, Sweat and Tears, *Blood, Sweat and Tears*
Mike Bloomfield, *Super Session*
Breakfast at Tiffany's
James Brown, *Live at the Apollo*
Tim Buckley, *Happy Sad*
Buffalo Springfield, *Buffalo Springfield Again*
Paul Butterfield, *East-West*
Bye Bye Birdie
The Byrds, *Fifth Dimension*
Camelot
Glen Campbell, *Wichita Lineman*
Captain Beefheart, *Safe as Milk*
Johnny Cash, *At Folsom Prison*
Johnny Cash, *The Essential*
Ray Charles, *Anthology*
Chopin, *Nocturnes*
Patsy Cline, *Greatest Hits*
Joe Cocker, *With a Little Help from My Friends*
Leonard Cohen, *The Songs*
Nat King Cole and George Shearing, *Nat King Cole Sings/George Shearing Plays*
Judy Collins, *Wildflowers*
John Coltrane, *A Love Supreme*
Sam Cooke, *The Man and his Music*
Aaron Copland, *Appalachian Spring*
Cream, *Disraeli Gears*
Crosby, Stills & Nash, *Crosby, Stills & Nash*
Eric Dolphy, *Out to Lunch!*

Donovan, *Donovan's Greatest Hits*
The Doors, *The Doors*
Dr. Zhivago
Bob Dylan, *Blonde on Blonde*
Bob Dylan, *Nashville Skyline*
Easy Rider
Duke Ellington with John Coltrane, *Duke Ellington & John Coltrane*
Bill Evans, *Waltz for Debby*
Fairport Convention, *Liege & Lief*
Fiddler on the Roof
The 5th Dimension, *Greatest Hits on Earth*
Ella Fitzgerald, *Complete Ella in Berlin*
The Four Seasons, *Anthology*
The Four Tops, *Anthology*
Aretha Franklin, *Lady Soul*
Aretha Franklin, *Queen of Soul*
Funny Girl
Judy Garland, *Judy at Carnegie Hall*
Stan Getz, *Getz/Gilberto*
Goldfinger
The Good, the Bad and the Ugly
Dexter Gordon, *Go!*
Grateful Dead, *Live/Dead*
Vince Guaraldi, *A Boy Named Charlie Brown*
Arlo Guthrie, *Alice's Restaurant*
Woody Guthrie, *The Greatest Songs*
Buddy Guy, *The Very Best*
Hair
Herbie Hancock, *Maiden Voyage*
Tim Hardin, *Reason to Believe*
Richie Havens, *Mixed Bag*
Isaac Hayes, *Hot Buttered Soul*
Jimi Hendrix, *Band of Gypsys*
Jimi Hendrix Experience, *Are You Experienced?*
Jimi Hendrix Experience, *Electric Ladyland*
Hitsville USA: The Motown Singles
Ian & Sylvia, *Northern Journey*
Etta James, *The Essential*
Jefferson Airplane, *Surrealistic Pillow*
Antonio Carlos Jobim, *Wave*
Tom Jones, *Tom Jones' Greatest Hits*
Janis Joplin, *Pearl*
Albert King, *Ultimate Collection*
B.B. King, *Live at the Regal*
King Crimson, *In the Court*
Kingston Trio, *Sold Out/String Along*
The Kinks, *Something Else*
Lawrence of Arabia
Led Zeppelin, *Led Zeppelin II*
Tom Lehrer, *That Was the Year That Was*
Love, *Forever Changes*
Taj Mahal/Ry Cooder, *Rising Sons*

1970s

Decade Index

1980s

Decade Index

Ray Lynch, *Deep Breakfast*
Madonna, *Immaculate Collection*
Madonna, *Like a Virgin*
Mahler, *Symphony No. 5*
Mannheim Steamroller, *Fresh Aire IV*
John Cougar Mellencamp, *American Fool*
John Cougar Mellencamp, *Scarecrow*
Metallica, *Master of Puppets*
Miami Vice
George Michael, *Faith*
Bette Midler, *Beaches*
Midnight Oil, *Diesel and Dust*
Morrissey, *Viva Hate*
Bob Mould, *Workbook*
Mozart, *Piano Concertos 19-23*
Mozart, *Requiem*
New Order, *Power, Corruption & Lies*
New Order, *Substance*
Stevie Nicks, *Bella Donna*
N.W.A, *Straight Outta Compton*
Orchestral Manoeuvers in the Dark, *The Best of OMD*
Ozzy Osbourne, *Blizzard of Ozz*
Dolly Parton, Linda Ronstadt & Emmylou Harris, *Trio*
Mandy Patinkin, *Mandy Patinkin*
Tom Petty, *Full Moon Fever*
Tom Petty/Heartbreakers, *Greatest Hits*
The Phantom of the Opera
Pixies, *Surfer Rosa*
The Pogues, *If I Should Fall from Grace with God*
The Pointer Sisters, *Break Out*
The Police, *Synchronicity*
The Pretenders, *Learning to Crawl*
The Pretenders, *The Pretenders*
Pretty in Pink
Prince, *1999*
Prince, *Purple Rain*
Prince, *Sign 'O' the Times*
Public Enemy, *It Takes a Nation*
Puccini, *La Bohème*
Raffi, *Baby Beluga*
Bonnie Raitt, *Nick of Time*
Ravel, *Boléro*
R.E.M., *Murmur*
The Replacements, *Let It Be*
The Replacements, *Tim*
Lionel Richie, *Can't Slow Down*
Roxy Music, *Avalon*
Run-D.M.C., *Raising Hell*
Rush, *Moving Pictures*
Sade, *Diamond Life*
Satie, *Gymnopédies, Gnossiennes*

Joe Satriani, *Surfing with the Alien*
Bob Seger & The Silver Bullet Band, *Against the Wind*
Michelle Shocked, *Short Sharp Shocked*
Show Boat
Paul Simon, *Graceland*
Squeeze, *Singles 45's and Under*
Siouxsie & the Banshees, *Kaleidoscope*
Slayer, *Reign in Blood*
Slick Rick, *The Great Adventures*
The Smiths, *The Queen Is Dead*
Sonic Youth, *Daydream Nation*
Bruce Springsteen, *Born in the USA*
Bruce Springsteen, *Bruce Springsteen & the E Street Band Live/1975-85*
Sting, *The Dream of the Blue Turtles*
The Stone Roses, *The Stone Roses*
George Strait, *Does Fort Worth Ever Cross Your Mind*
Barbra Streisand, *The Broadway Album*
Barbra Streisand, *Memories*
Sunday in the Park with George
Talking Heads, *Remain in Light*
Talking Heads, *Speaking in Tongues*
Tears for Fears, *Songs from the Big Chair*
10,000 Maniacs, *In My Tribe*
This Is Spinal Tap
Richard & Linda Thompson, *Shoot Out the Lights*
Top Gun
Randy Travis, *Storms of Life*
Tina Turner, *Private Dancer*
U2, *The Joshua Tree*
U2, *War*
Luther Vandross, *The Best*
Vangelis, *Chariots of Fire*
Van Halen, *1984 (MCMLXXXIV)*
Stevie Ray Vaughan & Double Trouble, *Greatest Hits*
Suzanne Vega, *Solitude Standing*
Violent Femmes, *Violent Femmes*
Andreas Vollenweider, *Down to the Moon*
Tom Waits, *Rain Dogs*
Grover Washington Jr., *Winelight*
Waterboys, *Fisherman's Blues*
Wham!, *Make It Big*
When Harry Met Sally
Lucinda Williams, *Lucinda Williams*
George Winston, *Autumn*
Steve Winwood, *Arc of a Diver*
X, *Wild Gift*
Dwight Yoakam, *Guitars, Cadillacs*
ZZ Top, *Eliminator*

1990s

Boyz II Men, *Boyz II Men, II*
Adams, *The Chairman Dances*
Afro-Celt Sound System, *Sound Magic Volume 1*
Air, *Moon Safari*
Aladdin
Alice in Chains, *Dirt*
Tori Amos, *Little Earthquakes*
Anonymous 4, *An English Ladymass*
Marc Anthony, *Marc Anthony*
Aphex Twin, *Selected Ambient Works*
Arrested Development, *3 Years, 5 Months & 2 Days in the Life of . . .*
J.S. Bach, *Six Unaccompanied Cello Suites*
Erykah Badu, *Baduizm*
Barenaked Ladies, *Stunt*
Beauty and the Beast
Beck, *Odelay*
Belle & Sebastian, *If You're Feeling Sinister*
Ben Folds Five, *Ben Folds Five*
Big Star, *Sister Lovers/Third*
Björk, *Debut*
Mary J. Blige, *My Life*
Mary J. Blige, *What's the 411?*
Boyz II Men, *Cooleyhighharmony*
Billy Bragg & Wilco, *Mermaid Ave.*
Toni Braxton, *Secrets*
Sarah Brightman, *Time to Say Goodbye*
Brooks & Dunn, *Brand New Man*
Garth Brooks, *No Fences*
Garth Brooks, *Ropin' the Wind*
Jeff Buckley, *Grace*
Buena Vista Social Club
Mary Chapin Carpenter, *Shooting Straight in the Dark*
Johnny Cash, *American Recordings*
Rosanne Cash, *Interiors*
Manu Chao, *Clandestino*
Tracy Chapman, *New Beginning*
The Chemical Brothers, *Dig Your Own Hole*
The Chieftains, *Long Black Veil*
Eric Clapton, *Unplugged*
Cocteau Twins, *Heaven or Las Vegas*
Natalie Cole, *Unforgettable*
Shawn Colvin, *A Few Small Repairs*
The Commitments
Counting Crows, *August and Everything After*
Crazy for You
The Crow
Sheryl Crow, *Tuesday Night Music Club*
The Crystal Method, *Vegas*
Cypress Hill, *Cypress Hill*

Daft Punk, *Homework*
D'Angelo, *Brown Sugar*
Deee-Lite, *World Clique*
Deep Forest, *Deep Forest*
De La Soul, *3 Feet High and Rising*
Iris DeMent, *My Life*
Depeche Mode, *Violator*
Ani DiFranco, *Living in Clip*
Digable Planets, *Reachin'*
Sasha & John Digweed, *Northern Exposure 2: East Coast Edition*
Celine Dion, *Let's Talk About Love*
Dixie Chicks, *Wide Open Spaces*
DJ Shadow, *Endtroducing . . .*
Dr. Dre, *The Chronic*
Dr. Octagon, *Dr. Octagonecologyst*
Missy Elliott, *Supa Dupa Fly*
Eminem, *The Slim Shady LP*
Enigma, *MCMXC A.D.*
En Vogue, *Born to Sing*
En Vogue, *Funky Divas*
Melissa Etheridge, *Yes I Am*
Everything But the Girl, *Amplified Heart*
Everything But the Girl, *Walking Wounded*
Cesaria Evora, *Miss Perfumado*
Faith No More, *The Real Thing*
Fatboy Slim, *You've Come a Long Way, Baby*
Flaming Lips, *Transmissions from the Satellite Heart*
Foo Fighters, *Foo Fighters*
Forrest Gump
Fugazi, *13 Songs*
The Fugees, *The Score*
Garbage, *Garbage*
Jerry Garcia/David Grisman, *Not for Kids Only*
Górecki, *Symphony No. 3*
David Gray, *White Ladder*
Macy Gray, *On How Life Is*
Green Day, *Dookie*
Patty Griffin, *Living with Ghosts*
Nanci Griffith, *Flyer*
Guns n' Roses, *Use Your Illusion I*
Guys and Dolls
Handel, *Messiah*
Handel, *Water Music*
Ben Harper, *Burn to Shine*
Emmylou Harris, *Wrecking Ball*
PJ Harvey, *Rid of Me*
Faith Hill, *Breathe*
Lauryn Hill, *The Miseducation*
Lena Horne, *An Evening with*
Whitney Houston, *The Bodyguard*
Ice Cube, *AmeriKKKa's Most Wanted*
Alan Jackson, *A Lot About Livin'*
Janet Jackson, *janet.*

Decade Index

2000s

SPECIAL FEATURES

Air Guitar
(Guitar excellence)
AC/DC, *Back in Black*
AC/DC, *Highway to Hell*
Aerosmith, *Pump*
Aerosmith, *Toys in the Attic*
The Allman Brothers, *Eat a Peach*
Bad Company, *Bad Company*
The Band, *The Band*
Jeff Beck, *Blow by Blow*
Black Sabbath, *Paranoid*
Mike Bloomfield, *Super Session*
Bon Jovi, *Slippery When Wet*
Boston, *Boston*
Paul Butterfield, *East-West*
Glen Campbell, *Wichita Lineman*
Johnny Cash, *At Folsom Prison*
Johnny Cash, *The Essential*
Cheap Trick, *Live at Budokan*
Eric Clapton, *Slowhand*
Eric Clapton, *Unplugged*
Albert Collins, *Ice Pickin'*
Albert Collins, Johnny Copeland and Robert Cray, *Showdown!*
Alice Cooper, *Greatest Hits*
Robert Cray, *Strong Persuader*
Cream, *Disraeli Gears*
Crosby, Stills, Nash & Young, *Four Way Street*
Deep Purple, *Machine Head*
Def Leppard, *Hysteria*
Def Leppard, *Pyromania*
Derek & the Dominos, *Layla*
Dire Straits, *Brothers in Arms*
Bob Dylan, *Blood on the Tracks*
The Eagles, *Their Greatest Hits*
The Eagles, *Hotel California*
Steve Earle, *Guitar Town*
Foo Fighters, *Foo Fighters*
Foo Fighters, *One By One*
Peter Frampton, *Frampton Comes Alive!*
Gipsy Kings, *Gipsy Kings*
Grateful Dead, *Live/Dead*
Guns n' Roses, *Appetite for Destruction*
Guns n' Roses, *Use Your Illusion I*
Buddy Guy, *The Very Best*
Ben Harper, *Burn to Shine*
Hedwig and the Angry Inch
Jimi Hendrix Experience, *Are You Experienced?*
Jimi Hendrix Experience, *Electric Ladyland*
High Fidelity
Hüsker Dü, *New Day Rising*
Iron Maiden, *Number of the Beast*

Elmore James, *The Sky Is Crying*
Waylon Jennings, *Honky Tonk Heroes*
Joan Jett & the Blackhearts, *I Love Rock 'n' Roll*
Journey, *Escape*
Kansas, *Point of Know Return*
Albert King, *Ultimate Collection*
B.B. King, *Live at the Regal*
B.B. King and Eric Clapton, *Riding with the King*
The Kinks, *Something Else*
Kiss, *Alive!*
Leo Kottke, *6- and 12-String Guitar*
Lenny Kravitz, *Are You Gonna Go My Way?*
Led Zeppelin, *Led Zeppelin II*
Led Zeppelin, *Led Zeppelin IV*
Ottmar Liebert, *Nouveau Flamenco*
Live, *Throwing Copper*
Los Lobos, *How Will the Wolf Survive?*
Lynyrd Skynyrd, *Pronounced Leh-Nerd Skin-Nerd*
Lynyrd Skynyrd, *Second Helping*
Taj Mahal/Ry Cooder, *Rising Sons Matrix*
Dave Matthews Band, *Live at Red Rocks 8.15.95*
John Mayall, *Bluesbreakers: John Mayall with Eric Clapton*
Metallica, *Master of Puppets*
Pat Metheny, *Pat Metheny Group*
Wes Montgomery, *Incredible Jazz Guitar of Wes Montgomery*
Nirvana, *Nevermind*
Ozzy Osbourne, *Blizzard of Ozz*
Pearl Jam, *Ten*
Pearl Jam, *Vitalogy*
Pearl Jam, *Vs.*
Tom Petty/Heartbreakers, *Damn the Torpedoes*
Tom Petty, *Full Moon Fever*
Tom Petty/Heartbreakers, *Greatest Hits*
Phish, *A Live One*
Prince, *Purple Rain*
Queen, *News of the World*
Queens of the Stone Age, *Songs for the Deaf*
Queensryche, *Empire*
Red Hot Chili Peppers, *Californication*
Rolling Stones, *Sticky Fingers*
Rush, *Moving Pictures*
Rush, *2112*
Santana, *Abraxas*
Santana, *Shaman*

Joe Satriani, *Surfing with the Alien Singles*
Slayer, *Reign in Blood*
Soundgarden, *Superunknown*
Steely Dan, *The Royal Scam*
Stone Temple Pilots, *Core*
The Strokes, *Is This It*
Styx, *The Grand Illusion*
Sugar, *Copper Blue*
System of a Down, *Toxicity*
Susan Tedeschi, *Just Won't Burn*
Television, *Marquee Moon*
This Is Spinal Tap
Van Halen, *1984 (MCMLXXXIV)*
Van Halen, *Van Halen*
Stevie Ray Vaughan & Double Trouble, *Greatest Hits*
The Who, *Who's Next*
Johnny Winter, *Johnny Winter*
Yes, *Fragile*
Dwight Yoakam, *Guitars, Cadillacs*
Neil Young & Crazy Horse, *Rust Never Sleeps*
Frank Zappa, *Apostrophe*

Avant-Garde

Aphex Twin, *Selected Ambient Works*
Bartók, *Concerto for Orchestra*
Bartók, *6 String Quartets*
Basement Jaxx, *Rooty*
Berlioz, *Symphonie Fantastique*
Björk, *Selmasongs*
Captain Beefheart, *Safe as Milk*
Manu Chao, *Clandestino*
Ornette Coleman, *Shape of Jazz to Come*
John Coltrane, *A Love Supreme*
Miles Davis, *Bitches Brew*
Devo, *Q: Are We Not Men?*
DJ Shadow, *Endtroducing . . .*
Eric Dolphy, *Out to Lunch!*
Dr. Octagon, *Dr. Octagonecologyst*
Brian Eno, *Before and After Science*
Flaming Lips, *Transmissions from the Satellite Heart*
Philip Glass, *Glassworks*
Hedwig and the Angry Inch
KLF, *The White Room*
Koyaanisqatsi
Kraftwerk, *Computer World*
Charles Mingus, *Mingus Ah Um*
Alan Parsons Project, *I Robot*
The Prodigy, *Music for the Jilted Generation*
Radiohead, *OK Computer*
The Roots, *Phrenology*
Satie, *Gymnopédies, Gnossiennes*
Sigur Rós, *'Agaetis Byrjun*
Sonic Youth, *Daydream Nation*
Stereolab, *Emperor Tomato Ketchup*

They Might Be Giants, *NO!*
Tricky, *Maxinquaye*
Frank Zappa, *Apostrophe*

Born in the USA

Adams, *The Chairman Dances*
Alabama, *Mountain Music*
American Graffiti
Animal House
Annie Get Your Gun
Apocalypse Now
Louis Armstrong, *Hello, Dolly!*
Arrested Development, *3 Years, 5 Months & 2 Days in the Life of . . .*
The Band, *The Band*
The Blues Brothers
Bon Jovi, *New Jersey*
Billy Bragg & Wilco, *Mermaid Ave.*
Johnny Cash, *At Folsom Prison*
Tracy Chapman, *Tracy Chapman*
Aaron Copland, *Appalachian Spring*
Crosby, Stills, Nash & Young, *Four Way Street*
Damn Yankees
John Denver, *Greatest Hits*
Neil Diamond, *The Jazz Singer*
Dixie Chicks, *Home*
Easy Rider
Forrest Gump
Marvin Gaye, *What's Going On*
Grateful Dead, *Steal Your Face*
Arlo Guthrie, *Alice's Restaurant*
Woody Guthrie, *The Greatest Songs*
Hair
Ice Cube, *AmeriKKKa's Most Wanted*
Indigo Girls, *Indigo Girls*
Robert Johnson, *The Complete Recordings*
Little Feat, *Feats Don't Fail Me Now*
Lynyrd Skynyrd, *Second Helping*
Manhattan
Curtis Mayfield, *Superfly*
Yo-Yo Ma, etc., *Appalachia Waltz*
Don McLean, *American Pie*
Meet Me in St. Louis
John Cougar Mellencamp, *Scarecrow*
Mos Def and Talib Kweli, *Black Star*
The Music Man
The Nitty Gritty Dirt Band, *Will the Circle Be Unbroken*
N.W.A, *Straight Outta Compton*
Phil Ochs, *I Ain't a 'Marchin' Anymore*
Oklahoma!
Peter, Paul & Mary, *Peter, Paul & Mary*
Public Enemy, *Fear of a Black Planet*
Public Enemy, *It Takes a Nation*

Michelle Shocked, *Short Sharp Shocked*
Show Boat
Simon & Garfunkel, *The Graduate*
Bruce Springsteen, *Born in the USA*
Bruce Springsteen, *The Rising*
The Weavers, *at Carnegie Hall*
West Side Story
Stevie Wonder, *Innervisions*
Woodstock
Neil Young, *After the Gold Rush*

Breakup

Big Brother and the Holding Company, *Cheap Thrills*
Clint Black, *Killin' Time*
Mary J. Blige, *My Life*
Sarah Brightman, *Time to Say Goodbye*
Rosanne Cash, *Interiors*
Chicago, *Chicago IX: Greatest Hits*
Patsy Cline, *Greatest Hits*
Rosemary Clooney, *Sings the Music of Cole Porter*
Shawn Colvin, *A Few Small Repairs*
The Commitments
Robert Cray, *Strong Persuader*
Crowded House, *Crowded House*
The Cure, *Boys Don't Cry*
Derek & the Dominos, *Layla*
Dido, *No Angel*
Bob Dylan, *Blood on the Tracks*
The Eagles, *The Long Run*
Gloria Estefan, *Greatest Hits*
Eurythmics, *Greatest Hits*
Everything But the Girl, *Walking Wounded*
Marianne Faithfull, *Broken English*
Fleetwood Mac, *Rumours*
The Four Tops, *Anthology*
Aretha Franklin, *Lady Soul*
Aretha Franklin, *Queen of Soul*
Vince Gill, *When I Call Your Name*
Patty Griffin, *Living with Ghosts*
Buddy Guy, *The Very Best*
High Fidelity
Etta James, *The Essential*
George Jones, *The Essential*
Janis Joplin, *Pearl*
Joy Division, *Substance*
The Judds, *Greatest Hits*
B.B. King, *Live at the Regal*
Lenny Kravitz, *Are You Gonna Go My Way?*
k.d. lang, *Ingenue*
Annie Lennox, *Diva*
Madonna, *Ray of Light*
Aimee Mann, *Magnolia*
John Mayer, *Room for Squares*
Jo Dee Messina, *I'm Alright*
Joni Mitchell, *Blue*

Alanis Morissette, *Jagged Little Pill*
Morrissey, *Viva Hate*
Sinéad O'Connor, *I Do Not Want What I Haven't Got*
Olive, *Extra Virgin*
Liz Phair, *Exile in Guyville*
Edith Piaf, *La Vie En Rose*
Portishead, *Dummy*
The Pretenders, *The Pretenders*
Pretty in Pink
Prince, *Purple Rain*
Bonnie Raitt, *Luck of the Draw*
LeAnn Rimes, *Blue*
Romeo + Juliet
Linda Ronstadt, *Heart Like a Wheel*
Todd Rundgren, *Something/Anything?*
Frank Sinatra, *In the Wee Small Hours*
Frank Sinatra, *Only the Lonely*
Elliot Smith, *XO*
The Smiths, *The Queen Is Dead*
George Strait, *Does Fort Worth Ever Cross Your Mind*
Richard & Linda Thompson, *Shoot Out the Lights*
Richard Thompson, *Rumor and Sigh*
Randy Travis, *Storms of Life*
Twin Peaks
Gillian Welch, *Revival*
Wilco, *Yankee Hotel Foxtrot*
Hank Williams, *40 Greatest Hits*
George Winston, *Autumn*
Tammy Wynette, *Stand by Your Man*
X, *Wild Gift*
Trisha Yearwood, *Hearts in Armor*
Dwight Yoakam, *Guitars, Cadillacs*
Dwight Yoakam, *This Time*
Neil Young, *After the Gold Rush*

Chill-Out

Air, *Moon Safari*
Amélie
Aphex Twin, *Selected Ambient Works*
The Association, *Greatest Hits*
Erykah Badu, *Baduizm*
Joan Baez, *Diamonds & Rust*
Chet Baker, *Chet Baker Sings*
Barber, *Adagio for Strings; Violin Concerto*
Bauhaus, *Mask*
Tony Bennett, *Playin' With My Friends*
Sarah Brightman, *Time to Say Goodbye*
Kate Bush, *Hounds of Love*
The Carpenters, *The Singles*
Rosanne Cash, *Interiors*
Close Encounters of the Third Kind

Cocteau Twins, *Heaven or Las Vegas*
Leonard Cohen, *I'm Your Man*
Coldplay, *Parachutes*
Lloyd Cole/Commotions, *Rattlesnakes*
Counting Crows, *August and Everything After*
D'Angelo, *Brown Sugar*
D'Angelo, *Voodoo*
Miles Davis with Gil Evans, *Sketches of Spain*
Deep Forest, *Deep Forest*
Dido, *No Angel*
Digable Planets, *Reachin'*
Nick Drake, *Bryter Later*
Nick Drake, *Pink Moon*
Bob Dylan, *Blood on the Tracks*
Bob Dylan, *Nashville Skyline*
Enya, *Watermark*
Everything But the Girl, *Amplified Heart*
Peter Gabriel, *Passion*
Stan Getz, *Getz/Gilberto*
Górecki, *Symphony No. 3*
David Gray, *White Ladder*
Emmylou Harris, *Wrecking Ball*
Antonio Carlos Jobim, *Wave*
Kruder & Dorfmeister, *K & D Sessions*
Peggy Lee, *Spotlight on Peggy Lee*
Ray Lynch, *Deep Breakfast*
Aimee Mann, *Magnolia*
John Mayer, *Room for Squares*
Loreena McKennitt, *Book of Secrets*
Sarah McLachlan, *Fumbling Towards Ecstasy*
Sarah McLachlan, *Surfacing*
Morcheeba, *Big Calm*
Van Morrison, *Astral Weeks*
Anne Murray, *Greatest Hits*
The Orb, *Adventures Beyond the Ultraworld*
Beth Orton, *Central Reservation*
Gram Parsons, *Grievous Angel*
Edith Piaf, *La Vie En Rose*
Roxy Music, *Avalon*
Jill Scott, *Who Is Jill Scott?*
Sigur Rós, *'Agaetis Byrjun*
Simon & Garfunkel, *The Graduate*
Elliot Smith, *XO*
Steely Dan, *Aja*
St. Germain, *Tourist*
Sundays, *Reading, Writing and Arithmetic*
A Tribe Called Quest, *Low End Theory*
A Tribe Called Quest, *People's Instinctive Travels*
Twin Peaks
Neil Young, *After the Gold Rush*

Cocktail Hour

Cannonball Adderley, *Somethin' Else*
Ain't Misbehavin'
Air, *Moon Safari*
A Little Night Music
Herb Alpert/Tijuana Brass, *Whipped Cream and Other Delights*
Amélie
An American in Paris
Anything Goes
J.S. Bach, *Brandenburg Concertos*
J.S. Bach, *State of Wonder*
Burt Bacharach, *Greatest Hits*
Chet Baker, *Chet Baker Sings*
Beethoven, *Piano Concertos 3 & 5*
Beethoven, *Piano Sonatas 8, 13 & 14*
Beethoven, *Symphonies 5 & 7*
Tony Bennett, *I Left My Heart in San Francisco*
Tony Bennett, *Playin' With My Friends*
George Benson, *Breezin'*
Art Blakey, *Moanin'*
Brahms, *Symphony No. 4*
Breakfast at Tiffany's
Sarah Brightman, *Time to Say Goodbye*
Dave Brubeck, *Time Out*
June Christy, *Something Cool*
Rosemary Clooney, *Sings the Music of Cole Porter*
Natalie Cole, *Unforgettable*
Nat King Cole, *Nat King Cole Story*
Nat King Cole and George Shearing, *Nat King Cole Sings/George Shearing Plays*
John Coltrane, *Blue Train*
Miles Davis, *Kind of Blue*
Miles Davis, *Miles Ahead*
Miles Davis with Gil Evans, *Sketches of Spain*
Neil Diamond, *The Jazz Singer*
Linda Eder, *It's No Secret Anymore*
Everything But the Girl, *Walking Wounded*
Ella Fitzgerald, *Best of the Songbooks*
Judy Garland, *Judy at Carnegie Hall*
Stan Getz, *Getz/Gilberto*
The Godfather
Herbie Hancock, *Maiden Voyage*
Handel, *Water Music*
Joe Jackson, *Night and Day*
Etta James, *The Essential*
Antonio Carlos Jobim, *Wave*
Tom Jones, *Tom Jones' Greatest Hits*
Kitaro, *Silk Road, Vol. 1*
Kruder & Dorfmeister, *K & D Sessions*

Lambert, Hendricks & Ross, *Sing a Song of Basie*
k.d. lang, *Shadowland*
Peggy Lee, *Spotlight on Peggy Lee*
Annie Lennox, *Diva*
The Mambo Kings
Manhattan
Johnny Mathis, *Johnny's Greatest*
Sergio Mendes, *Fool on the Hill*
Lee Morgan, *The Sidewinder*
Moulin Rouge!
Mozart, *Piano Concertos 19-23*
Mozart, *Symphonies 35–41*
The Music from Peter Gunn
Willie Nelson, *Stardust*
Beth Orton, *Central Reservation*
Oscar Peterson, *On the Town*
Edith Piaf, *La Vie En Rose*
The Pink Panther
Rachmaninoff, *Concerto No. 2*
Otis Redding, *The Otis Redding Story*
The Righteous Brothers, *Anthology*
Mstislav Rostropovich, *Dvorák; Tchaikovsky*
Sade, *Diamond Life*
Horace Silver, *Song for My Father*
Frank Sinatra, *In the Wee Small Hours*
Frank Sinatra, *Only the Lonely*
Sleepless in Seattle
Steely Dan, *Aja*
Stereolab, *Emperor Tomato Ketchup*
St. Germain, *Tourist*
The Supremes, *Anthology*
Swingers
Thievery Corporation, *The Mirror Conspiracy*
Twin Peaks
Van Cliburn, *Tchaikovsky; Rachmaninoff*
Vivaldi, *The Four Seasons*
Dionne Warwick, *The Dionne Warwick Collection*
George Winston, *Autumn*

Collaborations

Harry Belafonte and Lena Horne, *Porgy and Bess*
Tony Bennett, *Playin' With My Friends*
Billy Bragg & Wilco, *Mermaid Ave.*
Buena Vista Social Club
Nat King Cole and George Shearing, *Nat King Cole Sings/George Shearing Plays*
Albert Collins, Johnny Copeland and Robert Cray, *Showdown!*
Bing Crosby, *A Merry Christmas with Bing Crosby and The Andrews Sisters*

Miles Davis with Gil Evans, *Porgy and Bess*
Miles Davis with Gil Evans, *Sketches of Spain*
Duke Ellington with John Coltrane, *Duke Ellington & John Coltrane*
Jerry Garcia/David Grisman, *Not for Kids Only*
Stan Getz, *Getz/Gilberto*
Nanci Griffith, *Flyer*
B.B. King and Eric Clapton, *Riding with the King*
The Lion King
Taj Mahal/Ry Cooder, *Rising Sons*
John Mayall, *Bluesbreakers: John Mayall with Eric Clapton*
Les McCann/Eddie Harris, *Swiss Movement*
Gram Parsons, *Grievous Angel*
Dolly Parton, Linda Ronstadt & Emmylou Harris, *Trio*
Queens of the Stone Age, *Songs for the Deaf*
Diane Schuur, *Diane Schuur & The Count Basie Orchestra*
Frank Sinatra, *Duets*
Sarah Vaughan, *Sarah Vaughan With Clifford Brown*
West Side Story
Lester Young, *With the Oscar Peterson Trio*

Comebacks

AC/DC, *Back in Black*
Aerosmith, *Pump*
Louis Armstrong, *Hello, Dolly!*
Joan Baez, *Diamonds & Rust*
Chet Baker, *Chet Baker Sings*
Solomon Burke, *Don't Give Up On Me*
Johnny Cash, *American Recordings*
Tracy Chapman, *New Beginning*
Natalie Cole, *Unforgettable*
Marianne Faithfull, *Broken English*
Fleetwood Mac, *Fleetwood Mac*
Dexter Gordon, *Go!*
Michael Jackson, *Off the Wall*
Aimee Mann, *Magnolia*
Iggy Pop, *Lust for Life*
Elvis Presley, *Elvis (TV Special)*
Bonnie Raitt, *Nick of Time*
Roxy Music, *Avalon*
Santana, *Supernatural*
The Sting
Tina Turner, *Private Dancer*
ZZ Top, *Eliminator*

Compilations

Hitsville USA: The Motown Singles
A Night at Studio 54
Nuggets: Original Artyfacts

Special Feature Index

Cover Art

AC/DC, *Highway to Hell*
Air, *Moon Safari*
The Allman Brothers, *Eat a Peach*
Herb Alpert/Tijuana Brass, *Whipped Cream and Other Delights*
America, *History*
Aphex Twin, *Selected Ambient Works*
Basie Count, *The Complete Atomic Basie*
The Beatles, *Abbey Road*
The Beatles, *Revolver*
The Beatles, *Sgt. Pepper*
The B-52's, *The B-52's*
Big Brother and the Holding Company, *Cheap Thrills*
Art Blakey, *Moanin'*
Blondie, *Parallel Lines*
Boston, *Boston*
David Bowie, *Heroes*
David Bowie, *Ziggy Stardust*
Dave Brubeck, *Time Out*
A Chorus Line
June Christy, *Something Cool*
The Clash, *London Calling*
Leonard Cohen, *The Songs*
John Coltrane, *Blue Train*
Shawn Colvin, *A Few Small Repairs*
Chick Corea, *Return to Forever*
Elvis Costello, *My Aim Is True*
Cream, *Disraeli Gears*
Miles Davis, *Bitches Brew*
Deee-Lite, *World Clique*
De La Soul, *3 Feet High and Rising*
Devo, *Q: Are We Not Men?*
Nick Drake, *Pink Moon*
Bob Dylan, *Blood on the Tracks*
Earth, Wind & Fire, *That's the Way of the World*
Emerson, Lake and Palmer, *Brain Salad Surgery*
Bill Evans, *Waltz for Debby*
Evita
Fleetwood Mac, *Fleetwood Mac*
Funkadelic, *Maggot Brain*
Goldfinger
Grateful Dead, *American Beauty*
Guns n' Roses, *Appetite for Destruction*
Guns n' Roses, *Use Your Illusion I*
Herbie Hancock, *Maiden Voyage*
PJ Harvey, *Rid of Me*
Isaac Hayes, *Hot Buttered Soul*
Hedwig and the Angry Inch
Ice Cube, *AmeriKKKa's Most Wanted*
Janet Jackson, *janet.*
Jean-Michel Jarre, *Oxygene*
Jethro Tull, *Aqualung*

Elton John, *Goodbye Yellow Brick Rd.*
George Jones, *The Essential*
Joy Division, *Substance*
Carole King, *Really Rosie*
The Kinks, *Lola vs. the Powerman vs. the Money Go-Round*
Diana Krall, *The Look of Love*
Cyndi Lauper, *She's So Unusual*
Led Zeppelin, *Led Zeppelin IV*
Annie Lennox, *Diva*
Madonna, *Like a Virgin*
Curtis Mayfield, *Superfly*
Charles Mingus, *Mingus Ah Um*
Liza Minnelli, *Liza with a "Z"*
Joni Mitchell, *Hejira*
Van Morrison, *Astral Weeks*
Nas, *Illmatic*
New Order, *Power, Corruption & Lies*
Stevie Nicks, *Bella Donna*
Nine Inch Nails, *Downward Spiral*
Nirvana, *Nevermind*
No Doubt, *Tragic Kingdom*
N.W.A, *Straight Outta Compton*
The Orb, *Adventures Beyond the Ultraworld*
Pavement, *Crooked Rain*
Pearl Jam, *Vitalogy*
Tom Petty, *Full Moon Fever*
Pink Floyd, *Dark Side of the Moon*
Elvis Presley, *Elvis (TV Special)*
Prince, *Purple Rain*
The Prodigy, *Music for the Jilted Generation*
Public Enemy, *It Takes a Nation*
Radiohead, *OK Computer*
Rage Against the Machine, *Rage Against the Machine*
The Ramones, *Ramones*
Rancid, *And Out Come the Wolves*
Red Hot Chili Peppers, *Californication*
Lou Reed, *Transformer*
R.E.M., *Murmur*
The Replacements, *Tim*
Rocky
Rocky Horror Picture Show
Rolling Stones, *Some Girls*
Rolling Stones, *Sticky Fingers*
Sonny Rollins, *Saxophone Colossus*
Roxy Music, *Avalon*
Santana, *Abraxas*
The Sex Pistols, *Never Mind the Bollocks Here's the Sex Pistols*
Michelle Shocked, *Short Sharp Shocked*
Wayne Shorter, *Speak No Evil*
Simon & Garfunkel, *The Graduate*
Frank Sinatra, *Only the Lonely*

Special Feature Index

Lucinda Williams, *Lucinda Williams*
Johnny Winter, *Johnny Winter*

Debuts

Afro-Celt Sound System, *Sound Magic Volume 1*
Tori Amos, *Little Earthquakes*
Martha Argerich, *Début Recital*
Arrested Development, *3 Years, 5 Months & 2 Days in the Life of . . .*
Bad Company, *Bad Company*
Erykah Badu, *Baduizm*
Joan Baez, *Joan Baez*
Beastie Boys, *Licensed to Ill*
Ben Folds Five, *Ben Folds Five*
The B-52's, *The B-52's*
Björk, *Debut*
Clint Black, *Killin' Time*
Mary J. Blige, *What's the 411?*
Boogie Down Prod., *Criminal Minded*
Boston, *Boston*
Boyz II Men, *Cooleyhighharmony*
David Bromberg, *David Bromberg*
Brooks & Dunn, *Brand New Man*
Jackson Browne, *Saturate Before Using*
Jeff Buckley, *Grace*
The Cars, *The Cars*
Nick Cave/Bad Seeds, *From Her to Eternity*
Manu Chao, *Clandestino*
Tracy Chapman, *Tracy Chapman*
The Clash, *The Clash*
Leonard Cohen, *The Songs*
Coldplay, *Parachutes*
Lloyd Cole/Commotions, *Rattlesnakes*
Elvis Costello, *My Aim Is True*
Counting Crows, *August and Everything After*
The Cramps, *Songs the Lord Taught Us*
Crosby, Stills & Nash, *Crosby, Stills & Nash*
Sheryl Crow, *Tuesday Night Music Club*
Crowded House, *Crowded House*
The Crystal Method, *Vegas*
Cypress Hill, *Cypress Hill*
Daft Punk, *Homework*
D'Angelo, *Brown Sugar*
Terence Trent D'Arby, *Introducing*
Dead Kennedys, *Fresh Fruit for Rotting Vegetables*
Deee-Lite, *World Clique*
Deep Forest, *Deep Forest*
De La Soul, *3 Feet High and Rising*
Devo, *Q: Are We Not Men?*
Dido, *No Angel*
Digable Planets, *Reachin'*

DJ Shadow, *Endtroducing . . .*
The Doors, *The Doors*
Dr. Dre, *The Chronic*
Dr. Octagon, *Dr. Octagonecologyst*
Duran Duran, *Duran Duran*
Steve Earle, *Guitar Town*
Echo & the Bunnymen, *Crocodiles*
Missy Elliott, *Supa Dupa Fly*
Eminem, *The Slim Shady LP*
The English Beat, *I Just Can't Stop It*
En Vogue, *Born to Sing*
Eric B. & Rakim, *Paid in Full*
50 Cent, *Get Rich or Die Tryin'*
Foo Fighters, *Foo Fighters*
Garbage, *Garbage*
Go-Go's, *Beauty and the Beat*
Macy Gray, *On How Life Is*
Patty Griffin, *Living with Ghosts*
Guns n' Roses, *Appetite for Destruction*
Arlo Guthrie, *Alice's Restaurant*
Jimi Hendrix Experience, *Are You Experienced?*
Lauryn Hill, *The Miseducation*
Whitney Houston, *Whitney Houston*
Ice Cube, *AmeriKKKa's Most Wanted*
Indigo Girls, *Indigo Girls*
Jean-Michel Jarre, *Oxygene*
Norah Jones, *Come Away with Me*
Rickie Lee Jones, *Rickie Lee Jones*
Wynonna Judd, *Wynonna*
Keb' Mo', *Keb' Mo'*
Alicia Keys, *Songs in A Minor*
King Crimson, *In the Court*
Kris Kristofferson, *Kristofferson*
Cyndi Lauper, *She's So Unusual*
Annie Lennox, *Diva*
Ottmar Liebert, *Nouveau Flamenco*
Linkin Park, *Hybrid Theory*
Living Colour, *Vivid*
LL Cool J, *Radio*
Los Lobos, *How Will the Wolf Survive?*
Lyle Lovett, *Lyle Lovett*
Lynyrd Skynyrd, *Pronounced Leh-Nerd Skin-Nerd*
The Mamas and the Papas, *If You Can Believe Your Eyes and Ears*
Aimee Mann, *Whatever*
Massive Attack, *Blue Lines*
Matchbox 20, *Yourself or Someone Like You*
Maxwell, *Urban Hang Suite*
John Mayer, *Room for Squares*
MC 5, *Kick Out the Jams*
Kate & Anna McGarrigle, *Kate & Anna McGarrigle*
Natalie Merchant, *Tigerlilly*
Pat Metheny, *Pat Metheny Group*
George Michael, *Faith*

Moby Grape, *Moby Grape*
The Modern Lovers, *The Modern Lovers*
Morrissey, *Viva Hate*
Mos Def, *Black on Both Sides*
Mos Def and Talib Kweli, *Black Star*
Nas, *Illmatic*
Stevie Nicks, *Bella Donna*
No Doubt, *Tragic Kingdom*
Notorious B.I.G., *Ready to Die*
Olive, *Extra Virgin*
Ozzy Osbourne, *Blizzard of Ozz*
Mandy Patinkin, *Mandy Patinkin*
Pavement, *Slanted and Enchanted*
Pearl Jam, *Ten*
A Perfect Circle, *Mer de Noms*
Peter, Paul & Mary, *Peter, Paul & Mary*
Liz Phair, *Exile in Guyville*
Pharcyde, *Bizarre Ride*
Pixies, *Surfer Rosa*
The Police, *Outlandos d'Amour*
Portishead, *Dummy*
The Pretenders, *The Pretenders*
John Prine, *John Prine*
Procol Harum, *Procol Harum*
Rage Against the Machine, *Rage Against the Machine*
The Ramones, *Ramones*
R.E.M., *Murmur*
LeAnn Rimes, *Blue*
The Roches, *The Roches*
Sade, *Diamond Life*
Jill Scott, *Who Is Jill Scott?*
Slick Rick, *The Great Adventures*
Patti Smith, *Horses*
Snoop Dogg, *Doggystyle*
Phoebe Snow, *Phoebe Snow*
The Specials, *The Specials*
Steely Dan, *Can't Buy a Thrill*
Sting, *The Dream of the Blue Turtles*
The Stone Roses, *The Stone Roses*
Stone Temple Pilots, *Core*
Barbra Streisand, *The Barbra Streisand Album*
The Strokes, *Is This It*
Sugar, *Copper Blue*
Susan Tedeschi, *Just Won't Burn*
Television, *Marquee Moon*
Sundays, *Reading, Writing and Arithmetic*
They Might Be Giants, *Flood*
Randy Travis, *Storms of Life*
A Tribe Called Quest, *People's Instinctive Travels*
Tricky, *Maxinquaye*
Uncle Tupelo, *No Depression*
Van Halen, *Van Halen*
Velvet Underground, *The Velvet Underground and Nico*
Violent Femmes, *Violent Femmes*

Weather Report, *Weather Report*
Weezer, *Weezer*
Gillian Welch, *Revival*
Junior Wells, *Hoodoo Man Blues*
Johnny Winter, *Johnny Winter*
Wu-Tang Clan, *Enter the Wu-Tang*
Dwight Yoakam, *Guitars, Cadillacs*

Family Affair

(Albums appropriate for listeners of all ages)

ABBA, *Gold/Greatest Hits*
Alabama, *Mountain Music*
Aladdin
American Graffiti
Paul Anka, *Paul Anka Sings*
Annie
Louis Armstrong, *Hello, Dolly!*
The Association, *Greatest Hits*
The Beatles, *The Beatles 1962-1966*
Beauty and the Beast
The Bee Gees, *Children of the World*
The Bee Gees, *Saturday Night Fever*
Harry Belafonte, *Calypso*
Best of Schoolhouse Rock
The Big Chill
Sarah Brightman, *Time to Say Goodbye*
Bye Bye Birdie
Camelot
The Carpenters, *The Singles*
Natalie Cole, *Unforgettable*
Nat King Cole, *Nat King Cole Story*
Aaron Copland, *Appalachian Spring*
Jim Croce, *I Got a Name*
Bing Crosby, *A Merry Christmas with Bing Crosby and The Andrews Sisters*
Deee-Lite, *World Clique*
Deep Forest, *Deep Forest*
John Denver, *Greatest Hits*
Donovan, *Donovan's Greatest Hits*
The Eagles, *Their Greatest Hits*
E.T. The Extra-Terrestrial
Everly Brothers, *Cadence Classics*
Fiddler on the Roof
The Four Seasons, *Anthology*
Jerry Garcia/David Grisman, *Not for Kids Only*
Gershwin, *Rhapsody in Blue*
Vince Guaraldi, *A Boy Named Charlie Brown*
Hairspray
Hitsville USA: The Motown Singles
The Hollies, *Greatest Hits*
Buddy Holly, *The Best*
Jackson 5, *Anthology*
Janet Jackson, *Janet Jackson's Rhythm Nation 1814*
Michael Jackson, *Bad*
Michael Jackson, *Off the Wall*

Michael Jackson, *Thriller*
Billy Joel, *The Stranger*
Elton John, *Greatest Hits*
Norah Jones, *Come Away with Me*
The Judds, *Greatest Hits*
KC/Sunshine Band, *The Best*
The King and I
Carole King, *Really Rosie*
Kingston Trio, *Sold Out/String Along*
Kiss, *Alive!*
Alison Krauss, *Now That I've Found You*
Ottmar Liebert, *Nouveau Flamenco*
The Lion King
The Little Mermaid
Little Richard, *The Essential*
Ray Lynch, *Deep Breakfast*
The Mamas and the Papas, *If You Can Believe Your Eyes and Ears*
Mame
Mamma Mia!
Chuck Mangione, *Feels So Good*
Barry Manilow, *Greatest Hits*
Mannheim Steamroller, *Fresh Aire IV*
Bob Marley and the Wailers, *Legend*
Mary Poppins
John Mayer, *Room for Squares*
Yo-Yo Ma, etc., *Appalachia Waltz*
Meet Me in St. Louis
Muppet Movie
The Music Man
Mussorgsky, *Pictures at an Exhibition*
Willie Nelson, *Stardust*
The Nitty Gritty Dirt Band, *Will the Circle Be Unbroken*
Oliver!
Dolly Parton, Linda Ronstadt & Emmylou Harris, *Trio*
Peter, Paul & Mary, *Peter, Paul & Mary*
The Pink Panther
The Police, *Outlandos d'Amour*
Elvis Presley, *Elvis' Golden Records*
Raffi, *Baby Beluga*
LeAnn Rimes, *Blue*
Rocky
Sesame Street, *Platinum*
Singin' in the Rain
Sleepless in Seattle
The Sound of Music
The Sting
The Supremes, *Anthology*
They Might Be Giants, *Flood*
They Might Be Giants, *NO!*
Marlo Thomas and Friends, *Free to Be . . . You & Me*
Three Dog Night, *The Best*
Titanic

Andreas Vollenweider, *Down to the Moon*
The Weavers, *at Carnegie Hall*
West Side Story
Wham!, *Make It Big*
George Winston, *Autumn*
The Wizard of Oz

Fireworks

AC/DC, *Back in Black*
AC/DC, *Highway to Hell*
Aerosmith, *Pump*
Aerosmith, *Toys in the Attic*
Annie Get Your Gun
Apocalypse Now
Martha Argerich, *Début Recital*
J.S. Bach, *State of Wonder*
Bartók, *Concerto for Orchestra*
Jeff Beck, *Blow by Blow*
Beethoven, *Symphony No. 9*
Berlioz, *Symphonie Fantastique*
Bizet, *Carmen Suites; L'Arlesienne Suites*
Björk, *Selmasongs*
Black Sabbath, *Paranoid*
Boston, *Boston*
Maria Callas, *The Very Best*
The Chemical Brothers, *Dig Your Own Hole*
Aaron Copland, *Appalachian Spring*
The Crow
Def Leppard, *Hysteria*
Def Leppard, *Pyromania*
Celine Dion, *Let's Talk About Love*
Dire Straits, *Brothers in Arms*
DJ Shadow, *Endtroducing . . .*
Eric Dolphy, *Out to Lunch!*
Dreamgirls
8 Mile
Gloria Estefan, *Greatest Hits*
Garbage, *Garbage*
Gershwin, *Rhapsody in Blue*
Gypsy
Handel, *Water Music*
Hedwig and the Angry Inch
Jimi Hendrix, *Band of Gypsys*
Jimi Hendrix Experience, *Are You Experienced?*
Jimi Hendrix Experience, *Electric Ladyland*
Holst, *The Planets*
Iron Maiden, *Number of the Beast*
Janet Jackson, *Janet Jackson's Rhythm Nation 1814*
Kansas, *Point of Know Return*
Stan Kenton, *Kenton in Hi-Fi*
Linkin Park, *Hybrid Theory*
Lynyrd Skynyrd, *Second Helping*
Mahler, *Symphony No. 5*
Matrix
Metallica, *Master of Puppets*

Metallica, *Metallica*
Midnight Oil, *Diesel and Dust*
Charles Mingus, *Mingus Ah Um*
Moulin Rouge!
Mussorgsky, *Pictures at an Exhibition*
Nine Inch Nails, *Downward Spiral*
No Doubt, *Rock Steady*
Orff, *Carmina Burana*
Ozzy Osbourne, *Blizzard of Ozz*
Outkast, *Stankonia*
Charlie Parker, *Yardbird Suite*
Parliament, *Mothership Connection*
Mandy Patinkin, *Mandy Patinkin*
Pink Floyd, *The Wall*
Rachmaninoff, *Concerto No. 2*
Reservoir Dogs
Rimsky-Korsakov, *Scheherazade*
Rocky
Satie, *Gymnopédies, Gnossiennes*
Slayer, *Reign in Blood*
Soundgarden, *Superunknown*
Richard Strauss, *Also Sprach Zarathustra*
Stravinsky, *Petrushka*
Art Tatum, *Tatum Group Masterpieces, Vol. 1*
Top Gun
Van Cliburn, *Tchaikovsky; Rachmaninoff*
Wu-Tang Clan, *Enter the Wu-Tang*
Yes, *Fragile*

Grammy Winners

(* Album of the Year winner)

Ain't Misbehavin'
Alabama, *Mountain Music*
Aladdin
Annie
J.S. Bach, *Mass in B minor*
J.S. Bach, *Six Unaccompanied Cello Suites*
J.S. Bach, *State of Wonder*
Erykah Badu, *Baduizm*
Anita Baker, *Rapture*
Bartók, *Concerto for Orchestra*
Bartók, *6 String Quartets*
The Beatles, *Abbey Road*
The Beatles, *Sgt. Pepper**
Beauty and the Beast
Beck, *Odelay*
The Bee Gees, *Saturday Night Fever**
Pat Benatar, *Crimes of Passion*
Tony Bennett, *Playin' With My Friends*
George Benson, *Breezin'*
Berlioz, *Symphonie Fantastique*
Blood, Sweat and Tears, *Blood, Sweat and Tears**
Boyz II Men, *Cooleyhighharmony*

Breakfast at Tiffany's
Garth Brooks, *Ropin' the Wind*
Buena Vista Social Club
Solomon Burke, *Don't Give Up On Me*
Cabaret
Johnny Cash, *American Recordings*
Tracy Chapman, *Tracy Chapman*
Eric Clapton, *Unplugged**
Close Encounters of the Third Kind
Coldplay, *Parachutes*
Coldplay, *A Rush of Blood to the Head*
Natalie Cole, *Unforgettable**
Albert Collins, Johnny Copeland and Robert Cray, *Showdown!*
Phil Collins, *No Jacket Required**
Company
Aaron Copland, *Appalachian Spring*
Robert Cray, *Strong Persuader*
D'Angelo, *Voodoo*
Terence Trent D'Arby, *Introducing*
Miles Davis, *Bitches Brew*
Miles Davis with Gil Evans, *Sketches of Spain*
Dire Straits, *Brothers in Arms*
Dixie Chicks, *Home*
Dixie Chicks, *Wide Open Spaces*
Dreamgirls
Dr. Zhivago
Eminem, *The Eminem Show*
Eminem, *The Marshall Mathers LP*
Eminem, *The Slim Shady LP*
E.T. The Extra-Terrestrial
Flashdance
Fleetwood Mac, *Rumours**
Follies in Concert
The Fugees, *The Score*
Funny Girl
Peter Gabriel, *Passion*
Judy Garland, *Judy at Carnegie Hall**
Stan Getz, *Getz/Gilberto**
Gigi
The Godfather
Green Day, *Dookie*
Guys and Dolls
Gypsy
Hair
Hairspray
Emmylou Harris, *Wrecking Ball*
Isaac Hayes, *Shaft*
Don Henley, *The End of the Innocence*
Faith Hill, *Breathe*
Lauryn Hill, *The Miseducation**
Lena Horne, *An Evening with*
Vladimir Horowitz, *in Moscow*
Whitney Houston, *The Bodyguard**
India.Arie, *Voyage to India*
Indigo Girls, *Indigo Girls*

Special Feature Index

Guest Appearance
(Followed by guest name[s])

Special Feature Index

Daft Punk, *Discovery* (Romanthony, Todd Edwards)

D'Angelo, *Voodoo* (Roy Hargrove, Charlie Hunter, ?uestlove, etc.)

Miles Davis, *Bitches Brew* (including Chick Corea, John McLaughlin, Wayne Shorter)

Deee-Lite, *World Clique* (Bootsy Collins, Q-Tip, Horny Horns)

Derek & the Dominos, *Layla* (Duane Allman)

Celine Dion, *Let's Talk About Love* (The Bee Gees, Luciano Pavarotti, Barbra Streisand)

Nick Drake, *Bryter Later* (Richard Thompson, John Cale)

Dr. Dre, *The Chronic* (Snoop Doggy Dog)

The Eagles, *The Long Run* (Jimmy Buffett)

Missy Elliott, *Supa Dupa Fly* (Aaliyah, Busta Rhymes, Lil' Kim, etc.)

Eminem, *The Marshall Mathers LP* (Snoop Dogg, Sticky Fingaz, Xzibitz, etc.)

Gloria Estefan, *Greatest Hits* (Jon Secada)

Roberta Flack, *Softly With These Songs* (Maxi Priest, Luther Vandross, Donny Hathaway, etc.)

The Four Tops, *Anthology* (The Supremes)

Peter Gabriel, *Passion* (Nusrat Fateh Ali Khan, Youssou N'Dour, Baaba Mal, etc.)

Peter Gabriel, *So* (Kate Bush, Laurie Anderson, Bill Laswell)

Marvin Gaye, *Anthology* (Tammi Terrell, Mary Wells, Kim Weston)

Stan Getz, *Getz/Gilberto* (Astrud Gilberto)

Dizzy Gillespie, *At Newport* (Mary Lou Williams)

Benny Goodman, *B.G. in Hi-Fi* (Ruby Braff)

Macy Gray, *On How Life Is* (John Brion)

Nanci Griffith, *Flyer* (Adam Duritz, Mark Knopfler, U2, Indigo Girls)

Guns n' Roses, *Use Your Illusion I* (Alice Cooper)

Don Henley, *Building the Perfect Beast* (Lindsey Buckingham, Belinda Carlisle, Randy Newman, etc.)

Don Henley, *The End of the Innocence* (Bruce Hornsby, Axl Rose, Take 6, etc.)

Lauryn Hill, *The Miseducation* (Mary J. Blige, D'Angelo, Carlos Santana)

John Lee Hooker, *Ultimate Collection* (Bonnie Raitt)

Whitney Houston, *Whitney Houston* (Germaine Jackson, Teddy Pendergrass)

Ice Cube, *AmeriKKKa's Most Wanted* (Chuck D, Flavor Flav, Yo-Yo, etc.)

Indigo Girls, *Indigo Girls* (R.E.M., Hothouse Flowers, Luka Bloom)

Michael Jackson, *Bad* (Stevie Wonder, Siedah Garrett, the Winans)

Jay-Z, *The Blueprint* (Biz Markie, Eminem, Slick Rick, etc.)

Jesus Christ Superstar (Ian Gillan)

Jurassic 5, *Power in Numbers* (Big Daddy Kane, Kool Keith, Nelly Furtado)

KLF, *The White Room* (Tammy Wynette)

Cyndi Lauper, *She's So Unusual* (The Hooters)

John Lennon, *The John Lennon Collection* (Elton John)

Linkin Park, *Hybrid Theory* (The Dust Brothers)

Little Feat, *Feats Don't Fail Me Now* (Emmylou Harris, Bonnie Raitt)

Massive Attack, *Blue Lines* (Horace Andy, Neneh Cherry)

Massive Attack, *Protection* (Tracey Thorn, Craig Armstrong)

Johnny Mathis, *Johnny's Greatest* (Ray Coniff)

John Mayall, *Bluesbreakers: John Mayall with Eric Clapton* (Eric Clapton)

Alanis Morissette, *Jagged Little Pill* (Benmont Tench, Dave Navarro)

Mos Def, *Black on Both Sides* (Busta Rhymes, Talib Kweli)

Mott the Hoople, *All the Young Dudes* (David Bowie)

Bob Mould, *Workbook* (Anton Fier)

Oliver Nelson, *Blues/Abstract Truth* (Eric Dolphy)

Stevie Nicks, *Bella Donna* (Don Henley, Tom Petty)

The Nitty Gritty Dirt Band, *Will the Circle Be Unbroken* (Roy Acuff, Mother Maybelle Carter, Earl Scruggs, etc.)

No Doubt, *Rock Steady* (Prince, Lady Saw)

Notorious B.I.G., *Life After Death* (Krayzie Bone, Faith Evans, Carl Thomas, etc.)

Special Feature Index

Beth Orton, *Central Reservation* (Dr. John, Dr. Robert, Ben Watt, Terry Callier)

Outkast, *Aquemini* (Cee-Lo, Erykah Badu, George Clinton, etc.)

Outkast, *Stankonia* (Erykah Badu, Goodie Mob, Killer Mike, etc.)

Alan Parsons Project, *I Robot* (Allan Clarke, Steve Harley)

Tom Petty, *Full Moon Fever* (George Harrison, Roy Orbison, Jeff Lynne)

Pink Floyd, *The Wall* (Toni Tenille)

P!nk, *M!ssundaztood* (Linda Perry, Richie Sambora, Steven Tyler)

Iggy Pop, *Lust for Life* (David Bowie)

Prince, *Sign 'O' the Times* (Sheena Easton, Susanna Hoffs)

The Prodigy, *Music for the Jilted Generation* (Pop Will Eat Itself)

Linda Ronstadt, *Heart Like a Wheel* (Cissy Houston, Emmylou Harris, Maria Muldaur, etc.)

The Roots, *Phrenology* (Amiri Baraka, Nelly Furtado, Jill Scott, etc.)

Run-D.M.C., *Raising Hell* (Joe Perry, Steven Tyler)

Santana, *Shaman* (Seal, Michelle Branch, Placido Domingo, etc.)

Diane Schuur, *Diane Schuur & The Count Basie Orchestra* (Frank Foster)

Tupac Shakur, *All Eyez on Me* (Snoop Dogg, Dr. Dre, Redman, etc.)

Frank Sinatra, *Duets* (Luther Vandross, Anita Baker, Aretha Franklin, etc.)

Slick Rick, *The Great Adventures* (Jam Master Jay)

Patti Smith, *Easter* (Todd Rudgren, Lenny Kaye, Les Paul)

Steely Dan, *Aja* (Wayne Shorter)

Barbra Streisand, *Memories* (Donna Summer, Neil Diamond)

Matthew Sweet, *Girlfriend* (Lloyd Cole, Robert Quine, Richard Lloyd)

Talking Heads, *Remain in Light* (Brian Eno)

Talking Heads, *Speaking in Tongues* (Nona Hendryx)

Art Tatum, *Tatum Group Masterpieces, Vol. 1* (Benny Carter, Louie Bellson)

James Taylor, *October Road* (Ry Cooder)

Thievery Corporation, *The Mirror Conspiracy* (Bebel Gilberto)

Marlo Thomas and Friends, *Free to Be ... You & Me* (Alan Alda, Harry Belafonte, Carol Channing, etc.)

A Tribe Called Quest, *Low End Theory* (Ron Carter, Busta Rhymes)

Tricky, *Maxinquaye* (Alison Goldfrapp)

Tina Turner, *Private Dancer* (Jeff Beck)

U2, *Achtung Baby* (Brian Eno, Daniel Lanois)

Tom Waits, *Rain Dogs* (John Lurie, Keith Richards, Marc Ribot)

Stevie Wonder, *Songs/Key of Life* (Herbie Hancock, George Benson, Eddie "Bongo" Brown, etc.)

Stevie Wonder, *Talking Book* (Jeff Beck, David Sanborne, Deniece Williams, etc.)

Lester Young, *With the Oscar Peterson Trio* (Oscar Peterson)

Neil Young, *After the Gold Rush* (Nils Lofgren, Stephen Stills)

Warren Zevon, *Excitable Boy* (Linda Ronstadt, Jackson Browne, Karla Bonoff, John McVie, Mick Fleetwood)

Late Night

Cannonball Adderley, *Somethin' Else*

Air, *Moon Safari*

Tori Amos, *Little Earthquakes*

Aphex Twin, *Selected Ambient Works*

Anita Baker, *Rapture*

Chet Baker, *Chet Baker Sings*

Barber, *Adagio for Strings; Violin Concerto*

Beethoven, *Piano Sonatas 8, 13 & 14*

Belle & Sebastian, *If You're Feeling Sinister*

Big Star, *Sister Lovers/Third*

Art Blakey, *Moanin'*

Mary J. Blige, *My Life*

Toni Braxton, *Secrets*

Breakfast at Tiffany's

Jeff Buckley, *Grace*

Nick Cave/Bad Seeds, *From Her to Eternity*

Ray Charles, *Anthology*

The Chemical Brothers, *Dig Your Own Hole*

Chopin, *Nocturnes*

June Christy, *Something Cool*

Patsy Cline, *Greatest Hits*

Rosemary Clooney, *Sings the Music of Cole Porter*

Close Encounters of the Third Kind

Special Feature Index

Chris Isaak, *Heart Shaped World*
Janet Jackson, *janet.*
Journey, *Escape*
Diana Krall, *The Look of Love*
Lenny Kravitz, *Are You Gonna Go My Way?*
Kruder & Dorfmeister, *K & D Sessions*
k.d. lang, *Ingenue*
k.d. lang, *Shadowland*
Led Zeppelin, *Led Zeppelin II*
Peggy Lee, *Spotlight on Peggy Lee*
Annie Lennox, *Diva*
Madonna, *Ray of Light*
Massive Attack, *Blue Lines*
Massive Attack, *Protection*
Johnny Mathis, *Johnny's Greatest*
Maxwell, *Urban Hang Suite*
John Mayer, *Room for Squares*
George Michael, *Faith*
Moby, *Play*
Morcheeba, *Big Calm*
Van Morrison, *Moondance*
Oliver Nelson, *Blues/Abstract Truth*
Willie Nelson, *Stardust*
No Doubt, *Rock Steady*
Sinéad O'Connor, *I Do Not Want What I Haven't Got*
Olive, *Extra Virgin*
Roy Orbison, *The All-Time Greatest*
Orff, *Carmina Burana*
Beth Orton, *Central Reservation*
Parliament, *Mothership Connection*
The Pink Panther
Portishead, *Dummy*
Prince, *Purple Rain*
Prince, *Sign 'O' the Times*
Bonnie Raitt, *Nick of Time*
Ravel, *Boléro*
Otis Redding, *The Otis Redding Story*
Lionel Richie, *Can't Slow Down*
Romeo + Juliet
Roxy Music, *Avalon*
Sade, *Diamond Life*
Satie, *Gymnopédies, Gnossiennes*
Jill Scott, *Who Is Jill Scott?*
Seal, *Seal*
Frank Sinatra, *Sinatra Reprise*
Frank Sinatra, *Songs for Swingin' Lovers*
Snoop Dogg, *Doggystyle*
Dusty Springfield, *Dusty in Memphis*
Steely Dan, *Aja*
Thievery Corporation, *The Mirror Conspiracy*
TLC, *CrazySexyCool*
T. Rex, *Electric Warrior*
Tricky, *Maxinquaye*
Shania Twain, *Come on Over*
Twin Peaks
U2, *Achtung Baby*

U2, *The Joshua Tree*
Vangelis, *Chariots of Fire*
Grover Washington Jr., *Winelight*
Muddy Waters, *The Best*
When Harry Met Sally
Barry White, *All-Time Greatest Hits*
Cassandra Wilson, *New Moon Daughter*

Nature

Aphex Twin, *Selected Ambient Works*
Berlioz, *Symphonie Fantastique*
John Denver, *Greatest Hits*
Jerry Garcia/David Grisman, *Not for Kids Only*
Herbie Hancock, *Maiden Voyage*
Handel, *Water Music*
Holst, *The Planets*
Jean-Michel Jarre, *Oxygene*
Kitaro, *Silk Road, Vol. 1*
Koyaanisqatsi
Mannheim Steamroller, *Fresh Aire IV*
Yo-Yo Ma, etc., *Appalachia Waltz*
The Orb, *Adventures Beyond the Ultraworld*
Raffi, *Baby Beluga*
Smetana, *Má Vlast*
Vivaldi, *The Four Seasons*
Andreas Vollenweider, *Down to the Moon*
Waterboys, *Fisherman's Blues*
Weather Report, *Weather Report*
George Winston, *Autumn*

Number One

(Reached top spot on the Billboard Top 200 chart)
Boyz II Men, *Boyz II Men, II*
Aaliyah, *Aaliyah*
Alabama, *Mountain Music*
Herb Alpert/Tijuana Brass, *Whipped Cream and Other Delights*
Tori Amos, *Little Earthquakes*
AWB (Average White Band), *AWB*
Bad Company, *Bad Company*
Beastie Boys, *Licensed to Ill*
The Beatles, *Abbey Road*
The Beatles, *Revolver*
The Beatles, *Sgt. Pepper*
The Beatles, *The White Album*
The Bee Gees, *Saturday Night Fever*
Harry Belafonte, *Calypso*
George Benson, *Breezin'*
Big Brother and the Holding Company, *Cheap Thrills*
Björk, *Debut*
Blood, Sweat and Tears, *Blood, Sweat and Tears*

One-Hit Wonders

(The only hit album from the artist/band)

Party

Special Feature Index

Fats Waller, *Ain't Misbehavin'*
War, *War's Greatest Hits*
Grover Washington Jr., *Winelight*
Ween, *Chocolate and Cheese*
Hank Williams, *40 Greatest Hits*
ZZ Top, *Eliminator*

Rainy Day

Tori Amos, *Little Earthquakes*
Barber, *Adagio for Strings; Violin Concerto*
Belle & Sebastian, *If You're Feeling Sinister*
The Blues Brothers
Solomon Burke, *Don't Give Up On Me*
Ray Charles, *Anthology*
Leonard Cohen, *I'm Your Man*
Coldplay, *Parachutes*
The Crow
The Cure, *Boys Don't Cry*
Miles Davis, *Kind of Blue*
Dido, *No Angel*
Missy Elliott, *Supa Dupa Fly*
Everything But the Girl, *Amplified Heart*
Everything But the Girl, *Walking Wounded*
Fiddler on the Roof
Roberta Flack, *Softly With These Songs*
Judy Garland, *Judy at Carnegie Hall*
David Gray, *White Ladder*
Billie Holiday, *Lady Sings the Blues*
Manhattan
Loreena McKennitt, *Book of Secrets*
Natalie Merchant, *Tigerlilly*
Morrissey, *Viva Hate*
Willie Nelson, *Red Headed Stranger*
Sinéad O'Connor, *I Do Not Want What I Haven't Got*
Beth Orton, *Central Reservation*
Portishead, *Dummy*
Louis Prima, *Zooma Zooma*
R.E.M., *Murmur*
Seal, *Seal*
Nina Simone, *Wild Is the Wind*
Singin' in the Rain
Sleepless in Seattle
Elliot Smith, *XO*
The Smiths, *The Queen Is Dead*
Dusty Springfield, *Dusty in Memphis*
Cat Stevens, *Tea for the Tillerman*
Sundays, *Reading, Writing and Arithmetic*
Vivaldi, *The Four Seasons*
Wagner, *Der Ring des Nibelungen*
Dionne Warwick, *The Dionne Warwick Collection*
Gillian Welch, *Revival*
Hank Williams, *40 Greatest Hits*

Road

ABBA, *Gold/Greatest Hits*
AC/DC, *Back in Black*
AC/DC, *Highway to Hell*
Aerosmith, *Toys in the Attic*
Air, *Moon Safari*
The Allman Brothers, *Eat a Peach*
America, *History*
American Graffiti
Animal House
The Beach Boys, *Pet Sounds*
George Benson, *Breezin'*
Chuck Berry, *The Great Twenty-Eight*
The Big Chill
The Blues Brothers
Boston, *Boston*
Jackson Browne, *Running on Empty*
Dave Brubeck, *Time Out*
Cabaret
The Cars, *The Cars*
Johnny Cash, *At Folsom Prison*
Johnny Cash, *The Essential*
Cheap Trick, *Live at Budokan*
Aaron Copland, *Appalachian Spring*
Chick Corea, *Return to Forever*
Sheryl Crow, *Tuesday Night Music Club*
The Crystal Method, *Vegas*
John Denver, *Greatest Hits*
Depeche Mode, *Music for the Masses*
Dire Straits, *Brothers in Arms*
Dixie Chicks, *Wide Open Spaces*
The Doors, *The Doors*
The Doors, *L.A. Woman*
Dr. Dre, *The Chronic*
The Eagles, *Their Greatest Hits*
The Eagles, *Hotel California*
Steve Earle, *Guitar Town*
Easy Rider
Melissa Etheridge, *Yes I Am*
Forrest Gump
Jerry Garcia/David Grisman, *Not for Kids Only*
Godspell
Go-Go's, *Beauty and the Beat*
Guns n' Roses, *Use Your Illusion I*
Hair
Don Henley, *Building the Perfect Beast*
High Fidelity
Alan Jackson, *A Lot About Livin'*
Waylon Jennings, *Honky Tonk Heroes*
Robert Johnson, *The Complete Recordings*
Janis Joplin, *Pearl*
KC/Sunshine Band, *The Best*
B.B. King and Eric Clapton, *Riding with the King*

Special Feature Index

Rowdy
Animal House
Bad Brains, *I Against I*
Bartók, *6 String Quartets*
Beastie Boys, *Licensed to Ill*
Beastie Boys, *Paul's Boutique*
Pat Benatar, *Crimes of Passion*
Black Flag, *Damaged*
Bye Bye Birdie
The Clash, *London Calling*
The Commitments
Alice Cooper, *Greatest Hits*
Cypress Hill, *Cypress Hill*
Devo, *Q: Are We Not Men?*
Easy Rider
8 Mile
Eminem, *The Eminem Show*
Eminem, *The Marshall Mathers LP*
Eminem, *The Slim Shady LP*
Guns n' Roses, *Appetite for Destruction*
Guns n' Roses, *Use Your Illusion I*
Hairspray
High Fidelity
Holst, *The Planets*
Ice Cube, *AmeriKKKa's Most Wanted*
Billy Idol, *Rebel Yell*
Waylon Jennings, *Honky Tonk Heroes*
Joan Jett & the Blackhearts, *I Love Rock 'n' Roll*
Wynonna Judd, *Wynonna*
Albert King, *Ultimate Collection*
Led Zeppelin, *Led Zeppelin II*
LL Cool J, *Radio*
Lynyrd Skynyrd, *Pronounced Leh-Nerd Skin-Nerd*
Lynyrd Skynyrd, *Second Helping*
Meat Loaf, *Bat out of Hell*
Charles Mingus, *Mingus Ah Um*
Stevie Nicks, *Bella Donna*
Nuggets: Original Artyfacts
Orff, *Carmina Burana*
Outkast, *Stankonia*
P!nk, *M!ssundaztood*
Louis Prima, *Zooma Zooma*
Public Enemy, *It Takes a Nation*
Rent
Rocky Horror Picture Show
Rolling Stones, *Exile on Main Street*
Rolling Stones, *Sticky Fingers*
The Sex Pistols, *Never Mind the Bollocks Here's the Sex Pistols*
Stravinsky, *Petrushka*
A Tribe Called Quest, *Low End Theory*
Van Halen, *1984 (MCMLXXXIV)*
Van Halen, *Van Halen*
Stevie Ray Vaughan & Double Trouble, *Greatest Hits*
The Who, *Who's Next*
Johnny Winter, *Johnny Winter*
Dwight Yoakam, *Guitars, Cadillacs*
Lester Young, *With the Oscar Peterson Trio*
Neil Young & Crazy Horse, *Rust Never Sleeps*
ZZ Top, *Eliminator*

Spiritual
Anonymous 4, *An English Ladymass*
Arrested Development, *3 Years, 5 Months & 2 Days in the Life of . . .*
J.S. Bach, *Mass in B minor*
Barber, *Adagio for Strings; Violin Concerto*
Beethoven, *Symphony No. 9*
Burning Spear, *Marcus Garvey*
Johnny Cash, *At Folsom Prison*
John Coltrane, *A Love Supreme*
Bing Crosby, *A Merry Christmas with Bing Crosby and The Andrews Sisters*
Enigma, *MCMXC A.D.*
Enya, *Watermark*
Peter Gabriel, *Passion*
Godspell
Górecki, *Symphony No. 3*
Handel, *Messiah*
Lauryn Hill, *The Miseducation*
India.Arie, *Voyage to India*
Jesus Christ Superstar
Jethro Tull, *Aqualung*
Ray Lynch, *Deep Breakfast*
Madonna, *Ray of Light*
Bob Marley and the Wailers, *Burnin'*
Bob Marley and the Wailers, *Legend*
Sarah McLachlan, *Surfacing*
Van Morrison, *Astral Weeks*
Mozart, *Requiem*
Oliver Nelson, *Blues/Abstract Truth*
The Nitty Gritty Dirt Band, *Will the Circle Be Unbroken*
O Brother, Where Art Thou?
Dolly Parton, Linda Ronstadt & Emmylou Harris, *Trio*
Prince, *Sign 'O' the Times*
Stevie Wonder, *Songs/Key of Life*

Summer
Afro-Celt Sound System, *Sound Magic Volume 1*
Alabama, *Mountain Music*
Herb Alpert/Tijuana Brass, *Whipped Cream and Other Delights*
American Graffiti
The Association, *Greatest Hits*
The Beach Boys, *Pet Sounds*
The Bee Gees, *Children of the World*
Harry Belafonte, *Calypso*
George Benson, *Breezin'*

Jimmy Buffett, *Songs You Know by Heart*
Manu Chao, *Clandestino*
Jimmy Cliff, *The Harder They Come*
Alice Cooper, *Greatest Hits*
Chick Corea, *Return to Forever*
Creedence Clearwater Revival, *Chronicle*
Sheryl Crow, *Tuesday Night Music Club*
Bo Diddley, *The Chess Box*
Dirty Dancing
Dr. Dre, *The Chronic*
The Drifters, *All-Time Greatest Hits*
The Eagles, *Their Greatest Hits*
Steve Earle, *Guitar Town*
Easy Rider
8 Mile
Missy Elliott, *Supa Dupa Fly*
Everly Brothers, *Cadence Classics*
Cesaria Evora, *Miss Perfumado*
Fatboy Slim, *You've Come a Long Way, Baby*
The Four Seasons, *Anthology*
Stan Getz, *Getz/Gilberto*
Go-Go's, *Beauty and the Beat*
Grease
Hall & Oates, *Rock 'n' Soul, Part 1*
Don Henley, *Building the Perfect Beast*
INXS, *Kick*
Alan Jackson, *A Lot About Livin'*
Antonio Carlos Jobim, *Wave*
Journey, *Escape*
Keb' Mo', *Keb' Mo'*
Kruder & Dorfmeister, *K & D Sessions*
Lyle Lovett, *Lyle Lovett*
Shelby Lynne, *I Am Shelby Lynne*
Bob Marley and the Wailers, *Legend*
Massive Attack, *Blue Lines*
Matchbox 20, *Yourself or Someone Like You*
Jo Dee Messina, *I'm Alright*
Miami Vice
Bette Midler, *Beaches*
Moby Grape, *Moby Grape*
The Nitty Gritty Dirt Band, *Will the Circle Be Unbroken*
No Doubt, *Rock Steady*
Outkast, *Aquemini*
Red Hot Chili Peppers, *Californication*
The Righteous Brothers, *Anthology*
Rocky
Boz Scaggs, *Silk Degrees*
Snoop Dogg, *Doggystyle*
South Pacific
Bruce Springsteen, *Born in the USA*
Steve Miller Band, *Greatest Hits*

Rod Stewart, *Every Picture Tells a Story*
Sublime, *Sublime*
Matthew Sweet, *Girlfriend*
James Taylor, *Greatest Hits*
Vivaldi, *The Four Seasons*
Andreas Vollenweider, *Down to the Moon*
Lucinda Williams, *Lucinda Williams*
Steve Winwood, *Arc of a Diver*
Woodstock
Neil Young, *After the Gold Rush*

Sunday Morning

Ain't Misbehavin'
Amélie
An American in Paris
Paul Anka, *Paul Anka Sings*
Annie
Anything Goes
J.S. Bach, *Brandenburg Concertos*
J.S. Bach, *Six Unaccompanied Cello Suites*
J.S. Bach, *State of Wonder*
Burt Bacharach, *Greatest Hits*
The Beatles, *Rubber Soul*
Beethoven, *Piano Sonatas 8, 13 & 14*
Beethoven, *Symphonies 5 & 7*
Beethoven, *Violin Sonatas 9 & 5*
Harry Belafonte and Lena Horne, *Porgy and Bess*
Tony Bennett, *Playin' With My Friends*
George Benson, *Breezin'*
Mary J. Blige, *No More Drama*
Blood, Sweat and Tears, *Blood, Sweat and Tears*
Glen Campbell, *Wichita Lineman*
Candide
The Carpenters, *The Singles*
The Chieftains, *Long Black Veil*
A Chorus Line
Joe Cocker, *With a Little Help from My Friends*
John Coltrane, *A Love Supreme*
Company
Crazy for You
Blossom Dearie, *Blossom Dearie*
Iris DeMent, *My Life*
Doobie Brothers, *Best*
Dreamgirls
Bill Evans, *Waltz for Debby*
Evita
Fiddler on the Roof
The 5th Dimension, *Greatest Hits on Earth*
Ella Fitzgerald, *Best of the Songbooks*
Follies in Concert
Godspell
David Gray, *White Ladder*

Vince Guaraldi, *A Boy Named Charlie Brown*
Guys and Dolls
Gypsy
Hair
George Harrison, *All Things Must Pass*
Jascha Heifetz, *Beethoven & Mendelssohn: Violin Concertos*
Keith Jarrett, *The Köln Concert*
Elton John, *Greatest Hits*
Elton John, *Goodbye Yellow Brick Rd.*
Rickie Lee Jones, *Rickie Lee Jones*
Kiss Me, Kate
Alison Krauss, *Now That I've Found You*
Little Shop of Horrors
Ray Lynch, *Deep Breakfast*
Mame
Mamma Mia!
Manhattan Transfer, *The Best*
Mannheim Steamroller, *Fresh Aire IV*
John Mayer, *Room for Squares*
Yo-Yo Ma, etc., *Appalachia Waltz*
Bette Midler, *Beaches*
Joni Mitchell, *Court and Spark*
Mozart, *Don Giovanni*
Mozart, *Piano Concertos 19-23*
Mozart, *Symphonies 35–41*
Anne Murray, *Greatest Hits*
My Fair Lady
Oliver Nelson, *Blues/Abstract Truth*
The Nitty Gritty Dirt Band, *Will the Circle Be Unbroken*
Gram Parsons, *Grievous Angel*
Mandy Patinkin, *Mandy Patinkin*
Edith Piaf, *La Vie En Rose*
Elvis Presley, *From Elvis in Memphis*
Rachmaninoff, *Concerto No. 2*
Otis Redding, *The Otis Redding Story*
The Roches, *The Roches*
Mstislav Rostropovich, *Dvořák; Tchaikovsky*
Satie, *Gymnopédies, Gnossiennes*
Show Boat
Side by Side by Sondheim
Paul Simon, *There Goes Rhymin' Simon*
Simon & Garfunkel, *The Graduate*
Phoebe Snow, *Phoebe Snow*
South Pacific
Dusty Springfield, *Dusty in Memphis*
Cat Stevens, *Tea for the Tillerman*
Sting, *The Dream of the Blue Turtles*
Sweeney Todd
Matthew Sweet, *Girlfriend*
The Temptations, *Greatest Hits*
Sundays, *Reading, Writing and Arithmetic*

Richard Thompson, *Rumor and Sigh*
Van Cliburn, *Tchaikovsky; Rachmaninoff*
Vivaldi, *The Four Seasons*
Dionne Warwick, *The Dionne Warwick Collection*
Waterboys, *Fisherman's Blues*
George Winston, *Autumn*
Stevie Wonder, *Songs/Key of Life*

Teen Spirit

Alice in Chains, *Dirt*
American Graffiti
Animal House
Paul Anka, *Paul Anka Sings*
The Beach Boys, *Pet Sounds*
Beastie Boys, *Licensed to Ill*
The Beatles, *The Beatles 1962-1966*
Chuck Berry, *The Great Twenty-Eight*
Black Flag, *Damaged*
Boyz II Men, *Cooleyhighharmony*
The Breakfast Club
Bye Bye Birdie
Alice Cooper, *Greatest Hits*
Dirty Dancing
8 Mile
Everly Brothers, *Cadence Classics*
Fame
Flashdance
Footloose
The Four Seasons, *Anthology*
Go-Go's, *Beauty and the Beat*
Grease
Green Day, *Dookie*
Guns n' Roses, *Use Your Illusion I*
Hairspray
Hedwig and the Angry Inch
Buddy Holly, *The Best*
Janet Jackson, *Janet Jackson's Rhythm Nation 1814*
Alicia Keys, *Songs in A Minor*
Cyndi Lauper, *She's So Unusual*
Linkin Park, *Hybrid Theory*
Matchbox 20, *Yourself or Someone Like You*
John Mayer, *Room for Squares*
Alanis Morissette, *Jagged Little Pill*
Nirvana, *In Utero*
Nirvana, *Nevermind*
No Doubt, *Rock Steady*
Nuggets: Original Artyfacts
Pearl Jam, *Ten*
P!nk, *M!ssundaztood*
Pretty in Pink
Queens of the Stone Age, *Songs for the Deaf*
Rage Against the Machine, *Rage Against the Machine*
The Ramones, *Ramones*
The Ramones, *Ramones Mania*

Rancid, *And Out Come the Wolves*
Red Hot Chili Peppers, *Californication*
Rent
The Replacements, *Tim*
The Righteous Brothers, *Anthology*
LeAnn Rimes, *Blue*
Rocky Horror Picture Show
Romeo + Juliet
Smashing Pumpkins, *Siamese Dream*
The Stooges, *Funhouse*
The Stooges, *The Stooges*
TLC, *CrazySexyCool*
Tool, *Aenima*
Weezer, *Weezer*
West Side Story
White Stripes, *White Blood Cells*

Top Sellers

Gold

(500,000 or more sold)

Louis Armstrong, *Hello, Dolly!*
AWB (Average White Band), *AWB*
Joan Baez, *Diamonds & Rust*
Joan Baez, *Joan Baez*
Harry Belafonte, *Calypso*
Tony Bennett, *I Left My Heart in San Francisco*
David Bowie, *Station to Station*
David Bowie, *Ziggy Stardust*
The Breakfast Club
Jeff Buckley, *Grace*
Cabaret
Harry Chapin, *Verities & Balderdash*
Cheap Trick, *Live at Budokan*
The Chemical Brothers, *Dig Your Own Hole*
The Chieftains, *Long Black Veil*
The Clash, *The Clash*
Close Encounters of the Third Kind
Joe Cocker, *With a Little Help from My Friends*
Leonard Cohen, *The Songs*
Judy Collins, *Wildflowers*
John Coltrane, *Blue Train*
John Coltrane, *A Love Supreme*
Common, *Like Water for Chocolate*
Elvis Costello, *This Year's Model*
Robert Cray, *Strong Persuader*
Jim Croce, *I Got a Name*
Bing Crosby, *A Merry Christmas with Bing Crosby and The Andrews Sisters*
The Crystal Method, *Vegas*
Daft Punk, *Homework*
Miles Davis, *Bitches Brew*
Derek & the Dominos, *Layla*
Devo, *Q: Are We Not Men?*
Ani DiFranco, *Living in Clip*
Digable Planets, *Reachin'*

Dreamgirls
Dr. Zhivago
Steve Earle, *Guitar Town*
Easy Rider
Erasure, *Erasure Pop!*
E.T. The Extra-Terrestrial
Everything But the Girl, *Amplified Heart*
The 5th Dimension, *Greatest Hits on Earth*
Frankie Goes to Hollywood, *Welcome to the Pleasuredome*
Aretha Franklin, *Lady Soul*
Funny Girl
Judy Garland, *Judy at Carnegie Hall*
Marvin Gaye, *What's Going On*
Genesis, *Lamb Lies Down on B'way*
Stan Getz, *Getz/Gilberto*
Gigi
The Good, the Bad and the Ugly
Grateful Dead, *Live/Dead*
Hair
Emmylou Harris, *Pieces of the Sky*
Isaac Hayes, *Hot Buttered Soul*
Isaac Hayes, *Shaft*
India.Arie, *Voyage to India*
Joe Jackson, *Night and Day*
Jefferson Airplane, *Surrealistic Pillow*
Jesus Christ Superstar
KC/Sunshine Band, *The Best*
The King and I
B.B. King, *Live at the Regal*
King Crimson, *In the Court*
KLF, *The White Room*
Leo Kottke, *6- and 12-String Guitar*
Diana Krall, *Live in Paris*
k.d. lang, *Shadowland*
Tom Lehrer, *That Was the Year That Was*
Little Feat, *Feats Don't Fail Me Now*
The Mamas and the Papas, *If You Can Believe Your Eyes and Ears*
The Mambo Kings
Mame
Aimee Mann, *Magnolia*
Mannheim Steamroller, *Fresh Aire IV*
Bob Marley and the Wailers, *Burnin'*
Mary Poppins
Curtis Mayfield, *Superfly*
Don McLean, *American Pie*
Sergio Mendes, *Fool on the Hill*
Liza Minnelli, *Liza with a "Z"*
Joni Mitchell, *Hejira*
Moody Blues, *This is the Moody Blues*
Van Morrison, *Astral Weeks*
Morrissey, *Viva Hate*
Mos Def, *Black on Both Sides*
Randy Newman, *Little Criminals*

Special Feature Index

A Night at Studio 54
Harry Nilsson, *Nilsson Schmilsson*
Orchestral Manoeuvers in the Dark, *The Best of OMD*
Pet Shop Boys, *Very*
Liz Phair, *Exile in Guyville*
Pharcyde, *Bizarre Ride*
The Pink Panther
Portishead, *Dummy*
Elvis Presley, *From Elvis in Memphis*
Pretty in Pink
The Ramones, *Ramones Mania*
Rancid, *And Out Come the Wolves*
R.E.M., *Murmur*
The Righteous Brothers, *Anthology*
Rocky Horror Picture Show
Todd Rundgren, *Something/Anything?*
Frank Sinatra, *In the Wee Small Hours*
Frank Sinatra, *Only the Lonely*
Frank Sinatra, *Songs for Swingin' Lovers*
Slayer, *Reign in Blood*
The Smiths, *The Queen Is Dead*
Phoebe Snow, *Phoebe Snow*
South Pacific
The Spinners, *A One of a Kind Love Affair: The Anthology*
The Sting
Barbra Streisand, *The Barbra Streisand Album*
The Strokes, *Is This It*
The Supremes, *Anthology*
Matthew Sweet, *Girlfriend*
Talking Heads, *Remain in Light*
Sundays, *Reading, Writing and Arithmetic*
They Might Be Giants, *Flood*
Three Dog Night, *The Best*
Traffic, *John Barleycorn Must Die*
Trainspotting
A Tribe Called Quest, *People's Instinctive Travels*
Twin Peaks
2001: A Space Odyssey
Frank Zappa, *Apostrophe*

Platinum

(1 million or more sold)

Boyz II Men, *Boyz II Men, II*
Aaliyah, *Aaliyah*
ABBA, *Gold/Greatest Hits*
AC/DC, *Highway to Hell*
Aerosmith, *Pump*
Aerosmith, *Toys in the Attic*
Alabama, *Mountain Music*
Aladdin
Alice in Chains, *Dirt*
The Allman Brothers, *Eat a Peach*
America, *History*
American Graffiti

Annie
Marc Anthony, *Marc Anthony*
Arrested Development, *3 Years, 5 Months & 2 Days in the Life of . . .*
The Association, *Greatest Hits*
Bad Company, *Bad Company*
Erykah Badu, *Baduizm*
Anita Baker, *Rapture*
The Beach Boys, *Pet Sounds*
Beastie Boys, *Licensed to Ill*
Beastie Boys, *Paul's Boutique*
The Beatles, *Revolver*
The Beatles, *Rubber Soul*
Beauty and the Beast
Beck, *Odelay*
Jeff Beck, *Blow by Blow*
The Bee Gees, *Children of the World*
George Benson, *Breezin'*
The B-52's, *The B-52's*
Big Brother and the Holding Company, *Cheap Thrills*
The Big Chill
Björk, *Debut*
Clint Black, *Killin' Time*
Black Sabbath, *Paranoid*
Mary J. Blige, *My Life*
Mary J. Blige, *No More Drama*
Mary J. Blige, *What's the 411?*
Blondie, *Parallel Lines*
The Blues Brothers
Bon Jovi, *New Jersey*
David Bowie, *Changesbowie*
Boyz II Men, *Cooleyhighharmony*
Toni Braxton, *Secrets*
Sarah Brightman, *Time to Say Goodbye*
Brooks & Dunn, *Brand New Man*
Jackson Browne, *Running on Empty*
Dave Brubeck, *Time Out*
Buena Vista Social Club
Jimmy Buffett, *Songs You Know by Heart*
Camelot
Glen Campbell, *Wichita Lineman*
Mary Chapin Carpenter, *Shooting Straight in the Dark*
The Carpenters, *The Singles*
The Cars, *The Cars*
Johnny Cash, *At Folsom Prison*
Tracy Chapman, *New Beginning*
Tracy Chapman, *Tracy Chapman*
Chicago, *Chicago IX: Greatest Hits*
A Chorus Line
Eric Clapton, *Slowhand*
The Clash, *London Calling*
Patsy Cline, *Greatest Hits*
Coldplay, *Parachutes*
Natalie Cole, *Unforgettable*
Shawn Colvin, *A Few Small Repairs*
The Commitments
Alice Cooper, *Greatest Hits*

Special Feature Index

Elvis Costello, *My Aim Is True*

Counting Crows, *August and Everything After*

Cream, *Disraeli Gears*

Creedence Clearwater Revival, *Chronicle*

Crosby, Stills & Nash, *Crosby, Stills & Nash*

Crosby, Stills, Nash & Young, *Déjà Vu*

Crosby, Stills, Nash & Young, *Four Way Street*

The Crow

Sheryl Crow, *Tuesday Night Music Club*

Crowded House, *Crowded House*

Cypress Hill, *Cypress Hill*

D'Angelo, *Brown Sugar*

D'Angelo, *Voodoo*

Charlie Daniels Band, *Fire on the Mountain*

Terence Trent D'Arby, *Introducing*

Miles Davis, *Kind of Blue*

Deep Purple, *Machine Head*

Def Leppard, *Pyromania*

De La Soul, *3 Feet High and Rising*

John Denver, *Greatest Hits*

Depeche Mode, *Music for the Masses*

Neil Diamond, *The Jazz Singer*

Dido, *No Angel*

Dire Straits, *Brothers in Arms*

Dixie Chicks, *Home*

Donovan, *Donovan's Greatest Hits*

The Doors, *The Doors*

The Doors, *L.A. Woman*

Dr. Dre, *The Chronic*

Duran Duran, *Duran Duran*

Duran Duran, *Rio*

Bob Dylan, *Blonde on Blonde*

Bob Dylan, *Blood on the Tracks*

Bob Dylan, *Nashville Skyline*

The Eagles, *The Long Run*

Earth, Wind & Fire, *That's the Way of the World*

Electric Light Orchestra, *ELO's Greatest Hits*

Missy Elliott, *Supa Dupa Fly*

Eminem, *The Eminem Show*

Eminem, *The Marshall Mathers LP*

Eminem, *The Slim Shady LP*

Enigma, *MCMXC A.D.*

En Vogue, *Born to Sing*

En Vogue, *Funky Divas*

Enya, *Watermark*

Eric B. & Rakim, *Paid in Full*

Gloria Estefan, *Greatest Hits*

Melissa Etheridge, *Yes I Am*

Eurythmics, *Greatest Hits*

Faith No More, *The Real Thing*

Fame

Fatboy Slim, *You've Come a Long Way, Baby*

Fiddler on the Roof

Flashdance

Fleetwood Mac, *Fleetwood Mac*

Dan Fogelberg, *Phoenix*

John Fogerty, *Centerfield*

Foo Fighters, *Foo Fighters*

Footloose

Peter Frampton, *Frampton Comes Alive!*

The Fugees, *The Score*

Funkadelic, *One Nation Under a Groove*

Peter Gabriel, *So*

Garbage, *Garbage*

Gipsy Kings, *Gipsy Kings*

Go-Go's, *Beauty and the Beat*

Grateful Dead, *Workingman's Dead*

David Gray, *White Ladder*

Macy Gray, *On How Life Is*

Grease

Al Green, *Greatest Hits*

Guns n' Roses, *Use Your Illusion I*

Arlo Guthrie, *Alice's Restaurant*

Hall & Oates, *Rock 'n' Soul, Part 1*

Herbie Hancock, *Head Hunters*

George Harrison, *All Things Must Pass*

Jimi Hendrix, *Band of Gypsys*

Jimi Hendrix Experience, *Are You Experienced?*

Jimi Hendrix Experience, *Electric Ladyland*

Don Henley, *Building the Perfect Beast*

Faith Hill, *Breathe*

Lauryn Hill, *The Miseducation*

Ice Cube, *AmeriKKKa's Most Wanted*

Billy Idol, *Rebel Yell*

Indigo Girls, *Indigo Girls*

INXS, *Kick*

Iron Maiden, *Number of the Beast*

Chris Isaak, *Heart Shaped World*

Alan Jackson, *A Lot About Livin'*

Janet Jackson, *janet.*

Janet Jackson, *Janet Jackson's Rhythm Nation 1814*

Michael Jackson, *Bad*

Michael Jackson, *Off the Wall*

Jane's Addiction, *Ritual de lo Habitual*

Jay-Z, *The Blueprint*

Jethro Tull, *Aqualung*

Joan Jett & the Blackhearts, *I Love Rock 'n' Roll*

Billy Joel, *Piano Man*

Billy Joel, *The Stranger*

Elton John, *Goodbye Yellow Brick Rd.*

Special Feature Index

The Who, *Tommy*
The Who, *Who's Next*
Hank Williams, *40 Greatest Hits*
Wings, *Band on the Run*
George Winston, *Autumn*
Steve Winwood, *Arc of a Diver*
The Wizard of Oz
Woodstock
Wu-Tang Clan, *Enter the Wu-Tang*
Tammy Wynette, *Stand by Your Man*
Trisha Yearwood, *Hearts in Armor*
Yes, *Fragile*
Dwight Yoakam, *Guitars, Cadillacs*
Dwight Yoakam, *This Time*
Neil Young, *After the Gold Rush*
Neil Young, *Harvest*
Warren Zevon, *Excitable Boy*

Diamond

(10 million or more sold)

AC/DC, *Back in Black*
The Beatles, *Abbey Road*
The Beatles, *The Beatles 1962-1966*
The Beatles, *Sgt. Pepper*
The Bee Gees, *Saturday Night Fever*
Bon Jovi, *Slippery When Wet*
Boston, *Boston*
Garth Brooks, *No Fences*
Garth Brooks, *Ropin' the Wind*
Eric Clapton, *Unplugged*
Phil Collins, *No Jacket Required*
Def Leppard, *Hysteria*
Celine Dion, *Let's Talk About Love*
Dirty Dancing
Dixie Chicks, *Wide Open Spaces*
Doobie Brothers, *Best*
The Eagles, *Their Greatest Hits*
The Eagles, *Hotel California*
Fleetwood Mac, *Rumours*
Forrest Gump
Green Day, *Dookie*
Guns n' Roses, *Appetite for Destruction*
Whitney Houston, *The Bodyguard*
Whitney Houston, *Whitney Houston*
Michael Jackson, *Thriller*
Elton John, *Greatest Hits*
Carole King, *Tapestry*
Led Zeppelin, *Led Zeppelin II*
Led Zeppelin, *Led Zeppelin IV*
Led Zeppelin, *Physical Graffiti*
The Lion King
Madonna, *Immaculate Collection*
Madonna, *Like a Virgin*
Bob Marley and the Wailers, *Legend*
Matchbox 20, *Yourself or Someone Like You*
Meat Loaf, *Bat out of Hell*
George Michael, *Faith*
Alanis Morissette, *Jagged Little Pill*
Nirvana, *Nevermind*
No Doubt, *Tragic Kingdom*

Notorious B.I.G., *Life After Death*
Pearl Jam, *Ten*
Pink Floyd, *Dark Side of the Moon*
Pink Floyd, *The Wall*
Prince, *Purple Rain*
Lionel Richie, *Can't Slow Down*
Santana, *Supernatural*
Bruce Springsteen, *Born in the USA*
Bruce Springsteen, *Bruce Springsteen & the E Street Band Live/1975-85*
James Taylor, *Greatest Hits*
Titanic
TLC, *CrazySexyCool*
Shania Twain, *Come on Over*
U2, *The Joshua Tree*
Van Halen, *1984 (MCMLXXXIV)*
Van Halen, *Van Halen*
ZZ Top, *Eliminator*

Trendsetters

Cannonball Adderley, *Somethin' Else*
Air, *Moon Safari*
The Allman Brothers, *Eat a Peach*
Marc Anthony, *Marc Anthony*
Aphex Twin, *Selected Ambient Works*
Erykah Badu, *Baduizm*
Joan Baez, *Joan Baez*
Barber, *Adagio for Strings; Violin Concerto*
The Beach Boys, *Pet Sounds*
The Beatles, *Sgt. Pepper*
Beck, *Odelay*
The Bee Gees, *Saturday Night Fever*
Beethoven, *Symphonies 5 & 7*
Harry Belafonte, *Calypso*
The B-52's, *The B-52's*
Björk, *Debut*
Mary J. Blige, *What's the 411?*
Blondie, *Parallel Lines*
Boogie Down Prod., *Criminal Minded*
David Bowie, *Ziggy Stardust*
Boyz II Men, *Cooleyhighharmony*
Dave Brubeck, *Time Out*
Johnny Cash, *American Recordings*
Tracy Chapman, *Tracy Chapman*
The Chemical Brothers, *Dig Your Own Hole*
The Clash, *The Clash*
Leonard Cohen, *The Songs*
Elvis Costello, *My Aim Is True*
The Crow
Miles Davis, *Bitches Brew*
Miles Davis, *Kind of Blue*
De La Soul, *3 Feet High and Rising*
Depeche Mode, *Music for the Masses*
Devo, *Q: Are We Not Men?*

Special Feature Index

DJ Shadow, *Endtroducing . . .*
Fats Domino, *My Blue Heaven*
The Doors, *The Doors*
Nick Drake, *Pink Moon*
Dr. Dre, *The Chronic*
Duran Duran, *Duran Duran*
Bob Dylan, *Nashville Skyline*
8 Mile
Missy Elliott, *Supa Dupa Fly*
Eminem, *The Marshall Mathers LP*
Enigma, *MCMXC A.D.*
Brian Eno, *Before and After Science*
En Vogue, *Funky Divas*
Erasure, *Erasure Pop!*
Eric B. & Rakim, *Paid in Full*
Flashdance
Aretha Franklin, *Lady Soul*
The Fugees, *The Score*
Funkadelic, *Maggot Brain*
Gang of Four, *Entertainment!*
Marvin Gaye, *What's Going On*
Genesis, *Lamb Lies Down on B'way*
Go-Go's, *Beauty and the Beat*
Goldfinger
The Good, the Bad and the Ugly
Grateful Dead, *Workingman's Dead*
Green Day, *Dookie*
Guns n' Roses, *Appetite for Destruction*
Woody Guthrie, *The Greatest Songs*
Herbie Hancock, *Maiden Voyage*
Isaac Hayes, *Shaft*
Jascha Heifetz, *Beethoven & Mendelssohn: Violin Concertos*
John Lee Hooker, *Ultimate Collection*
Howlin' Wolf, *Moanin' in the Moonlight*
Hüsker Dü, *New Day Rising*
Michael Jackson, *Bad*
Ahmad Jamal, *At the Pershing*
Jane's Addiction, *Ritual de lo Habitual*
Jean-Michel Jarre, *Oxygene*
Keith Jarrett, *The Köln Concert*
Waylon Jennings, *Honky Tonk Heroes*
B.B. King, *Live at the Regal*
Carole King, *Tapestry*
The Kinks, *Lola vs. the Powerman vs. the Money Go-Round*
Kraftwerk, *Trans-Europe Express*
Lenny Kravitz, *Are You Gonna Go My Way?*
Kris Kristofferson, *Kristofferson*
Cyndi Lauper, *She's So Unusual*
The Little Mermaid
Madonna, *Like a Virgin*
The Mambo Kings
Bob Marley and the Wailers, *Burnin'*
Massive Attack, *Blue Lines*

John Mayall, *Bluesbreakers: John Mayall with Eric Clapton*
Curtis Mayfield, *Superfly*
Metallica, *Master of Puppets*
Pat Metheny, *Pat Metheny Group*
Joni Mitchell, *Blue*
Moby, *Play*
The Modern Lovers, *The Modern Lovers*
Moody Blues, *This is the Moody Blues*
Lee Morgan, *The Sidewinder*
Alanis Morissette, *Jagged Little Pill*
Van Morrison, *Astral Weeks*
Moulin Rouge!
Muppet Movie
Nas, *Illmatic*
Willie Nelson, *Red Headed Stranger*
New Order, *Power, Corruption & Lies*
Nine Inch Nails, *Downward Spiral*
Nirvana, *Nevermind*
Notorious B.I.G., *Ready to Die*
N.W.A, *Straight Outta Compton*
Laura Nyro, *Eli and the Thirteenth Confession*
Beth Orton, *Central Reservation*
Outkast, *Aquemini*
Parliament, *Mothership Connection*
Gram Parsons, *Grievous Angel*
Pavement, *Slanted and Enchanted*
Pet Shop Boys, *Very*
Edith Piaf, *La Vie En Rose*
Pink Floyd, *Dark Side of the Moon*
Pixies, *Surfer Rosa*
Portishead, *Dummy*
Prince, *1999*
Public Enemy, *It Takes a Nation*
Radiohead, *OK Computer*
Rage Against the Machine, *Rage Against the Machine*
The Ramones, *Ramones*
The Replacements, *Let It Be*
Sonny Rollins, *Saxophone Colossus*
Run-D.M.C., *Raising Hell*
Pete Seeger, *We Shall Overcome*
The Sex Pistols, *Never Mind the Bollocks Here's the Sex Pistols*
Tupac Shakur, *All Eyez on Me*
Horace Silver, *Song for My Father*
Frank Sinatra, *Songs for Swingin' Lovers*
Slick Rick, *The Great Adventures*
Patti Smith, *Horses*
Snoop Dogg, *Doggystyle*
Sonic Youth, *Daydream Nation*
Star Wars
Steely Dan, *Can't Buy a Thrill*
The Sting
The Stone Roses, *The Stone Roses*
The Stooges, *Funhouse*

Donna Summer, *Dance Collection*
Matthew Sweet, *Girlfriend Swingers*
James Taylor, *Sweet Baby James*
Marlo Thomas and Friends, *Free to Be . . . You & Me*
Tool, *Aenima*
Trainspotting
T. Rex, *Electric Warrior*
2001: A Space Odyssey
Uncle Tupelo, *No Depression*
Vangelis, *Chariots of Fire*
Suzanne Vega, *Solitude Standing*
Velvet Underground, *The Velvet Underground and Nico*
Andreas Vollenweider, *Down to the Moon*
Weather Report, *Weather Report*
The Weavers, *at Carnegie Hall*
Wilco, *Yankee Hotel Foxtrot*
Hank Williams, *40 Greatest Hits*
George Winston, *Autumn Woodstock*
Wu-Tang Clan, *Enter the Wu-Tang*
Yes, *Fragile*
Neil Young, *After the Gold Rush*

Tribute

Billy Bragg & Wilco, *Mermaid Ave.*
Rosemary Clooney, *Sings the Music of Cole Porter*
Natalie Cole, *Unforgettable*
Ella Fitzgerald, *Best of the Songbooks*
Lambert, Hendricks & Ross, *Sing a Song of Basie*

U.S. City Sounds

Atlanta/Athens

The Allman Brothers, *Eat a Peach*
Arrested Development, *3 Years, 5 Months & 2 Days in the Life of . . .*
The B-52's, *The B-52's*
Toni Braxton, *Secrets*
Indigo Girls, *Indigo Girls*
Outkast, *Aquemini*
Outkast, *Stankonia*
R.E.M., *Automatic for the People*
R.E.M., *Murmur*
TLC, *CrazySexyCool*

Austin/Dallas/Houston

Clarence "Gatemouth" Brown, *Texas Swing*
Dixie Chicks, *Home*
Dixie Chicks, *Wide Open Spaces*
Steve Earle, *Guitar Town*
Nanci Griffith, *Flyer*
Lyle Lovett, *Lyle Lovett*
Willie Nelson, *Red Headed Stranger*
Willie Nelson, *Stardust*

George Strait, *Does Fort Worth Ever Cross Your Mind*
Stevie Ray Vaughan & Double Trouble, *Greatest Hits*
Johnny Winter, *Johnny Winter*

Boston

Aerosmith, *Pump*
Aerosmith, *Toys in the Attic*
Boston, *Boston*
The Cars, *The Cars*
Dinosaur Jr, *You're Living All Over Me*
The Modern Lovers, *The Modern Lovers*
Morphine, *Cure for Pain*
Pixies, *Surfer Rosa*
Susan Tedeschi, *Just Won't Burn*

Chicago

Mike Bloomfield, *Super Session*
The Blues Brothers
Paul Butterfield, *East-West*
Chicago, *Chicago IX: Greatest Hits*
Common, *Like Water for Chocolate*
Buddy Guy, *The Very Best*
Howlin' Wolf, *Moanin' in the Moonlight*
Liz Phair, *Exile in Guyville*
Smashing Pumpkins, *Mellon Collie and the Infinite Sadness*
Smashing Pumpkins, *Siamese Dream*
Styx, *The Grand Illusion*
Muddy Waters, *The Best*

Detroit

8 Mile
Eminem, *The Eminem Show*
Eminem, *The Marshall Mathers LP*
Eminem, *The Slim Shady LP*
The Four Tops, *Anthology*
Marvin Gaye, *Anthology*
Marvin Gaye, *What's Going On*
Hitsville USA: The Motown Singles
John Lee Hooker, *Ultimate Collection*
Jackson 5, *Anthology*
MC 5, *Kick Out the Jams*
Parliament, *Mothership Connection*
Iggy Pop, *Lust for Life*
Smokey Robinson, *Anthology*
Bob Seger & The Silver Bullet Band, *Against the Wind*
Bob Seger & The Silver Bullet Band, *Night Moves*
The Stooges, *Funhouse*
The Stooges, *The Stooges*
The Supremes, *Anthology*
The Temptations, *Greatest Hits*

Los Angeles

The Beach Boys, *Pet Sounds*
Beck, *Odelay*

Singles
Soundgarden, *Superunknown*
Twin Peaks

Work-Out

ABBA, *Gold/Greatest Hits*
Afro-Celt Sound System, *Sound Magic Volume 1*
The Bee Gees, *Children of the World*
The Bee Gees, *Saturday Night Fever*
Chuck Berry, *The Great Twenty-Eight*
The B-52's, *The B-52's*
Big Brother and the Holding Company, *Cheap Thrills*
Blondie, *Parallel Lines*
Bon Jovi, *Slippery When Wet*
Cabaret
The Cars, *The Cars*
Chic, *Dance Dance Dance*
Daft Punk, *Homework*
8 Mile
En Vogue, *Funky Divas*
Gloria Estefan, *Greatest Hits*
Fame
Fatboy Slim, *You've Come a Long Way, Baby*
Flashdance
Footloose
The Four Seasons, *Anthology*
Funny Girl
Grease
Hairspray
Handel, *Water Music*
INXS, *Kick*
Janet Jackson, *Janet Jackson's Rhythm Nation 1814*
Joan Jett & the Blackhearts, *I Love Rock 'n' Roll*
KC/Sunshine Band, *The Best*
Little Richard, *The Essential*
Madonna, *Ray of Light*
Matrix
George Michael, *Faith*
Kylie Minogue, *Fever*
A Night at Studio 54
No Doubt, *Rock Steady*
Paul Oakenfold, *Tranceport*
Olive, *Extra Virgin*
The Pointer Sisters, *Break Out*
Pretty Woman
Prince, *Purple Rain*
Queen, *Classic Queen*
The Ramones, *Ramones Mania*
Rocky
Rolling Stones, *Some Girls*
Squeeze, *Singles 45's and Under*
The Strokes, *Is This It*
Donna Summer, *Dance Collection*
Top Gun
Vangelis, *Chariots of Fire*
Van Halen, *1984 (MCMLXXXIV)*

Alphabetical
Page Index
by Album Name

Alphabetical Page Index by Album Name

Alphabetical Page Index by Album Name

Alphabetical Page Index by Album Name

Alphabetical Page Index by Album Name

Alphabetical Page Index by Album Name

Alphabetical Page Index by Album Name

Alphabetical Page Index by Album Name

Alphabetical Page Index by Album Name

Alphabetical Page Index by Album Name

Alphabetical Page Index by Album Name

Alphabetical Page Index by Album Name

Alphabetical Page Index by Album Name

Alphabetical Page Index by Album Name

Alphabetical Page Index by Album Name

Alphabetical Page Index by Album Name

Alphabetical Page Index by Album Name

Alphabetical Page Index by Album Name

Alphabetical Page Index by Album Name

Alphabetical Page Index by Album Name

subscribe to zagat.com

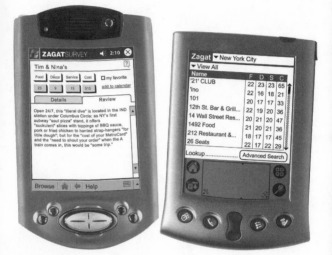